APPLE PASCAL:
A Problem Solving Approach

APPLE PASCAL:
A Problem Solving Approach

Terry L. Dennis
Rochester Institute of Technology

West Publishing Company
St. Paul   New York   Los Angeles   San Francisco

Copyediting: Pamela S. McMurry
Design: The Quarasan Group, Inc.
Composition: Master Typographers, Inc.
Cover Design: Delor Erickson

Credits: The photographs on pages 3, 6, 7, 8, and 9
were provided by Apple Computer, Inc.

Library of Congress Cataloging in Publication Data

Dennis, Terry L.
   Apple Pascal.

   Bibliography: p.
   Includes index.
   1. Apple computer—Programming.   2. UCSD Pascal
(Computer program language)   I. Title.
QA76.8.A66D46   1985   001.64'2   84-20928
Softcover: ISBN 0-314-85228-X
Hardcover: ISBN 0-314-92881-2

To
Matt,
Sara and
Rachel

Table of Contents

4

Introduction to Procedures 77

5

An Approach to Problem Solving and Program Development 105

6

Graphics 121

⑦

Repetition   141

⑧

Program Control Through Conditional Branching   165

12

Arrays 269

13

Records 303

17

Recursion, Searching, and Sorting   405

18

Additional Apple Features—Graphics and Sound   433

Preface

This book was written for Apple computer users who want to learn how to program in Pascal. It was designed to be used in introductory Pascal courses or by individuals who want to learn Pascal on their own. Although the book is structured around the Apple computer, users of other computers with the UCSD Pascal system should have little difficulty using this book.

This book should do three things for you. First, it will familiarize you with the UCSD Pascal system, which includes an Editor for writing programs, a Compiler for compiling and running programs, and a Filer for organizing disk files. Second, it will introduce you to a problem-solving approach to programming through a structured, top-down method of program development. And third, it will teach you Pascal syntax and how to write programs in Pascal.

These objectives will be accomplished by providing you with a great deal of hands-on experience with the computer. Almost every chapter involves actual programming exercises on the computer. Chapter 5 outlines the steps that should be followed to develop a problem-solving approach to programming and illustrates how structured, top-down programs are developed. This problem-solving approach is then applied to example problems in the following chapters. The book also begins with a simple problem and a program to solve it and expands on this program in subsequent chapters. As you progress through this book, you will see the sophistication and complexity of this program increase as your knowledge of the Pascal language grows.

Why Pascal?

Pascal is only one of many programming languages available today. Most microcomputers come with some version of BASIC included, either stored permanently in the computer's read only memory (ROM) or externally on a disk supplied with the computer. Given the variety of programming languages and the ready availability of BASIC, one might wonder, why Pascal? There are a variety of responses to that question, but the most frequently mentioned reasons refer to the fact that Pascal is a highly structured language, and that, in general, people who learn Pascal tend to develop better programming skills than those who learn other languages.

Because of the way Pascal requires programs to be written, it is often much easier to look at a Pascal program for the first time and understand what it will do than it is with many other programming languages. Pascal is designed to enable programmers to write in a logical and straightforward fashion. This facilitates the coding of programs, which are more likely to be logically correct. Because of this structure, Pascal lends itself to problem-solving and allows programmers to subdivide large, complex programs into smaller, simpler modules that are easier to program. Pascal is also an excellent language for handling data files, since it is capable of supporting complex data structures.

Despite the fact that Pascal was originally intended as a teaching language rather than a serious programming language, it has become one of the most popular languages today for professional applications programmers and software houses. Furthermore, many educators believe that it is much easier for a person to learn other programming languages once they have learned Pascal. And finally, my personal experience has shown that if you write in another language such as BASIC and then master Pascal, you will begin to write BASIC programs that are more structured and logical.

Apple Pascal

The Pascal language was originally developed as a programming language in 1968 by Niklaus Wirth, a Swiss computer scientist, in an effort to help students learn proper programming skills. Wirth wanted a language that would lend itself to a systematic approach to programming and named his new language after the seventeenth century mathematician, Blaise Pascal. The first Pascal compiler was completed in 1970. Standard Pascal refers to the version of the language adopted by the International Standards Organization and described by Kathleen Jensen and Niklaus Wirth in their *Pascal User Manual and Report* (Springer-Verlag, 1974).

In 1975, Dr. Kenneth L. Bowles and his associates at the University of California San Diego developed a new version of Pascal that was based on Standard Pascal but included an operating system and a number of enhancements to the original version. This new version is known as UCSD Pascal. The system was extremely portable in nature and worked very well with microcomputers. The system, called a P-System, included an editor that could be used for writing and editing programs and a file maintenance section for housekeeping purposes as well as the Pascal compiler. UCSD Pascal also provided a number of enhancements that added graphics, sound, and string (a literal string of characters) handling capabilities to the language.

Apple Pascal is based on UCSD Pascal as developed by Bowles. There are a few enhancements to the language that are designed primarily to take advantage of special features that the Apple computer offers. In most respects, however, Apple Pascal is identical to UCSD Pascal and UCSD Pascal is based on and uses most of the same programming terminology and structure found in Standard Pascal. The current Advanced Placement in Computer Science test is based on Standard Pascal. Students using this book to prepare for the Advanced Placement test should remember that the graphics, sound, and string-handling enhancements found in UCSD and Apple Pascal are not contained in Standard Pascal.

Organization

The organization of this book follows a format I have used successfully for a number of years in workshops and seminars. My intention is to give you as much hands-on experience as possible. I have attempted to follow a learning sequence that would be logical for someone actually using the computer, e.g., you learn how to enter programs on the computer you are using before you begin programming, and you cannot write a second program before you know how to save your first one.

Chapter 0 is an optional introduction to computers and programming for those readers who have had little or no prior experience with the computer.

Chapter 1 introduces you to the P-System, beginning with simple Filer commands and then moving to the Editor, where you learn the basic editing commands. At the end of the chapter you will enter and run an actual program.

Chapter 2, one of the few hands-off chapters, introduces the normal structure of a Pascal program. The program written in chapter 1 is analyzed, and some of the different data types used by Pascal are explained.

Chapter 3 tells you how to prepare a storage disk for your programs and discusses methods of saving and moving files (programs) on disks. This chapter also includes housekeeping functions such as removing unwanted files from a disk and obtaining a listing of the files stored on a disk.

Chapter 4 introduces you to procedures, Pascal's modular subprograms. It also covers additional Editor commands and clarifies data input and output procedures. After completing these chapters, you should have a working knowledge of the p-System and the basic structure of a Pascal program.

Chapter 5 outlines a problem-solving approach to programming, beginning with the definition of the problem, then moving through the development of an algorithm and the actual coding of the program to the final testing of the finished program. Once you have completed this chapter, you are ready to go on to the chapters that expand your knowledge of the Pascal language.

Chapter 6 introduces Apple Pascal graphics. This chapter is included early in the book so that both text and graphics examples can be included in the following chapters. If you have no desire to work with graphics, this chapter and the graphics examples can be omitted. However, many of the students and teachers I have worked with enjoy working with graphics, where the visual image on the screen shows clearly whether a program is working properly.

Chapter 7 covers the different methods Pascal uses to achieve repetition in a program, including the FOR..DO, REPEAT..UNTIL, and WHILE..DO structures. Chapter 8 discusses Boolean expressions and the conditional branching statements IF..THEN, IF..THEN..ELSE, and CASE..OF.

Chapter 9 covers the use of parameters to pass values to and from procedures and expands on the concept of modular programs. Parameters allow programmers to subdivide large programs into smaller procedures that can be written separately without depending on the use of identical variable names. Chapter 10 goes on to the use of parameters with both built-in and user-defined functions.

Chapter 11 begins a discussion of scalar data types and the manner in which Pascal allows users to define their own data types. It concludes by covering sets and the use of sets and set operations in programs. Chapter 12 expands on data structures through the introduction of single and multidimensional arrays. Records, a more complex data type, are then introduced in chapter 13, and chapter 14 details the creation of data files and Pascal's ability to store data in or retrieve it from these disk files. The concept of pointer variables is included in chapter 15 for those who wish to explore this topic.

Chapter 16 introduces a number of built-in string-handling functions that allow us to combine, delete, and perform other manipulations on string variables. Chapter 17 discusses searching and sorting routines. Both linear and binary search procedures are covered, and examples of six of the more popular sorting routines are provided. Chapter 18 concludes the book with a further discussion of graphics commands and an introduction to Pascal's ability to use the sound available on the Apple.

Thus, chapters 1 through 5 constitute an introduction to the P-System, the structure of Pascal programs, and a problem-solving approach to writing Pascal programs. Chapters 6 through 10 contain graphics and much of the Pascal language syntax used to write programs. Chapters 11 through 15 discuss the various data structures available in Pascal, from the simple scalar types through the more complex arrays and records, and the use of files for data storage and retrieval. Chapters 16 through 18 then conclude with a discussion of some of the extras available with Apple (and UCSD) Pascal, such as string-handling functions, additional graphics, and sound, as well as examples of the more commonly used searching and sorting routines.

As you progress through this book, you will frequently be instructed to enter and run Pascal programs. It would be possible to complete this book without ever doing so, but you would lessen the learning experience that these hands-on examples are meant to provide. It is therefore suggested that you make the effort to actually enter and run the example programs and to develop your own programs as well. The practice will increase both your knowledge of the system and your programming skills.

There are several places in this book where you are also asked to write a program on your own and are then given an example solution or program. The programs shown are meant to be guides; if your program does not match the example program exactly, that does not mean that yours is wrong. While names used to identify variables will probably be identical only by chance, the logic of the program should be similar. The final test should always be, did the program run correctly?

Acknowledgments

I would like to thank the many people who contributed in some manner to this book. Included prominently in that group are the following reviewers: Gabriel Barta, University of New Hampshire; George Beekman, Oregon State University; Kolman Brand, Nassau Community College; Eileen Entin, Wentworth Institute; Steve Gregory, Bowling Green; Ernie Phillips, Northern Virginia Community College; Ron Young, Harrisburg Community College; Dan Fredrickson, Seattle Public Schools; Bruce Givner, Irvine Unified School District; Bob Hartman, Kent Meridian High School; David Hoerger, Cottage Grove High School; Larry Insel, Broward Community Schools; Brother Charles Jackson, Bellarmine Prep School; Michael Marcotte, Union Catholic Regional High School; Dennis C. Ehn, Boston Computer Society. They offered many helpful suggestions along the way. I would also like to thank the many teachers who attended workshops and seminars and allowed me to test this book on them. They were not only understanding of the many early typos, but offered both suggestions and much appreciated support. My thanks are also extended to Gordon Goodman, who first urged me to learn Pascal, Steve Kurtz, for his early encouragement and help, Patrick Fitzgerald, my editor, and Kim Theesfeld and the many others at West involved in the preparation of this book. I would also like to thank my father and children, who gave me the time and understanding necessary to finish this project. And finally, I would especially like to thank my wife, Laurie, whose contributions cannot be properly acknowledged in the space allowed by my editor.

APPLE PASCAL:

A Problem Solving Approach

Introduction to Computers and Programming

This chapter is numbered zero because it is optional. It contains a brief, simplified introduction to the computer, covering such topics as hardware, software, programming languages, language processors, and programming. If you have had prior computer experience and simply wish to learn to program in Pascal, you may want to skip this chapter. Because this book is written for the Apple® II series of microcomputers (the Apple II+, IIe, and IIc), discussions about computers will focus specifically on the Apple rather than on computers in general, although most of the material applies equally well to any computer or microcomputer.*

The computer is best viewed as a tool. There is nothing magic about it; its major strengths are its speed and accuracy. The Apple can do thousands of calculations per second without making a mathematical mistake. But it can only do what we tell it to do, through the programs we provide.

0.1 Hardware
      Central Processing Unit
      Memory
      Auxiliary Storage
      Input Devices
      Output Devices
0.2 Software
0.3 Programming Languages
0.4 Language Processors
0.5 Programming

* Apple is a registered trademark of Apple Computer, Inc.

0.1 HARDWARE

Hardware is the term used to describe the actual machine we are using, with all of its various components. The Apple hardware consists of five main components: the central processing unit, memory, auxiliary storage, input devices, and output devices.

Central Processing Unit

The central processing unit (CPU) is the computer's "brain." The CPU does two jobs. First, it controls all the activities of the computer and its components, such as making sure program instructions are executed in the proper sequence, and directing output to the monitor. The CPU's second job is to perform all of the arithmetic and logical operations carried out by the computer. The arithmetic operations include addition and subtraction (multiplication and division are achieved through repeated additions or subtractions). The logical operations are comparisons, e.g., comparing two pieces of data (A and B) to see if they are equal, if A is greater than B, or if B is greater than A. Again, the major advantage of the computer is its speed and accuracy. The Apple's CPU is its 6502 microprocessor chip, shown in figure 0–1. This microprocessor is capable of performing over 100,000 arithmetic operations per second.

Figure 0–1. The 6502 Microprocessor

Memory

The Apple's memory is an ordered sequence of storage locations, each capable of holding a separate piece of information. Because the computer stores information electronically, the smallest memory unit is called a **bit**, which stands for **binary digit**. You can think of a bit as an electronic switch that is either on or off. If the switch is closed or on, we can represent it with the binary digit 1: if the switch is open or off, we can represent it with a 0. To store data using these bits, we could use one bit of memory to store two letters of the alphabet, e.g., 1 (on) = A and 0 (off) = B. But two letters would not be enough to be useful. If we added a second bit in sequence with the first, we could represent four letters, as shown in exhibit 0–1.

Exhibit 0–1. Two Sequential Bits

Bit One	Bit Two	Letter
Off	On	A
Off	Off	B
On	On	C
On	Off	D

The addition of a third bit would increase the number of letters to 8, a fourth bit to 16, and so on. To represent all of the 128 keyboard characters, would require seven bits ($2^7 = 128$). The Apple (and most other microcomputers) use a combination of eight bits.

This combination of eight bits makes up the unit of memory known as the **byte**. It may be easier to remember that one byte of memory will store one character of data. We typically refer to the size of a microcomputer's memory in terms of the number of bytes it contains. You will frequently hear this shortened to the number of K that a computer has. One K stands for approximately one-thousand (actually 1,024) bytes of memory. Thus, when we say the Apple IIc has 128K of memory, we are saying it has about 128,000 bytes (actually 131,072 bytes) of memory.

Our examples showing how letters could be stored were for illustrative purposes only. The Apple uses its own version of the ASCII (American Standard Code for Information Interchange) code, a **binary code** used by many computers to represent the keyboard characters. The actual ASCII code for the letter A is 1000001. While only seven bits are required for the ASCII code, a byte contains eight bits. The eighth bit is used by the computer for error checking.

While it helps to know that the Apple uses a binary code to store characters, you do not need to convert characters to binary code to use the computer. When you type the letter A, the Apple automatically converts it into the proper code. You might type the letter A as part of a program statement, e.g., ARC = 6, or you might type it as data, e.g., A (in response to a prompt requesting you to choose a letter from A to Z). The computer does not distinguish between these two very different uses. In each case, the letter A is stored using the same code. The two letters are simply stored in different parts of memory. The computer uses some memory locations for programs and other locations for data (and still others for graphics, etc.). Moreover, when you write programs using Apple Pascal, the computer takes care of all this memory organization on its own (with the help of the Pascal operating system).

The Apple's memory, physically located within its micro-chips, is divided into two parts, **ROM** and **RAM**. ROM stands for *read-only memory* and is used to store information that is a permanent part of memory. The information on the Apple's ROM chips contains information that the computer uses frequently; it cannot be changed or altered. For example, Apple computers contain the BASIC language in ROM. Whenever you turn the Apple on, the BASIC language is there, ready to be used (unless your Apple has a language card installed and you have loaded some other language such as Pascal).

RAM, or *random-access memory*, is used to store programs and data. Whenever a program is entered into the computer's memory, it is stored in RAM. Because RAM is the usable portion of a microcomputer's memory, the size of the RAM is what we refer to when we discuss the size of a computer's memory (e.g., 64K). RAM is not permanent memory, however. When the Apple is turned off, all of the information stored in RAM is erased.

The primary fact you should remember about the computer's memory is that it is a temporary storage place for parts of the Pascal operating system, your program, and any data your program may use. The computer, with the help of your program, keeps track of where each data item is stored in the computer's memory. Like the mail boxes in the post office, each memory location in the computer's memory has its own unique address. The computer uses this address to store data in that particular location or to retrieve data from it. When a second piece of data is stored in a particular memory location, it replaces any data already stored there.

Auxiliary Storage

In addition to the Apple's main or internal memory, the Apple also uses auxiliary storage to store programs and data in a more permanent fashion. The Apple's auxiliary storage device is the **disk drive**. The disk drive(s) allows the computer to write programs or data onto a storage medium known as a **floppy disk**.

A disk drive and a floppy disk are shown in figures 0–2 and 0–3, respectively.

The disk drive is an electromechanical device that rotates the floppy disk under a magnetic **read/write head**. As the disk rotates under this head, the data is magnetically written onto or read from the disk. The data is stored on the disk in the same binary notation that is used in the computer's main memory.

The floppy disk is a thin, circular disk coated with a magnetic medium (similar to recording tape). The disks are approximately 5¼ inches in diameter and are encased in a more rigid, square jacket. The jacket has a small oval opening or slot about 1½ inches long by ½ inch wide that allows the read/write head to pass over the disk. The disk also has a large hole in its center. The spindle of the disk drive fits into this hole, just as the spindle of a record player fits into a record. A smaller hole located just to the right of the center hole is called the **pilot hole**. This hole serves as a reference point on the disk. Most floppy disks also have a square notch cut into the right-hand side of the disk. This notch accommodates a microswitch in the drive, enabling the head to write on the disk as well as read from it. If a disk does not have this notch or if it is covered with a small tab called a **write-protect tab**, then the microswitch remains off, the write head cannot be activated and the disk is said to be **write-protected**. Disks containing important programs or data are often write-protected so that they cannot be accidentally erased or written over.

Figure 0–2. Disk Drive

Figure 0–3. The Floppy
Disk

Floppy disks are very sensitive and should be treated with
care to avoid the loss of programs or data stored on them. They
should be kept away from heat, cold, magnetic fields, and sharp
objects, and should only be handled by their top or label edge.
When not in use, they should be kept in their protective dust
covers or envelopes.

Input Devices

The primary input device for the Apple is its keyboard. The
keyboard allows the user to enter information directly into the
computer by simply typing it. The Apple takes the information
from the keyboard, converts it into ASCII code, and stores it in
memory either as part of a program or as data. The keyboards
of the Apple II+, Apple IIe, and the Apple IIc differ slightly
and are shown in figure 0–4.

Figure 0–4.

The Apple II+ Keyboard

The Apple IIe Keyboard

The Apple IIc Keyboard

Output Devices

There are two common output devices for the Apples. The first and primary device is the **monitor** or CRT (cathode ray tube). A monitor is similar to a normal television set, but without the tuner. (It is possible to use a television set as a monitor with the proper adapter, an RF Modulator.) Some monitors also have sharper displays than the normal television set, especially around the edges of the screen. Television displays are also limited to 40 characters per line, while monitors can display 80 (if the Apple has an 80-column card). Monitors typically come in black and white, green or amber phosphors, or color.

Normally, anything typed into the computer from the keyboard is echoed (displayed) on the monitor screen. Program output can also be sent to the monitor by the program.

The second output device is the printer. The printer is optional, but it does provide a means of obtaining a **hard copy** of a program or output. The most common types of printers used with the Apple are the thermal printer, shown in figure 0–5, and the dot matrix printer, shown in figure 0–6.

0.2 SOFTWARE

Software is the term used to describe the programs that tell the computer what to do. There are two basic types of software, **systems software** and **applications software**. *Systems software* refers to the types of programs that control the computer and allow users to write and/or execute other programs. Operating systems such as UCSD Pascal and Apple DOS are examples of systems software. *Applications software* refers to the types of

Figure 0–5. Apple Silentype Printer

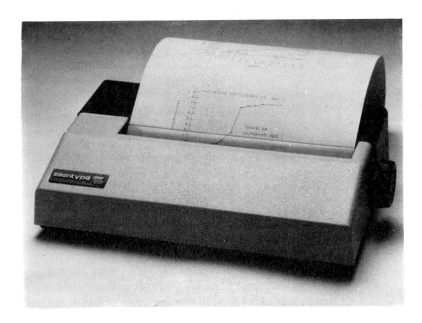

Figure 0–6. Apple
Dot Matrix Printer

programs that tell the computer to perform the tasks desired by
the user. Computer games, spreadsheets, and word processing
programs are all types of applications software.

0.3 PROGRAMMING LANGUAGES

As we have already seen, the computer only understands instructions that are in binary form and that tell it to carry out
detailed commands in a specified order, for example, we might
want to tell the computer to take one value from a designated
memory location and a second value from another designated
memory location, add the values together, and store the result
in a third memory location. While the CPU has no trouble
following such instructions when they are written in **machine
language** or **code** (binary code), we humans have a great deal of
difficulty writing instructions in that form.

To make things easier for human programmers, a number
of **high-level languages** have been developed to allow programmers to write programs in a form closer to English than to
machine language. Over one hundred high-level languages have
been developed. Four of the more popular languages are BASIC,
Pascal, COBOL, and FORTRAN.

0.4 LANGUAGE PROCESSORS

Programmers can use high-level languages to write programs,
but the CPU can understand only machine code or machine
language. To make the transition between the high-level lan-

guage and the machine language, the computer uses a program known as a **language processor**, which converts a program written in a higher level language into machine code. There are two different types of language processors, **compilers** and **interpreters**. A compiler converts the higher level language program into a machine language program. As it compiles the program into code, the compiler also checks the program for syntax errors that would prevent the program from running properly. FORTRAN is an example of a compiled language.

An interpreter executes a program by taking each program instruction separately and executing it (thereby acting as an interpreter between the program and the CPU). BASIC is an example of an interpreted language. Interpreters can also be used with the intermediate code produced when some languages are compiled.

Apple Pascal is a compromise between compiled and interpreted languages. Pascal programs are first compiled into an intermediate code known as **p-code**. This p-code is then interpreted into machine language when the p-code program is executed (run) by the computer. While it takes time to compile a program, compiled programs typically execute much faster than interpreted programs since they are either already in machine language or closer to it.

0.5 PROGRAMMING

A computer can do many tasks for us in a very fast and efficient manner. All we need is a program designed to accomplish our task. Remember, a **program** is simply a list of instructions, typically written in a higher level language, that tells the computer what to do. **Programming** is the process of creating a program. As you will learn, there is more to this process than simply sitting down at the keyboard and entering a program.

The remainder of this book is designed to give you the knowledge and experience to write your own programs in Pascal. It will introduce you not only to the correct Pascal **syntax**, but to a **problem-solving approach** to writing programs as well.

If you have not had any prior experience using the Apple, it should not be a major problem, but you may want to review the introductory or tutorial material supplied with the Apple before proceeding.

1

Getting Started—Introduction to the UCSD Pascal P-System

This book is an introduction to the UCSD Pascal language system on the Apple computer. As the book introduces new topics, it will not necessarily give you all of the information on a particular topic; you will be given only what is necessary to complete the chapter or to understand a concept. Additional information will be added as you progress through the book and the Pascal language. This structured presentation should make new concepts easier to understand, since they will be immediately applied in the programs you will write.

1.1 GETTING STARTED—BOOTING THE APPLE AND THE COMMAND LINE

The book has both **hands-on** chapters, which allow you to carry out the instructions on your Apple, and **hands-off** chapters, which cover definitions, terminology, and/or concepts and are to be read for understanding without using your Apple.

Most of the chapters are of the hands-on type and will begin with the instruction to "boot the Pascal system." The term **booting** comes from the expression "pulling yourself up by your bootstraps" and refers to the fact that the entire UCSD Pascal language system must be read into the Apple's memory each time you begin. The procedures you will follow to boot your system and the Pascal disks you will use are explained in the following sections, but they depend on whether you have one disk drive or two. The section pertaining to a one-drive system begins with an illustration of one drive;

the section pertaining to a two-drive system begins with an illustration of two drives.

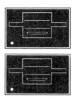

Whenever the book contains two separate sections for these two types of systems, you should read the appropriate section for your system and skip the other one.

Before beginning, however, you should follow the procedure given in appendix A and make copies of your Apple Pascal disks. Do that now, then put the original disks in a safe place and use the copies. Do not write-protect the copies; Apple Pascal must be able to write on the system disks.

This chapter is a hands-on chapter, so you should begin by booting the Pascal system into your Apple using the instructions in one of the following sections.

Booting the Apple with One Disk Drive:

Using the Apple computer with one disk drive, insert your copy of the APPLE3: disk into the drive and turn your Apple on. When the red light on the drive goes off, remove the APPLE3: disk and insert the APPLE0: disk, then press the RESET key in the upper right corner of the keyboard (if you have the newer Apple Pascal version 1.2, simply press the RETURN key when prompted to do so). If nothing happens when you press RESET, hold down the CTRL key (left edge of the keyboard) and press the RESET. This should boot the Pascal system into your Apple.

Booting the Apple with Two Disk Drives:

If your Apple has two disk drives, insert your copy of APPLE1: into drive one and APPLE2: into drive two and turn the Apple on. This should boot the Pascal system into your Apple.

The COMMAND line

When you boot the Pascal system, you will see the following message (or a similar one) identifying the UCSD Pascal system used by your computer:

```
WELCOME APPLE0, TO APPLE II Pascal 1.1
BASED ON UCSD PASCAL II.1
CURRENT DATE IS 30-NOV-81
APPLE COMPUTER INC. 1979, 1980
U.C. REGENTS 1979
```

The message, version number, and date may be slightly different on your screen. This is no cause for concern. After the message appears, it will be followed with the followin line at the top of the screen:

```
COMMAND: E(DIT, R(UN, F(ILE, C(OMP, L(IN
K, X(ECUTE, A(SSEM, D(EBUG, ? [1, 1]
```

This line, known as the COMMAND prompt line, is the entry point into the UCSD Pascal system. If you have an Apple with a 40-column display, you will only see the top (unshaded) line on your screen. If your Apple has an 80-column display, you will see the top line and the line shaded in color all on one line. In this book, 80-column prompts will sometimes be displayed on two lines, one unshaded, one shaded, due to space considerations. If you have a 40 column display, you can only see half of the COMMAND prompt. To see the right (shaded in color) half of the prompt, hold down the CTRL key (located on the left side of the keyboard) and press the A key (in the future, this will be referred to as CTRL-A). The CTRL key is much like the shift key on a typewriter, i.e., you have to hold the CTRL key down while you press the A key (or any other key referred to with CTRL-).

Having done a CTRL-A, you should now be looking at the right (shaded) half of the COMMAND line. To return to the left half of the COMMAND line again, do another CTRL-A. You should now be back where you started. The Pascal system is designed to use a page or screen that is 80 characters wide. If your screen will only show 40 characters at a time, you can only see half of the Pascal page, usually the left half. By using CTRL-A, you can shift from left to right and back again. When you make the shift, you do not simply shift from left to right on the top line, however; the shift is for the entire half page, from top to bottom. Obviously, if you have an 80-column display, you can ignore the CTRL-A (in fact, it won't do anything), since you see both halves of the screen at once. The illustrations in this book will generally be in the form shown above, i.e. the first 40 columns will be unshaded and the last 40 will be shaded. This will allow those of you with 80-column displays to see the full page while showing those with 40-column displays what they will see normally (unshaded text) and what they will see when they use CTRL-A (shaded text). CTRL-A reminders will be included in the first few chapters of this book; if you have an 80-column display, be patient (or sympathetic) and ignore them.

This chapter will not cover all the commands in the COMMAND line because they are not all needed at this point. Before leaving the COMMAND line, however, remember that this line is the entry point into the Pascal system. The UCSD system is often compared to a tree with branches. COMMAND is the trunk of the tree. When you leave COMMAND, you proceed out one of the branches to another part of the Pascal system; when you finish with that part or branch, you must always return to the trunk (COMMAND). The UCSD Pascal system has two major branches that we will use frequently: the Filer and the Editor. The Filer branch is used primarily for housekeeping functions related to the storage of programs, while the Editor is used to write and/or edit programs. Because learning UCSD Pascal involves learning how to use the UCSD p-System as well as how to program in Pascal, this chapter will focus on these two branches and some of their subbranches or **modes**.

1.2 THE UCSD PASCAL FILER ▄▄▄▄▄▄▄▄▄▄▄▄▄▄▄▄▄▄▄▄▄▄▄▄▄▄▄▄▄▄▄▄

We will now leave the COMMAND line. You should be looking at the left half of the COMMAND line. One of the commands available to you is F(ILE. Press the F key. The screen should clear and then the COMMAND line should be replaced by:

```
FILER: G, S, N, L, R, C, T, D, Q, [1.1]
```

This line tells you that you have left the COMMAND level of the system and entered the Filer. The Filer line contains additional commands that are available as part of the Filer level; notice the similarity to the COMMAND line. Also note that when you type a letter representing a command such as F for F(ILE, you do not have to hit the return key before the system acts on your instructions. This will happen whenever you type such a command.

D(ate Set

Now you can proceed with some of the Filer commands. Type a D. The Filer line should disappear and be replaced by the message:

```
DATE SET: (1..31)(JAN..DEC)-(00..99)
TODAY IS 30-NOV-81
NEW DATE ?
```

At this point, there is no prompt line (list of commands) at the top of the screen, because there is no other level you can move to from here, other than returning to the Filer. The instructions in the three lines on the screen tell us that typing the letter D while at the Filer level allows us to change the date to today's date. While this may seem like a small point, it is the starting point for work on the Pascal system—the system will later date any work you do with the current date in the system. Thus, if you always begin by updating the date, you can look back later and see when you wrote a particular program or created a data file. It is not absolutely necessary to set the correct date, it is simply a reference point for later use.

   The instructions on the screen tell you exactly how to enter the date and in what form. You should first type a number between 1 and 31 corresponding to the day of the month, then a hyphen, then a three-letter abbreviation for the month, another hyphen, and finally the last two digits of the current year, e.g., 15-JAN-85. If you make any mistakes while you are typing the date, you can easily correct them by using the left arrow key (←) to back up or erase. The **cursor** (a solid square of light) shows you where you are. Once you have moved the cursor back to your mistake, simply begin typing again. After you have correctly typed the current date, press the RETURN key to enter the date into the computer. The line

THE DATE IS 15-JAN-85

will appear directly below the NEW DATE? prompt (showing the date you entered), and the Filer prompt will reappear at the top of the screen, indicating that you have been returned to the Filer level.

It is not necessary to enter all three components each time you wish to change the date. Typing the day and pressing RETURN will enter that day, leaving the month and year unchanged. Entering the day and month and RETURN leaves the year unchanged.

To clear the screen of the remaining Date text after returning to the Filer level, press RETURN and you will be left with just the Filer prompt. You can use RETURN in this way anytime you are at the Filer level (indicated by the prompt at the top of the screen) and you want to clear the screen of text remaining from your previous actions.

N(ew

Now type the letter N. This instruction moves you from the Filer prompt level and the message

WORKFILE CLEARED

will appear for a few seconds before you are returned to the Filer prompt. The letter N stands for New and tells the computer you wish to clear the workfile so that you can enter a new program or some other text into the computer's memory. If there is already a program (or text) in your workfile when you give the New command, the computer will always ask you the question

THROW AWAY CURRENT WORKFILE?

as a precaution before erasing it. This prevents you from accidentally erasing a program you want saved. If you type the letter N (for no), the computer will return to the Filer prompt without erasing the workfile. You must answer with a Y (for yes) to erase your current workfile.

This is a good time to examine the manner in which the computer saves text or programs for you. There are three terms that you should become familiar with: **buffer**, **workspace**, and **workfile**. The buffer or memory buffer is a part of the computer's memory used for temporary storage. When you enter programs or text into the computer, they are stored in the buffer as you enter them. When you finish your entry and press CTRL-C to accept it, the contents of the buffer are transferred into another part of the computer's memory, the workspace. As an analogy, think of this paragraph as the workspace, and imagine that it was saved in the following way: as each sentence was typed, the characters went into a buffer, one at a time; when the period was typed to complete the sentence, however, the entire sentence was automatically added to the existing workspace (paragraph). Once the paragraph was completed, checked for errors, and a decision was made to save it permanently (since the buffer memory and workspace are cleared each time the computer is turned off), it was copied into a workfile on a disk for more permanent storage.

When the workfile is written onto a disk, it is automatically given the name SYSTEM.WRK.TEXT by the Pascal system. Figure 1–1 shows the relationships between the buffer, the workspace, and the workfile.

Figure 1–1. Buffer, Workspace & Workfile Relationships

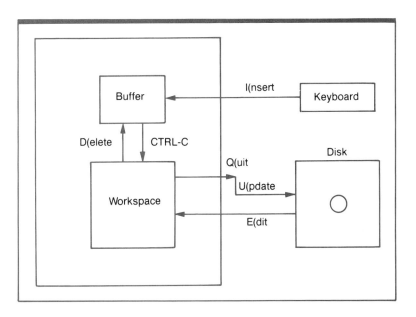

Programs (or text) entered from the keyboard go into the buffer (and also onto the screen). When we decide to save an entry, it is transferred from the buffer into the workspace. When we have finished our entry, we can make a more permanent copy by having the p-System store it as a file on a disk. As the arrows in figure 1–1 indicate, a file can also be copied (read) from a disk into the workspace, and text from that file can be moved from the workspace into the buffer. The exact manner in which these transfers take place will be explained shortly. Using the New command clears the workspace in the computer's memory and erases the SYSTEM.WRK.TEXT file from the disk.

You are now ready to leave the Filer level. Type the letter Q, which stands for Quit and tells the computer to quit or leave the Filer system. You will now see that the Filer prompt

is gone and you are bac
prompt line. You now
and have cleared the wc
gram. We will begin by
be solved by hand or by
Pascal.

1.3 THE PROBLEM

Mr. Matthews, a tenth gra
to calculate the final grade
has announced that the fin
all weighted differently: tl   counts 20%, the
class project counts 30%, and the final exam counts 50%. A
student named Rachel received an 84 on her notebook, a 94 on
her class project, and an 82 on her final exam. Mr. Matthews
now wants to determine Rachel's final grade.

Solving this problem does not really require a computer
program. The final grade can be determined by multiplying
each score by the percentage or weight and then adding the resulting components:

	score	× weight	= component
notebook	84	20%	16.8
class project	94	30%	28.2
final exam	82	50%	41.0
final grade			86.0

Thus, Rachel's final grade is an 86.

1.4 A PASCAL PROGRAM

The program to solve this problem will be our first example of
a Pascal program:

```
PROGRAM ONE;

CONST
   WGTNOTES = 0.20;
   WGTPROJ = 0.30;
   WGTFINAL = 0.50;

VAR
   NOTES,PROJECT,FINAL,GRADE:REAL;
   NAME:STRING;

BEGIN
   NOTES := 84;
   PROJECT := 94;
   FINAL := 82;
   NAME := 'RACHEL';
```

```
   GRADE := WGTNOTES*NOTES + WGTPROJ*PROJ
   ECT + WGTFINAL*FINAL;
   WRITELN ('FINAL GRADE = ',GRADE);
   WRITELN ('FOR: 'NAME)
END.
```

The terms in this program will be explained in chapter 2. In this chapter you will learn how to enter and run a program before learning the actual details of program writing. The program in this example will run, so you should concentrate on the method used to enter, correct, and run the program.

1.5 THE UCSD PASCAL EDITOR

To enter the program into your workspace, you must be in the Pascal Editor. Since a glance at the top of the screen shows that you are at the COMMAND level, you can move into the Editor by typing the letter E for E(DIT. Type an E now. The COMMAND prompt disappears, just as it did when you entered the Filer system, and the word EDIT appears:

```
)EDIT:
```

Below this prompt is the message

```
NO WORKFILE IS PRESENT. FILE? ((RET) FO
R NO FILE (ESC-RET) TO EXIT)
   :
```

Use CTRL-A to look at the shaded half of the "no workfile" message, then CTRL-A back. The message is telling you that there is no workfile currently in the computer's memory (you already knew this since you executed the New command in Filer to clear the workspace). FILE? asks you to name a file if you wish to copy an existing file from the disk into the workspace. (RET) tells you to hit the RETURN key if you wish to begin work on a new workfile, and (ESC-RET) tells you to hit the ESC key and then hit the RETURN key if you really didn't want to be here in the first place (you may occasionally hit the wrong keys). Since you do want to be here and you do want to begin entering a new program, hit the RETURN key. The preceding message should disappear and you should be left with the EDIT prompt line with a blank screen below it:

```
)EDIT: A(DJUST C(PY D(LETE F(IND I(NSERT J
(MP R(PLACE, Q(UIT X(CHNG Z(AP, [1.1]
```

I(nsert

The screen below the EDIT prompt displays the contents of the workspace memory. At the moment, both the screen and the memory are blank (empty). Type the letter I. The EDIT prompt should be replaced by the Insert prompt line

```
)INSERT: TEXT [(BS) A CHAR,(DEL) A LINE]
[(ETX) ACCEPTS, (ESC) ESCAPES]
```

You are now in the Insert mode of the Editor. The line following the cursor now represents the buffer memory; you can write anything you want on it, just as you write on a blackboard. The (BS) tells you that you can correct an unwanted character by backspacing (using the left arrow key ←). The (ESC) lets you leave the insert mode if you typed the wrong key and didn't really want to be in the Insert mode in the first place. A discussion of the other commands will be postponed for now. Type a row of approximately ten Xs (XXXXXXXXXX). You can do this by pressing the letter X key and the REPT key at the same time. If you have an Apple IIe or an automatic repeating feature, simply hold the X key down; there is no REPEAT key on the Apple IIe since it's not needed. The Xs you typed are now in the buffer memory. Press the (ESC) key. The screen should now be blank with the EDIT prompt at the top. Pressing (ESC) clears the buffer and returns you to the Editor without saving the text you inserted, i.e., without transferring it from the buffer to the workspace. This is only useful when you enter the Insert mode unintentionally or when you decide you don't want what you typed to become part of your workfile after all. This also means that you must be careful not to hit the (ESC) key accidentally when you do want to save your entry.

Let's go back to Insert; press the letter I. Now type the number 1 followed by the words THIS INSERTION. Press RETURN and enter 2WILL SERVE AS, and RETURN again. Continue until your entry looks like the one shown in exhibit 1–1, with the cursor after the period at the end of the sixth line. If you hit (RET) and the cursor is below the 6, simply press

Exhibit 1–1. Sample Entry

```
1THIS INSERTION
2WILL SERVE AS
3AN EXAMPLE OF
4A PROGRAM WE
5MIGHT ENTER
6SOMETIME.
```

the left arrow (←) key once and you will "backspace" to the end of line 6. You can now use the [(ETX) ACCEPTS] command. The keyboard does not have an ETX key, but the same result can be achieved by typing a CTRL-C (hold the CTRL key down while typing the letter C). Type a CTRL-C now. This causes the computer to move everything you have typed from the buffer into the workspace memory or "accept" it. When you type the CTRL-C, you also leave the Insert mode and move back to the EDIT level, as shown by the EDIT prompt line, which should reappear at the top of the screen.

Cursor Moves

We will now explore ways to move the cursor and change the text you have entered into the buffer or workspace. The example you typed has little in common with an actual Pascal program, but this is a good time to explore ways in which we can move the cursor over a page of text. All of the move commands are executed at the EDIT level. The cursor is now at the end of the program. To move it to the right, press the right arrow key; to move to the left, press the left arrow key (notice that at the EDIT level, the left arrow key does not erase, it simply moves the cursor). With the cursor at the end of line 6, press the right arrow key (→). The cursor doesn't move. This is because your workspace contains no text to the right of or below the cursor. You can only move the cursor over text that already exists within your workspace. Now press the left arrow key (←) and the REPEAT key or (on an Apple IIe hold the arrow key down) until the cursor is over the 4 on the fourth line. As you have seen, the cursor moves up to the previous line when you reach the end of a line. Press the space bar (SPACE) a few times. This acts like the right arrow, moving you to the right one space each time. Now press the (RET). Each time you press (RET), you move down to the beginning of the next line.

To move to a higher line, you could repeatedly press the left arrow key (or hold it down to invoke the auto-repeat on the IIe or II-c) until you reach the left margin and then backspace once more to move to the end of the line above. Moving up and down the screen this way is a slow process, however. We can speed the process up by using CTRL-L or CTRL-O (or the up and down arrow keys if you have a IIe or IIc and your version of Apple Pascal supports them). CTRL-L causes the cursor to move down one line each time you type it; CTRL-O causes the cursor to move up one line. We now have six ways to move the cursor. The left arrow moves to the left one space at a time; the right arrow moves to the right one space at a time; the CTRL-L moves down one line; and the CTRL-O moves up one line; the SPACE key moves to the right, space by space; and, finally the RETURN key moves the cursor to the beginning of the next line. Try using each of these commands to move the cursor around the screen. Be careful to only use these six commands.

Using these commands, place the cursor over the 1 on the first line. Now type the number 6 (it won't appear on the screen) followed by the Space Bar. Notice that the cursor moved 6 spaces to the right (over the I in the word INSERTION). Press the number 4 followed by **(RET)**. The cursor should now be over the number 5 on line 5. Pressing a number followed by a moving command will cause that command to be repeated the designated number of times.

Once you feel comfortable with the cursor moves, you will be ready to erase this example from the workspace and move on. To do this, type the letter Q to tell the system you are ready to leave (Quit) the Editor. The EDIT prompt will be replaced by the Quit prompt

```
)QUIT:
     U(PDATE THE WORKFILE AND LEAVE
     E(XIT WITHOUT UPDATING
     R(ETURN TO THE EDITOR WITHOUT UPDATING
     W(RITE TO A FILE NAME AND RETURN
```

The APPLE1: and a newer version of the APPLE0: disk also include a fifth line

```
     S(AVE WITH SAME NAME AND RETURN
```

These commands will be discussed later in this section under the heading "Leaving the Editor." Right now we just want to get rid of the example. To do this, type the letter E to Exit the Editor. This will return you to the COMMAND level. (Some versions of Apple Pascal may give the prompt THROW AWAY CHANGES SINCE LAST UPDATE? when you try to Exit the Editor. Again, this is a protection against pressing the wrong key. Responding by typing Y will complete the Exit.) Then type E again to return to the Editor. When the EDIT prompt reappears, you will see there is no workfile present, since we exited without updating the workfile—this has the effect of returning the workfile to the condition it was in when we originally entered the Editor (in this case, blank). Hit the **(RET)** now to prepare the Editor for a new program.

Entering the Program

It's time to begin entering our program, which is shown on the next page.

```
PROGRAM ONE;

CONST
  WGTNOTES = 0.20;
  WGTPROJ = 0.30;
  WGTFINAL = 0.50;

VAR
  NOTES,PROJECT,FINAL,GRADE:REAL;
  NAME:STRING;

BEGIN
  NOTES := 84;
  PROJECT := 94;
  FINAL := 82;
  NAME := 'RACHEL';
  GRADE := WGTNOTES*NOTES + WGTPROJ*PROJ
ECT + WGTFINAL*FINAL;
  WRITELN ('FINAL GRADE = 'GRADE);
  WRITELN ('FOR: ',NAME)
END.
```

Press the letter I to enter the Insert mode, then type in the first line (PROGRAM ONE;). Before you hit the RETURN key, check the line to make sure there are no mistakes. If there are, use the left arrow key to go back and correct them. Once you are sure the line is correct, hit the RETURN key. The cursor should now be at the beginning of the next line. Hit the RETURN key again. This produces a blank line and makes the program easier to read. Type the second line (CONST). If it is correct, press RETURN, then press the space bar twice and type the third line (WGTNOTES = 0.20;). From this point on, you should assume there is a RETURN at the end of each line—you will not be specifically instructed to type RETURN. If there is a blank line between two lines, two RETURNs are called for.

Notice that when you hit the RETURN key after typing the third line, the cursor returned to a position directly below the W in WGTNOTES, indented two spaces. This automatic indentation feature allows you to enter a program with indented lines without having to continuously space to the proper starting point on the line. The cursor will always return to a point directly below the first character on the previous line. Type the next two program lines and RETURN to leave a blank line. Automatic indentation becomes a disadvantage when you get to the sixth program line (VAR), since you do not want that line to be indented. To move the cursor back out to the left-hand margin, press the left arrow key twice. Do not enter VAR yet.

When you type the line VAR and hit RETURN, you have

entered four characters in your workspace: the letters V, A, and R and the (RET) character. You cannot see the (RET), but it is there. To test this, press the left arrow key a third time. You should see the cursor move up one line. This is because you have erased the (RET) which caused the cursor to move to that line. Press the left arrow again and the cursor should move to the end of the WGTFINAL = 0.50; line, since you have removed another (RET) instruction. RETURN twice to move the cursor back down and backspace twice to the left margin. Now enter the VAR line and continue until the end of the program, indenting and spacing as shown in the example.

When you get to the 4th line of text, "GRADE : = ...", you will see the cursor vanish off the right side of a 40-column screen as you near the end of the line. It has moved into the right half of the page; you can CTRL-A to that side to see what you are typing, but remember to CTRL-A back after you hit RETURN.

After entering the entire program, type CTRL-C to enter the program into your workspace. Check the program to make sure it is correct. Have you included semicolons at the ends of the lines where they belong (and omitted them from the lines where they don't belong)? If you have made any mistakes, the following section will explain how you can correct them.

D(elete

Using the cursor move commands, move the cursor so that it is directly over the V in VAR. Type the letter D. This is the command for the Delete mode within the Editor. The EDIT prompt has been replaced with the Delete prompt:

```
>DELETE: <> <MOVING COMMANDS> [<ETX> TO
[DELETE, <ESC> TO ABORT]
```

The (MOVING COMMANDS) prompt tells you that the left or right arrow keys will move the cursor and delete any characters that the cursor passes over. You can use the RETURN key to delete the entire line beginning at the cursor position, including the (RET) at the end of the line. If you hit the ESC key, you return to the EDIT level without making any changes, even if you have already typed some deletions. The deletions (i.e. the characters deleted) go from the workspace into the buffer, so if you change your mind while in Delete mode and press ESC to abort the deletion, the Editor copies the deletions back into the workspace.

If you enter CTRL-C (which is the Apple II version of the ETX command), you accept the deletion, and return to the EDIT level. The deletion is still in the buffer (temporarily), but it is gone from the workspace. (The buffer memory is automatically cleared whenever the Insert or Delete mode is entered.)

Try the Delete mode now. Hit the right arrow key twice; the V and A should disappear from the word VAR. Do a CTRL-C to accept this change. The text should now have the single letter R on the sixth line of text. Use the CTRL-L to move down two lines, then the CTRL-O to return. (You may make other moves if you wish, but return the cursor to a position directly over the letter R.) Now type the letter I to reenter the Insert mode and type the letters V and A again. Use CTRL-C to accept this entry and return to the EDIT level. The program should now be back in its correct form.

Leaving the Editor

You are now ready to leave the Editor. Type the letter Q. The EDIT prompt is replaced by the Quit prompt

```
)QUIT:
     U(PDATE THE WORKFILE AND LEAVE
     E(XIT WITHOUT UPDATING
     R(ETURN TO THE EDITOR WITHOUT UPDATING
     W(RITE TO A FILE NAME AND RETURN
     S(AVE WITH SAME NAME AND RETURN (on two-drive
     system only)
```

You now have four (or five) choices. If you did not really mean to leave the Editor, you can return by typing the letter R. If you type E, you will leave the Editor without updating, that is, without saving what you have entered in your workspace. This has the effect of erasing everything you have entered in the workspace. (The only time E(xit will be used is when you have entered the Editor to see what is there and then wish to leave without making any changes. In this case, your workfile is not erased because it was entered previously and you made no changes (updates.) The letter U updates (saves) whatever is in the workspace both in the computer's memory and in a work-file space on the disk (in the file named SYSTEM.WRK.TEXT). The W(rite and S(ave commands will be discussed in a later chapter. Type U to save the program and leave the Editor. The list of EDIT commands will be replaced by

```
WRITING...
```

and the message

```
YOUR FILE IS 372 BYTES LONG
```

will flash briefly on the screen (probably too briefly for you to clearly read the entire line).

1.6 RUNNING THE PROGRAM

As you can see from the prompt line at the top of the screen, you are now back at the COMMAND level. Type the letter R to enter the RUN mode. The prompt disappears and the word

```
COMPILING...
```

appears on the screen followed by

```
APPLE Pascal COMPILER II.1 [B2B] (or a similar version)
( 0)..
```

and then (if you have made no mistakes)

```
ONE [2030] WORDS
(15).....
23 LINES
SMALLEST AVAILABLE SPACE 2030 WORDS
```

(The number of words shown may vary.) If you did make a mistake, the second part of your message might look more like

```
VAR
LINE 8, ERROR 14: (SP)(CONTINUE), (ESC)(
TERMINATE), E(DIT
```

The instructions mean: hit the space bar **(**SP**)** to continue compiling (this not necessarily a good idea with a mistake in the program); hit the ESC key to leave the compiler and return to the COMMAND prompt; or type the letter E to return to the Editor. If you have this sort of message, type E. You will soon see

```
)EDIT
READING....
```

followed by a message related to your error on the prompt line with the program shown below. If, for example, you omitted the semicolon after WGTFINAL = 0.50, the message would read:

```
';' EXPECTED (POSSIBLY ON LINE ABOVE).
TYPE (SP)
```

The cursor would be at the end of the word VAR. Although the messages are not always this clear, this one identifies a missing semicolon. A list of error messages is provided in Appendix D. To make the correction in this example, you could type the space as instructed (to return you to the Editor prompt) and then just move the cursor to the end of the line and use Insert

Insert to add the semicolon (I ; CTRL-C). After the correction has been made and accepted, you can type Q U R to quit, update, and run again and receive the first message shown.

At this point the computer has taken the program that was written in text and compiled it (translated it) into a Pascal code (commonly called p-code) that the computer can understand. The compiled program (in code) will also be saved in a separate workfile named SYSTEM.WRK.CODE.

Once the program has been compiled with no errors, the compiling messages will leave the screen and the word RUNNING...will appear near the top of the screen, followed after a few seconds by the answer:

```
RUNNING...
FINAL GRADE = 8.60000E1
FOR: RACHEL
```

As soon as the answer appears and the program stops running, the COMMAND prompt line will reappear at the top of the screen. The answer is in a form called **scientific notation** (which will be discussed in the next chapter), but it is the same 86.0 that the hand calculation produced. You might note that when you typed R for Run, the Pascal system did two distinct things. It first compiled the program into p-code, then it ran (executed) the p-code program.

This concludes the hands-on portion of this chapter. If you intend to stop, you can remove the Pascal disk(s) and turn the Apple off.

1.7 SUMMARY

Once the Pascal system has been booted in your computer, you are at the COMMAND level. From this level you can proceed to either FILER, EDIT, or RUN. Filer allows you to change the date using the D(ate set mode or clear your workfile by using N(ew. Typing a Q(uit returns you to COMMAND. EDIT (the Editor) allows you to I(nsert your program or D(elete sections of it. When you Q(uit the Editor, you can U(pdate your workfile, E(xit without updating, or R(eturn to the Editor. RUN tells the Pascal system to Compile and Run your program. These commands are shown schematically in figure 1–2. You also learned that you can move the cursor about in the Editor using the keys shown in figure 1–3 as well as the SPACE to move right and the RETURN to move to the beginning of the next line.

If you have a 40-column display and can only see half of the screen at one time, CTRL-A lets you shift from one half to the other and back. Since you now know how CTRL-A works, the constant reminders in the text to use CTRL-A to look at

Figure 1–2. Current Pascal Commands

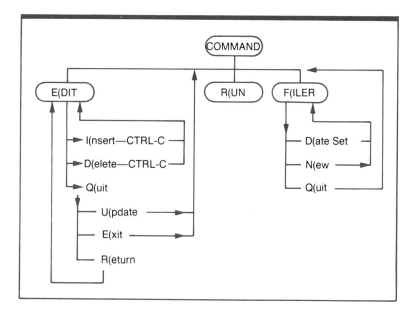

Figure 1–3. Cursor Moves

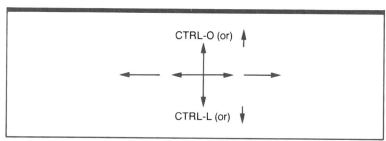

the other half of the screen will now be omitted. The complete line of material will be shown in the text, even if it exceeds 40 characters. The shading of the right half of the page will continue as a reminder to use the CTRL-A feature.

Review Questions

1. What three branches of the COMMAND level did you use in this chapter?

2. What is the purpose of the Editor in the Pascal System?

3. What is the purpose of the Filer in the Pascal System?

4. a) If you are in the Filer, what key do you press to return to the COMMAND level?
   b) Does the same key return you to the COMMAND level from the Editor?

5. If you are at the COMMAND level, what keys must you press to change the date to March 20, 1985, and return to the COMMAND level?

6. You are in the D(ate Set mode and the Current Date is July 14, 1985. If you wish to change the date to July 16, 1985, what entry would you make?

7. a) What does the N(ew command do?
b) Why is there an additional prompt (question) if you have an existing workfile?

8. When you are in the Editor, there are six keys you can press to move the cursor around the screen. Name them and explain how they cause the cursor to move.

9. If you are in the I(nsert mode and you make a typing mistake, e.g., VAE when you meant VAR, how would you correct it?

10. You are at the EDIT level and discover you made a typing mistake, e.g., VAE when you meant VAR. How would you correct it?

11. If you just entered the D(elete mode:
(a) what happens when you press the right arrow key?
(b) what happens when you press the left arrow key?
(c) what happens when you press the RETURN key?

12. The UCSD System often prompts you to press ETX, but no such key exists on the Apple keyboard. What key(s) can you press to achieve the same result?

13. When you are in the Editor, you are often told you can press the the ESC key. What is the purpose of this key?

14. The Q U R sequence of keystrokes will become a very familiar one as you use UCSD Pascal. When would you be likely to use them, and what do they stand for?

15. You are in the Editor and have just finished entering a new program. You are about to leave the Editor when you realize that you forgot to change the date before you began. Since you want this program to have the current date, you press D for D(ate Set. What will the prompt line show? Why?

16. You have just finished inserting your program into the buffer. What key(s) must be pressed to return to the COMMAND level if you want to include your insertions in the workfile?

17. You are at the COMMAND level and wish to begin entering a new program. If there is no existing workfile, what keys must you press before you can begin typing your program?

18. What name does the computer automatically give to the workfile?

19. What is the Editor's buffer memory? How is it related to the workspace memory?

20. What is the difference between the workspace and the workfile?

2

Introduction to a Pascal Program

In chapter 1, you had some hands-on experience in finding your way around the Pascal system. This chapter does not require you to use the computer; it will teach you some of the terminology associated with Pascal programming and explain the hows and whys of the program you ran in chapter 1.

2.1 REVIEW

To review the program in chapter 1, the weights were 20% for the notebooks, 30% for the class project, and 50% for the final exam, while the respective grades for each component were 84, 94, and 82. Multiplying the weights by the grades and adding the results gave a final grade of 86. The Pascal program used to solve this problem is shown in exhibit 2–1. The numbers in the square brackets [ ] are not part of the program. They are line numbers that have been included as references for discussion of the program.

Exhibit 2–1. Example Program ONE

```
[ 1]      PROGRAM ONE;
[ 2]
[ 3]      CONST
[ 4]         WGTNOTES = 0.20;
[ 5]         WGTPROJ = 0.30;
[ 6]         WGTFINAL = 0.50;
[ 7]
[ 8]      VAR
[ 9]         NOTES, PROJECT, FINAL, EARN: REAL;
[10]         NAME:STRING;
[11]
[12]      BEGIN
[13]         NOTES := 84;
[14]         PROJECT := 94;
[15]         FINAL := 82;
[16]         NAME :='RACHEL';
[17]         GRADE := WGTNOTES*NOTES + WGTPROJ*PROJ
           ECT + WGTFINAL*FINAL;
[18]         WRITELN ('FINAL GRADE = ',GRADE);
[19]         WRITELN ('FOR: ',NAME)
[20]      END.
```

When this program was run on the computer, it produced the following results:

```
FINAL GRADE = 8.60000E1
FOR: RACHEL
```

This problem and the example program are your introduction to programming in Pascal. Since most Pascal programs follow a similar format, a closer examination of this particular program will aid in the understanding of Pascal terminology and the structure of all Pascal programs.

2.2 IDENTIFIERS

An **identifier** is a name or reference. If we wanted to use two unique variables in a Pascal program, we could call them X and Y. The names X and Y are called identifiers; they help us and the computer identify the variables we are using. Pascal does not limit the use of identifiers to variables, however; identifiers are also used to name programs, subprograms, constants, and other Pascal program components that we will encounter in later chapters.

Before proceeding with an analysis of the example program, we will first learn how identifiers are used and the rules for forming identifiers. The first identifier in the example program was the program name, ONE. (Identifiers can also be used for **procedures**, which are subsections of programs, but there are no procedures in the example program). Identifiers are also used to name memory locations where data is stored for later use; data is then stored in or retrieved from those locations by referring to their names (identifiers).

We can think of the computer memory as a long row of square boxes (like a row of post office boxes). Each box holds one piece of data. If a letter of the alphabet is written next to the rows of boxes and the columns are numbered, as is done in figure 2–1, any box can be identified by simply stating the letter and number that intersect at that box. In figure 2–1, box A0 is the leftmost box in the row. Box A3 is the fourth box from the left. The designations A0 and A3 are identifiers that allow the computer to remember which box data is stored in.

Fortunately, the Pascal language does not require the user to understand the specifics of a computer's memory or to remember a long row of storage locations. The user simply specifies names, called identifiers, and the computer sets aside a unique memory location for each name. This uniqueness is important, because each box or location can hold only one piece

Figure 2–1. Memory Analogy

	0	1	2	3	4	...
A	A0			A3		

of information or data at a time. If the number 14 is stored in location A0, the value 14 would be retrieved any time the identifier A0 was used. If the computer is later instructed to store the number 42 in location A0, it would erase the 14 and replace it with 42. Now the value 42 will be retrieved any time the identifier A0 is used. Once a data value is assigned to (stored in) a memory location, it will remain there until it is replaced (intentionally or accidentally) or until the program ends.

When selecting names to use as identifiers, there are three rules that must be followed:

1. Identifiers must start with a letter. Any letter from A to Z can be used.

2. The first letter can be followed with any combination of letters (A to Z) or digits (0 to 9) or the underscore (_) (which is only on the IIe keyboard).

3. Identifiers cannot be **reserved words**, i.e., words that have special significance to the Pascal compiler. For example, the word PROGRAM is a reserved word that indicates the beginning point in the program. (Appendix B contains a list of all reserved words.)

The rules for forming identifiers are illustrated in the **syntax diagram** in figure 2–2. (This practice of introducing new Pascal syntax through the use of a syntax diagram will be followed throughout the book.)

The proper syntax for an identifier can be determined by following the arrows in the syntax diagram. Rectangular boxes contain easily recognized or previously defined parts of the structure, while reserved words or punctuation marks are shown in circles or ovals. Following the arrows in figure 2–2, we can see that a Pascal identifier must begin with a letter, then there is a choice: we can exit with a one-letter identifier, or we can move through one or more of the loops, adding additional letters, digits, or the underscore.

The following identifiers are all acceptable:

```
RATE        HOURS        A1        B97CU6M        X
```

Figure 2–2. Identifier

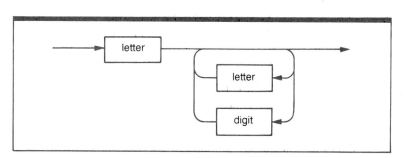

These identifiers all begin with a letter, and those with more than one character follow the beginning letter with a combination of letters and/or digits.

The following sequences would not be acceptable as identifiers:

```
RATE OF PAY    (spaces are not allowed)
B9.73          (decimal is not a letter or digit)
1A             (does not begin with a letter)
A-1            (hyphen is not a letter or digit)
```

One word of caution in selecting names or identifiers—while there is no limit on the length of the sequence, most Pascal compilers and computers do have a limit on the number of characters they use for identification purposes. Many computers only use the first eight characters in the identifier and thus would treat DATABASENOTES and DATABASEPROJECT as identifying the same memory location. Thus using these two names could result in the loss of one set of data, as discussed earlier, although the compiler will catch this with an "identifier declared twice" error message.

2.3 PROGRAM DEFINITION STATEMENT

The first line in this program

```
PROGRAM ONE;
```

is called the program definition statement. All programs begin with such a statement. Program definition statements typically contain two items: the word PROGRAM, a reserved word, tells the computer that this is the beginning of the program and the program name or identifier. The program definition statement ends with a semicolon, indicating that additional statements follow. The program definition statement, therefore, takes the following form:

```
PROGRAM name;
```

The program definition statement in our example follows this form. It begins with the word PROGRAM, the next word, ONE, is the identifier or name of this particular program, and it ends with a semicolon(;). The syntax diagram for the program definition statement is shown in figure 2–3.

Figure 2–3. Program Definition Syntax Diagram

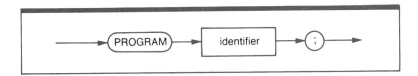

2.4 CONSTANTS

Continuing with our example program, the next four lines of text make up the constant declaration statement:

```
CONST
   WGTNOTES = 0.20;
   WGTPROJ = 0.30;
   WGTFINAL = 0.50;
```

The word CONST is a reserved word that tells the compiler to set aside memory locations for named values that will not change throughout the program. WGTNOTES, WGTPROJ, and WGTFINAL are the identifiers used to name the three constants in this program. The compiler will now allocate memory locations for the values of WGTNOTES, WGTPROJ, and WGTFINAL. The value 0.20 is associated with the constant WGTNOTES and will be stored in that identified memory location. Thus, whenever WGTNOTES is used in the program, the computer will return a value of 0.20.

You may wonder why constants are used at all when the actual number could be used. The answer is related to the whole approach to programming. In the example program, the number 0.20 could have been used directly without ever defining a constant named WGTNOTES, but this is a simple program. If the program were longer and more complex, WGTNOTES might be used several times in the program. What if we wanted to change the weights for the various components? We would have to locate and change the number 0.20 each time it occurred in the program—but this assumes that the number 0.20 is only associated with the weight for the notebook. What if it is also used as the weight for a term paper? The changes quickly become more difficult and time consuming. On the other hand, if all constants that may change in value at some future date (but not while the program is running) are identified with their associated values in the beginning of a program, future changes will be greatly simplified; only the constant declaration statement will need to be changed.

The constant declaration statement takes the following form:

```
CONST name = value;
```

Note that the constant declaration statement, like the program definition statement, ends with a semicolon to indicate that more statements follow. The constant declaration statement is illustrated in Figure 2–4. The "constant" in the syntax diagram can be a value (number), an identifier that represents an already

Figure 2–4. Constant Declaration Syntax Diagram

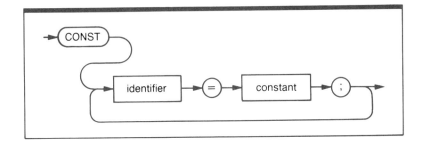

Figure 2–5. Constant Syntax Diagram

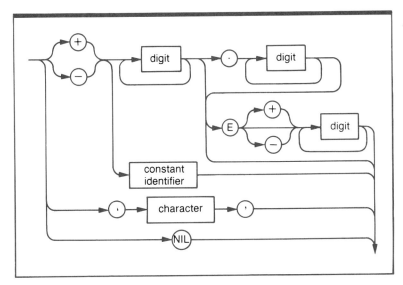

declared constant, a keyboard character (enclosed in single quotes), or the word NIL. Figure 2–5 is an expanded syntax diagram illustrating the various possible contents of the "constant" rectangle.

2.5 SPACING

Since the general form of the constant declaration statement does not look exactly like the statements in the example program, this is a good point to mention spacing. The Pascal compiler ignores spaces before or after reserved words or identifiers (but not within them). The programmer can take advantage of this fact when writing the program. By using space wisely, the program becomes easier to read and correct (if necessary). The first five lines of the example program could have been written:

```
PROGRAM ONE;CONST WGTNOTES = 0.20; WGTPROJ =
0.30;WGTFINAL = 0.50;
```

or

```
PROGRAM ONE;

CONST WGTNOTES = 0.20;WGTPROJ = 0.30;WGTFINA
L = 0.50;
```

but these forms make it more difficult to separate the different sections of the program, and they are more difficult to read. Because programs occasionally have to be corrected or changed (not always by their original author) they should be formatted in a manner that makes them easy to read and understand.

2.6 VARIABLES

A **variable** is the name given to a memory location that contains a data value that may change or vary during the execution of the program. The location is defined by its variable name or identifier. To use memory space efficiently, the computer must be told how many locations to allocate for variable storage. By using a variable declaration statement to name all variables prior to their use, an efficient allocation can be achieved. Lines [8]–[10] in the example program show a variable declaration statement:

```
VAR
   NOTES, PROJECT, FINAL, GRADE:REAL;
   NAME:STRING;
```

The word VAR is a reserved word that tells the compiler that the identifiers that follow are the names of variables. NOTES, PROJECT, FINAL, GRADE, and NAME are the variable names used in this program. The compiler will allocate five memory locations for variable values. The variable name lists are followed by colons and the words REAL and STRING. These words define the types of the variables that are listed. It is necessary to identify the type of each variable because different types require different amounts of memory. Again, the purpose is the efficient allocation of the available memory. There are five basic types of variables and each has its own reserved word identifier: INTEGER, REAL, BOOLEAN, CHAR (character), and STRING.

In our example program, the first four variables, NOTES, PROJECT, FINAL, and GRADE are all of the Real type, and the fifth, NAME, is a String variable. Space was again used to separate the word VAR from the variable list. The variable declaration statement has the general form:

```
VAR  variable name list:type;
```

Figure 2–6. Variable
Declaration Syntax
Diagram

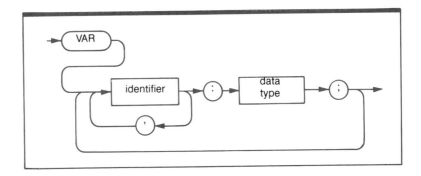

The syntax diagram is shown in Figure 2–6. As with our other statements, this statement ends with a semicolon.

2.7 DATA TYPES

The five most common Pascal data types—Integer, Real, Boolean, Char, and String—will be discussed in this section. Additional data types will be included as we need them in later chapters.

Integer

In Apple Pascal integer values are whole numbers, typically ranging from -32768 to $+32767$, although the size may vary from computer to computer. Integer variables can take only whole values; thus, 12, 30900, and -3 would be acceptable while 1.64, 5084723 (too large), and 0.05 would not. When programming, care must be taken to use integer variables correctly. If AVERAGE is defined as an integer variable, the expression

```
AVERAGE := 10/3
```

(where the slash (/) represents division) will not result in an integer value. Apple Pascal recognizes this and would not even permit the computer to try to carry out the division. If you tried to compile a program with this statement in it, you would get a compiler error message—TYPE CONFLICT OF OPERANDS—which means you have the wrong data type for this operation. (Later in this chapter you will learn how to perform division with integers.)

Real

Real values are numbers with allowable decimal parts. They can range in size from approximately 3.0E38 (3.0×10^{38}) down to 1.0E–38 (1.0×10^{-38}). The values 12, 0.62, and 129754.86

can all be used with real variables. Note that while the number 120 is a whole number, it can still be defined as a real value type. While real values can be large, they are not limitless.

In most cases, the number of significant figures that are stored for a value will be determined by the particular computer you are using. If AVERAGE is defined as a real variable, the expression

```
AVERAGE := 10/3
```

will result in AVERAGE = 3.3333333333333.... Since the computer cannot store an infinite string of 3s, the actual result it gives might be AVERAGE = 3.33333. Apple Pascal uses six significant digits. While the accuracy lost is not great, it can occasionally produce rounding errors. Thus, if AVERAGE is multiplied by 3, the result might be 9.99999 rather than 10.

Boolean

Boolean data types are special types that can take one of two values: TRUE or FALSE. They are used when we want to be able to select alternative actions depending upon a prior condition. For example, if a Boolean variable ANS is true, the program may do one thing, and if ANS is false, it may do something different. Boolean values are stored in memory as 1 (true) or 0 (false).

In addition to storing Boolean values for Boolean data types, the computer uses Boolean values whenever it makes logical comparisons. For example, if we have an Integer data type X with a value of 3, and we make a logical comparison such as (X > 2), this expression will be evaluated as TRUE by the computer. The use of Boolean comparisons will be discussed further in detail in later chapters.

Char (Character)

Char data types are single characters from the keyboard (i.e., the "value" of any character on the keyboard, upper- or lower-case, could be stored as a Char data type). They are normally used to store data that will be used literally rather than in the calculation of variable values. The characters shown below enclosed in single quotes

```
'A'   '7'   '+'   'f'
```

are all Char values. Char values are especially useful to allow single character verbal answers such as Y or N to be input, or to allow specific letters, numbers, or symbols to be output.

String

The String data type is similar to the Char type, except that a string can contain a series (string) of characters. Two strings are shown below enclosed in single quotes.

```
'WHAT IS YOUR ANSWER?'   'HELLO'
```

2.8 PROGRAM BLOCK STATEMENTS

The next section of the program contains **executable** program statements. This section is preceded by the reserved word BEGIN and followed by the reserved word END. BEGIN is not followed by a semicolon for the same reason CONST and VAR are not—it is not an independent statement (it has been placed on a separate line for clarity). All of the statements between BEGIN and END have been indented to show where the execution of the program statements begins and where it ends. The group of statements starting with the BEGIN statement [12] and ending with the END statement [20] is called a program block.

2.9 ASSIGNMENT STATEMENTS

The first five statements in the program block ([13]–[17]) are assignment statements:

```
NOTES := 84;
PROJECT := 94;
FINAL := 82;
NAME := 'RACHEL';
GRADE := WGTNOTES*NOTES + WGTPROJ*PROJ
ECT + WGTFINAL*FINAL;
```

An assignment statement is not necessarily the same as an algebraic equality. In the case of an assignment statement, everything to the right of the := symbol is evaluated, then that value is placed in the variable location identified on the left of the := symbol. Thus, the first statement above can be translated, "Replace the current value of the variable NOTES with the value 84."

The effect of an assignment statement is easier to see if the problem is modified somewhat. Suppose the teacher wanted to see what would happen to the final grade if the notebook grade were 10% higher; this could be done by adding the following statement after the "NOTES := 84;" statement:

```
NOTES := NOTES * 1.10;
```

This is obviously not an algebraic equality; it is, however, an acceptable program statement. It will replace the current value of NOTES with the value of NOTES times 1.1 (92.4).

The general form of an assignment statement is:

result := *operand*;

or

result := *operand   arithmetic operator   operand*;

as is illustrated in the syntax diagram in figure 2–7. These forms can also be changed into the more familiar

identifier := *expression*;

As with other statements, these statements are followed by a semicolon.

In the first assignment statement in our example program, the variable NOTES takes the value of the result and 84 is called the operand. Our modified assignment statement NOTES := NOTES * 1.10) has the second form: the variable NOTES still takes the value of the result, the current value of NOTES is the first operand, the asterisk (*) is the arithmetic operator for multiplication, and the value 1.10 is the second operand.

Program statement [17]

```
GRADE := WGTNOTES*NOTES + WGTPROJ*PROJ
ECT + WGTFINAL*FINAL;
```

is also an assignment statement. It contains an arithmetic expression that must be evaluated, and you will learn how it is evaluated in section 2.10.

The Use of Decimal Points in Constants and Variables

The numbers in the program statements demonstrate another feature of the Pascal language and compiler: a number cannot begin or end with a decimal point. In the constant WGTNOTES,

Figure 2–7. Assignment Statement Syntax Diagram

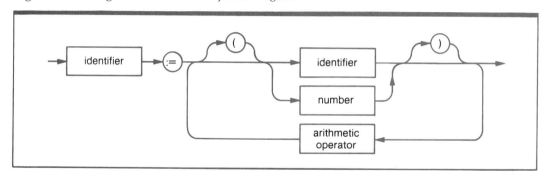

Figure 2–8. Unsigned Numbers

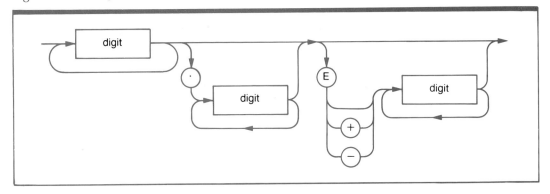

the decimal was preceeded by the digit 0 (0.20). NOTES : = 84; is also acceptable since it does not use a decimal point. Thus, X: = 3.0; Y: = 0.4; and Z: = 5; are all acceptable assignment statements, while X: = 3.; and Y: = .4; are not. Figure 2–8 shows a syntax diagram for unsigned numbers.

2.10 ARITHMETIC OPERATORS

The fundamental arithmetic operators are shown in exhibit 2–2. More than one arithmetic operator can be used in an expression (as in statement [17] GRADE := …), but some precautions must be taken to ensure that the desired results are actually obtained. When an assignment statement is encountered by the computer, the operations in the line are processed in a specific order determined by rules of **precedence**. The statement is processed in the following manner: all multiplications or divisions are carried out as they occur, moving from left to right; then (2) all additions and subtractions are carried out as they occur, again moving from left to right. For example, we might try to write the following expression

$$\frac{4 + 2}{5 - 3} \times 3 - 2$$

as

$$4 + 2 / 5 - 3 \times 3 - 2$$

The value of the first expression would be 7, but the computed value of the second expression would be -6.6. Evaluating the second expression following the rules of precedence, 2/5 is evaluated as 0.4, then 3×3 is set equal to 9, leaving

$$4 + 0.4 - 9 - 2$$

The second pass carrys out the additions and subtractions and adds 0.4 to 4, producing 4.4, then subtracts 9, leaving -4.6, and finally subtracts 2, for a result of -6.6.

Exhibit 2–2. Arithmetic Operators

Arithmetic Operator	Arithmetic Function
+	Addition
−	Subtraction
*	Multiplication
/	Division

Because of the precedence rule, this expression must be modified with parentheses to achieve the desired result. The computer processes all expressions in parentheses first (using the same rules of precedence in each set of parentheses). Thus, writing the expression as

$$(4 + 2) / (5 - 3) \times 3 - 2$$

would produce the correct result. When in doubt, you can always use extra sets of parentheses, for example,

$$(((4 + 2) / (5 - 3)) \times 3) - 2$$

would also produce the correct result.

If you are familiar with another programming language, you may have noticed that Apple Pascal does not have an exponential symbol. A method for handling exponentials will be introduced in a later chapter.

Special Division Operators for Integers—DIV and MOD

While most of the arithmetic operators just described work for both Real and Integer values, the division operator (/) will not work with Integer data types. X/Y can be used only when X and Y are both Real. For example, if X is equal to 10 and Y is equal to 3, the result will be equal to 3.33333 (note that there are six significant digits). If X and Y were both Integer data types, however, the result would also have to be an Integer value, but X/Y produces a Real value. As we pointed out earlier, attempting to compile this expression would result in a compiler error.

To overcome this problem, Pascal provides two additional arithmetic operators just for Integer division: DIV and MOD. DIV is Pascal's operator for Integer division. If X and Y are both Integer values, the expression X DIV Y will give the integer part of the quotient, for example, if X equals 10 and Y equals 3, X DIV Y will equal 3.

The MOD operator is used when we want to know the remainder of the division operation. The expression X MOD Y tells the computer to divide X by Y and return the remainder rather than the quotient. Using the same values as in the example above, X MOD Y would equal 1.

Exhibit 2–3. The DIV
and MOD Operators

Expression	Value
13 DIV 5	2
13 MOD 5	3
25 DIV 6	4
25 MOD 6	1
4 DIV 7	0
4 MOD 7	4
10 MOD 5	0

When evaluating an Integer expression containing DIV and MOD, Pascal uses the same precedence used with Real values, i.e., all multiplication, DIV, and MOD operations are performed first, then all addition and subtraction operations. Expressions enclosed in parentheses arc again evaluated first.

2.11 WRITING OUTPUT

The last two statements in the program block ([18] & [19]) are used to output the results of the weighted average calculation and the name of the student:

```
WRITELN ('FINAL GRADE = ',GRADE);
WRITELN ('FOR: ',NAME)
```

The reserved word WRITELN is used to output a line of data. This means that a return will be issued and cause the cursor to move to the next line after the last data item has been output, although the data will not necessarily fill the line. (The reserved word WRITE is also used to output data. The difference between WRITELN and WRITE will be discussed further in chapter 4.) The syntax diagram for both WRITE and WRITELN is shown in figure 2–9.

WRITELN is followed by an output list enclosed in parentheses. The output list is a list of all constants, variables, or strings to be output. In the example, 'FINAL GRADE = ' is a

Figure 2–9. WRITELN (and Write) Statement Syntax Diagram

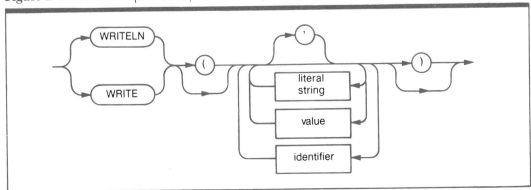

string, so all characters between the first and last apostrophes are output verbatim. The purpose of the string is to make the output easier to read. Instead of outputting

```
8.60000E1
```

on a blank screen, using the string produces

```
FINAL GRADE = 8.60000E1
```

This answer is much easier to interpret. Since the next item in the list, GRADE, is the name of a variable, the value of that variable is output. Notice that this statement is followed by a semicolon.

The last WRITELN statement is included for clarification

```
WRITELN ('FOR: ',NAME)
```

character string associated with) the variable NAME. Since RACHEL was previously assigned to NAME, the result is

```
FOR: RACHEL
```

However, there is one important difference in this statement: it is *not* followed by a semicolon! Because it is the last statement that will be executed, it is followed only by the word END, which, as previously noted, completes the group of statements between BEGIN and itself (END). END is followed with a period (.), which indicates to the Pascal compiler that this is the end of the entire program.

2.12 EXPONENTIAL NOTATION

Finally, we will discuss the form of the numerical results of this program

```
FINAL GRADE = 8.60000E1
```

Because the variable GRADE is a real data type, the answer is expressed in **floating point notation** (also called **scientific notation** or **exponential notation**). Floating point notation is commonly used when writing large numbers with many zeros in them. The E in our program's answer stands for exponent and the number to the right of the E is the exponent to which the number 10 is to be raised; the number to the left of the E is then multiplied by that power of 10. Thus the exponent indicates how many places the decimal point should be moved to express the number in standard notation. For example:

$$1.725E2 = 1.725 \times 10^2 = 1.725 \times 100 = 100 = 172.5$$
$$5.29E-2 = 5.29 \times 10^{-2} = 5.29 \times (1/100) = 0.0529$$

Exhibit 2–4. Examples of Exponential Conversions

Exponential Notation	Standard Notation
5.34000E3	5340.000
6.91700E-2	0.069170
9.82360E5	982360.0
1.20000E-5	0.000012

If the exponent is positive, the decimal point is moved to the right; if it is negative, the decimal point is moved to the left. Thus, in GRADE, since the exponent is 1 (positive), the decimal point should be moved one place to the right, producing an answer of 86.0000 (or 86). Exhibit 2–4 gives some examples of exponential conversions.

2.13 SUMMARY

We have seen that a simple Pascal program can have the following general outline:

> program definition statement
> constant definition statement
> variable declaration statement
> program block (statements)

Putting each of these sections in the correct general form, we have

    PROGRAM name

    CONST name = value;

    VAR name list : type;

    BEGIN

        (program statements such as:)
        result := = operand;   (or)
        result := = operand   arithmetic operator   operand;
        WRITELN (string, constant, variable)

    END.

Obviously, the program statements can be any mixture of assignment and/or output statements. In later chapters, the number and type of program statements will be expanded.

The following table summarizes the Pascal language terms we have learned in this chapter. This Summary of Pascal Syntax table will appear at the end of every chapter (except chapter three). The new terms presented in each chapter will be highlighted in blue.

SUMMARY of Pascal Syntax

Reserved Words	Built-in Procedures	Built-in Functions	Library Units
PROGRAM CONST VAR BEGIN WRITELN END DIV MOD NIL	WRITE		

			Boolean Constants
			FALSE TRUE

			Integer Constants

1. What is an identifier?

2. What is the first word in every Pascal program?

3. What is a constant? What is the reserved word used to declare constants? What is the purpose of declaring constants in a program?

4. What is the purpose of indenting statements in a Pascal program?

5. What purpose does the semicolon (;) serve in a Pascal program?

6. What is the difference between a variable and a constant?

7. Write the variable declaration statement that would declare the real variables X and Y and the string variable NAME.

8. What is the difference between an integer and a real data type?

9. What is the difference between a Char and a string data type?

10. What is a Boolean data type?

11. a) What are the six arithmetic operators used in Pascal?
b) What is their order of precedence?

12. a) What are the special operators used for integer data types?
b) Explain how they work.

13. What is a program block? How can you tell where it begins and ends?

14. What is meant by scientific notation? Why do you think Pascal outputs values in scientific notation?

15. Pascal programs have a certain structure or order. What is that structure?

1. Tell which of the following identifiers are acceptable and which are not. For those that are not acceptable, tell why.
a) ITEM12.4   f) 2GOOD
b) NANCY   g) BEGIN
c) X38JR   h) NUMBER ONE
d) BAM!
e) AVERYLONGONE

2. Evaluate the following expressions:
a) 4 + 6 / 2   c) 3 + 5 * 3 − 1
b) 7 * 2 + 4   d) 2 + 6 * 4 / 2

3. Evaluate the following expressions:
a) (4 + 6) / 2 − 3   d) 5 * (9 − (2 + 3)) / (6 * (3 + 1))
b) 5 * (7 − 4) / (2 + 1)
c) (10 − 8 * 2) / 2 * (4 − 1)

4. Convert the following to standard numerical notation:
a) 9.32E1   d) 6.3E-1
b) 1.54E-3   e) 8.925E6
c) 4.576E4

5. Write the following numbers in scientific notation:
a) 123   d) 0.065
b) 72.604   e) 0.0008139
c) 1397826

6. Evaluate the following expressions (assume A = 5 and B = 7):
a) A + B * 3   d) A + B − 3 / A * 2
b) B − A / 10   e) (A + B − 3) / (A * 2)
c) (B − A) / 10

7. If X = 2, Y = 5, and Z = 4, evaluate each of the following expressions:
a) 3 * X + 2 * Y   d) 6 * (Z / X) * Y
b) (3 * X + 2) * Y   e) 6 * (Z / (X * Y))
c) 6 * Z / X * Y

8. Evaluate the following expressions:
a) 14 DIV 5   d) 18 MOD 3
b) 9 DIV 12   e) 19 MOD 4
c) 17 MOD 15

9. Convert the following to Pascal syntax. Assume all variables are Real data types.

a) $\dfrac{A}{2}$ d) $F\left(\dfrac{G + H}{7}\right)$

b) 5B + 6C

c) $\dfrac{2D}{E}$ e) $4A - \dfrac{5C}{2B}$

10. Convert the following to Pascal syntax. Assume all variables are Integer data types.

a) $\dfrac{A}{2}$ d) $F\left(\dfrac{G + H}{7}\right)$

b) 5B + 6C

c) $\dfrac{2D}{E}$ e) $4A - \dfrac{5C}{2B}$

11. Write a program that will output "NOW OR NEVER".

12. Write a program that will assign a value to A and 15.2 to a variable and then output the result.

13. If A is a variable, write a program that will output ANSWER = and value of A.

---

14. What will the result of the following statements look like:
a) `WRITELN (145);`
b) `WRITELN ('ANSWER IS ',345.67);`
c) `WRITELN;`
d) `WRITELN ('ONE ',55,'TWO',999'S',999);`
e) `WRITELN (0.000364);`

15. What will the following program segments do:

```
a) BEGIN
     A := 6;
     B := 8;
     WRITELN ('RESULT = ',A)
   END.

b) BEGIN
     A := 9;
     B := 12;
     WRITELN ('RESULT = ',A+B)

c) BEGIN
     X := 4;
     Y := 20;
     Z := 5 * X + 2 * Y;
     WRITELN ('RESULT = ',Z)
   END.
```

16. Some of the following expressions are incorrect. Identify the incorrect expressions and tell why they are incorrect.
a) `C := A + 2B`   d) `C := B + .4 * A`
b) `C := 4 - A * 3 / B`   e) `C := C - B + A / C`
c) `C  = 5 / A`

17. What errors do you find in the following program?

```
PROGRAM 2B;

CONST
  A := .8;

VAR
  B,C;REAL

BEGIN
  B = 12;
  C = 6;
  WRITELN ('RESULT = ',A * B + C);
END
```

3 Moving Files to and from Disks

This chapter will cover a number of Pascal Editor and Filer commands dealing with disk storage. We will begin with L(ist, which allows you to list the contents of a disk. We will then look at V(olumes, which tells the Apple to check itself to see what devices are available for use (disk drives, printer, and so forth). Then we will use an existing Pascal program named FORMATTER to format a blank disk, and we will use the C(hange command to give the newly formatted disk a name. We will also learn how to save and retrieve files to and from our system disk (APPLE0: or APPLE1:) or a storage disk. The chapter will also discuss the K(runch command, which rearranges files on a disk to create larger storage spaces, and the E(xtended Directory Listing option, which provides a more extensive list of disk contents. This is a hands-on chapter, so boot the Pascal system, and we'll begin.

3.1 L(IST

Move from the COMMAND level to the Filer (by pressing the F key), then press the L key. This stands for L(ist and tells the system that you want to see a listing of the files stored on the disk in your disk drive. The Filer prompt line will be replaced with the question

        DIR LISTING OF ?

requesting the name of the disk you want to list. Enter APPLE0: for a one-drive system (the Pascal APPLE0: disk should be in the disk drive) or APPLE1: for a two-drive system. The screen will clear, then the name of the disk you requested will appear, followed by a list of the files saved on that disk, their lengths, and the dates they were entered on the disk (this is why you learned to set the date in chapter 1). At the end of the list is a statement telling the number of files that have been listed out of the total number on the disk (10/10 means 10 of the 10 files have been listed) and the amount of space remaining. When there are more files on a disk than can be listed at one time, the first 22 files will be listed and the instruction TYPE(SPACE) TO CONTINUE will appear above the list. Each time you press the spacebar, the next 22 files will be listed on the screen until all files and the summary statement have been displayed. The listing should look something like exhibit 3–1. The file SYSTEM.WRK.TEXT is the workfile you created in chapter 1; its date should be the date you entered. The SYSTEM.WRK. CODE file is the p-code file that was created when you com-

Exhibit 3–1. Disk Directory Listing

```
APPLE0:
SYSTEM.PASCAL            36              4-MAY-79
SYSTEM.MISCINFO          1              4-MAY-79
      .                                      .
      .                                      .
      .                                      .
SYSTEM.WRK.TEXT          4              25-OCT-84
SYSTEM.WRK.CODE          2              25-OCT-84

   10/10 FILES, 35 UNUSED, 35 IN LARGEST
```

piled your workfile. It is important to remember that any files that you created from the editor will automatically be given the suffix .TEXT and any files created from the compiler will be given the suffix .CODE. When the directory listing has been completed, the Filer prompt line should reappear at the top of your screen. Whenever you want to see which files you have on a disk or how much space you have left, you can enter Filer and L)ist the contents of any disk you name, provided that disk is in one of your disk drives.

Now repeat the process (press L), but when you are asked

    DIR LISTING OF ?

type *:(RET). The asterisk (*) represents the system disk, i.e., the disk used to boot the system—the APPLE0: disk for a single-drive system or the APPLE1: for a two-drive system.

Press L again, but this time just enter a colon (:) and (RET). You should get another listing of your system disk, because typing the colon without any disk name tells the computer to refer to the default disk. In normal use, the default disk and the system disk are the same. Thus, a simple L : (RET) will give you a disk directory listing.

While you are still in the Filer, change the date (type the letter D) if it differs from your last entry.

3.2 V)OLUMES

While you are still in Filer, type a question mark (?). On some systems, this will cause the computer to display additional Filer prompts (FILER: W, B, E, K, M, P, V, X, Z [1.1]). If your particular Apple does not display these extra prompts, don't worry, they're still available. Type V for V)olumes, which requests a listing of the Volumes that are **on-line** (connected to the Apple). One of the listings shown in exhibit 3–2 (or something similar) should appear on the screen. The first item (CONSOLE:) is the name given to the monitor and the second item (SYSTERM:) is really the keyboard. Any volume with a pound sign (#) preceding the volume name is a block-structured

Exhibit 3–2. Volumes On-Line Display

One Drive System	Two Drive System
VOLS ON-LINE:	VOLS ON-LINE:
1 CONSOLE:	1 CONSOLE:
2 SYSTERM:	2 SYSTERM:
4 # APPLE0:	4 # APPLE1:
6 PRINTER:	5 # APPLE2:
ROOT VOL IS — APPLE0:	6 PRINTER:
PREFIX IS — APPLE0:	ROOT VOL IS — APPLE1:
	PREFIX IS — APPLE1:

device (a disk). Thus, volume 4 refers to the disk in Drive 1. If you have two drives connected to your Apple, volume 5 refers to the disk in Drive 2. If your Apple contains an interface card for a printer, volume 6 will show it, even if it's not connected to the printer.

Knowing the volume numbers for the various devices can be useful. If a friend gives you a disk with information on it but forgets to tell you the volume name of the disk, you could do a listing of #4:, i.e.

```
DIRECTORY LISTING OF ?#:<RET>
```

would direct the Apple to list the contents of any disk it found in Drive 1. Remember that the colon is always part of the name of the volume, just as it is with the Apple Pascal disks.

3.3 WRITING YOUR PROGRAM (TEXT FILES) TO THE SYSTEM DISK FROM THE EDITOR

As you have been writing or modifying the example programs from this book, they have been automatically saved in the SYSTEM.WRK.TEXT file each time you Quit the Editor by Updating. Although this is advantageous, it means you can only have one program in the workfile at any time. If you want to modify the program in the workfile and also save the original version, you have to save the original under another file name. That's exactly what the Editor's W(rite option lets you do. Let's try it now. Q(uit the Filer and move to the Editor. Program ONE should appear on the screen. Now type Q to Q(uit; when the menu of choices appears, type W, which represents the fourth option available from Q(uit, i.e., W(RITE TO A FILE NAME AND RETURN. The prompt

```
NAME OF OUTPUT FILE (<CR) TO RETURN)--
>
```

will appear.

 Type APPLE0:ONE and hit **(RET)** or

 Type APPLE1:ONE and hit **(RET)**;
The disk drive will spin and the messages

```
WRITING..
YOUR FILE IS 908 BYTES LONG.
DO YOU WANT TO E(XIT FROM R(ETURN TO
THE EDITOR ?
```

will appear on the screen. Note that there was no need to add the suffix .TEXT after the file name. That is because the only type of file that can exist within the Editor is a text file. The system automatically adds the suffix when it writes to the file. Type E to E(xit. Then enter Filer and type L : (RET) to obtain a listing; make sure that the new file ONE.TEXT is on your system disk.

Thus, the Editor's W(rite function allows us to write the program in the workspace onto a disk using any file name we wish. File names may be a maximum of 15 characters in length including periods and suffixes. Some special characters are unacceptable; it is best to use only alphabetic or numeric characters. This file will always be a text file, with the .TEXT suffix added by the computer.

The following sections contain information on formatting, naming, and storing your programs on a storage disk. Since the procedures are different for one- and two-drive systems, sections 3.4 through 3.10 are included twice, once with instructions for a one-drive system and once for a two-drive system. You should read the instructions that pertain to your particular computer and skip the duplicate set. (If you have a two-drive system, skip to page 65 now.)

3.4 APPLE PASCAL UTILITY PROGRAMS

As you look at the listing for APPLE0: you can see that there is a limited amount of space available for you to save additional programs. Because of this, you will want to use some storage disks to hold the various programs you write. The following procedures will show you how to format those disks in a manner that the Pascal system can understand and use. Unfortunately, with only one disk drive you will have to change the disk in the disk drive frequently.

Formatting a New Disk

Type Q to Q(uit the Filer and return to the COMMAND level. Now type X, which stands for eX(ecute. The screen will clear and the message

```
EXECUTE WHAT FILE ?
```

will appear. Remove APPLE0: from the drive and replace it with APPLE3: Then type in APPLE3:FORMATTER and (RET). You will see

```
APPLE DISK FORMATTER PROGRAM
FORMAT WHICH DISK (4, 5, 9..12) ?
```

Remove APPLE3: from the drive and replace it with a new disk. Then answer by typing the number 4, which, you may remember, stands for the disk in volume 4 (Drive 1). The drive should clatter and spin and the message

```
NOW FORMATTING DISKETTE IN DRIVE 4
```

should appear followed shortly by

```
FORMAT WHICH DISK (4, 5, 9..12) ?
```

If you want to format more disks, put another new disk into the drive and repeat the process. When you are finished, place APPLE0: back in the drive and hit (RET). The message

```
PUT SYSTEM DISK IN #4 AND PRESS RETURN
```

followed by

```
THATS ALL FOLKS...
```

or simply the THATS ALL FOLKS... message tells you you're done. You now have one or more disks formatted for Pascal. Those disks now have the volume name BLANK:. When the FORMATTER program formats a disk, it automatically names it BLANK:. Since you would probably prefer a more meaningful name, you will want to change the volume name.

Changing the Volume Name on a Disk

APPLE0: should be in the disk drive and you should be at the COMMAND level. Type F to enter Filer and then C for C(hange. The question

```
CHANGE ?
```

asks what you want to change. Remove APPLE0:, reinsert one of your BLANK: disks, and type BLANK: and (RET). You will be prompted with

```
CHANGE TO WHAT ?
```

and should respond with whatever name you want to give to that particular volume (disk). Since you will have to type the volume name whenever you want to refer to that disk, you should select a fairly short name. For this example, however, let's use STORAGE: as the name. You can go back later and use C(hange to rename the disk anything you prefer. Type STORAGE: and (RET). The computer will tell you it was successful in renaming the disk by giving you the message

```
BLANK:            --)STORAGE:
```

3.5 WRITING A TEXT FILE TO A STORAGE DISK
FROM THE EDITOR ▬▬▬▬▬▬▬▬

You now have a storage disk available to hold any files or programs you wish to put there. We can also use the Editor's W(rite function to store text files on this storage disk. Remove the disk from the drive and reinsert APPLE0:. Type Q E to Q(uit the Filer and return to the Editor. Your example program should still be there. Type Q and then W, to W(rite to a file. Then replace APPLE0: with your newly formatted and renamed disk. Respond to the prompt by typeing in the name of your new disk volume and a file name, e.g.

```
NAME OF OUTPUT FILE (<CR> TO RETURN —
>STORAGE:ONE
```

and press **(RET)**. The disk drive should whir and the example program should be written onto your new disk. The message

```
WRITING..
YOUR FILE IS 908 BYTES LONG
DO YOU WANT TO E(XIT FROM OR R(ETURN TO
THE EDITOR?
```

tells you the program was successfully written onto the storage disk. If you want to check this (1) put APPLE0: back in the drive; (2) type E to exit; (3) type F for Filer; (4) switch the disks once more so that your new disk is in the drive; and (5) type L and STORAGE: to verify that ONE.TEXT did get copied onto your disk. Once you have made that verification, you should reload APPLE0: into the drive and press return.

3.6 SAVING WORKFILES TO A STORAGE DISK
USING S(AVE FROM THE FILER ▬▬▬▬▬▬▬

If you are in the Filer and want to write the contents of your workfile to a storage diskfile, you do not have to go to the Editor to use the W(rite function. There are two Filer methods you can use; both methods use the Filer S(ave Function, and they will be covered in this section and the following one.

The first method uses the S(ave function to save the workfile onto your STORAGE: disk. Since you are already in Filer, type S for S(ave and then, when prompted with

```
SAVE AS ?
```

enter the volume name and file name, for example:

```
STORAGE:EXAMPLE(RET)
```

The disk will whir again, find APPLE0: disk rather than the STORAGE: disk, and prompt with

```
PUT IN STORAGE:
TYPE <SPACE> TO CONTINUE
```

At this point, place your storage disk in the drive and press the space bar. The drive will whir again, and the message

```
APPLE0:SYSTEM.WRK.TEXT
--> STORAGE:EXAMPLE.TEXT
```

will appear. This message may or may not be followed shortly by a second message inserted above the first

```
APPLE0:SYSTEM.WRK.CODE
NO SUCH VOL ON-LINE <SOURCE>
```

(Whether or not this message appears depends on your version of Pascal.) The message means that the computer tried to go back and save the code file as well but was unable to do so. Type L for L(ist and then STORAGE:**(RET)**; you should see the ONE.TEXT and EXAMPLE.TEXT files listed on your STORAGE: disk.

3.7 SAVING WORKFILES FROM FILER

We can also use the Filer's S(ave option to save the workfile onto the system disk, but this method works in a slightly different fashion. Place APPLE0: back in the drive and press S for S(ave. The SAVE AS? prompt will appear again. Enter the name EXAMPLE and press **(RET)**. Notice that we supplied no disk volume name or suffix. When no disk name is supplied, the system uses the default disk (APPLE0:) No suffix is given because we want to save both of the SYSTEM.WRK files (TEXT and CODE). After the drive whirs for a moment, the message

```
TEXT FILE SAVED & CODE FILE SAVED
```

tells you that both the TEXT and CODE workfiles have been successfully saved. Typing L:**(RET)** should now show a listing that includes the files ONE.TEXT, EXAMPLE.TEXT, and EXAMPLE.CODE on your system disk. Note that the SYSTEM.WRK files are gone, however. Whenever you use S(ave with the system disk, the text and code files are saved under the file name you specify and the workfiles are cleared.

3.8 TRANSFERRING FILES

The Pascal system also gives us the ability to transfer files between disks or from a disk to a printer. These procedures will be covered in the next sections.

Transferring Files to a Storage Disk

What if you wanted to save a code file on the storage disk as well? The S(ave and W(rite functions won't do this with a one-drive system, but there is another Filer option that will: the Transfer option allows us to copy a file from one disk to another. We'll try it now. Press T for T(ransfer. The prompt

```
TRANSFER ?
```

will appear on the screen, requesting the name of the file you want to transfer. Enter the file name EXAMPLE.CODE and press (RET). The drive will find the file on the disk and then prompt

```
TO WHERE ?
```

Answer with STORAGE:EXAMPLE.CODE and (RET) (if you gave your storage disk some other name, use that name rather than STORAGE:. The system will look for the storage disk and, not finding it, will prompt

```
PUT IN STORAGE:
TYPE <SPACE> TO CONTINUE
```

Put your storage disk in the drive and press the space bar. The transfer will be made and the message

```
APPLE0:EXAMPLE.CODE
--> STORAGE:EXAMPLE.CODE
```

will show that the transfer has been completed successfully. When you use T(ransfer, you must supply the suffix for both the original and new files.

Transferring Files to the Printer

If you have a printer attached to your Apple, you can also use the T(ransfer function to obtain a listing of your program. Turn your printer on, make sure it's properly connected, and press T. Answer the TRANSFER? prompt with STORAGE:ONE.TEXT and (RET). When the prompt TO WHERE? appears, answer with PRINTER: and (RET). The disk should whir and your printer should begin printing the text file. When the transfer is completed, the message

```
STORAGE:ONE.TEXT
--> PRINTER:
```

should appear. You can then remove your printed copy of the program from the printer and turn it off (Silenttype thermal printers have no ON/OFF switch).

3.9 REMOVING A FILE FROM A DISK

You now have program ONE saved on your storage disk and on your system disk (under the filenames ONE and EXAMPLE on both). Since four copies of the same program is a few too many, we'll delete the EXAMPLE.TEXT files. We can do this with the Filer option R(emove, which allows us to delete a file from a disk. You should still be in Filer with the storage disk in the drive. Press R for R(emove. When you see

```
REMOVE WHAT FILE ? or REMOVE ?
```

enter STORAGE:EXAMPLE.TEXT and **(RET)**. The Apple should respond with

```
STORAGE:EXAMPLE.TEXT          -->REMOVED
UPDATE DIRECTORY?
```

which gives you a chance to change your mind. If you answer N (no), the file will not be deleted (removed) and you will be returned to Filer. If you type Y, the directory will be updated and the file will be gone. Type Y, then use L(ist to verify that the File has been removed. Repeat the process to remove the EXAMPLE.CODE file from the storage disk. Now let's do the same thing with the system disk. Remove the storage disk and replace it with APPLE0:. Use R(emove to get rid of the ONE. TEXT file. Once the file is removed, verify it with L(ist. (Do not remove the EXAMPLE files on the system disk.)

R(emove lets us remove files from any disk, but it should not be used to delete the SYSTEM.WRK files. To delete these files (there are two, .TEXT and .CODE) you should use the N(ew option from chapter 1. When you have an existing workfile (you shouldn't now because S(ave erased it) and you press N for N(ew, the message

```
THROW AWAY CURRENT WORKFILE ?
```

gives you a chance for second thoughts before deleting your workfile, just as UPDATE DIRECTORY? did with R(emove. A Y (yes) response will produce the WORKFILE CLEARED message we saw in chapter 1. An N (no) returns you to the Filer without deleting the workfiles.

3.10 MOVING FILES BACK TO THE WORKFILE

There may be times when you want to modify files you have saved on your system disk or your storage disk. To do so, you must copy the program file back into the workfile. You can do this by using either the T(ransfer function or a new Filer function named G(et.

Transferring a File from a Storage Disk to the Workfile

When you want to run a program located on a storage disk, you must first move it to the system disk on a one-drive system. One way to do this is to transfer the program (file) back to the system disk. You are in Filer, so type T for T(ransfer. Place your storage disk in the drive and then answer the prompt

    TRANSFER ?

with the name of your storage disk followd by ONE.TEXT, e.g., STORAGE:ONE.TEXT. Press (RET) and the drive will whir until the prompt

    TO WHERE ?

appears. Answer APPLE0:SYSTEM.WRK.TEXT and (RET). The drive will whir again and

    PUT IN APPLE0:
    TYPE (SPACE) TO CONTINUE

will appear. Put APPLE0: back in the drive and press the space bar. You should soon see

    STORAGE:ONE.TEXT
    --) APPLE0:SYSTEM.WRK.TEXT

with the Filer prompt at the top of the screen. You have now successfully recovered the file from the storage disk. Type Q to move to the COMMAND level, and then I for I(nitialize. The system will reinitialize itself (loading the SYSTEM.WRK file into memory in the process) and inform you that it has been successful with

    SYSTEM RE-INITIALIZED

Type E to enter the Editor and you should again be looking at Program ONE.

Using G(et from Filer to Move a Program to the Workfile

We will now look at an additional way to move files back to the workfile. First press Q E F to Q(uit, E(xit, and move to the Filer. Then press N (N(ew) and Y (yes) to clear the workfile. We are now ready to use G(et. When our system disk contains a file that we want to use as our workfile, we can use the Filer function G(et in much the same manner that we used S(ave. Press G for G(et. The prompt

    GET?

should appear. Enter the file name EXAMPLE and press **(RET)**. The disk will whir and the message

```
TEXT & CODE FILE LOADED
```

will appear. Type L:**(RET)**. If they are loaded, why are there no SYSTEM.WRK files listed in the directory? Because the SYS-TEM.WRK TEXT file is not created until the file in the work-space is updated. At this point, the computer has simply been instructed by G(et to regard the EXAMPLE files as the work-files. If we were at the COMMAND level and pressed R for Run, the EXAMPLE.CODE file would be executed. If we were to move to the Editor, the workfile EXAMPLE.TEXT would be read into the workspace. Once we left the Editor using U(pdate, however, a new workfile (SYSTEM.WRK.TEXT) would exist and would replace the EXAMPLE file as the workfile.

Although we used N(ew to clear the workfile before using G(et, this step is not really necessary. If we use G(et when a workfile already exists, the message

```
THROW AWAY CURRENT WORKFILE?
```

will appear allowing us to enter N (no) to forget the whole thing or Y (yes) to clear the existing workfiles and G(et new ones.

This concludes this chapter's information on file-handling chores with one disk drive. The next few pages cover the same material for systems with two disk drives. To complete this chapter, skip to section 3.11, which begins on page 72.

3.4 APPLE PASCAL UTILITY PROGRAMS

As you look at the listing for APPLE1: you can see that there is a limited amount of space available for you to save addi-tional programs. Because of this, you will want to use some storage disks to hold the various programs you write. The fol-lowing procedures will show you how to format those disks in a manner that the Pascal system can understand and use.

Formatting a New Disk

Type Q to Q(uit the Filer and return to the COMMAND level. Now type X, which stands for eX(ecute. The screen will clear and the message

```
EXECUTE WHAT FILE ?
```

will appear. Remove APPLE2: from Drive 2 and replace it with APPLE3:. Then type in APPLE3:FORMATTER and **(RET)**. You will see

```
APPLE DISK FORMATTER PROGRAM
FORMAT WHICH DISK (4, 5, 9..12) ?
```

Remove APPLE3: from the drive and replace it with a new disk. Then answer by typing the number 5, which, you may remember, stands for the disk in volume 5 (Drive 2). The drive should clatter and spin and the message

```
NOW FORMATTING DISKETTE IN DRIVE 5
```

should appear followed shortly by

```
FORMAT WHICH DISK (4, 5, 9..12) ?
```

If you want to format more disks, put another new disk into the drive and repeat the process. When you are finished, hit **(RET)**. The message

```
THATS ALL FOLKS...
```

tells you you're done. You now have one or more disks formatted for Pascal. Those disks all have the volume name BLANK:. When the FORMATTER program formats a disk, it automatically names it BLANK:. Since you would probably prefer a more meaningful name, you will want to change the volume name.

Changing the Volume Name on a Disk

APPLE1: should be in Drive 1, your BLANK: disk should be in Drive 2, and you should be at the COMMAND level. Type F to enter Filer and then C for C(hange. The question

```
CHANGE ?
```

asks what you want to change. Type BLANK: and **(RET)**. You will be prompted with

```
CHANGE TO WHAT ?
```

and should respond with whatever name you want to give to that particular volume (disk). Since you will have to type the volume name whenever you want to refer to that disk, you should select a fairly short name. For this example, however, let's use STORAGE: as the name. You can go back later and use C(hange to rename the disk anything you prefer. Type STORAGE: and **(RET)**. The computer will tell you it was successful in renaming the disk by giving you the message

```
BLANK:    --)STORAGE:
```

3.5 WRITING A TEXT FILE TO A STORAGE DISK FROM THE EDITOR

You now have a storage disk available to hold any files or programs you want to put there. We can also use the Editor's W(rite function to store text files on this storage disk. Type Q E to Q(uit the Filer and return to the Editor. Your example program should still be there. Type Q and then W, to W(rite to a file. Then type in the name of your new disk volume and a file name, e.g.

```
NAME OF OUTPUT FILE (<CR> TO RETURN --
>STORAGE:ONE
```

and press **(RET)**. The disk drive should whir and the example program should be written onto your new disk. The message

```
WRITING..
YOUR FILE IS 908 BYTES LONG
DO YOU WANT TO E(XIT FROM OR R(ETURN TO
THE EDITOR?
```

tells you the program was successfully written onto the storage disk. If you want to check this (1) type E to exit; (2) type F for Filer; and (3) type L and STORAGE: **(RET)** to verify that ONE. TEXT did get copied onto your disk.

3.6 SAVING WORKFILES TO A STORAGE DISK USING S(AVE FROM THE FILER

If you are in the Filer and want to write the contents of your workfile to a storage diskfile, you do not have to go to the Editor to use the W(rite function. There are two Filer methods you can use; both methods use the Filer S(ave function, and they will be covered in this section and the following one.

The first is the S(ave function to write the workfile onto your STORAGE disk. Since you are already in Filer, type S for S(ave and then, when prompted with

```
SAVE AS ?
```

enter the volume name and file name, for example:

```
STORAGE:EXAMPLE<RET>
```

The drive will whir, and the message

```
APPLE1:SYSTEM.WRK.TEXT
--> STORAGE:EXAMPLE.TEXT
```

will appear. After a short pause and more whirring, a second message will appear

```
APPLE1:SYSTEM.WRK.CODE
--> STORAGE:EXAMPLE.CODE
```

3.7 SAVING WORKFILES FROM FILER

We can also use the Filer's S(ave option to save the workfile onto the system disk, but this method works in a slightly different fashion. Press S for S(ave and when the SAVE AS? prompt appears again, enter the name EXAMPLE and press **(RET)**. Notice that we supplied no disk volume name or suffix. When no disk name is supplied, the system uses the default disk (APPLE1:) No suffix is given because we want to save both of the SYSTEM.WRK files (TEXT and CODE). After the drive whirs for a moment, the message

```
TEXT FILE SAVED & CODE FILE SAVED
```

tells you that both the TEXT and CODE workfiles have been succcssfully saved. Typing L:**(RET)** should now show a listing that includes the files ONE.TEXT, EXAMPLE.TEXT, and EXAMPLE.CODE on your system disk. Note that the SYSTEM.WRK files are gone, however. Whenever you use S(ave with the system disk, the text and code files are saved under the file name you specify and the workfiles are cleared.

3.8 TRANSFERRING FILES

The Pascal system also gives us the ability to transfer files between disks or from a disk to a printer. These procedures will be covered in the next sections.

Transferring Files to a Storage Disk

While the S(ave option is very useful for saving workfiles, it will not work for other files on the disk. If you wish to copy files other than the workfiles to your storage disk, you must use still another option that resides within Filer, the T(ransfer option. Press T for T(ransfer. The prompt

```
TRANSFER ?
```

will appear on the screen, requesting the name of the file you want to transfer. Enter the file name EXAMPLE.CODE and press **(RET)**. The drive will find the file on the disk and then prompt

```
TO WHERE ?
```

Answer with STORAGE:EX.CODE and **(RET)** (if you gave your storage disk some other name, use that name rather than STORAGE). The transfer will be made and the message

```
APPLE1:EXAMPLE.CODE
--) STORAGE:EX.CODE
```

will show that the transfer has been completed successfully. You can type L #5: **(RET)** to verify it. When you use T(ransfer, you must supply the suffix for both the original and new files.

Transferring Files to the Printer

If you have a printer attached to your Apple, you can also use the T(ransfer function to obtain a listing of your program. Turn your printer on, make sure it's properly connected, and press T. Answer the TRANSFER? prompt with STORAGE:ONE.TEXT and **(RET)**. When the prompt TO WHERE? appears, answer with PRINTER: (be sure to include the colon), and **(RET)**. The disk should whir and your printer should begin printing the text file. When the transfer is completed, the message

```
STORAGE:ONE.TEXT
--> PRINTER:
```

should appear. You can then remove your printed copy of the program from the printer and turn it off (Silenttype thermal printers have no ON/OFF switch).

3.9 REMOVING A FILE FROM A DISK

You now have program ONE saved on your storage disk and on your system disk (under the filenames ONE and EXAMPLE on both). Since four copies of the same program is a few too many, we'll delete the extra files. We can do this through the use of the Filer option R(emove, which allows us to delete a file from a disk. You should still be in Filer with the storage disk in the drive. Press R for R(emove. When you see

```
REMOVE WHAT FILE ? or REMOVE ?
```

enter STORAGE:EXAMPLE.TEXT and **(RET)**. The Apple should respond with

```
STORAGE:EXAMPLE.TEXT     -->REMOVED
UPDATE DIRECTORY ?
```

which gives you a chance to change your mind. If you answer N (no), the file will not be deleted (removed) and you will be returned to Filer. If you type Y, the directory will be updated and the file will be gone. Type Y, then use L(ist to verify that the File has been removed. Now let's do the same thing with the system disk. While the STORAGE: disk is still in Drive 2, R(emove the EXAMPLE.CODE and EX.CODE files from STORAGE: as well. Then use R(emove to delete the ONE.TEXT file on APPLE1:. Once the file is removed, verify it with L(ist.

R(emove lets us remove files from any disk, but it should not be used to delete the SYSTEM.WRK files. To delete these files (there are two, .TEXT and .CODE) you should use the N(ew option from chapter 1. When you have an existing work-file (you shouldn't now because S(ave erased it) and you press N for N(ew, the message

```
THROW AWAY CURRENT WORKFILE ?
```

gives you a chance for second thoughts before deleting your workfile, just as UPDATE DIRECTORY? did with R(emove. A Y (yes) response will produce the WORKFILE CLEARED message we saw in chapter 1. An N (no) returns you to the Filer without deleting the workfiles.

3.10 MOVING FILES BACK TO THE WORKFILE

There may be times when you want to modify files you have saved on your system disk or your storage disk. To do so, you must copy the program file back into the workfile. There are three ways to accomplish this: you can use the T(ransfer function; you can read the file directly into the editor's workspace; or you can use a new Filer function named G(et. The T(ransfer method will not be discussed since it is the most cumbersome and thus it is the least desirable.

Reading a File from a Storage Disk

When you want to edit a program located on a storage disk, you can load it into your workspace directly from the Editor. You should make sure your workspace is cleared (by pressing N(ew), place the storage disk in Drive 2, and then type Q(uit and E(dit to leave the Filer and move to the Editor. When you see the prompt

```
NO WORKFILE IS PRESENT. FILE? (<RET> FO
R NO FILE <ESC-RET> TO EXIT):
```

you can enter the disk volume name and the file name, e.g.

```
STORAGE:ONE
```

The disk drive will whir, the message READING.. will appear briefly, and the program will then appear on the screen.

Using G(et from Filer to Move a Program to the Workfile

Now we will look at the third method for moving files back to the workfile when you have two disk drives. First press Q E F Q(uit, E(xit, and move to the Filer. Then press N (N(ew) and Y (yes) to clear the workfile. We are now ready to use G(et.

When our system disk or storage disk contains a file that we want to use as our workfile, we can use the Filer function G(et in much the same manner that we used S(ave. Press G for G(et. The prompt

```
GET?
```

should appear. Enter the file name EXAMPLE and press **(RET)**. The disk will whir and the message

```
TEXT & CODE FILE LOADED
```

will appear. Type L:**(RET)**. If they are loaded, why are there no SYSTEM.WRK files listed in the directory? Because the SYSTEM.WRK.TEXT file is not created until the file in the workspace is updated. At this point, the computer has simply been instructed by G(et to regard the EXAMPLE files as the workfiles. If we were at the COMMAND level and pressed R for R(un, the EXAMPLE.CODE file would be executed. If we were to move to the Editor, the workfile EXAMPLE.TEXT would be read into the workspace. Once we left the Editor using U(pdate, however, a new workfile (SYSTEM.WRK.TEXT) would exist and would replace the EXAMPLE file as the workfile.

With two disk drives, you can also use G(et to move your files from the storage disk in Drive 2 to the APPLE1: disk in Drive 1. But you must leave the storage disk in Drive 2 until the program has been read into the Editor. The Pascal compiler is stored in a file on the APPLE2: disk to leave more space on the APPLE1: disk; therefore, you cannot compile any programs without the APPLE2: disk in Drive 2.)

Although we used N(ew to clear the workfile before using G(et, this step is not really necessary. If we use G(et when a workfile already exists, the message

```
THROW AWAY CURRENT WORKFILE?
```

allows us to enter N (no) to forget the whole thing or Y (yes) to clear the existing workfiles and G(et new ones.

Saving Workfiles from the Editor

You may remember that when you Q(uit the Editor, you were offered a fifth option, S(ave. If you have used G(et to designate a file as the workfile and then made modifications to that file, Quitting the Editor by using S(ave rather than U(pdate will cause the program in the workspace to be saved under the existing workfile name (rather than SYSTEM.WRK.TEXT). (If the file is a new one, i.e., if you did not use G(et, the file will be saved under the normal SYSTEM.WRK.TEXT designation.)

Before the old workfile (e.g., ONE.TEXT) is updated, however, you will be asked if you want to PURGE OLD APPLE1: ONE BEFORE S(AVE? Responding Y causes the new version to overwrite the old version; responding N causes the new version to be written to the disk before the old file is erased. While this method is safer, it requires more space on the disk.

This concludes the sections of this chapter dealing with the file-handling chores for systems with two disk drives. To complete this chapter, proceed to the next section (3.11).

3.11 KRUNCHING A DISK

While you are learning how to move files around, you should learn one additional housekeeping task. L(ist the system disk's directory (L:(RET)). At the bottom of the listing, you will see a summary similar to the one below:

```
12/12 FILES, 26 UNUSED, 18 IN LARGEST
```

The disk is organized into 280 blocks, each block holding up to 512 bytes of information. As you continue to U(pdate, W(rite, S(ave, or T(ransfer files onto the disk, there are fewer and fewer unused blocks available on the disk. When Pascal writes a file onto the disk, it does so by writing it into adjacent unused blocks. Referring to the above directory summary, you will see the disk has 26 unused blocks, "18 in largest." This means that while there are 26 unused blocks on the disk, the largest area of adjacent unused blocks is only 18 blocks long. It is important to check this occasionally, because if you try to U(pdate or W(rite a file that is larger than the "largest" figure (18 in this case), you will get a message

```
WRITING..
```

followed in short order by the following message above WRITING..

```
ERROR: WRITING OUT THE FILE PLEASE PRES
S (SPACEBAR) TO CONTINUE
```

It can be extremely frustrating to have just completed entering a long program in the Editor and to receive this message—it means you cannot U(pdate your workfile. If you had no other formatted disk available, it would also mean you could not leave the Editor without losing your latest entries. Fortunately, you can recover from this circumstance. Unfortunately, to do so you would have to: W(rite the file to STORAGE: (or any other formatted disk with enough space); E(xit the Editor; move room available through R(emove or T(ransfer; then T(ransfer the file from STORAGE: back to your system disk; and finally, reinitialize (or use G(et if you have two drives).

It is also a good idea to use T(ransfer or R(emove to keep your system disk from becoming too full. (This is especially important on one-drive systems, where the SYSTEM.COMPILER file is on APPLE0:. There were only 35 unused blocks available on the APPLE0: disk before you ever used it; the remainder of the disk contains the system files (Pascal, Editor, Filer, and so forth). Two-drive system users will find a little more space on APPLE1: (75 blocks initially) because the COMPILER file is on APPLE2:.

Let's return to our example where we had 26 unused blocks, but only 18 adjacent blocks to write files on. We can make those additional 8 blocks available by using a Filer utility called K(runch. K(runch does exactly that—it crunches the existing files together, leaving all of the unused blocks adjacent to each other. Try it now. Press K. The prompt

    CRUNCH ?   or   CRUNCH WHAT DISK ?

asks you to identify the disk you wish to K(runch. Since it is the system disk, enter :(RET) or *(RET) (or APPLE0: (one-disk drive) or APPLE 1: (two-disk drive). A second prompt

    FROM END OF DISK, BLOCK 280 ? (Y/N)

asks you if you wish to begin at the end of the disk. Type Y(RET). The drive will whir and the computer will keep you abreast of its progress, for example

    MOVING FORWARD
    SYSTEM.WRK.TEXT MOVED
    SYSTEM.WRK.CODE MOVED

(the actual files listed will vary) until it is finished and the message

    APPLE0: CRUNCHED

        or

    APPLE1: CRUNCHED

appears. When it has, type L : (RET) to List. You should now see a message similar to

    12/12 FILES 26 UNUSED, 26 IN LARGEST

Thus, all of the unused blocks are now adjacent and available. It is a good idea to use K(runch on a regular basis simply to give yourself the largest possible usable space on your system disk. While we have concerned ourselves most with the system disk because of its limited space, K(runch may be used with any disk by specifying the correct disk name when prompted with CRUNCH WHAT DISK ?

3.12 EXTENDED LIST

Move from the COMMAND level to the Filer (press the F key), then press the E key. This stands for E(xtended Directory List and instructs the system to list the files stored on your disk drive. This is very similar to the L(ist command and the Filer prompt will be replaced with the question

    DIR LISTING OF ?

which, as you know from the L(ist command, requests the name of the disk you want to list. Type a colon and (RET). The screen will look similar to exhibit 3–3.

One of the differences between the L(ist command and the E(xtended list command is that the E(xtended list shows not only the files on the disk, but also the unused areas. While both commands cause the file name, number of blocks used, and last modification date to be listed, the E(xtended list command also includes the starting block address and the file type for each file. (The E(xtended list for the Apple IIe, which has an 80-column display, may be slightly different, showing a column with bytes per block (usually 512) as well.)

3.13 SUMMARY

In this chapter, you have learned how to use a number of additional Filer functions. The L(ist function gives you a listing of the disk directory. The V(olumes function causes the Pascal system to take an inventory and tell you what equipment is currently available on your system. C(hange allows you to change the name of a volume (disk). S(ave is used when you want to store the workfiles under another name. Both the TEXT and CODE files are saved if you are saving on the sys-

Exhibit 3–3. Extended Directory Listing

```
APPLE0:
SYSTEM.PASCAL      36       4-MAY-79      6 DATA
SYSTEM.MISCINFO     1       4-MAY-79     42 DATA
SYSTEM.COMPILER    71      30-MAY-79     43 CODE
SYSTEM.EDITOR      45      29-JAN-79    114 CODE
SYSTEM.FILER       28      24-MAY-79    159 CODE
      .
      .
(UNUSED)           26                   254
11/11 FILES 30 UNUSED, 26 IN LARGEST
```

tem disk or if you have two drives; only the TEXT file is saved if you are saving to a storage disk with only one drive. The R(emove function permits you to delete files from your disks. The T(ransfer function allows you to copy files from one disk to another or from a disk to the printer. G(et can be used to designate a file from the system disk (or from a storage disk with a two-drive system) as the workfile. The K(runch function moves files together on the disk, giving you the largest number of adjacent unused blocks for storing new files. Finally, the E(xtended Directory Listing function gives a directory listing of a disk and includes information not shown when the normal L(ist function is used.

The chapter also introduced you to an additional EDIT command, W(rite, which enables you to copy the text in the EDIT workfile onto a disk under any name you choose. (Some systems also have an Editor S(ave function.) You also learned how to execute the FORMATTER program to format a new disk.

The commands that you should know at this point are shown in figure 3–1. You should now be feeling more comfortable with the UCSD system and with the basic structure of Pascal programs. At the same time, you should always feel free to refer back to prior material as needed. Comfort and ease with Pascal will grow gradually with practice and experience.

Figure 3–1. Summary of Commands

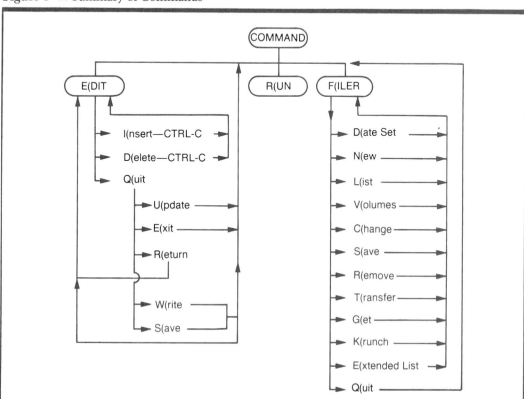

Review Questions

1. How many files on your system disk have a name beginning with the word SYSTEM?

2. There are four responses to the prompt DIR LISTING OF ? that will cause the contents of your system disk to be listed. What are they?

3. What V(olumes are currently on-line on your Apple?

4. You are in the Editor and you want to copy your current program (from the workspace) to your system disk under the file name MYPROG.TEXT. How would you accomplish this (as easily as possible)?

5. You are at the COMMAND level and want to give a newly formatted disk the volume name DISK1. How would you do this?

6. You are in the Filer and type S and then MAYBE (RET). What will happen?

7. Is it possible to use the S(ave command from the Filer to save a TEXT and CODE file to a storage disk?

8. How would you copy a CODE file from your system disk to a storage disk?

9. Once you had copied the CODE file mentioned in (8), how would you delete it from your system disk?

10. You currently have TEXT and CODE files with the name FAST on your system disk and you want to use them as your workfile. Can you do this? If so, how?

11. When you do a directory listing of your system disk, you find there are 34 blocks unused, but only 9 "in largest." What does "in largest" mean?

12. In reference to question 11, is it possible to use all 34 unused blocks to store a large program? If not, is there something you can do to consolidate the unused blocks?

13. What are the basic differences between the L(ist and the E(xtended List Filer options?

14. Not all of the Filer options may be listed on the Filer prompt line. How can we see what additional options are available to us?

15. What is the difference between Saving a workfile to a storage disk and Transferring it?

4

Introduction to Procedures

This chapter contains a large amount of information on various topics. It begins with a discussion of the COMMAND level's C(ompile and eX(ecute functions, which allow us to compile a text file into p-code and execute a code file. It then introduces a number of additional Editor functions. Procedures, small subprograms that can be used repeatedly by the main program, are also explained. The chapter concludes with more detailed explanations of the input (READ and READLN) and output (WRITE and WRITELN) statements. This is a hands-on chapter, so boot Pascal into the system.

4.1 COMPILING A TEXT FILE (PROGRAM) INTO CODE

There will be times when we have a text file (other than the workfile) stored on a disk and we want to compile it into a CODE file. Since the R(un command only works with the workfile, we will use another command, C(ompile, which tells the Apple to compile a TEXT file into a CODE file. Because C(ompile automatically tries to compile the workfile, we must first use the Filer's N(ew option to clear any existing workfile.

We will use our EXAMPLE file to illustrate the use of C(ompile. Since we already have an existing EXAMPLE.CODE file, we will have to go to the Filer and delete it before we can proceed. Do that now. (While you are in Filer, use N(ew to clear the workfile if one exists, and set a new Date if it has changed.) Then return to the COMMAND level.

Once you are back at the COMMAND level, press C for C(ompile. You will be prompted with

```
COMPILE WHAT TEXT?
```

Respond with the file name EXAMPLE and (RET). No suffix is needed since only text files can be compiled. You will then see

```
TO WHAT CODEFILE?
```

which prompts for a filename for the code file. You now have three options: you can press (RET), enter a filename identical to the name of the text file, or you can enter a different filename.

Pressing (RET) without entering a filename causes the system to use the default name SYSTEM.WRK.CODE, overwriting any file already existing under that name. Entering the identical name, in this case, EXAMPLE, will give you text and code files with the same name. If you want to have an identical name, you can save yourself some typing by simply entering a "wildcard" symbol—the dollar sign ($)—and pressing (RET). The $ instructs the system to give the code file the same name (including the same disk volume name) as that of the text file. You can also enter a unique name to give your code file a different name from the text file. In each case, no suffix is necessary. The computer automatically adds the .CODE suffix. Let's use the second option. Enter the dollar sign ($) and (RET)to compile an EXAMPLE.CODE file. You should see the same compiling messages you normally see when you press R(un.

4.2 EXECUTING A CODE FILE

Once we have a program compiled into a code file, we can use the eX(ecute command to run the program. The R(un command cannot be used, however—it can only be used to run SYSTEM.-WRK.CODE files. We used the eX(ecute command in chapter 3 when we ran the FORMATTER program. Now we'll use it to execute our newly compiled EXAMPLE file. Press X and answer the EXECUTE WHAT FILE? prompt with EXAMPLE. The .CODE suffix is unnecessary, since the computer executes only code files. You should see the same results that we obtained in chapter 1, since we have made no changes in the actual program.

The ability to compile and/or execute files independently gives us some flexibility with regard to storing files. To save space, we could simply store the code files for our programs on the system (or any other) disk. We can run (execute) them at any time. On the other hand, we could store all of our program text files on a storage disk without saving the code files. This avoids filling up disk space with seldom-used programs. Keeping the program text files gives us the opportunity to modify programs at a later date, and we can always compile the text files when we wish to execute the program.

4.3 ADDITIONAL EDITOR FUNCTIONS

Now that we have explored the C(ompile and eX(ecute commands, press F to move to the Filer, G to G(et a workfile, answer with EXAMPLE, and then Q(uit Filer and enter the Editor. The program ONE should appear on the screen with the cursor blinking in the upper left corner and the EDIT prompt line at the top of the screen. You are now ready to make changes in the program if you wish.

Recall that in the original problem for which this program was written, the teacher wanted to determine the final grade for a student named Rachel. Suppose the teacher had grade data for two students, Rachel and Sara. Sara's grades were 92 on the notebook, 86 on the class project, and 90 on the final exam (Rachels grades for the same items were 84, 94, and 82). We will modify the program to determine the final grade for both students.

As we move through the book, we will often make modifications to existing programs, especially this grading program. In this section you will be introduced to six additional Editor functions that may be helpful when making those modifications.

CTRL-Z Mode

CTRL-Z is a screen display command similar to CTRL-A. If you have an 80-column display, you may skip this section.

When you are entering lines that are over 40 characters long, you must CTRL-A to see the right end of your statement and then CTRL-A back again after hitting the RETURN key. There is another option: the CTRL-Z. Holding down the CTRL key and typing the letter Z causes the system to enter a **horizontal scroll mode**. To see how this works, move the cursor down to the GRADE : = ... line, then press the right arrow key and the REPT key to move the cursor from left to right. As you near the right side of the screen, the text characters on the screen should begin to move or scroll to the left. You can still only see 40 characters at a time, but now the 40 characters on the screen are determined by the cursor location rather than whether they are on the left or right side of the page. CTRL-A takes you out of the CTRL-Z mode (but does not necessarily leave you on the left side of the page). You will probably find it convenient to use horizontal scrolling whenever you have to enter statements over 40 characters long.

J(ump

Before proceeding with our program revisions, we will discuss two additional cursor-moving functions found in the Editor. The first is the J(ump function. Whenever you reenter the Editor, the workfile is written onto the screen and the cursor is placed over the first character (upper left-hand corner of the screen). When you have a program (for example, ONE) that is too long to fit on the screen, you can use CTRL-L to scroll down the program, but if you simply wish to move to the other end of the program, you can use the J(ump function, which lets you "jump" to the end of the file in the Editor. Press J and the prompt will change to

```
>JUMP: B(EGINNING E(ND M(ARKER (ESC)
```

If you type B you will automatically be placed at the beginning of your program. Typing E will automatically move you to the end of the program. Try it now. Press E—you should be looking at the end of the program. Type J B and you should be back at the beginning. Marker will not be covered at this time; since your program does not contain any markers, do not press M when you use J(ump.

P(age

The P(age function is similar to the J(ump function in that it allows you to move over the text in the Editor more rapidly than the CTRL-O or CTRL-L options. Pressing P for P(age causes the cursor to move approximately one "page" (screen) down the file each time it is pressed. J(ump can take you to either end of a file, but P(age can be used to move through a file quickly. Our present file is not long enough for the P(age function to be very useful, but you may want to remember it in later chapters.

C(opy B(uffer

C(opy B(uffer is an Editor function that allows us to copy (duplicate) or move text within a file. Move the cursor until it is directly over the N in the NOTES : = 84; statement. Now press D for D(elete and hit the return key 7 times, deleting the seven program statements between BEGIN and END. Then press ESC to return to the EDIT mode without deleting. The lines should reappear. The seven statements temporarily deleted from the workspace were added to the buffer. Remember, both insertions and deletions go into the buffer. Text is inserted into the buffer and then transferred to the workspace when you press CTRL-C, and text is also deleted from your workspace and transferred to the buffer whenever you use D(elete. You should now be at the EDIT level again. Type the letter C, which stands for C(opy, and the prompt line will change to

```
)COPY: B(UFFER F(ROM FILE (ESC)
```

which instructs you to type B if you want to copy from the buffer memory, type F if you want to copy from a file, and type ESC if you want to return to EDIT without copying. Type the letter B to copy the contents of the buffer. The seven statements that you deleted a few moments ago have now been copied from the buffer to the workspace and you have those seven statements in your program twice. (You will have to scroll down the screen to see the second set of statements, since they extend below the bottom of the screen.) Thus, you can duplicate text by first deleting it into the buffer, pressing ESC, and then copying it from the buffer (C B). Remember, however, that you can only copy whatever you have first deleted into the buffer. Remember too, that whenever the D(elete or I(nsert keys are pressed, whatever is in the buffer will be erased.

The C(opy B(uffer function can also be used to move text within a file. The text is first deleted and the deletion accepted (CTRL-C); then the cursor is moved to the location where you want the text, and you can C(opy it into that location from the B(uffer.

A(djust

When you C(opy from the B(uffer, the text you copy into your program is often not indented properly with respect to the rest of your program. There is an Editor formatting function, A(djust, that will solve that problem. Simply place the cursor on the first line to be adjusted and press A. The prompt

```
)ADJUST: L(JUST R(JUST C(JUST (LEFT,RIGH
T,UP,DOWN-ARROWS) [(ETX) TO LEAVE]
```

will appear. Now press the left or right arrow keys to move the line of text to the left or right. When the line is properly indented, press CTRL-C to return to the EDIT level. (You may have noted that CTRL-C is the only way to leave A(djust; you cannot use ESC with this function.)

If you want to adjust several lines, you needn't change them one at a time. After you have correctly positioned the first line (and before you press CTRL-C), use CTRL-O or CTRL-L to move up or down the screen. As you move vertically, each line you move to will be adjusted the same number of spaces (left or right) as the previous line. You can also stop on any line and use the arrow keys to make further adjustments. When you have finished, you can then CTRL-C to accept all the changes at once.

The L, R, and C options allow you to left-justify (move all text against the left margin), which is the normal mode in the Editor, right-justify (move all text so they end at the right margin), or center text (on the 80-column page). We will not use these editing options with Pascal programs.

eX(change

The eX(change function can be used to change characters of your text by overwriting the old ones. Let's try it now. Move the cursor until it is over the 8 in the second NOTES : = 84; statement and press the X key. This key takes you into the eX(change mode, which allows you to exchange characters on a one-for-one basis (similar to a simultaneous delete and insert). The prompt line at the top of the screen

```
)EXCHANGE: TEXT [(BS) A CHAR] [(ESC) ESC
APES: (ETX) ACCEPTS]
```

tells you to backspace (left arrow) to correct a mistyped character, to press ESC to leave eX(change without making changes, and to CTRL-C to accept your changes.

Type the number 92 and then CTRL-C to accept. This changes the second NOTES from Rachel's 84 to Sara's 92. Change the remaining two grades to 86 and 90 using the eX(change mode. Now use D(elete and I(nsert to change NAME

:= from 'Rachel' to 'Sara'. Why can't you use eX(change on this change? If you said because Sara is two characters shorter than Rachel, you are correct. Using eX(change to enter Sara would replace "Rach" but leave the remaining "el." There is one more change that must be made before this new program will compile and run successfully. Before reading ahead, see if you can find it.

The final change that must be made is the addition of a semicolon at the end of the first WRITELN ('FOR: ',NAME) statement. Insert the semicolon if you haven't already done so, then use Q U R to Q(uit, U(pdate, and R(un this program. You should get the answers

```
FINAL GRADE = 8.60000E1
FOR: RACHEL
FINAL GRADE = 8.92000E2
FOR: SARA
```

This seems like a lot of program for such a small amount of output. Perhaps it can be made more efficient. Return to the Editor.

4.4 PROCEDURES

As you can easily imagine, the program would get quite long if there were 10 students. The last three statements in the program statement block are repeated twice in the current program and would have to be repeated ten times for a class of ten. Fortunately, this repetition is avoidable. Pascal provides for special blocks of statements called **procedures**, which allow you to write a set of instructions once and then have the computer execute them repeatedly at any point in the program. A procedure is identified by the reserved word PROCEDURE followed by the name (identifier) of the procedure; this statement is called a procedure declaration statement and it must precede any use of the procedure within the program.

It may be easier to understand how a procedure works by looking at an example, so the next step will create one in our program. Move the cursor over the G in either of the GRADE = ... assignment statements, enter D(elete, press RETURN three times, then CTRL-C to accept. The assignment statement and the two WRITELN statements should now be in the buffer. Move the cursor up to the blank line between NAME:STRING; and BEGIN and use C and B to copy the three lines from the buffer. Use the I(nsert and D(elete modes to change the remainder of the program until it looks like the one in exhibit 4–1. (When you want to add a line that is not indented like the one above it, place the cursor at the end of the existing line, press I for insert, RETURN to move to the next line, and then use the left arrow key to move toward the left margin. Attempt-

Exhibit 4-1. Program
TWO

```
PROGRAM TWO;

CONST
   WGTNOTES = 0.20;
   WGTPROJ = 0.30;
   WGTFINAL = 0.50;

VAR
   NOTES,PROJECT,FINAL,GRADE:REAL;
   NAME:STRING;

PROCEDURE CALCULATE;
   BEGIN
      GRADE := WGTNOTES*NOTES + WGTPROJ*PR
      OJECT = WGTFINAL*FINAL
   END; (*CALCULATE*)

PROCEDURE WRITEOUT;
   BEGIN
      WRITELN ('FINAL GRADE = ',GRADE);
      WRITELN ('FOR: ',NAME)
   END; (*WRITEOUT*)

BEGIN
   NOTES := 84;
   PROJECT := 94;
   FINAL := 82;
   NAME := 'RACHEL';
   CALCULATE;
   WRITEOUT;
   NOTES := 92;
   PROJECT := 86;
   FINAL := 90;
   NAME := 'SARA';
   CALCULATE;
   WRITEOUT
END.
```

ing to use the left arrow key without a RETURN will not work,
since there are no spaces to back over in the existing line.) Go
ahead and make the changes now. Although it was not absolutely necessary, the program name has been changed to TWO
(eX(changing a TWO for the ONE).

Notice that we have established two procedures in this program, CALCULATE and WRITEOUT. The ninth statement is a
procedure declaration statement that declares the procedure
CALCULATE. This statement is followed by the procedure
block, which begins with the word BEGIN and ends with the
word END. The word END is followed by a semicolon rather

Figure 4–1. Procedure
Syntax Diagram

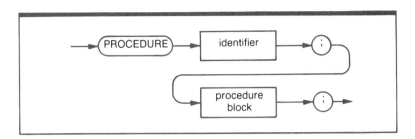

than a period to tell the compiler that there is more to follow. Any time this procedure is **called** or referred to in another part of the program, this block of statements will be executed and GRADE will be calculated. The second procedure, WRITEOUT, contains the WRITELN statements that output the answers.

Within the main program block are the identifiers CALCULATE and WRITEOUT. These names call the procedures when the program is run and cause them to be executed. Thus, Rachel's component grades and name are assigned to the variables first, the procedure CALCULATE is called and executed to determine Rachel's final grade, and the procedure WRITEOUT is called to output the answers; then the entire process is repeated for Sara. Type Q U R to compile and run this program. The answers should be the same as the ones you obtained previously.

Procedures, therefore, allow you to break up a large program into smaller parts or to establish program blocks that can be easily repeated at other points in the program. Although both of the procedures in this program were called in the main program block, procedures can also be called from other procedures. The only restriction is that a procedure must be declared before it is called. A procedure declaration statement and procedure block have the form shown in figure 4–1.

4.5 COMMENTS

Type E to return to the EDIT mode. Look at the END statements for the two procedures:

```
END; (*CALCULATE*)

END; (*WRITEOUT*)
```

They both contain **comments**. Comments are words or statements inserted into the program to clarify it for the reader; they are ignored by the Pascal compiler when the program is compiled, since they are meant for the user and not the computer. Comments must be enclosed by (* and *) (or { and } if you are using the Apple IIe) so that the compiler can recognize them as comments rather than program statements. While too many comments can clutter a program and make it more difficult to read, enough comments should be used to clarify the purpose of each section of the program. In the example program, the comments (*CALCULATE*) and (*WRITEOUT*) were placed after the END statements in the procedures to make it clear where the procedures ended. The addition of a comment after the program definition statement, for example

```
PROGRAM ONE;
(*DETERMINES FINAL GRADE*)
```

would tell another user of this program what the program does.

4.6 READING INPUT FROM THE KEYBOARD

This section deals with reading input from the keyboard using the READ and READLN statements and some of the errors that can result from improper input.

READ and READLN

You can see that our program does all the teacher asked it to do. It calculates the final grades for Rachel and Sara. Once the teacher has these figures, however, the program has little further use in its present form. What the teacher would really like is a program that is more universal in its application, i.e., one in which the assignment statements do not have to be rewritten each time another student's grade is to be calculated. We can write a program like this by using READ or READLN statements in place of the assignment statements; these read statements instruct the computer to read values from the keyboard. We will add a procedure called ENTRY to our program; it will allow data to be entered from the keyboard.

Insert the following procedure between the variable declaration statements and the CALCULATE procedure

```
PROCEDURE ENTRY;
(*READS 3 GRADES AND A NAME FROM KEYBOARD*)
  BEGIN
    READLN (NOTES,PROJECT,FINAL);
    READLN (NAME);
  END; (*ENTRY*)
```

The READLN statement instructs the computer to read a line (the end of the line is designated by the RETURN). The statement begins with the reserved word READLN and is followed by a variable list (and the ever-present semicolon). The first

Figure 4–2. READ and READLN Syntax Diagram

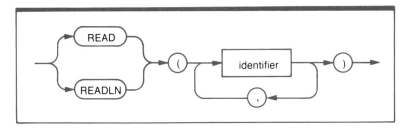

statement instructs the computer to read the values of three variables from a line. The second calls for one variable value (in this case a string) to be read. Figure 4–2 shows the proper syntax for the READ and READLN statements.

In the Pascal language, reading values from the keyboard can easily cause errors because of the manner in which values are read. Extreme caution is therefore advised whenever you write a program that requires someone else to input data from a keyboard.

When this procedure is executed, it will expect four values from the keyboard. In the first READLN, three real variables are to be read. When you begin to enter the value, each single entry (character) will be read. Thus, when you type the number 19, the digits 1 and 9 are read. As long as you continue to type digits or a decimal point (period) followed by more digits, the value of the variable will be exactly what you have typed. The computer will assume you have come to the end of the entry value when you type either a SPACE or a RETURN (the computer treats them in the same way). No other character can be used to end an entry value. It is important to understand this if you wish to avoid input errors. Typing

```
84 94 82<RET>  or  84<RET>94<RET>82<RET>
```

will assign the values of 84, 94, and 82 to the variables NOTES, PROJECT, and FINAL respectively. Why does either form work? Because, as we pointed out, the computer treats the RETURNs between the values as if they were SPACEs. The RETURN at the end of the line is necessary since READLN ends the line with the RETURN character. Why didn't the line end with the first RETURN (after 84)? Because the READLN statement treats the RETURNs as SPACEs until it has read three values. If you find this confusing, you are beginning to understand the reason for extreme care when using READ and READLN statements.

Input Errors

What would have happened if you had typed

```
84,94,82<RET>
```

Since the comma after the 84 is neither a digit nor a decimal, the computer would have correctly assumed the first value ended with the digit four and would have assigned the value 84 to NOTES. Unfortunately, since the comma is not a SPACE nor a RETURN, it would not have been totally ignored. It would be treated as the first character of the value for PROJECT, and since PROJECT is a real variable and the comma is a character, it would have caused an error and the termination of the program. This creates a real trap when data is input from the keyboard. What happens when you intend to type the digit 3 and you accidentally hit the E key? If you answered that the program would be terminated due to an input error, you understand the problem. But what if you meant to type the digit 3 and you accidentally typed 2? In this case there is no program termination, since 2 is digit. But how do you change the 2, which you don't want, to a 3, which you do want? The answer, unfortunately, is you don't. If you try to correct the 2 by backspacing over it (←), you will find that the backspace or left arrow is a character to the computer (just like the RETURN), and that this character is not a digit!

In the second READLN statement

```
READLN (NAME);
```

the variable being read is a string variable, so spaces do not represent the end of the variable entry—they are just spaces within the string. Thus, any characters from the beginning of the entry to the RETURN character are included in the string (provided the length does not exceed 80 characters).

The READ statement is similar to the READLN statement. The basic difference is that the READ statement ends after the last variable value has been entered whether a RETURN character is present or not. The statements

```
READ (NOTES,PROJECT,FINAL);
READLN (NAME);
```

could have been used in place of the two READLN statements shown previously, and would give the same results with the following entry

```
84 94 82RACHEL(RET)
```

In this case, the R in Rachel signals the end of the FINAL value and is also treated as the beginning of NAME, but since NAME is a string variable, this is acceptable. If the entry had been

```
84 94 82 RACHEL(RET)
```

the space after 2 (in 82) would have been assigned to NAME, i.e., ⌷RACHEL, a seven-character string with a blank for the first character.

Returning to the program, D(elete the assignment statements in the main program block and I(nsert the ENTRY procedure calls so that the main block looks like

```
BEGIN
  ENTRY;
  CALCULATE;
  WRITEOUT;
  ENTRY;
  CALCULATE;
  WRITEOUT
END.
```

Type Q U R to Q(uit, U(pdate, and R(un this new version of the program. After compiling, RUNNING...appears at the top of the screen with the cursor under the R. The program is waiting for data to be input from the keyboard.

Program Termination Errors

Since mistakes in data entry do happen, you might as well be prepared. Type 5 and then press the left arrow key. The program will stop immediately and the message

```
IO ERROR: BAD INPUT FORMAT
S#1, P#2, I# 183
TYPE <SPACE> TO CONTINUE
```

will appear on your screen. The message indicates that the program has been terminated due to an input error. (IO stands for input/output.) There is no reason to panic; follow the directions and press the space bar. The drives will begin reading your Pascal diskettes, the screen will clear, and the message

```
SYSTEM RE-INITIALIZED
```

will appear near the top of the screen followed quickly by the COMMAND prompt line above it. The Pascal system has now recovered from the mistake and is ready to begin again. You can type R to R(un again and try to avoid any entry mistakes (intentional or otherwise) this time. Now type 84 94 82(RET) RACHEL(RET). The screen should show

```
RUNNING...
84 94 82
RACHEL
FINAL GRADE = 8.60000E1
FOR: RACHEL
```

with the cursor directly under the F (The entries have been shaded for clarity). Type 92**(RET)**86**(RET)**90 **(RET)**SARA**(RET)**. The screen should continue with

```
92
86
90
SARA
FINAL GRADE = 8.92000E2
FOR: SARA
```

and the COMMAND prompt should reappear at the top of the screen. This indicates that the program has been completed.

4.7 USING WRITELN STATEMENTS FOR CLARIFICATION OF INPUT

When the program began running, you could tell it was waiting to read data because: (1) RUNNING... was at the top of the screen, not the prompt line; and (2) the cursor (white square) was on the second line of the screen, indicating that the computer was ready to accept input. If you were not familiar with the program, however, you would not know what type of input was expected or how to input it correctly. For someone not familiar with the program, entering the data correctly would be almost impossible. To avoid this difficulty, you can add a set of instructions to help the user input data correctly. Return to the EDIT mode and change the Entry procedure as shown in exhibit 4–2.

The first WRITELN statement, with no variable lists or strings after it, causes a blank line to be printed. The next three WRITELN statements cause the instructions to be printed on the first three lines. Three statements were used

Exhibit 4–2. Procedure ENTRY

```
PROCEDURE ENTRY;
  BEGIN
    WRITELN;
    WRITELN ('ENTER GRADES UNDER THE');
    WRITELN ('APPROPRIATE TITLE WITH SPACES');
    WRITELN ('BETWEEN THEM, THEN TYPE RETURN');
    WRITELN;
    WRITELN ('  COMPONENTS');
    WRITELN ('NOTE PROJ FINAL');
    WRITELN ('---- ---- -----');
    READLN (NOTES,PROJECT,FINAL);
    WRITELN;
    WRITE ('ENTER NAME AND TYPE RETURN:');
    READLN (NAME)
  END; (*ENTRY*)
```

instead of one long one to make the instructions easier to read—each of the three lines is less than 40 characters long and will therefore appear completely on the screen (a single longer line would use the full 80-character Pascal page width and disappear off the right-hand side of the screen). The next WRITELN statement is again used for spacing to make the output easier to read. The next three lines provide a heading for the input and the following READLN reads that input. A WRITELN is again used for spacing. The WRITE statement is used with the name entry instructions rather than the WRITELN so that the entry may be made on the same line as the instruction (and to illustrate the difference between the two statements). A final READLN statement reads the name.

As long as you are making changes that will make the program easier to read and use, change the WRITEOUT procedure to:

```
PROCEDURE WRITEOUT;
  BEGIN
    WRITELN;
    WRITELN (NAME, '''S FINAL GRADE ='
    ,GRADE:8:2);
    WRITELN
  END (*WRITEOUT*);
```

In the second WRITELN, the student's name will be written followed by an apostrophe S ('S), then there is an explanation of what will be written next (FINAL GRADE =), and then the value of GRADE will be written. Because an apostrophe is used to denote the beginning or end of a string, two consecutive apostrophes are necessary to output an apostrophe within the string. In this case, there are three consecutive apostrophes—one to mark the beginning of the string and the next two to output an apostrophe. It is somewhat unusual to have a string begin with an apostrophe—a more typical string might be 'SAM''S GRADE'. Again, the single apostrophe marks the beginning and end of the string and the double apostrophe (not a quote) causes a single apostrophe to be written on the screen.

Once you have made these changes, type Q U R to check their effect. Your results should look like those in exhibit 4–3 (the input data is shaded). The teacher now has a program that allows him to input data for any two students, and it is complete with instructions on how to enter the data. In addition, the results are in a much more readable form. The next section will discuss the change in the form of the results, so type E to return to the Editor and move the cursor down until the WRITEOUT Procedure is on the screen.

Exhibit 4–3. Program
TWO Results

```
ENTER GRADES UNDER THE
APPROPRIATE COMPONENT WITH SPACES
BETWEEN THEM, THEN TYPE RETURN

   COMPONENTS
NOTE PROJ FINAL
____ ____ _____
 84   94   82(RET)

ENTER NAME AND TYPE RETURN:RACHEL(RET)

RACHEL'S FINAL GRADE = 86.00

ENTER GRADES UNDER THE
APPROPRIATE COMPONENT WITH SPACES
BETWEEN THEM, THEN TYPE RETURN

   COMPONENTS
NOTE PROJ FINAL
____ ____ _____
 92   86   90(RET)

ENTER NAME AND TYPE RETURN:SARA(RET)

SARA'S FINAL GRADE = 89.20
```

4.8 FORMATTING OUTPUT

Note the addition to the second WRITELN statement after GRADE—colon, 8, colon, 2 (:8:2). This caused the output to be written in a special form called a **format**. The first colon followed by the number 8 instructed the computer to print the value of GRADE in the next 8 spaces; the second colon and the number 2 instructed the computer to output a value with only two digits to the right of the decimal point.

When you allocate spaces for a formatted output, remember to leave a space for the sign (+ or −) of the number and a space for the decimal point. The computer will always allocate the first space in the format field for the sign, even though it does not print a plus sign in front of positive numbers. When printing negative numbers, the first space is saved for the sign even though the minus sign will be moved to the right and printed just prior to the first digit, no matter where that digit falls within the format field. The general form of the format is

variable name:number of spaces:places to the right of the decimal

If you wish to allocate a particular number of spaces for your

Exhibit 4–4. Formatted Outputs

Statement	Resulting Output	[Line]
WRITELN (15.35:7:3)	□15.350	[1]
WRITELN (-23.0:8:2)	□□-23.00	[2]
WRITELN (123.456:8:2)	□□123.46	[3]
WRITELN (-123.432:9:2)	□□-123.43	[4]
WRITELN (123456.78)	□1.23457E5	[5]
WRITELN (123456.789:15)	□□□□□□1.23457E5	[6]
WRITELN (123456.78:12:2)	□□□123457.□□	[7]
WRITELN (123456.78:4:2)	□123457.	[8]
WRITELN (12345678901)	□12345678901	[9]
WRITELN ('STRING':10)	□□□□STRING	[10]
WRITELN ('STRING':3)	STR	[11]

answer without specifying the number of decimal places, simply omit the second colon and digit.

Examples of formatted WRITELN outputs and the results are shown in exhibit 4–4. The open boxes represent the spaces. The first two lines are fairly straightforward. Line [3] shows that when there are fewer decimal places in the format than in the actual number, the number is rounded. Line [4] shows a negative number. The fifth through ninth lines are variations on the same theme.

Line [5] is an unformatted large number, which is rounded and printed with 6 digits in scientific notation. Why does the number begin in the second space? Because the first space was left for the plus sign, even though it is not printed. In line [6], the same number is formatted to 15 spaces; it gives the same numerical result, but the number is right-justified, i.e., moved to the right so that the last digit is printed in the 15th space. Line [7] shows a large real number that is to be printed in 12 spaces with 2 decimal places. Because the resulting number is over 6 digits long, however, it is rounded to 6 digits. Notice that the number appears to be printed in ten spaces, right-justified. The computer is actually using twelve spaces, since there are two spaces to the right of the decimal. It is just that the numbers were not printed (not even 00) because the entire number exceeded 6 digits. Line ([8]) shows the same number formatted for 4 spaces with 2 decimal places. Since this format is impossible, the computer ignores it and prints as much of the number as it can, left-justified. The ninth line shows a very long unformatted number that seems to be printed exactly as it was written, without rounding. The reason for this is that this particular number differs from all of the preceding numbers in one respect. Can you tell how? This number is an Integer (type). The computer does not round integers as it does real numbers. This is an important point to remember when you desire a great deal of accuracy in your figures and wish to avoid possible rounding errors. This point will be expanded in a later chapter.

The tenth and eleventh lines show how formatting affects a string. In the first case, the string was printed as expected, right-justified within ten spaces. In the second case, the formatted space was shorter than the length of the string and the result was the truncation of the string after the first three characters. As you look at line [11], it appears that the strings begin one space to the left of the numbers. This is not actually the case, but it appears to be so because with numbers, the first space is always left for a plus (+) or minus (−) sign. When there are more than enough spaces to hold the actual number and sign, the sign is placed to the immediate left of the first digit (as in lines [2] and [4]).

4.9 SOME DIFFERENCES BETWEEN WRITE AND WRITELN

You may have noticed that both WRITE and WRITELN were used in the ENTRY Procedure. Each of these statements, whose syntax diagrams are shown in figure 4–3, directs output to be written to the screen. The basic difference is that WRITE does not issue a carriage return when it is completed, while WRITELN does.

We can write a simple program to illustrate how this works. Press Q E F to Q(uit, E(xit without U(pdating, and enter the Filer. Type S TWO to S(ave the workfile under the name TWO (text and code). Then type N Y Q E and **(RET)** (N for N(ew to clear the workfile, Yes response to THROW AWAY..., Q to Q(uit the Filer, E to return to the Editor, and finally, **(RET)** to acknowledge that there is no workfile present). Now press I (I(nsert) and enter the program shown in exhibit 4–5. After using CTRL-C to accept, enter Q U R. After compiling, you should see

Figure 4–3. WRITE and WRITELN Syntax Diagram

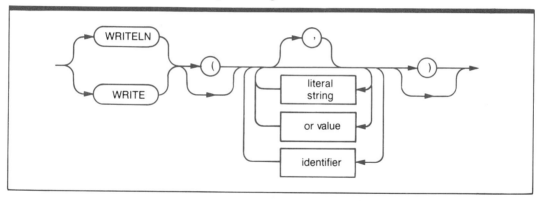

Exhibit 4–5. Program
RITE

```
PROGRAM RITE;

BEGIN
   WRITELN;               (*SKIPS A LINE*)
   WRITE ('THIS');        (*WRITES A WORD*)
   WRITE ('IS ALL');
   WRITE ('ON ONE LINE.');
   WRITELN;               (*ISSUES (CR)*)
   WRITELN;               (*SKIP LINE*)
   WRITELN ('THIS');      (*WRITES A LINE*)
   WRITELN ('IS');
   WRITELN ('NOT')
END.
```

```
RUNNING..

THIS IS ALL ON ONE LINE.

THIS
IS
NOT
```

The first WRITELN produces the space between Running..
and the first written output. The output THIS IS ALL ON ONE
LINE. is accomplished by the next four statements—three
WRITEs and one WRITELN. Note that a space is included at the
end of each of the first two strings to achieve the proper spacing. Thus, the first WRITE statement causes the word THIS
followed by a space to be printed, but no carriage return is
issued. This leaves the cursor over the sixth character position
on the line. When the second WRITE statement is executed, it
begins with the letter I in the sixth space and continues from
there. The square brackets show how each of the WRITE or
WRITELN statements in this program works:

```
[(RET)]
[THIS ][IS ALL ][ON ONE LINE.][(RET)]
[(RET)]
[THIS(RET)]
[IS(RET)]
[NOT(RET)]
```

While WRITELN statements are often more practical because the output is physically separated and therefore easier to
read, there are times when WRITE statements are useful. For
example, in the example program in chapter 3, we used a WRITE
statement to request a response from the user. The WRITE
statement was preferable in this case because the cursor re-
mained on the line immediately following the request (question). This positioning makes things easier for the user, and it

is the same format that the Pascal operating system uses for its questions, i.e., the cursor remains on the line following the question mark in TRANSFER ?, CHANGE ?, REMOVE ?, and so forth.

4.10 WRITING OUTPUT TO A PRINTER

If you have a printer connected to your Apple, there will be times when you want to have a printed (hard) copy of your program or program output. You can obtain a printed copy of your program by going to the Filer and Transferring the file containing your program (probably SYSTEM.WRK.TEXT) to PRINTER:. If you want to send program output to the printer, however, you must tell the computer to do this in your program. This is done by adding a variable of type INTERACTIVE or TEXT and then including a REWRITE statement in the body of your program; this will redirect the output from WRITE or WRITELN statements. The REWRITE statement has the form

REWRITE (*fname, fileID*);

where *fname* is the identifier associated with the file to which output will be directed and *fileID* is the specific name given to that file. If we want the output sent to the printer, we would use the fileID PRINTER:, which Apple Pascal recognizes (assuming that Volume (printer) is on-line, i.e., connected and turned on). Thus, REWRITE (OUT, 'PRINTER:') assigned the fileID PRINTER: to the identifier OUT. When a WRITE or WRITELN statement begins with a reference to OUT, the output will be sent to the printer rather than to the screen. The V(olume name for the screen is CONSOLE:, but it is not necessary to REWRITE to the CONSOLE: since this is the automatic default for all Apple Pascal WRITE and WRITELN statements.

The following example program uses the REWRITE statement to send output to the printer:

```
PROGRAM HARDCOPY;

VAR
  OUT:INTERACTIVE;

BEGIN
  REWRITE (OUT, 'PRINTER:'); (*REDIRECTS
    OUTPUT*)
  WRITELN (OUT, 'THIS OUTPUT SHOULD GO');
  WRITELN (OUT, 'TO THE PRINTER, CREATING');
  WRITELN (OUT, 'WHAT IS KNOWN AS HARD COPY.');
  CLOSE (OUT)
END.
```

We declare the variable OUT as INTERACTIVE (or TEXT) in the variable declaration section of the program, then use RE-WRITE to assign PRINTER: to OUT. The inclusion of the file name OUT in each of the three WRITELN statements sends the output of those statements to the file, i.e., the printer. The CLOSE statement closes the file (OUT); the CLOSE statement is not really necessary in this case, but closing files opened by a REWRITE statement is a good habit to get into. We will discuss the use of REWRITE further in chapter 14 with regard to writing to files.

4.11 READ AND READLN STATEMENTS REVISITED

READ and READLN statements are similar to WRITE and WRITELN statements. The READ statement reads to the end of the input variable only and the cursor remains on the same line, while the READLN statement reads until it finds the carriage return.

Let's test some variations on these statements. Type F N Y Q E (RET) I. The operating system will remember these commands and execute them in order, even if they are all typed at once. If you can tell what will happen without looking back, you should be able to find your way around the Pascal system with little trouble. If you are not sure, there is no need to look them all up—they stand for F(iler, N(ew, Yes (in answer to THROW AWAY CURRENT WORKFILE ?), Q(uit, E(ditor, (RET) (to begin a new workfile), and I(nsert. Now enter the following program:

```
PROGRAM CHKR;

VAR
  CHARACTER:CHAR;
  STG:STRING;
  Y:REAL;

BEGIN
  READ (CHARACTER);
  WRITELN ('CHARACTER: ',CHARACTER);
  READLN (CHARACTER);
  WRITELN ('CHARACTER: ',CHARACTER);
  READ (Y,CHARACTER,STG);
  WRITELN (Y,CHARACTER,STG);
  WRITELN ('Y = 'Y:6:2);
  WRITELN ('CHARACTER: ',CHARACTER);
  WRITELN ('STRING: ',STG)
END.
```

CTRL-C to accept, correct any typing errors or omissions, Q(uit, U(pdate, and R(un. In this program there are no WRITE statements preceding the READ statements to help us know what the computer expects, so we will have to refer back to the program listing as needed. The program declares a Character variable, a String variable, and a Real variable. When the program compiles, we see the normal RUNNING.. message and then the cursor stops below the R. The computer is waiting for a character to be input from the keyboard. Type X and the screen will show

```
RUNNING..
XCHARACTER: X
```

The computer read the character X that you typed, moved the cursor to the second space on the line, and executed the WRITELN statement. This spacing is not a very desirable one— we just want to show how the instructions are carried out. The location of the cursor shows that the computer is waiting again, so type the word SAW and **(RET)** (the **(RET)** is necessary because this is a READLN statement). The result should be

```
SAW(RET)
CHARACTER: S
```

because the computer was instructed to read a character. It read the first character entered from the keyboard (S) and ignored everything else (except the **(RET)**).

The next line gets tricky. Type

```
123.45A STRING OF LETTERS(RET)
```

and you should see:

```
123.45A STRING OF LETTERS  [your input]
 1.23450E2A STRING OF LETTERS
Y = 123.45
CHARACTER: A
STRING: STRING OF LETTERS
```

A review of the discussion in chapter 3 reveals that the Real variable Y ended with the first nonnumeric (and nondecimal point) character, the letter A. The letter A was read as the character CHARACTER and not part of the string STG, which begins with the space before the S in STRING and ends at the **(RET)**.

Let's carry our example one step further. Type R to run the program again, then enter X and SAW**(RET)** as before. Now enter the letter Z. As you can see from

```
Z
IO ERROR: BAD INPUT FORMAT
S# 0, P# 255, I# 10674
TYPE (SPACE) TO CONTINUE
```

it is important to remember that Pascal is intolerant. When it expects a Real number, it will **not** accept a letter. Hit the space bar as instructed, then the disk will whir and

```
SYSTEM RE-INITIALIZED
```

will put things back in order.

4.12 SUMMARY

In this chapter you learned how to use the C(ompile command to compile a text file into a code file, which can then be executed (run) by using the eX(ecute command. You also learned the additional Editor functions: CTRL-Z causes the text to scroll horizontally as the cursor moves across a 40-column screen; C(opy B(uffer enables you to copy or move text within your file; eX(change is used to replace characters in the file with characters typed from the keyboard (overstriking); A(djust is used to change the indentation on lines of text; J(ump allows you to move directly to the beginning or end of a file; and P(age moves down a long program approximately one "page" or screen at a time. You should now be familiar with the following Filer and Editor commands shown in figure 4–4 and the Pascal terms in the Summary of Pascal Syntax table.

In this chapter, you also learned how to declare and then call a PROCEDURE, how to leave clarifying (*comments*) in your program, how to use READ or READLN statements to read data from the keyboard while avoiding common data entry errors, what causes and how to recover from program terminating errors, that WRITELN statements with literal strings can be used to tell the user of the program what is expected by the program, how to format output, and the differences between READ and READLN and WRITE and WRITELN statements.

In summary, you have learned a great deal thus far. As you progress through the book, do not hesitate to return to the first few chapters to refresh your memory or to review any of these topics.

Review Questions

1. What is the function of the Editor's J(ump command?

2. What is the function of the P(age command?

3. What procedure would you follow to copy (duplicate) a line of your program ten lines below the original line?

4. What procedure would you follow to move a line in your program down ten lines?

5. When you moved the line in question 4, the indentation was not correct for the new location. What is the easiest way to change it?

SUMMARY of Pascal Syntax

Reserved Words	Built-in Procedures	Built-in Functions	Library Units

PROGRAM
  CONST
  VAR
  PROCEDURE
BEGIN
END
DIV
MOD
NIL
	WRITE
	WRITELN
	READ
	READLN		

			Boolean Constants
			FALSE TRUE
			Integer Constants

6. You have a program with the name FRED in it, but you want to change it to MARY. What's the easiest way to accomplish this?

7. What is a procedure? When might you use one?

8. What is the purpose of a Pascal comment?

9. What will the following statements do?
a) READLN (A,B,C);
b) READ (NAME);

10. You want to input the values 55, 43, 78, and JANE in response to the statements shown in question 9. Specify exactly how you would enter these values from the keyboard.

11. What is the basic difference between a READ statement and a READLN statement?

12. When you began to make the entries referred to in question 10, you made a mistake and tried to use the left arrow key to go back and change it. When you pressed **(RET)** at the end of the line, however, you got an IO ERROR message. What can you do now?

13. What is the basic difference between the WRITE and WRITELN statements?

14. Formulate a general rule for deciding when it would be advantageous to use a procedure.

Programming Exercises

1. If X = 34.8137, what would the Apple write out for the value of X when each of the following is included in a WRITE statement?

a) X   c) X:5   e) X:8:1
b) X:12   d) X:10:3   f) X:12:5

2. Write a program to multiply 4.56 by 9.72 and output the results.

3. Modify the program in exercise 2 so that it outputs

4.56 × 9.72 =

with the result correct to two decimal places.

4. Write a program which reads two values from the keyboard, adds them together, multiplies the result by the first value, and then outputs that result.

5. Modify the program in exercise 4 so that a first-time user would be prompted to enter the correct data.

6. Modify the program from exercise 5 again so that the program outputs the first result (addition) and the final result; both results should be clearly labeled and displayed to the nearest two decimal places.

7. Modify the program from exercise 6 again so that all calculations are performed in a separate procedure.

Diagnostic Exercises

8. A, B, and C are all Real variables, and the following entries are made from the keyboard:

```
12  72.3  86  97.4
608
39.21  25
```

What values for these variables would be read into memory for each of the following READ and READLN statements?

a) READ (A,B,C)

b) READ (A,B);
   READLN (C)

c) READLN (A,B);
   READLN (C)

d) READLN (A);
   READLN (B);
   READLN (C)

9. A is an Integer, B a Real, and C a Char data type, and the following entry is made from the keyboard:

```
15  12.64  BAD
```

What values for these variables would be read into memory in each of the cases shown below?

a) READLN (A,B,C)

b) READ (A,B,C)

c) READ (A,B);
   READLN (C)

d) READ (A);
   READ (B);
   READ(C)

10. Given the following variable declarations:

```
I:INTEGER;
R:REAL;
C:CHAR;
S:STRING;
```

and the following entry from the keyboard

```
92,17.3,BAD
```

what will be output to the screen by the following program block?

```
BEGIN
   READLN(I,R,C,S);
   WRITELN(I,R);
   WRITELN(C)
END.
```

11. a) If the input to exercise 10 was:

```
92,17.3,BAD
```

what would be output to the screen?

b) If the input was:

9217.3BAD

what would be output to the screen?

12. A program contains the following procedures:

```
PROCEDURE A;
  BEGIN
    WRITE('HERE IS A ')
  END;

PROCEDURE B;
  BEGIN
    WRITE('B TOO ')
  END;
```

What would be the results of the following program block?

```
BEGIN
  A;
  WRITE('AND ');
  B
END.
```

13. Given the procedures from exercise 12, what would be the results of the following program block?

```
BEGIN
  A;
  WRITELN;
  WRITELN('AND ');
  B
END.
```

Problems

14. A local retailer has advertised a discount of 27% off all merchandise in the store. Write a program that will allow the store's employees to enter a current price and then return the new discounted price.

15. The volume of a cube is represented by the formula

$$V = W * L * H$$

where V is volume, W is width, L is length, and H is height. Write a program that will prompt the user for each dimension (in feet) and then calculate the volume and output the result to the nearest tenth of a cubic foot.

16. Sales tax is based on the selling price of an item. Write a program that will allow the user to input a selling price and will then calculate and output the original selling price, the sales tax, and the total price (selling price plus tax) if the sales tax rate is 7%.

17. Modify the program in exercise 16 so that the input, calculations, and output are all performed by separate procedures.

5

An Approach to Problem Solving and Program Development

In chapter 1 you were introduced to the p-System, Apple Pascal, and some of the more useful Filer and Editor commands. Chapter 2 showed you the form a Pascal program takes and introduced you to the different data types. Chapter 4 showed how programs could be segmented into smaller subprograms known as procedures. Now that you are beginning to get a feel for Pascal, we'll take a little time to discuss a useful approach to writing Pascal programs. This chapter, therefore, will be a hands-off chapter.

5.1 PROGRAM DEVELOPMENT STEPS

Because of its structure, Pascal is an excellent programming language for problem-solving applications; it was originally designed to help students develop problem-solving programs. Therefore, before proceeding further in learning about Pascal or the UCSD system, we will introduce some useful steps for developing problem-solving programs. Our method will follow these steps:

1. Definition of the problem
   a Clearly define the problem
   b Define what the output of a successful solution should be
2. Develop the solution (using a top-down approach) by:
   a Dividing the problem into smaller, independent subproblems or modules
   b Developing step-by-step procedures (algorithms) for solving the problem, written in a narrative programming shorthand (pseudocode)
3. Continue to subdivide and refine the modules
4. Write (code) the program in Pascal
5. Compile, run, and test the program
6. Document the program

If you follow these steps when you approach a programming problem, you will find that you are developing and refining your problem-solving skills as well as your proficiency in Pascal. You may discover that good programming skills are more a way of thinking or a method of approaching a problem than they are knowledge of the language. We will use the **top-down** programming method; this method will be discussed later in the chapter after the tools it requires have been developed.

5.2 DEFINITION OF THE PROBLEM

The first step is to define the problem clearly. This step can be broken down into two parts: the first is a statement of the problem and the second is a description of what the results (output) of a successful solution will be. We can use Mr. Matthews' grade problem as an example again. Mr. Matthews wanted a program that would calculate a student's final average based on the weighted results of three separate grades. This is a fairly straightforward problem; we already have a clear statement of the problem and the output should be a final average (identified as such) and the student's name.

5.3 ALGORITHMS

In this book, we will think of an **algorithm** as a series of steps that, when followed, will produce a solution to a problem. Some algorithms are relatively simple and straightforward, others are more complex. As we develop algorithms, we will always keep the constraints of the Pascal language and the computer in mind.

We will continue with the grading problem as our example. The final average can be expressed as the sum of the three component scores (notebook, project, and final exam), each multiplied by the appropriate component weight—this forms the basis of the algorithm for this problem. We can refine it into more clear-cut steps by stating that the final average is determined by:

1. establishing the weights for each component;
2. getting the student's name and grades for each component;
3. multiplying the student's notebook grade by the weight assigned to notebooks (20%);
4. multiplying the student's project grade by the weight assigned to projects (30%);
5. multiplying the student's final exam grade by the weight assigned to the final exam (50%);
6. summing the results of steps 3, 4, and 5;
7. outputing the results.

Using this algorithm and referring to our first example program, the constant declarations established the weights for the three components, i.e., step 1:

```
CONST
   WGTNOTES = 0.20;
   WGTPROJ = 0.30;
   WFTFINAL = 0.50;
```

and the four assignment statements at the beginning of the program accomplished step 2:

```
NOTES := 84;
PROJECT := 94;
FINAL := 82;
NAME := 'RACHEL';
```

The assignment statement

```
GRADE := WGTNOTES*NOTES + WGTPROJ*PROJ
ECT + WGTFINAL*FINAL;
```

performed steps 3 through 6, and finally the WRITELN statements were used for step 7:

```
WRITELN ('FINAL GRADE = ',GRADE);
WRITELN ('FOR: ',NAME)
```

We could simplify steps 3–6 and make them more universal by saying that we will determine a weighted average by:

3. multiplying a component grade by the component's assigned weight;
4. adding the result from step 3 to a sum; and
5. repeating steps 3 and 4 until all of the components have been included (at this point the sum of the weights should be 100%).

Either of these algorithms would accomplish the desired results.

We may also encounter problems that can be divided into a number of smaller problems. In these cases, we can develop separate algorithms to solve each subproblem. For example, consider the following problem. We want to determine the cost of carpeting a number of rooms, some square and some round, where the dimensions (side or radius) of the rooms are stated in feet and the cost of various carpet materials is stated in dollars per square yard—this statement is the definition of the problem. Our output should give the number of square rooms and round rooms, the total area in square yards, the material cost/yard, and the total cost of carpeting the rooms. The last figure (total cost) will be the actual problem solution; the other output values will help us to understand the results and check for errors. We could think of the algorithm for this problem as having five distinct steps:

1. determine the number of square rooms and the number of round rooms;
2. for each square room:
  a input side measurement (length or width);
  b determine the number of square yards of material required;
  c add the yards of material to the total requirements;
3. for each round room:
  a input radius measurement;
  b determine the number of square yards of material required;
  c add the yards of material to the total requirements;

4. determine the cost by multiplying the cost of the material by the total number of square yards required (the result of steps 2 and 3);

5. output the result.

Notice, however, that we could establish distinct algorithms for steps 2b and 3b as:

2b **(1)** multiply the length of the room by its width;
   (2) divide the result by 9 (to convert to square yards);
3b **(1)** multiply the radius by itself;
   (2) multiply the result of step 3.b.1 by pi (3.1416);
   (3) divide the result by 9 (to convert to square yards);

The important point is that if we followed each of these steps each time, we would achieve the correct results for any room dimension or material cost. The algorithm provides us with a logical, step-by-step procedure to follow.

5.4 USING PSEUDOCODE TO DEVELOP SOLUTIONS

Once you have written an algorithm that helps you solve a problem, you must then convert it into Pascal code, i.e., instructions to the computer in the proper Pascal syntax. A great deal of time and effort can be saved when writing the Pascal code if you make it a habit to write your algorithms in **pseudocode**. Pseudocode is a narrative algorithm that incorporates some of the reserved words and structure of the Pascal language. There are no hard and fast syntax requirements for pseudocode; the more familiar you are with the Pascal language, the easier it will be to develop algorithms in pseudocode. There are some general guidelines that you should follow, however.

- Write the algorithm in a structured form similar to the one the program will eventually take, i.e., the steps should be in a logical and sequential order.
- Use indentation to show subsections, just as you would in a program.
- Include procedure and variable identifiers as the algorithm becomes more clearly defined.
- Use easily understood terms such as "get", or "input" for input, "output" for output, and "call..." for a procedure call.

Some programmers believe the pseudocode algorithm should also include the declaration of all variables, while others do not. This book will side with the latter group.

An algorithm written in pseudocode should provide a logical method for solving the problem, and the pseudocode should make the algorithm easier to translate into Pascal code. This means that the pseudocode algorithm and the Pascal code should both be written *before* you move to the EDITOR and begin to enter a program. For very simple programs, the algorithm may be straightforward and the coding quite easy, and it might even take more time to prepare an algorithm in pseudocode before coding the actual program. Taking the time to write the pseudocode algorithm will develop better programming habits, but there is always the temptation to take shortcuts on simple programs. On more complex problems, however, these steps will usually shorten the overall programming process.

In spite of this strong plea for proper program development, you will notice that there are cases in this book where a program is given without the development of an algorithm or any pseudocode. This is usually done because the program is being presented as an example to illustrate a particular facet of Pascal, rather than as a problem-solving exercise. It does not mean that the problem-solving approach outlined in this chapter was not used when the example was originally developed; in many cases the pseudocode algorithm has been intentionally omitted in order not to distract from the topic being illustrated. The lack of algorithms in some of the examples, therefore, should not be construed to mean that they are unimportant.

5.5 THE TOP-DOWN APPROACH TO PROGRAMMING

Along with algorithms written in pseudocode, **top-down** design is another useful approach to Pascal programming (or programming in any other language). Top-down design really applies to a problem-solving approach as much as it applies to programming. It consists of breaking a large problem into smaller, independent modules or subproblems. Each of those subproblems can then be divided into still smaller modules. Each subdivision represents a level of refinement of the original problem. Then an algorithm and program segment can be developed for each subproblem. When all these modules (program segments) are combined into the larger program, they should solve the original problem. The idea behind the top-down approach is that smaller problems are easier to solve than large ones and smaller program segments are easier to write. Thus, we begin with the "big picture" and then refine the problem, adding details as we move down. That's exactly what we did with the grading problem in chapter 4. Figure 5–1 illustrates the hierarchical structure used in a top-down design; it shows three levels (level 0 and two levels of refinement).

The uppermost level in top-down design is usually referred to as Level 0. In our example grading problem, Level 0 would be a statement of the problem—determine the weighted aver-

Figure 5–1. Hierarchical Structure

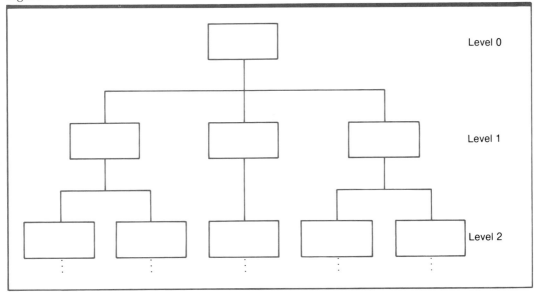

age for any student given component grades and weights. Moving down to Level 1, we could break this problem into three modules:

1. input of data;
2. calculation of the student's average; and
3. output of the results.

Notice that these three independent segments look much like the three procedures, ENTRY, CALCULATE, and WRITEOUT we used in chapter 4.

Our next level of refinement would begin to add detail. For example, the first segment (input of data) could be refined further at Level 2 as:

1. define weights;
2. input component scores;
3. input student's name;

and a still further refinement of this segment might lead to these Level 3 pseudocode statements:

```
define component weights
    notes = 20%
    project = 30%
    final exam = 50%
input component scores
    (prompt for scores)
    get notes score
    get project score
    get final exam score
```

> input student's name
> (prompt for name)
> get name

The two statements referring to prompts are shown in parentheses because they might be considered a further refinement. The pseudocode statements "get..." are flexible; they can be coded using assignment statements or as READLN statements. If we decide to "get" these values from the keyboard, the prompt statements could be added as a further refinement.

Let's apply top-down design to our carpet cost problem. We won't actually enter a Pascal program and try to run it, but we will use the top-down approach to refine the problem to a point where we can convert it to Pascal code. A Level 0 statement would be "Determine the total cost of carpeting a number of square or round rooms, where the number of rooms, room sizes, and cost of carpeting can vary from problem to problem." A Level 1 refinement might look like this:

1. input data;
2. calculate cost;
3. output results.

Level 2 would then begin to add some detail as shown below. We will assume the program is **interactive** (i.e., accepts values from the keyboard), and we will call the program CARPET-COST.

CARPETCOST;

1. input data:
     input data on the number of each type of room and the cost/yard of the carpet;
2. calculate cost:
     calculate area of square rooms;
     calculate area of round rooms;
     add areas of both types of rooms;
     calculate cost as cost/yard * total area;
3. output results:
     output data on number of rooms of each type, areas, cost of carpeting; (for clarification)
     output total cost;

Level 3 would add further refinements, expanding on Level 2 to produce something like this:

CARPETCOST;

1. input data:
     input number of square rooms;
     input number of round rooms;
     input carpet cost/yard;
     input side dimension for each square room;
     input radius for each round room;

2. calculations:

> initialize total area = 0 (since we will add the area of each room to this figure, we must begin with a value of zero); for each square room:
>
> > call SQUARE (input size);
> > call SQUAREA (calculate square area);
> > call ADDON (add area to total);
>
> for each round room:
>
> > call ROUND (input size);
> > call RDAREA (calculate round area);
> > call ADDON (add area to total);
> > cost = area (in sq. yds) × cost/yard

3. output results:

> output number of square rooms;
> output number of round rooms;
> output total area;
> output cost/yard;
> output total cost.

Notice that in the calculation subsection, we used the word **call** followed by a name to indicate that the program would call a procedure to handle that particular entry or calculation, even though these procedures have not been written yet. Our Level 4 refinements will add these procedures.

CARPETCOST;

1. define PI = 3.14;

> INITIAL (input initial data):
>
> > prompt for cost of carpeting;
> > get cost of carpet (MATCOST);
> > prompt for number of square rooms;
> > get number of square rooms (NUMSQ);
> > prompt for number of round rooms;
> > get number of round rooms (NUMRD);
>
> SQUARE (input size data for square room);
>
> > prompt for side value;
> > get side value (SIDE).
>
> ROUND (input size data for round room);
>
> > prompt for radius value;
> > get radius value (RADIUS).

2. initialize TOTAREA (total area) = 0

> SQAREA (calculate square room area):
>
> > AREA = SIDE * SIDE;
> > AREA = AREA / 9 (converts to sq. yds.);
>
> RDAREA (calculate round room area):
>
> > AREA = PI * RADIUS * RADIUS;
> > AREA = AREA / 9 (converts to sq. yds.);
>
> ADDON (add each area to total):
>
> > TOTAREA = TOTAREA + AREA;

for each square room:
    call SQUARE (input);
    call SQAREA (calculate square area);
    call ADDON (add area to total);
for each round room:
    call ROUND (input);
    call RDAREA (calculate round area);
    call ADDON (add area to total);
COST = TOTAREA * MATCOST;

3. RESULTSOUT (output results):
    output number of square rooms (NUMSQ);
    output number of round rooms (NUMRD);
    output total area (TOTAREA);
    output cost/yard (MATCOST);
    output total cost (COST).

While we might have some difficulty now with the "for each...
room" sections of this program, you can see that conversion of
this pseudo code into Pascal code would not be too difficult.
You can also see that we have added and used some of the procedure and variable identifiers that will be used in the actual
Pascal program. For example, the program would probably take
a form similar to the one shown in exhibit 5–1. While most of
the statements for the procedures and a large part of the main
program must still be coded, enough of the program is shown to
illustrate the translation from pseudocode to the actual program.

Exhibit 5–1.
PROGRAM
CARPETCOST

```
PROGRAM CARPETCOST;

CONST
  PI = 3.14;

VAR
  NUMSQ,NUMRD:INTEGER;
  MATCOST,AREA,TOTAREA,COST:REAL;

PROCEDURE INITIAL; (*ENTRY OF INITIAL VALUES*)
  BEGIN
    WRITE ('ENTER CARPET COST (PER SQ. YD.)');
    WRITELN;
    WRITE ('ENTER NUMBER OF SQUARE ROOMS');
    READLN (NUMSQ);
    WRITELN;
    WRITE ('ENTER NUMBER OF ROUND ROOMS');
    READLN (NUMRD);
    WRITELN
  END;                    (* INITIAL *)

PROCEDURE SQUARE;
  BEGIN
  END;
```

```
PROCEDURE ROUND;
   BEGIN
   END;

PROCEDURE SQAREA;
   BEGIN
   END;

PROCEDURE RDAREA;
   BEGIN
   END;

PROCEDURE ADDON;
   BEGIN
   END;

BEGIN                    (* MAIN PROGRAM *)
   TOTAREA := 0;
   INITIAL;

      (* AND SO ON UNTIL THE PROGRAM IS CO
      MPLETE *)

   WRITELN ('TOTAL COST = ',COST:8:2)
END.                     (* MAIN PROGRAM *)
```

5.6 ADDING COMMENTS TO THE ACTUAL PASCAL PROGRAM

Programs that are written in a top-down manner using a pseudocode algorithm tend to be easier to understand, change, and/or correct. They tend to be organized in a more logical (or structured) fashion than programs written "at the keyboard." Comments, which we mentioned in chapter 4, also make programs easier to understand and use. Comments in a program are ignored by the Pascal compiler; they are intended strictly for the programmer or program user. They are identified (and enclosed) by two kinds of parenthesis (* *) or { } and can appear anywhere within the program. At the end of a line, they can appear before or after the semicolon. As a matter of personal preference, the comments in the examples in this book appear after the semicolon.

Programs that contain comments are usually easier to follow than programs without them. The liberal use of comments makes it much easier to understand or debug a program. Comments can be used to mark the beginning and/or end of each segment of the program, e.g., END; (* INITIAL *) makes it clear where the procedure INITIAL ends, and END. (* MAIN PROGRAM *) marks the end of the main program. They are also useful to mark the beginning and end of a repetitive loop (this topic will be covered in detail in chapter 7). Comments should also be used to highlight parts of a program that may need to be changed in the future.

5.7 TESTING THE PROGRAM

Once we have written a program we can easily check for syntax errors by compiling it and check for run-time errors by running it. But what about logical errors, i.e., errors in the logic rather than the syntax of the program. Logical errors are programming errors which the computer can carry out. For example, a program statement designed to multiply the length of a room by its width to determine its area might be erroneously written as AREA: = LENGTH *LENGTH. This statement contains no syntax errors; the program will compile, and, when run, will produce a result. The result, however, will be wrong—the result of a logical (programmer) error. The only way we can find possible logical errors is by testing the program, i.e., by inputting values and checking the results against results we have calculated by hand.

To test our grading program, we could enter identical component scores (e.g. 85, 85, and 85); the result should be 85, regardless of the weights. Likewise, since the weights for notes and the project combined (20% + 30%) are equal to the weight for the final exam (50%), entries of 80, 80 and 100 should give a result of 90.

In the carpet cost problem, we could first test the program by inputting one square room with a side of 3 feet, no round rooms, and a cost/yard of $2. Our answer should then be $2. We could then try no square rooms, one round room with a radius of 3 feet, and a cost/yard of $2. Our answer should be $6.28. Our third test could include both of these rooms, with an expected result of $8.28.

Testing programs helps us catch any logical or nonsyntax errors we might have missed. It should always be the last step in the programming process.

5.8 DOCUMENTATION OF THE PROGRAM

Once we have a program running correctly, we can add one final nonprogramming step—**program documentation**. Documentation means a handwritten (or typed) description of the program, including:

1. the file name (usually the same as the program name) and the disk volume;
2. the problem being solved;
3. the expected input for the program; and
4. the output produced by the program.

The documentation should be extensive enough so that another user (familiar with Apple Pascal) could take the documentation and the disk and successfully use the program. You will also find this helpful when you return to a program you haven't used for a long time.

5.9 SUMMARY

In this chapter, we examined an approach to problem-solving that involves a logical and systematic method for solving any problem. This approach uses top-down design, beginning with a statement of the problem to be solved, then subdividing the problem into smaller, independent modules that can each be subdivided further as necessary. The problem and each of these lower-level modules can then be stated in terms of an algorithm that outlines the steps necessary for the solution of the problem or subproblem. The algorithm is written in pseudocode, a narrative version of the steps to be followed; the algorithm takes the style, form, and some of the terminology of a Pascal program. Once the refined algorithm is completed, the pseudocode can be translated into Pascal code, which is then entered into the computer through the EDITOR.

As the program is entered, comments can be added to the program statements to clarify where one segment of the program ends and the next begins, or to explain what operations take place at a given point in the program. These comments are strictly to assist anyone attempting to understand or alter the program. After the program is complete, it can be compiled (converted to p-code) and run using the R(un command at the COMMAND level. Once the program is completed, it is tested using various inputs and by checking the results for accuracy. Test inputs frequently include extreme values to ensure that the program will run with any acceptable input value. When this testing is completed documentation is prepared which describes what the program is intended to do and the input and output formats for future users.

Review Questions

1. What is the first step in solving a problem?

2. What is an algorithm?

3. When developing algorithms, we always start at Level 0. What is the Level 0 algorithm?

4. What does **pseudocode** mean?

5. What is the top-down approach to program development? Is it more effective for very simple or very complex programs? Why?

SUMMARY of Pascal Syntax

Reserved Words	Built-in Procedures	Built-in Functions	Library Units

PROGRAM
  CONST
  VAR
  PROCEDURE
BEGIN
END
 	
DIV
MOD
NIL
	WRITE
	WRITELN
	READ
	READLN		

			Boolean Constants
			FALSE TRUE
			Integer Constants

6. How many levels of refinement should there be in an algorithm? Is it possible for some branches to have more levels than others?

7. What is the purpose of testing a program?

8. What is the purpose of program documentation? When would program documentation be especially important?

9. Program documentation can be internal to the program or external. Explain.

10. Do Pascal's procedures contribute to or hinder good top-down program design? Explain.

Programming Exercises

1. Develop an algorithm to calculate the number of square feet of wall space in a room.

2. Modify the algorithm from exercise 1 to allow interactive input of the room dimensions.

3. Code a program from the algorithm developed in exercise 2.

4. Test the program from exercise 3 using a room 12 feet wide, 21 feet long, and 8 feet high.

5. Write an algorithm to determine the volume of a cube.

6. Develop an algorithm to determine and output the change due a customer when the amount of the sale and the cash tendered are input.

7. Code and test a program based on the algorithm developed in exercise 6.

8. We want to wallpaper the room discussed in exercises 1–4. The room has a door 6.5 feet high by 3 feet wide and two windows, each 2 feet wide by 3.5 feet high. Modify your algorithm to determine the number of square feet of wallpaper needed (excluding these openings and assume that no wallpaper will be wasted).

9. When we went to the wallpaper store, we found that wallpaper is sold in rolls containing 5 square yards of wallpaper. Modify the algorithm developed in exercise 3 or 8 to determine how many rolls of wallpaper should be purchased.

10. The wallpaper in exercise 9 costs $12.85 per roll. In addition, the paste necessary to complete the job costs $3.40, a brush costs $5.95, and a wallpaper knife costs $3.50. The salesperson has also advised us to purchase 10% more wallpaper than needed on a square yard basis to allow for waste, matching, and so forth. Modify the algorithm further to determine the total cost of this project.

11. Code the algorithm developed in exercise 10.

6

Graphics

In this chapter we will leave our teacher and his grade calculating program (which we have stored under the filename TWO (.TEXT and .CODE)) and explore the capabilities of Apple Pascal graphics. The chapter begins with a brief discussion of the graphics used in Apple Pascal, so you don't need to boot the Pascal system yet.

6.1 TURTLEGRAPHICS

TURTLEGRAPHICS, a set of programs (procedures and sub-routines) in the Apple Pascal system library, gives the Apple its graphics capabilities. The name Turtle derives from the work done at Massachusetts Institute of Technology with a robotic "turtle" that could be instructed to move a certain distance or to turn a specified angle. As the turtle moved, it could leave a "trail" by lowering a pen onto the paper it was moving over. Thus, when the pen was lowered and the turtle moved, the pen left a trail showing where the turtle had been. By giving the turtle instructions to move or turn, children could make it draw pictures (its trail) on a large sheet of paper. Apple Pascal's TURTLEGRAPHICS uses the same principle to draw pictures on the monitor's screen.

The graphics procedures are not included in the portion of the Pascal language we have been using. They are stored in a special Pascal system library on the system disk. To use them, therefore, we must tell the Apple to retrieve them from the disk. We do this with the USES statement, which has the form

USES *procedures;*

where USES is a reserved word that tells the Apple to add the designated procedures from the system library and *procedures* is the name of the group of procedures to be used; the syntax diagram is shown in figure 6–1. The USES statement is placed immediately after the program definition statement.

The graphics procedures is called TURTLEGRAPHICS; therefore, we must place the statement

USES TURTLEGRAPHICS;

immediately after the program definition statement whenever we want to use the graphics procedures.

Figure 6–1. USES Statement Syntax Diagram

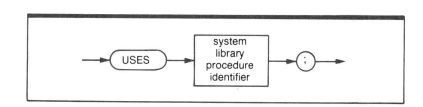

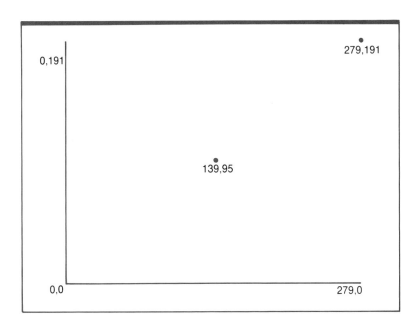

6.2 THE GRAPHICS SCREEN

The Apple holds two different screen images within its memory. One image is for text and the other for graphics. The Pascal graphics screen is a rectangle 280 units wide and 192 units high. You can think of it as a piece of graph paper with an X (horizontal) and Y (vertical) axis. The lower left corner of the screen is the origin (X = 0, Y = 0), and the upper right corner of the screen is represented by X = 279, Y = 191. The center of the screen would be approximately X = 139, Y = 95. The coordinates of the center and corner points (X,Y) are shown in figure 6–2. The actual screen is totally blank with no axes or coordinates displayed so figure 6–2 should serve as a useful reference until you become accustomed to the graphics screen.

FOCUS
On Problem
Solving

Suppose we want to draw a simple shape, a square, on the Apple screen. We'll apply our problem-solving approach to this problem. Assume we have a mechanical turtle that will follow our directions and leave a trail (line) wherever it goes. The problem is to give the turtle a set of directions that will cause it to move in a square pattern. See if you can write the algorithm for this problem before proceeding.

Our algorithm might begin (Level 0) as:

1. Draw a Square.

and then be refined at Level 1 to:

1. Draw a Square:
   a. prepare the turtle; (put on paper, hook-up, etc.)
   b. lower the pen;

c. move a distance; (draw side 1)
d. turn left; (90 degrees)
e. move a distance; (draw side 2)
f. turn left;
g. move a distance; (draw side 3)
h. turn left;
i. move a distance; (draw side 4)

Once our algorithm has been developed, we can code the program and test it. Some of the program commands that will be needed weren't included in the algorithm because we haven't defined them yet. All the new statements in the program will be clarified later.

Boot Pascal, move to Filer, enter a new D(ate, and then use N(ew to clear the workfile. Now Q E (RET) I to Q(uit Filer, move to the Editor, begin a new workfile, and enter the I(nsert mode. Enter the program in exhibit 6–1. When you have entered the program, CTRL-C to accept the insertions, check it to make sure there are no missing semicolons or other errors, and then Q U R to Q(uit, U(pdate, and R(un the program. If you have made no mistakes, you should see a square drawn on the screen with the lower left-hand corner of the square in the center of the screen (see figure 6–3 on p. 126). When you are ready to proceed, you can press the **(RET)** key. The screen should clear and the COMMAND prompt line should reappear. Let's return to the Editor and take another look at the program.

The first line is the program definition statement (PROGRAM SQUARE) and the second is the USES TURTLE-GRAPHICS instruction, which we discussed in section 6.1. ∎

Exhibit 6–1. Program SQUARE

```
PROGRAM SQUARE;

USES TURTLEGRAPHICS;

BEGIN (*DRAW SQUARE*)
   INITTURTLE;
   PENCOLOR(WHITE);
   MOVE (50);
   TURN (90);
   MOVE (50);
   TURN (90);
   MOVE (50);
   TURN (90);
   MOVE (50);
   READLN;
   TEXTMODE
END. (*DRAWSQAURE*)
```

Figure 6–3. Program
SQUARE Results

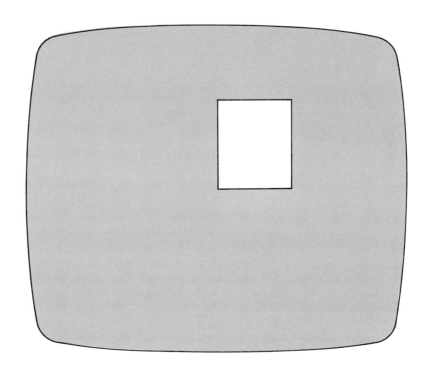

6.3 INITTURTLE

The first line of the main program block, INITTURTLE; is a special graphics built-in procedure that "initializes" the graphics screen. INITTURTLE is usually used before any graphics commands in a program. It does the following: (1) clears the graphics (image) screen; (2) sets the image to full screen; (3) displays the graphics screen on the monitor; (4) places the Turtle in the middle of the screen facing right; and (5) raises the Turtle's pen (by setting the PENCOLOR equal to NONE) so that it will not leave a trail when it first moves.

6.4 PENCOLOR

The second line of the program block, PENCOLOR(WHITE), sets the PENCOLOR equal to WHITE. This is the equivalent of telling the Turtle to lower its pen (with white ink in it) so that it will leave a white trail on the black screen as it moves along. Obviously, the PENCOLOR WHITE will produce a green or yellow trail on green or amber phosphorus monitors. On color monitors, however, we can use the full range of Pascal colors. The pen colors (or modes) available are:

WHITE	BLACK	GREEN
WHITE1	BLACK1	VIOLET
WHITE2	BLACK2	ORANGE
		BLUE

The PENCOLOR statement takes the form:

PENCOLOR *(color)* or PENCOLOR *(penmode)*

Notice that in the list of colors, we have not only WHITE, but also WHITE1 and WHITE2 (as well as three choices of black). This selection is necessary because of the way monitors produce color displays (and the way your Apple sends those color signals to the monitor). WHITE and BLACK give exactly what you would expect, white and black lines. If you are using white or black in combination with green or violet lines, however, and want the lines to be the same width (and in the same position on the screen), you must use WHITE1 or BLACK1. Similarly, if you are using white or black in combination with orange or blue lines and want them to have the same width (and position), you must use WHITE2 or BLACK2. Once you set the PENCOLOR, it remains that color until you change it.

In addition to the colors we have mentioned, there are two additional penmodes available—NONE and REVERSE. Remember that INITTURTLE sets the PENCOLOR to NONE, the equivalent of raising the Turtle's pen. Thus you would specify PENCOLOR (NONE) to move the Turtle without leaving a trail, i.e., to leave the screen over which the Turtle moved unchanged.

REVERSE penmode can cause the colors on the screen to be "reversed" as the line is drawn; BLACK becomes WHITE and WHITE becomes BLACK. The REVERSE penmode is useful when you are drawing a line over different colored backgrounds. If you are drawing a white line on a black background and move into a section of the screen with a white background, a white line will not be visible. In REVERSE penmode, the white line will change to a black one as you begin moving over the white background. In addition to WHITE and BLACK, GREEN and VIOLET, ORANGE and BLUE, WHITE1 and BLACK1, and WHITE2 and BLACK2 are the other reversing combinations.

Because of the way some monitors produce colors, vertical lines may sometimes be displayed in a color other than the one you specified in penmode. If true and consistent color is crucial, you can sometimes change the displayed color by changing the X coordinate of the line by one unit (add or subtract 1 to X). This color variation or "bleeding" is usually caused by your monitor rather than your program.

6.5 MOVE

The third line in the program block uses the built-in procedure MOVE, which instructs the Turtle to move forward (in the direction it is currently facing) a specified distance on the screen. Thus, MOVE (50) instructs the Turtle to move forward a distance of 50. Because the graphics screen is 280 units wide by 192 units high, a horizontal move of 50 will be slightly more than 1/6 the screen width, while a vertical move of 50 will be slightly more than 1/4 the screen height. Unlike graphics programs written in BASIC, Apple Pascal graphics allows moves that take the Turtle completely off the screen without resulting in program-ending error messages. Although the Turtle can MOVE or TURN off the screen, you will not be able to see the results of those moves until the Turtle moves back within the displayable limits of the screen. This ability can be used to produce some extremely interesting effects.

The Turtle can be instructed to move backwards (back up) by using a negative MOVE distance, e.g., MOVE (−50). All distances used in the MOVE procedure are Integer values. The MOVE statement has the form

MOVE *(distance)*

where *distance* is a positive or negative Integer value.

The third program line, therefore, instructs the Turtle to move forward 50 units. Since INITTURTLE placed the Turtle in the center of the blank screen facing toward the right, and since PENCOLOR(WHITE) put the Turtle's pen down, the Turtle will move 50 units to the right, leaving a white line behind it.

6.6 TURN

Moving to the next program line, you may have already guessed that TURN is a built-in procedure that instructs the Turtle to turn a specified number of degrees. The 90 in the parentheses following TURN tells the Turtle how many degrees to turn. Positive degrees (e.g., 90) specify turns to the left (counterclockwise) while negative degrees (e.g., −90) specify turns to the right (clockwise). A 90 degree turn would be a left turn; a −90 turn would be a right turn. Since the Turtle can turn through the full 360 degree circle, a turn of 270 would give the same result as a turn of −90. A turn of 180 or −180 degrees would turn the Turtle around. Since we use TURN (90) in the procedure, we are telling the Turtle to do a leftface.

The TURN statement has the form

TURN *(degrees)*

where the number of degrees is limited to Integer values normally ranging from 0 (no turn) through 359 or –359. (The number of degrees can actually exceed 360 or −360, but there is nothing to be gained by doing so.) When the Turtle turns, it rotates the specified number of degrees from its current direction. Thus, if the Turtle is facing up (on the screen), a TURN (90) instruction will cause it to face left; if the Turtle is facing left, a TURN (90) instruction will cause it to face down (on the screen). Obviously, a little planning is required to achieve the desired results on the graphics screen.

At this point the Turtle has drawn a line 50 units long across the screen (to the right) and has performed a left turn, so it is facing upward. The next TURN and MOVE statements cause the Turtle to draw a vertical line up (toward the top of the screen), make a left turn, draw a horizontal line across the screen to the left, make another left turn, and draw a vertical line back down the screen to its starting point, completing the square.

The next line in the program is a more familiar one, READLN;. This line is included to force the computer to wait for the (RET) before executing the next statement. The Apple executes commands so quickly that without the READLN; the square would appear on the graphics screen for less than one second before the next statement, TEXTMODE, would execute, returning the text screen image to the monitor.

6.7 TEXTMODE AND GRAFMODE

As we just mentioned, the last statement in the program, TEXT-MODE, instructs the Apple to change the image on the monitor from the graphics screen to the text screen. With a two-drive system (APPLE1: the system disk), the system automatically returns to the text screen when the program terminates. Thus, the TEXTMODE statement is not really necessary with a two-drive system. On the other hand, a one-drive system (APPLE0: the system disk) does not return to the text screen automatically. Therefore, if the TEXTMODE statement is not included, the graphics image will remain on the monitor screen even after the program has terminated. The COMMAND prompt will be at the top of the text screen image, but that screen will not be displayed on the monitor. The only way to recover from this omission is to reboot the Pascal system. To avoid this problem, we usually use the TEXTMODE statement in combination with (and following) a READLN statement. It would also be possible to use a simple READ statement, which would terminate the graphics display whenever any key was pressed.

Although we did not use it in the SQUARE program, there is a second screen command, GRAFMODE, which works the same way TEXTMODE does. GRAFMODE places the graphics screen image on the monitor. Although GRAFMODE is similar to INITTURTLE, it simply places the existing graphics screen image on the monitor—it does not clear the previous graphics image from the screen, nor does it center the Turtle on the screen. The GRAFMODE command is useful when you have a graphics display on the graphics screen and you want to recall it to the monitor's screen within a text program.

6.8 DRAWING A CUBE

Now that you know what the statements do, let's change the square to a cube and make a few other modifications to the program. But first, enter Filer and S(ave the program as SQUARE. Once you get the TEXT FILE AND CODE FILE SAVED message, Q(uit Filer, go to the Editor, and change the program to the one shown in exhibit 6–2. When you have entered the program and checked it for mistakes, Q U R to see the results of your work. You should see a cube similar to the one shown in figure 6–4 near the center of your screen.

Exhibit 6–2. Program CUBE

```
PROGRAM CUBE;

USES TURTLEGRAPHICS;

BEGIN (*DRAW CUBE*)
  INITTURTLE;
  MOVETO (80,60);
  PENCOLOR(WHITE);
  MOVE (50); (*DRAW SQUARE*)
  TURN (90);
  MOVE (50);
  TURN (90);
  MOVE (50);
  TURN (90);
  MOVE (50); (*END SQUARE*)
  PENCOLOR(NONE);
  TURN (90);
  MOVE (50);
  PENCOLOR(WHITE);
  TURN (45); (*DRAW SIDE*)
  MOVE (50);
  TURN (45);
  MOVE (50);
  TURN (135);
  MOVE (50); (*END SIDE*)
  PENCOLOR(NONE);
  TURN (180);
  MOVE (50);
  PENCOLOR(WHITE);
  TURN (135); (*DRAW TOP*)
  MOVE (50);
  TURN (45);
  MOVE (50); (*END TOP*)
  READLN;
  TEXTMODE
END. (*DRAW CUBE*)
```

Figure 6–4. Program
CUBE Results

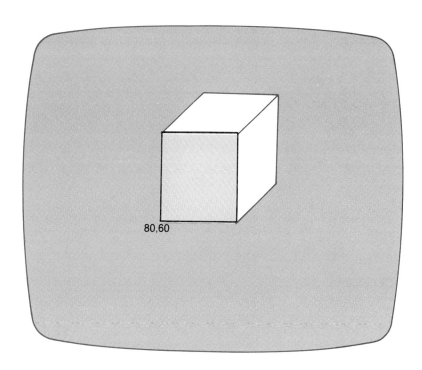

80,60

6.9 MOVETO AND TURNTO—CARTESIAN
GRAPHICS COMMANDS ▬▬▬▬▬▬▬▬▬▬▬

Program CUBE contains a new graphics command, MOVETO
(80,60). The MOVETO instruction has the form

```
MOVETO (X,Y)
```

where (X,Y) specifies X and Y (Cartesian) coordinates on the
graphics screen. Unlike MOVE, which specifies a move of a particular distance, MOVETO specifies a move to a particular
point on the screen. The point is designated by the X and Y
coordinates within the parentheses. The direction the Turtle is
facing does not change, nor does the PENCOLOR. Using
MOVETO with the pen down, e.g., PENCOLOR(WHITE), will
draw a line from the Turtle's current position to the coordinates
specified by the MOVETO. Thus, MOVETO (80,60) in the
CUBE program moves the Turtle from the center of the graphics
screen (139,95) down and to the left, to X = 80, Y = 60. Because PENCOLOR is NONE, no line is left on the screen by
this move; its purpose is simply to give us more space above
and to the right of the starting point for drawing the cube.
This move is illustrated in figure 6–5 (on p. 132).

After moving to this new starting point, the PENCOLOR is
set to WHITE and the square is drawn. Then the PENCOLOR is
set to NONE, and the Turtle is turned and moved back to the
lower right-hand corner of the square. We could have used

Figure 6–5. MOVETO in PENCOLOR(NONE) MODE

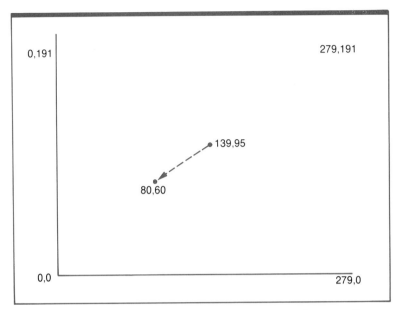

MOVETO (130,60) (since X = 130, Y = 60 are the coordinates of the lower right-hand corner of the square) instead of the MOVE (50) command. Either command would reposition the Turtle on the right side of the square. Once the Turtle is in position to begin drawing the side view of the cube, we use PENCOLOR(WHITE) to turn the pen back on.

Since we moved the Turtle along the bottom edge of the square when moving to the lower right corner, we could have left the PENCOLOR equal to WHITE; the new line would have been drawn over the existing line with no change in appearance on the screen. The procedure in our program—turning the pen off, moving it, and then turning the pen back on—was used simply to acquaint you with it.

The next steps in drawing the side of the cube are shown in figure 6–6. After the side has been drawn, the pen is turned off

Figure 6–6. Drawing the Side of the Cube

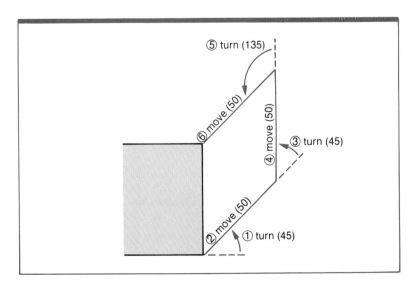

Figure 6-7. Drawing
the Top of the Cube

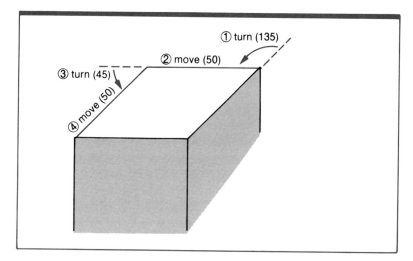

and the Turtle turns around and retraces its path to the upper
right corner of the side. (Again, we could have left the pen on
since the Turtle was simply retracing its steps.) The pen is then
turned back on and the top is drawn (figure 6–7). This completes the cube.

The TURNTO command is similar to the MOVETO com-
mand. It specifies a turn to a specific direction rather than turning a number of degrees. This statement has the form

TURNTO *(direction)*;

where *direction* is an Integer value between 0 and 359. An angle
of zero (0) faces the Turtle toward the right, 90 straight up, 180
toward the left, and 270 straight down. The advantage of
TURNTO over TURN is that you do not have to keep track of
the Turtle's current angle. For example, if you are using TURN
and want the Turtle to face left when it is currently facing
right, you would use TURN (180). If the Turtle was facing up,
however, you would use TURN (90). With TURNTO, you simply use TURNTO (180), no matter what direction the Turtle
was facing; the Turtle would always face left after this command. Some of the more common TURNTO directions (angles)
are shown in figure 6–8 (but any Integer number of degrees can
be used).

Figure 6-8. Common
TURNTO Angles

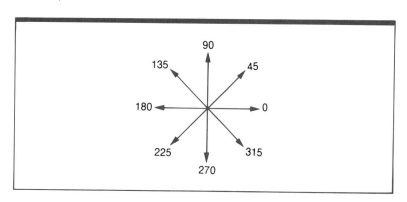

Let's return to the MOVETO command for a moment. Remember that MOVETO directs the Turtle to move to a particular point on the screen, regardless of the direction the Turtle is facing. Thus, it would have been possible to draw the cube using only MOVETO commands, with no TURN commands. This would require some planning, however. Here is your chance to try it: get a piece of paper, sketch the cube on it, and then label the coordinates at each corner—keep the starting point at 80,60 (X = 80, Y = 60) and the sides 50 units long. Identifying the first point on the side (the lower right-hand corner) requires caution, since we want to draw a diagonal line (the hypotenuse of an imaginary triangle) 50 units long. Hint: to save you these calculations, each side of the imaginary triangle is approximately 35 units, i.e., 35 units to the right and then 35 units up.

Your sketch should look something like the one shown in figure 6–9. Now let's write a program to draw the cube using this method. Exhibit 6–3 shows this program, which we have named CUBE2. Move to Filer, S(ave the first CUBE program under the name CUBE, use N(ew to clear the workfile, then return to the Editor, enter the program in exhibit 6–3 and run it. Once again, you should have the cube on the screen.

Now that you have become more familiar with some of the graphics commands, move to Filer and S(ave CUBE2. Then clear the workfile (N(ew). Now G(et (see section 3-10 if you've forgotten how) SQUARE.

Figure 6–9. Sketch of Cube with Corner Coordinates

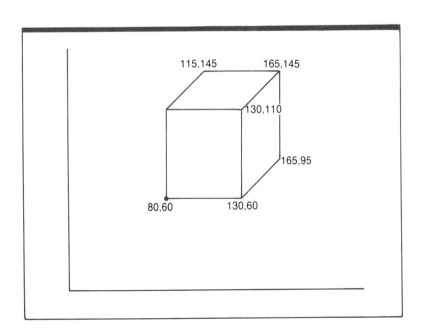

Exhibit 6–3. Program
CUBE2

```
PROGRAM CUBE2;

USES TURTLEGRAPHICS;

BEGIN (*DRAW CUBE*)
  INITTURTLE;
  MOVETO (80,60);
  PENCOLOR(WHITE);
  MOVETO (130,60); (*DRAW SQUARE*)
  MOVETO (130, 110);
  MOVETO (80, 110);
  MOVETO (80, 60); (*END SQUARE*)
  MOVETO (130, 60);
  MOVETO (165, 95); (*DRAW SIDE*)
  MOVETO (165,145);
  MOVETO (130,110); (*END SIDE*)
  MOVETO (165, 145);
  MOVETO (115,145); (*DRAW TOP*)
  MOVETO (80,110); (*END TOP*)
  READLN;
  TEXTMODE
END. (*DRAW CUBE*)
```

6.10 SCALING GRAPHICS DISPLAYS

Q(uit the Filer and eX(ecute SQUARE. The square should appear on the graphics screen. Although the turtle moved 50 units for each side, notice that the square appears to be taller than it is wide. It is. This happens because the Pascal screen uses 280 units horizontally and only 192 units vertically and because your monitor screen is slightly wider than it is high (although the edges—sides, top, and bottom—of the monitor screen are not used completely for graphics displays). Thus the dots on your monitor are closer together horizontally than vertically, and a horizontal move of 50 pixels (dots) will result in a slightly shorter line than a vertical move of 50 pixels. The ratio of the vertical distance to the horizontal distance can be approximated by a ratio of 5/4. Thus, if we want our square display to appear truly square, we must adjust our distances. Multiplying 50 by 5/4 gives us 62.5. Since we are limited to Integer values, we will use 63. Hit (RET) to exit the program and E for EDIT. The SQUARE program should appear on the screen. Change (eX(change) the 50 to 63 in the first and third MOVE statements, then Q U R to see the results. Note that when you U(pdated the workfile, you created a new SYSTEM.WRK.TEXT file (before the update, the SQUARE program was in the computer's workfile memory as a result of G(et, but there was no SYSTEM.WRK.TEXT file on the system disk).

You should now be looking at a graphic square that looks square (don't measure it; it's not perfect, but it comes close). Whenever it is important that a graphics display appear geometrically correct, you should remember to adjust the horizontal or vertical lines to the proper scale by multiplying horizontal distances by 5/4 (1.25) or vertical distances by 4/5 (0.80). Be sure to convert the resulting distances to the nearest Integer values. Now hit (RET) to move back to the text screen, F for Filer, and S(ave this new scaled version as SQUARE.

Now let's return to the Editor and modify the SQUARE program once more. This time we'll make the square drawing block into a procedure (remember D(elete and then C(opy Buffer?) and then use it to create a design. Enter the program in exhibit 6–4, and when it is ready, type Q U R. If everything went well, you should have three overlapping squares. If you want to practice on your own, add two more squares on an upper-left to lower-right diagonal.

Exhibit 6–4. Program DESIGN

```
PROGRAM DESIGN;

USES TURTLEGRAPHICS;

PROCEDURE DRAWSQUARE;
  BEGIN
    MOVE (63);
    TURN (90);
    MOVE (50);
    TURN (90);
    MOVE (63);
    TURN (90);
    MOVE (50);
    TURN (90);
  END; (*DRAWSQUARE*)

BEGIN
  INITTURTLE;
  MOVETO (30,30);
  PENCOLOR(WHITE);
  DRAWSQUARE;
  PENCOLOR(NONE);
  MOVETO (78,68);
  PENCOLOR(WHITE);
  DRAWSQUARE;
  PENCOLOR(NONE);
  MOVETO (126,106);
  PENCOLOR(WHITE);
  DRAWSQUARE;
  READLN;
  TEXTMODE
END.
```

Once you have finished, you should S(ave or T(ransfer these files to your STORAGE: disk (see sections 3.6 or 3.8 to review these processes). You may also wish to T(ransfer the SQUARE, CUBE, and CUBE2 files at this time and then R(emove them from your system disk to insure yourself enough space for future files. When you have finished these housekeeping chores, clear the workfile. Do you remember how? If you used N(ew, you're correct.

6.11 SUMMARY

In this chapter you learned how to access the Apple Pascal graphics routines (USES TURTLEGRAPHICS), how to initialize the graphics screen (INITTURTLE), how to shift from the text screen to graphics (GRAFMODE) and vice versa (TEXTMODE), you practiced using Filer's G(et to load files into workfile memory. You also learned how to draw shapes or designs on the graphics screen using the following statements:

```
MOVE (distance)
TURN (degrees)
MOVETO (X,Y)
TURNTO (angle)
PENCOLOR (penmode)
```

The following table shows a summary of the Pascal syntax that you have learned thus far. The shaded words were covered in this chapter. This summary table will appear at the end of each of the remaining chapters with the new words that were presented in that chapter highlighted.

Review Questions

1. What is the "Turtle" in Apple graphics?

2. What statement must be included in any Apple Pascal program that uses the Apple graphics routines?

3. What are the dimensions of the Apple graphics screen? Where is the point (0,0) located on the monitor screen?

4. What does the statement INITTURTLE do when it is included in a program?

5. What is the purpose of PENCOLOR(mode)? How many different modes are available on the Apple?

6. What are the differences between the MOVE and the MOVETO statements?

7. Will the statement MOVE(400) cause an error to occur in Apple Pascal? Why or why not?

8. What is the difference between the TURN and TURNTO statements?

SUMMARY of Pascal Syntax

Reserved Words	Built-in Procedures	Built-in Functions	Library Units
PROGRAM	WRITE		TURTLEGRAPHICS
USES	WRITELN		
CONST	READ		
VAR	READLN		
PROCEDURE	INITTURTLE		
BEGIN	PENCOLOR		
DIV	MOVE		
MOD	TURN		
NIL	MOVETO		
	TURNTO		
	TEXTMODE		
	GRAFMODE		

	Boolean Constants
	FALSE
	TRUE

	Integer Constants

9. If we have used INITTURTLE and wish to return to the text screen, what statement would we include in our program?

10. How does GRAFMODE differ from INITTURTLE?

11. What is the purpose of PENCOLOR(NONE), i.e., what does this statement do and why would it be used?

12. Would a program that moved the turtle 100 units from left to right on your screen move it the same distance in inches as a program that moved it 100 units up and down? Why or why not?

13. Why does the Apple offer three different modes for the colors WHITE and BLACK?

14. The *argument* in the TURN*(argument)* statement specifies what units? Can this argument be negative? Can it be a fraction?

15. Can the argument in MOVE(argument) be negative? If yes, what will the result be?

Programming Exercises

1. What statement would you use to make the turtle:
   a. go ahead 20 units?
   b. turn left?
   c. turn right?
   d. back up 60 units?
   e. turn around?

2. What will happen when each of the following statements is executed?
   a. MOVE (60)
   b. MOVE (-30)
   c. TURN (120)
   d. TURN (-135)

3. What will happen when each of the following statements is executed?
   a. MOVETO (80,100)
   b. MOVETO (150,10)
   c. MOVETO (600,500)
   d. TURNTO (150)

4. Write a program segment that will draw a horizontal line:
   a. from the center of the screen to the right-hand edge.
   b. from the center of the screen to the left-hand edge.

5. Develop an algorithm to draw a triangle on the screen.

6. Code and test the program from the algorithm developed in exercise 5.

Diagnostic Exercises

Sketch what you think would appear on the screen if the following segments were executed (assume INITTURTLE and PEN-COLOR(WHITE) precede each segment).

7.
```
MOVE (60);
TURN (45);
MOVE (60);
```

8.
```
TURN (-90);
MOVE (-80);
TURN (-90);
MOVE (80);
```

9.
```
MOVETO (200,140);
MOVETO (80,140);
MOVETO (140,95);
```

10.
```
MOVETO (239,155);
PENCOLOR (NONE);
MOVETO (39,155);
PENCOLOR (WHITE);
MOVETO (239,35);
```

11.
```
MOVE (70);
TURN (-144);
MOVE (70);
TURN (-144);
MOVE (70);
TURN (-144);
MOVE (70);
TURN (-144);
MOVE (70);
```

12. Write a program with a procedure that moves the turtle around a square centered on the screen. (Use MOVE and TURN with the variable parameters *distance* and *angle*, i.e. MOVE(DISTANCE) and TURN(ANGLE)).

Problems

13. Change the program created in exercise 12 so that a diamond (a square standing on its corner) is drawn. (Hint: you should only have to change or add one statement.)

14. Write a program that will draw a border around the graphics screen.

15. Using the procedure developed in exercise 12, can you draw three concentric squares?

16. Using the procedure developed in exercise 12, create a large square containing four smaller squares (two squares side-by-side on top of two similar squares).

7 Repetition

In this chapter you will learn how to repeat a program segment by using the FOR..DO, REPEAT..UNTIL, and WHILE..DO sequences. Now that you are more familiar with the Pascal system, some of the explicit command sequences that have been included previously will be omitted and more simple instructions will be used in their place. For example, in prior chapters, when you were in the Editor, you were told to Q U F L : (RET)—that is, Q(uit, U(pdate, move to the Filer, type L for L(ist, enter a colon (:), and (RET) to list the directory of the system disk. In the future, you will simply be told to move to Filer and L(ist the system disk. Or you may be told to clear the workfile and enter a new program. If you are not sure how to proceed on any of these commands, you can always refer to the preceding chapters. Boot your Apple and let's begin.

7.1 A NEW PROBLEM—A MODIFIED PROGRAM

Our teacher from chapters 1–5 has returned with a new problem. His program, TWO, worked fine when he wanted to calculate a final average for Rachel and Sara, in fact, it worked so well that he would like to use it for his entire class, all 28 students. He remembered that when he went from one student to two, he duplicated the following sequence in the main program block:

```
ENTRY;
CALCULATE;
WRITEOUT;
```

He could duplicate this twenty-six more times to get a total of twenty-eight, but he feels there must be a better way. There is.

Go to Filer, G(et TWO, and then move to the Editor. Change the name of the program to LOOP and delete the first occurrence of the three lines shown above. Then add the line COUNT:INTEGER to the end of the variable declarations:

```
VAR
   NOTES,PROJECT,FINAL,GRADE:REAL;
   NAME:STRING;
   COUNT:INTEGER;
```

Now modify the main program block by changing it from

```
BEGIN
   ENTRY;
   CALCULATE;
   WRITEOUT
END.
```

to

```
BEGIN (* LOOP PROGRAM *)
  FOR COUNT := 1 TO 4 DO
    BEGIN (* FOR..DO *)
       ENTRY;
       CALCULATE;
       WRITEOUT
    END (* FOR...DO *)
END. (* LOOP PROGRAM *)
```

7.2 REPEATING A SET OF STATEMENTS
USING THE FOR..DO SEQUENCE ▬▬▬▬▬▬▬▬▬▬▬

Let's look at the new program block you just created. Before we go into the mechanics of the loop, let's look at the statements in this program segment and make sure the use of the semicolon is clear. There is no semicolon at the end of the FOR COUNT : = 1 TO 4 DO statement because it is considered to be the beginning of the "statement" that follows (there is no semicolon after BEGIN for the same reason). The following "statement" is actually a **compound statement**, because it is a number of statements that are to be executed together. The compound statement begins with the BEGIN (* FOR..DO *) statement and ends with the END (* FOR..DO *) statement immediately after the WRITEOUT line. Note that although WRITEOUT is no longer the last statement in the program block, it does not end with a semicolon. That is because it is now the last statement in the compound statement; the END statement concluding the compound statement is considered part of the previous line, so no semicolon is necessary. There is no semicolon after the END, since it is followed by the program block END line. It is never necessary to place a semicolon on any line preceding an END.

The compound statement takes the form

```
BEGIN

   (* BODY OF STATEMENTS *);

END;
```

The syntax diagram for compound statements is shown in figure 7–1. The body of statements between BEGIN and END is typically a number of statements, although it would be acceptable to have just one statement in the body.

Figure 7–1. Compound Statement Syntax Diagram

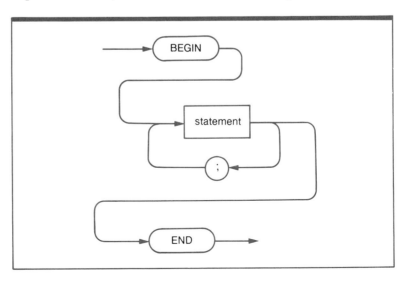

The FOR COUNT := 1 TO 4 DO statement is known as a FOR statement or a FOR..DO statement. It tells the computer to "do" (execute) the following compound statement a specific number of times—in this case four. The Integer variable COUNT is assigned the value 1 and the compound statement is executed. COUNT is then incremented (assigned the next value) to 2, then 3, and finally 4. Each time a new value is assigned to COUNT, the compound statement is executed again. The FOR statement has the form

FOR *identifier* := *expression 1* TO *expression 2* DO
statement;

Its syntax diagram is shown in figure 7–2. The identifier, also known as a counter variable because it is used to count the passes through the loop, must be an ordinal type variable, i.e., either Integer, Char, or Boolean. For now, we will use Integer variables. *Expression 1* is the initial value of the counter variable, and *expression 2* is its final value. The expressions used to assign the initial and final values to the counter variable must also be ordinal. It is possible to use variables for either or both expressions, for example,

```
START := 4;
FINISH := 9;
FOR COUNT := START TO FINISH DO
   WRITELN (COUNT);
```

Thus, the initial value is 4, the final value is 9, and the loop will be executed six times. The output of this segment would be

```
4
5
6
7
8
9
```

The number of times a loop will be executed can be determined from

(final value − initial value) + **1**

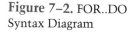

Figure 7–2. FOR..DO
Syntax Diagram

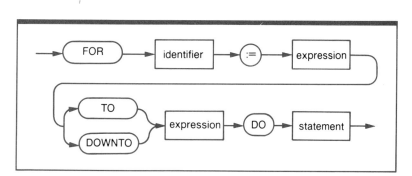

In the preceding example, $(9 - 4) + 1 = 6$, so the loop is repeated six times. The expressions for the initial and final values are evaluated between the FOR and DO; this means that the values are determined before the loop begins. If the loop was modified to

```
START := 4;
FINISH := 9;
FOR COUNT := START TO FINISH DO
  BEGIN (* FOR..DO *)
    FINISH := 20;
    WRITELN (COUNT)
  END; (* FOR..DO *)
```

the loop would still be executed only six times. Changing the value of the variable FINISH within the loop has no effect on the number of times the loop is executed, since the final value was established using the value of FINISH when it was encountered between the FOR and DO.

Note that in the example

```
START := 4;
FINISH := 9;
FOR COUNT := START TO FINISH DO
  WRITELN (COUNT);
```

there was only one statement in the loop, WRITELN(COUNT);. In that case, a compound statement was not necessary, but we did use a semicolon to mark the end of this statement. Actually, the semicolon separates this statement from the next statement (which may be a null statement). The statement in the FOR..DO loop can be a single statement or a compound statement.

We should consider one other point before leaving this discussion of FOR..DO loops. Look at the following example:

```
START := 4;
FINISH := 9;
FOR COUNT := START TO FINISH DO
  BEGIN
    COUNT := COUNT + 1;
    WRITELN(COUNT)
  END; (* FOR..DO *)
```

It contains a statement that could produce erroneous results: the counter variable is assigned a new value within the loop. This would cause an error in some systems, but Apple Pascal permits this statement. It may produce unexpected results, however. In this example, the program would write

```
5
7
9
```

Each pass through the FOR..DO loop increments the counter value by 1. When 1 is added to COUNT within the loop, the resulting value is incremented on the next pass. If an assignment in the loop changes the counter value beyond the final value, the loop will terminate. On the other hand, if the counter is either reduced in value (e.g., COUNT := COUNT − 1) or assigned a constant value within the FOR..DO range (e.g., COUNT := 5), the computer will never reach the final value, causing the program to "hang" in an endless loop. When this happens, the only solution is to hold down the CTRL and SHIFT keys simultaneously and press the P key. This is referred to as CTRL-@—it interrupts the program with the message

```
PROGRAM INTERRUPTED BY USER
S# ?, P# ?, I# ??
TYPE (SPACE) TO CONTINUE
```

Pressing the space bar brings the

```
SYSTEM REINITIALIZED
```

message and the COMMAND prompt line at the top of the screen. The Pascal system has just been rebooted.

What would happen if the value of START was greater than the value of FINISH? In that case, the loop would not be executed at all, since the ending condition is met before the loop is ever executed. There are times, however, when we may want to loop from a higher START value to a lower FINISH value. We can do this using second form of the FOR..DO statement:

FOR *identifier* : = *expression 1* DOWNTO *expression 2* DO
statement;

In this form, we have replaced TO with DOWNTO. As you can probably guess, this statement will decrement the counter variable downward (assigning the next lower value) from *expression 1* to *expression 2*. For example,

```
FOR COUNT := 9 DOWNTO 4 DO
    WRITELN(COUNT);
```

would be executed

(initial value − final value) + 1

times or (9 − 4) + 1 = 6 times.

Let's return to our newly modified program, LOOP, which is shown in its entirety in exhibit 7–1.

Exhibit 7–1. Program
LOOP

```
PROGRAM LOOP;

CONST
  WGTNOTES = 0.20;
  WGTPROJ = 0.30;
  WGTFINAL = 0.50;

VAR
  NOTES,PROJECT,FINAL,GRADE:REAL;
  NAME:STRING;
  COUNT:INTEGER;

PROCEDURE ENTRY;
  BEGIN
    WRITELN;
    WRITELN ('ENTER GRADES UNDER THE');
    WRITELN ('APPROPRIATE TITLE WITH SPA
CES');
    WRITELN ('BETWEEN THEM, THEN TYPE RE
TURN');
    WRITELN;
    WRITELN (' COMPONENT');
    WRITELN ('NOTE PROJ FINAL');
    WRITELN ('____ ____ _____';
    READLN (NOTES,PROJECT,FINAL);
    WRITELN;
    WRITE ('ENTER NAME AND TYPE RETURN:'
); READLN (NAME)
END (* ENTRY *);

PROCEDURE CALCULATE;
  BEGIN
    GRADE := WGTNOTES*NOTES + WGTPROJ*PR
OJECT + WGTFINAL*FINAL
  END (* CALCULATE *);

PROCEDURE WRITEOUT;
  BEGIN
    WRITELN;
    WRITELN (NAME, '''S FINAL GRADE = ',
GRADE:8:2);
    WRITELN
  END (* WRITEOUT *);

BEGIN (* MAIN BLOCK *)
  FOR COUNT := 1 TO 4 DO
    BEGIN (* FOR..DO *)
      ENTRY;
      CALCULATE;
      WRITEOUT
    END (* FOR..DO *)
END. (* MAIN BLOCK *)
```

It now becomes apparent that we have made a further modification in the program. We have written it for a class size of 4 rather than 28. The reason for this is simple: the programming principles are exactly the same, but you will only have to enter 4 sets of grades, not 28, to see if the program runs properly. And now it is time to find out. R(un the program. You need to enter four sets of data (each set contains three grades and a name) and obtain a final grade for each student. (Aren't you glad we didn't use 28?)

7.3 MAKING THE FOR..DO LOOP MORE FLEXIBLE

The LOOP program that we wrote has one definite drawback: it will work for a class size of 28 (or 4), but if the class size changes, the final value in the FOR..DO line of the program must be changed. We would prefer programs that do not have to be changed frequently. One way to solve this problem is to make the final value for the loop a variable that can be input at the beginning of the program. What changes would have to be made to the LOOP program to accomplish this? Try to think this question through and note the changes before proceeding.

Let's see how well you did. You may not have made the changes in the same sequence or used exactly the same identifiers or wording, but see if your modifications accomplish the goal, i.e., allow the teacher to input any class size and then loop successfully. To allow entry of the proper class size, we should insert some sort of prompt statement as the first line in the main program block, then follow it with a statement that accepts input from the keyboard (and then perhaps a WRITELN statement for spacing), for example:

```
BEGIN
  WRITE ('INPUT CLASS SIZE --) ');
  READLN (SIZE);
  WRITELN;
```

Once the value for the variable SIZE is read, it can be used as the final value for the loop

```
FOR COUNT := 1 TO SIZE DO
```

This leaves only one additional chore, including the variable SIZE (an Integer) in the variable declaration statement

```
COUNT,SIZE:INTEGER;
```

Make the changes and run the program. Once the program is working to your satisfaction, S(ave LOOP and clear the workfile.

7.4 AN ALTERNATIVE APPROACH—THE
REPEAT..UNTIL SEQUENCE

Our SQUARE program from chapter 6 (exhibit 7–2) is another candidate for a looping sequence. G(et (or T(ransfer) SQUARE return to the Editor. Modify the program as shown in exhibit 7–3.

Exhibit 7–2. Program
SQUARE

```
PROGRAM SQUARE;

USES TURTLEGRAPHICS;

BEGIN (*DRAWSQUARE*)
  INITTURTLE;
  PENCOLOR(WHITE);
  MOVE (50);
  TURN (90);
  MOVE (50);
  TURN (90);
  MOVE (50);
  TURN (90);
  MOVE (50)
END. (*DRAWSQUARE*)
```

Exhibit 7–3. Program
SQUARE Modified
(SQUARE2)

```
PROGRAM SQUARE2;

USES TURTLEGRAPHICS;

VAR
  SIDE:INTEGER;

BEGIN (*DRAW SQUARE*)
  INITTURTLE;
  PENCOLOR(WHITE);
  SIDE := 0;
  REPEAT
    SIDE := SIDE + 1;
    MOVE (50);
    TURN (90)
  UNTIL SIDE = 4;
  READLN;
  TEXTMODE
END. (*DRAWSQUARE*)
```

In SQUARE2 we have added a variable named SIDE and set its initial value equal to zero. Setting the initial value of a variable equal to zero (or any other value) is called **initializing** the variable. Since the value of any variable is initially undefined, it is always necessary to initialize variables that reference themselves (SIDE : = SIDE + 1).

We have also added the REPEAT..UNTIL sequence. This sequence has the form

REPEAT *statement(s)* UNTIL *Boolean expression;*

The syntax diagram for this sequence is shown in figure 7–3. All of the statements between the REPEAT and UNTIL statements are part of a loop that is repeated until the Boolean expression following the UNTIL statement becomes TRUE. Thus, on the first pass through the loop, SIDE becomes 1 and the first side of the square is drawn. Since SIDE does not equal 4, the loop is repeated. SIDE becomes 2, the second side of the square is drawn, and since SIDE is still not equal to 4, the process is repeated again with SIDE now equal to 3. On the next pass through the loop, however, SIDE becomes equal to 4 (SIDE: = SIDE + 1). Does the loop terminate at this point? No. The fourth side is drawn, and then the UNTIL comparison is made; now SIDE is equal to 4 and the loop is terminated. At this point, execution of the program proceeds to the next statement (READLN). Notice that the statement that was repeated was a compound statement, but BEGIN and END statements were not necessary because REPEAT marked the beginning of the statement and UNTIL marked its end. That is also why there are no semicolons after REPEAT or TURN (90). Could we have included BEGIN and END? Yes. The segment

```
REPEAT
  BEGIN
    SIDE := SIDE + 1;
    MOVE (50);
    TURN (90)
  END
UNTIL SIDE = 4;
```

would also be valid, although the BEGIN and END statements are unnecessary.

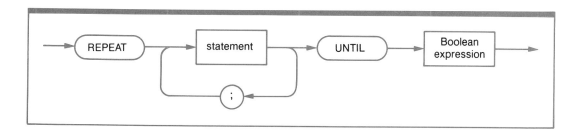

You may have noticed that the loop allowed the Turtle to turn at the end of the square, even though it was not going to move again. If we did not want the Turtle to make that extra turn, we could use the segment

```
REPEAT
  SIDE := SIDE + 1;
  MOVE (50);
  TURN (90)
UNTIL SIDE = 3;
MOVE (50); (*DRAWS THE 4TH SIDE*)
```

You should note that the terminating condition (SIDE = 3) or (SIDE = 4) is a **Boolean expression** (a comparison) that is either TRUE or FALSE; also note that it contains an equal sign (=) rather than an assignment symbol (: =). SIDE = 4 compares the value of SIDE with the constant 4. If they are equal, the expression evaluates as TRUE; if they are not equal, the expression evaluates as FALSE. The Boolean operators in exhibit 7–4 can be used for these comparisons. In each case, the expression (comparison) evaluates as either TRUE or FALSE. The repetitive loop will continue to be executed as long as the expression is FALSE. When it becomes TRUE, the loop is terminated. You should note that since the comparison is made at the end of the REPEAT..UNTIL sequence, the program will always make at least one pass through the loop, i.e., the statements in the loop will be executed at least once, even if the expression is TRUE at the beginning of the sequence.

Using a REPEAT..UNTIL loop with our grading program would result in a program segment similar to

```
WRITE ('INPUT CLASS SIZE --> ');
READLN (SIZE);
WRITELN;
COUNT := 0;
```

Exhibit 7–4. Boolean Operators

Operator (Symbol)	Meaning
=	Equals
<>	Not Equal to
>	Greater Than
<	Less Than
> =	Greater Than or Equal to
< =	Less Than or Equal to

```
REPEAT
  COUNT := COUNT + 1;
  ENTRY;
  CALCULATE;
  WRITEOUT
UNTIL COUNT = SIZE;
```

Although this program segment would work, as would the new version of SQUARE, both would be more efficient using a FOR..DO loop than with a REPEAT..UNTIL. This is because REPEAT..UNTIL loops require a counter variable, i.e., a variable that we increment to the next higher number with each pass through the loop. The FOR..DO loop does this automatically and we don't even have to initialize the counter.

Using Flag Values to Terminate a Process

If the FOR..DO loop is more efficient and easier to use, why do we even have the REPEAT..UNTIL option? The FOR..DO loop works best in situations where we know (or the computer knows) exactly how many times we want to pass through the loop. REPEAT..UNTIL, however, is a better loop to use when the number of passes through the loop is undefined. For example, suppose our teacher wants to have his program calculate grades for any number of students, i.e., he does not want to count the number of students and enter the class size at the beginning of the program. He wants a program he can stop at any time. This could be accomplished through a REPEAT.. UNTIL loop:

```
REPEAT
  ENTRY;
  CALCULATE;
  WRITEOUT
UNTIL NAME = 'STOP';
```

Using this segment, the program will continue to loop until the teacher enters the word STOP in place of a student name. Because the program also requests three scores, he will have to enter fictitious scores and allow the computer to calculate a fictitious grade for the student named STOP before the loop will be terminated. Then the teacher can use the program to calculate grades for any number of students without having to know (or specify) the number when he begins.

There is another, similar method of terminating this loop. Instead of using the fictitious name STOP, we could have used fictitious grades to produce a final grade that would terminate the program. With this method, however, we would have to be careful to produce a final grade that would be unlikely to occur with a real student. This fictitious grade would then act as a **flag**, telling the computer (through the expression in the UNTIL statement) that we wished to terminate the loop. What grade would serve as a good flag? We would expect real grades to range from 0 to 100 on a typical grading scale, so we should pick a grade that falls outside that range. A grade of 999 would certainly meet that criterion. Thus, we could write

```
REPEAT
   ENTRY;
   CALCULATE;
   WRITEOUT
UNTIL GRADE = 999;
```

and enter three scores of 999 to produce that final grade. However, the computer, because of the manner in which it stores numbers and because of occasional rounding errors, sometimes gives us results other than those we expect. In this case, entering three scores of 999 might produce a computer result of 999.000001 or 998.999999. While these numbers are both very close to 999, they are not (exactly) equal to 999 and would not cause the loop to terminate. To be on the safe side, therefore, we should use the statement

```
UNTIL GRADE > 100;
```

Either of the figures mentioned above (999.000001 and 998.999999) satisfy this expression, but no student grade would. Again, the teacher will have to make one extra set of entries— the set with scores of 999, 999, and 999 and a fictitious name (or just a **(RET)** when prompted for the name) to terminate the loop.

FOCUS
On Problem Solving

In these examples, we entered a fictitious name or artificial scores to terminate the loop. The REPEAT..UNTIL loop is also very useful for terminating a loop on the basis of a value calculated within the loop. For example, write a program that will write a number and the value of that number squared (multiplied by itself), beginning with the number 1 and proceeding upwards, one number at a time, until the squared value exceeds 1000. You can try writing the algorithm and program yourself, or continue reading.

Our Level 1 algorithm might be

1. initialize digit;
2. repeat:
   a. increment digit;
   b. square digit;
   c. output results;
   until the squared value exceeds 1000.

At Level 2, we might have

1. initialize DIGIT to 0;
2. REPEAT:
   a. add 1 to DIGIT;
   b. square DIGIT;
   c. output DIGIT and SQUARED;
   UNTIL SQUARED is greater than 1000.

A program that would accomplish this task might look something like

```
PROGRAM TASK;

VAR
  DIGIT,SQUARED:INTEGER;

BEGIN
  DIGIT := 0; (*INITIALIZE DIGIT*)
  REPEAT
    DIGIT := DIGIT + 1;
    SQUARED := DIGIT * DIGIT;
    WRITELN (DIGIT:8,SQUARED:8)
  UNTIL SQUARED > 1000
END.
```

If you wish, you can clear your workfile, enter the above program, and run it.

The important point in this example is that the process will continue until the calculated value of SQUARED reaches the limit we have set. This is obviously a more practical use of REPEAT..UNTIL than our first examples. ■

7.5 ANOTHER APPROACH—THE WHILE..DO SEQUENCE

The WHILE..DO sequence is a looping process similar to RE-PEAT..UNTIL. It will repeat a loop an undefined number of times. While the REPEAT..UNTIL loop uses a Boolean expression to terminate the loop, the WHILE..DO uses a Boolean expression to enter the loop. The WHILE..DO statement has the form

```
WHILE Boolean expression DO
```

and is followed by a compound statement that comprises the loop to be repeated (in the same fashion as the FOR..DO loop). Figure 7–4 shows the syntax diagram for the WHILE..DO sequence. When the Boolean expression is evaluated as TRUE,

Figure 7–4. WHILE..DO
Syntax Diagram

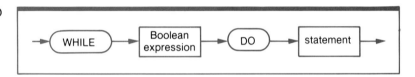

the loop is executed. When the expression is evaluated as FASLE, the entire loop is bypassed. Let's look at a version of the TASK program that uses the WHILE..DO loop.

```
PROGRAM TASK;

VAR
  DIGIT,SQUARED:INTEGER;

BEGIN (* TASK *)
  DIGIT := 0; (*INITIALIZE DIGIT*)
  SQUARED := 0; (*INITIALIZES SQUARED*);
  WHILE SQUARED ( 1000 DO
    BEGIN (* WHILE..DO *)
      DIGIT := DIGIT + 1;
      SQUARED := DIGIT * DIGIT;
      WRITELN (DIGIT:8,SQUARED:8)
    END (* WHILE..DO *)
END. (* TASK *)
```

The expression SQUARED (1000 is evaluated at the beginning of the WHILE statement, and since it is TRUE (SQUARED was initialized as 0, which is less than 1000), the loop is entered (executed). The loop will continue to be executed as long as the value of SQUARED is less than 1000. Alter the TASK program and run it again to see whether it produces the same results.

Notice the difference between this loop and the REPEAT.. UNTIL loop. In REPEAT..UNTIL, the evaluation was done at the end of the loop, which meant the loop was always executed at least once. In the WHILE..DO loop, the evaluation is done at the beginning of the loop. Thus, if the expression is FALSE when the WHILE statement is reached, the loop will never be executed. Evaluation at the beginning of the loop can have some disadvantages, however. Consider the grading program we have been working with. In the REPEAT..UNTIL loop, we could terminate the program by entering a special name such as "STOP" or a set of scores producing a grade of 999. If we tried to use a similar structure with a WHILE..DO statement, we could run into a problem. Look at the following program block; can you see where the problem could occur?

```
BEGIN (* PROGRAM *)
   WHILE NAME <> 'STOP' DO
      BEGIN (* WHILE..DO *)
         ENTRY;
         CALCULATE;
         WRITEOUT
      END (* WHILE..DO *)
END. (* PROGRAM *)
```

You are right if you said that NAME is not read until the ENTRY procedure (in the loop) but the expression containing NAME is evaluated prior to the loop. In particular, NAME is undefined the first time the expression is evaluated. Although the program will still run properly—the value of NAME, while undefined, is not equal to STOP—it is safer in most cases to initialize the value of the entry variable prior to the WHILE..DO statement. This is especially true when using a numerical variable that you expect to be equal to zero. Variables that have had no value assigned to them within the program (unassigned variables) will not necessarily have a zero value in Apple Pascal. It is safest to initialize.

When we initialize numerical variables, we frequently set them equal to zero. We initialize String or Char variables similarly, but instead of setting them equal to zero, we set them equal to nothing or **null** through assignment statements such as NAME := ''. What you see on the right-hand side of the assignment is not a quotation mark, it is two apostrophes with no space between them. Since the string is contained between the apostrophes, the string NAME is initialized as a string with no characters in it—this is known as a **null string**.

Thus, the REPEAT..UNTIL and the WHILE..DO statements allow us to repeat loops an undefined number of times. One provides a means for terminating the loop when a certain condition is met, while the other provides a means of entering or executing the loop when a condition is met.

7.6 USING LOOPS TO DRAW A DESIGN

Let's consider one more example that uses loops. Look at the program listing in exhibit 7–5. The DRAWSQUARE procedure is fairly straightforward and serves as an example of the FOR..DO loop, but what does the main program block do? Why is the value of Y initialized to a negative number, a coordinate (−15) is not even on the graphics screen? Why was 131 selected as the limiting value for the WHILE expression? And what does the REPEAT..UNTIL loop do? Clear the TASK program from your workfile (save it if you wish), then enter and run this program. Did it do what you expected?

Exhibit 7–5. Program
DESIGN2

```
PROGRAM DESIGN2;

USES TURTLEGRAPHICS;

VAR
  SIDE,X,Y,PAUSE:INTEGER;

PROCEDURE DRAWSQUARE;
  BEGIN
    PENCOLOR(WHITE);
    FOR SIDE := 1 TO 4 DO
      BEGIN (* FOR..DO *)
        MOVE (50);
        TURN (90)
      END (* FOR..DO *)
  END; (* DRAWSQUARE *)

BEGIN (*DESIGN*)
  INITTURTLE;
  X := 10; (*INITIALIZE X COORDINATE*)
  Y := -15; (*INITIALIZE Y COORDINATE*)
  WHILE Y ( 131 DO
    BEGIN (* WHILE..DO *)
      X := X + 25;
      Y := Y + 25;
      PENCOLOR(NONE);
      MOVETO (X,Y);
      DRAWSQUARE;
      PAUSE := 0;
      REPEAT
        PAUSE = PAUSE + 1
      UNTIL PAUSE = 1500
    END; (* WHILE..DO *)
  READLN;
  TEXTMODE
END. (*DESIGN*)
```

If you have studied the program and answered the questions in the preceding paragraph, let's take a moment to review the answers. What does the main program block do? Briefly, it uses the Turtle to draw a series of squares on the graphics screen. Why is the value of Y initialized to a negative number? Although -15 is not a coordinate on the graphics screen, Y is incremented by 25 BEFORE the Turtle is moved. Thus, the Turtle's beginning coordinates for the first square are X = 35 and Y = 10. The selection of the starting point was somewhat arbitrary; we wanted a position in the lower-left corner of the screen, but X = 30 and Y = 15 (or any other nearby points) would have been equally acceptable. Why was 131 selected as the limiting value in the expression WHILE Y (131? Like the beginning point, this figure is somewhat arbitrary, but the reasoning behind the selection was something like this: (1) the maximum visible Y coordinate is 191; (2) the square is 50 units high, so the beginning lower coordinate would have to be 191 − 50 or 141 to keep the square on the screen; and (3) since we started 10 units from the bottom edge of the screen (actually 11 because of the Y = 0 coordinate), we decided to stop approximately 10 units from the top edge (141 − 10 = 131). Because the Y values begin at 10 and are incremented by 25 each time, we could check the coordinates mentally or on a piece of paper (10, 35, 60, 85, 110, and 135). When the fifth square is drawn, Y = 110. This is less than 131 and the loop is entered again. A sixth square is drawn beginning at Y = 135, and the loop is not entered again since 135 is not less than 131. The sixth square goes from Y = 135 to Y = 185, leaving a margin of 6 units at the top of the screen (191–185) rather than 10. Not perfectly symmetrical, but close enough! Why was Y selected as the limiting value rather than X? Simple, there are fewer Y coordinates; if the squares fit on the Y axis, they will surely fit on the X axis since there is more space there.

7.7 MAKING THE COMPUTER SLOW DOWN OR PAUSE

And finally, what does the REPEAT..UNTIL loop do? In one sense, nothing at all. It increments the variable PAUSE from 1 to 1500, but PAUSE is not used anywhere in the graphics procedures. On the other hand, this loop accomplishes its intended purpose. That purpose should have been evident from the variable's name, PAUSE, (if not from the title to this section) because that's exactly what this loop does. It makes the computer "count" from 1 to 1500 by ones after drawing each square. This slows the process down and allows you to see each square being added to the display. This is a common programming technique for making the computer pause briefly (or slow down its visible execution). The number selected as the terminating value determines the length of the pause.

Could a FOR..DO loop have been used instead? Of course. The following pause uses a FOR..DO loop:

```
FOR PAUSE := 1 TO 1500 DO
   BEGIN
   END; (* PAUSE LOOP *)
```

There are no statements between the BEGIN and END lines because we don't want the computer to do anything but cycle (silently) for a few seconds. We could have omitted the BEGIN and END statements completely and just used FOR PAUSE := 1 TO 1500 DO; since the semicolon identifies the end of the statement. Since this program already had a FOR..DO example in it, however, the REPEAT..UNTIL loop was used.

7.8 SUMMARY

In this chapter, you learned to use the FOR..DO statement to create a loop that will repeat an action a specified number of times. The compound statement, which is frequently used with the FOR..DO, was also discussed. Repetitive loops can also be constructed using REPEAT..UNTIL and WHILE..DO. These statements use a Boolean expression to determine when the loop is terminated (REPEAT..UNTIL) or entered (WHILE..DO). The equality and inequality symbols used in Boolean expressions were also introduced. The chapter discussed the initialization of variables, the use of variables as counters, and the null string. And finally, you were shown how to make a program pause briefly during execution, and how to terminate a program which is running through the use of CTRL-@ (CTRL, SHIFT and P Keys simultaneously).

Review Questions

1. What is a compound statement?

2. What is the form of the FOR..DO statement?

3. Can variables be used to control the number of iterations of a FOR..DO statement? Constants?

4. The FOR..DO statement can increment or decrement the index (counter) variable. Explain.

5. You should not change the value of the index variable of FOR..DO loop within the loop, e.g., I: = 9 if I is the index. Why?

6. If the FOR..DO loop uses a variable for its stopping expression, the value of that variable can be altered within the loop without affecting the looping process. Explain.

7. Can a FOR..DO loop be incremented by 1? 2? − 1? 1.5? Explain why or why not.

8. What is the form of the REPEAT..UNTIL statement?

9. How does the REPEAT..UNTIL statement differ from the FOR..DO statement?

10. BEGIN and END are not used in a REPEAT..UNTIL statement. Why not?

11. Can a REPEAT..UNTIL loop be incremented by 1? 2? − 1? 1.5? Explain why or why not.

12. What is a REPEAT..UNTIL counter variable? How is it used?

13. Name the six Boolean operators used in the looping control expressions.

14. What form does the WHILE..DO statement take?

SUMMARY of Pascal Syntax

Reserved Words	Built-in Procedures	Built-in Functions	Library Units
PROGRAM	WRITE		TURTLEGRAPHICS
USES	WRITELN		
CONST	READ		
VAR·	READLN		
PROCEDURE			
FOR..DO	PENCOLOR		
TO	MOVE		
DOWNTO	TURN		
REPEAT	MOVETO		
UNTIL	TURNTO		
WHILE..DO	TEXTMODE		
BEGIN	GRAFMODE		*Boolean Constants*
END			
DIV			FALSE
MOD·			TRUE
NIL			
			Integer Constants

15. What is meant by a **flag** value? Give an example of the use of a flag value.

16. How does the WHILE..DO statement differ from the REPEAT..UNTIL statement.

17. Can a variable used in a WHLE..DO Boolean expression be altered within the loop?

18. What is a pause loop? What does it do?

Programming Exercises

1. Write a FOR..DO loop that indexes and outputs the value of I from:
a) 1 to 5
b) 5 to 1
c) 10 to 15

2. Write a FOR..DO loop that will output 5 asterisks (* * * * *).

3. Write a REPEAT..UNTIL loop to output 5 asterisks (* * * * *).

4. Write a segment using REPEAT..UNTIL that will sum the digits from 1 to 20 and output the result.

5. Write a segment using a WHILE..DO statement that will allow you to input a digit N (with a value from 1–5) and then loop N–1 times.

Diagnostic Exercises

What will be output by each of the following segments?

```
6. FOR I := 1 TO 10 DO
      WRITE(I);
```

```
7. FOR I := 1 TO 10 DO
      BEGIN
         WRITELN(I);
         I := I*2
      END;
```

```
8. STOP := 12;
   FOR I := 6 TO STOP + 2 DO
     BEGIN
        WRITELN(I);
        STOP := STOP - 1
     END;
```

```
9. START := 8;
   FOR I := START TO 5 DO
      WRITELN(I);
```

10. ```
    I := 0;
    REPEAT
      I := I + 1;
      WRITELN(I)
    UNTIL I > 10;
    ```

11. ```
    I := 0;
    REPEAT
      I := I + 1;
      WRITELN(I)
    UNTIL I = 11;
    ```

12. ```
    I := 0;
    REPEAT
      I := I + 1;
      FOR J := 1 TO I DO
        WRITE('* ');
      WRITELN;
    UNTIL I >= 7;
    ```

13. ```
    I := 0;
    WHILE I < 10 DO
      BEGIN
        I := I + 1;
        WRITELN(I)
      END;
    ```

14. ```
    I := 10
    WHILE I < 10 DO
      BEGIN
        I := I + 1;
        WRITELN(I)
      END;
    ```

Problems

15. A constant, STAR, has been set equal to '*'. Using a loop or loops, write a program segment that will output

    ```
    *
    * *
    * * *
    * * * *
    * * * * *
    ```

16. n factorial ($n!$) is the value of n times $n-1$, $n-2$, and so on down to 1. For example, $4! = 4(3)(2)(1) = 24$. Write a program to calculate the value of 7!
    ```

17. Write a program that uses a loop or loops to output

```
        *
      * * *
     * * * * *
    * * * * * * *
   * * * * * * * * *
```

18. Write the algorithm for a program that will output

```
        *
      *   *
     *       *
    *           *
   * * * * * * * * *
```

19. Code and run the program from the algorithm developed in problem 18.

20. A vehicle reaches a speed of 2 miles/hour after one second and doubles its speed every second thereafter. Using a REPEAT..UNTIL statement, determine how many seconds it will take until the vehicle's speed exceeds 200 miles/hour. How fast will the vehicle be traveling at that point?

8

Program Control Through Conditional Branching

In this chapter you will learn about additional control structures that can be used in Pascal programs. These structures, sometimes known as **conditional transfers**, are very similar to the REPEAT..UNTIL and WHILE..DO statements from chapter 7. They cause execution of a program segment whenever a Boolean condition is met. These new statements, however, are not looping statements—they are used for control within the program rather than for repetitive looping. The statements covered in this chapter are the IF..THEN statement, the IF..THEN..ELSE statement, and the CASE..OF statement.

8.1 THE IF..THEN STATEMENT

In chapter 7 we attempted to control the grading program by repeating the loop until the name STOP was entered. At that point, a meaningless grade was still calculated and we were told that STOP's grade was equal to some artificial value. But the program did not stop until the end of the loop; it still executed the CALCULATE and WRITEOUT procedures before existing the loop. The IF..THEN statement gives us a means of control so that we can avoid those additional executions. The IF..THEN statement has the form

IF *Boolean expression* THEN *statement;*

Its syntax diagram is shown in figure 8–1. When the IF..THEN statement is executed, the Boolean expression is evaluated first. If the expression is TRUE, the statement following the THEN is executed. If the expression evaluates as FALSE, the statement is not executed. Suppose we want to execute several statements if the Boolean expression is TRUE—we can use a compound statement.

We can use an IF..THEN statement in the grading program by changing the compound statement in the loop from

```
BEGIN
  ENTRY;
  CALCULATE;
  WRITEOUT
END
```

to

```
BEGIN
  ENTRY;
  IF NAME <> 'STOP' THEN
    BEGIN
      CALCULATE;
      WRITEOUT
    END
END
```

Figure 8–1. IF..THEN Syntax Diagram

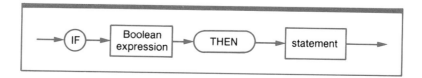

Boot Pascal, S(ave the DESIGN2 program if you want to keep it, clear the workfile, G(et the LOOP program, and move to the Editor. Enter the modifications so that the main program block looks like this:

```
BEGIN (*MAIN BLOCK*)
  REPEAT
    ENTRY;
      IF NAME <> 'STOP' THEN
        BEGIN
          CALCULATE;
          WRITEOUT
        END
  UNTIL NAME = 'STOP'
END. (*MAIN BLOCK*)
```

When you have made these modifications, update the file and run the program. Enter a few real grades and names, then three zeros separated by spaces, followed by the name STOP. This time, the CALCULATE and WRITEOUT procedures should not be executed, since the Boolean expression evaluated as FALSE. Notice that we want the program to run normally until NAME is equal to STOP, so we used the "negative" comparison ( ) (not equal to). This causes the expression NAME ( )'STOP' to evaluate as TRUE until STOP is entered, then NAME equals STOP so the expression is evaluated as FALSE.

While this new version eliminates the unnecessary calculations and output, you still have to input three artificial scores before stopping the program. Let's see if we can change that. Using D(elete and then C(opy Buffer (chapter 4, section 4.3), move the three lines

```
WRITELN;
WRITE('ENTER NAME AND TYPE RETURN');
READLN(NAME)
```

from the bottom of the ENTRY procedure to the top. Move to the end of the READ(NAME) line, I(nsert a semicolon, type **(RET)** to move down (while still in I(nsert mode) and add the lines

```
IF NAME <> 'STOP' THEN
  BEGIN
```

CTRL-C to accept the insertions, then move to the end of the procedure and I(nsert an END statement between the READLN statement and the END (*ENTRY*); line. For consistency, you should also delete the semicolon from the end of the READLN statement, since it is now followed by the END statement. The ENTRY procedure should now look like the one in exhibit 8–1.

Exhibit 8–1. Procedure
ENTRY

```
PROCEDURE ENTRY;
  BEGIN
    WRITELN;
    WRITE ('ENTER NAME AND TYPE RETURN:');
    READLN (NAME);
    IF NAME <> 'STOP' THEN
      BEGIN (* IF..THEN *)
        WRITELN;
        WRITELN ('ENTER GRADES UNDER THE
        ');
        WRITELN ('APPROPRIATE TITLE WITH
        SPACES');
        WRITELN ('BETWEEN THEM, THEN TYP
        E RETURN');
        WRITELN;
        WRITELN (' COMPONENT');
        WRITELN ('NOTE PROJ FINAL');
        WRITELN ('____ ____ _____');
        READLN (NOTES,PROJECT,FINAL)
      END (* IF..THEN *)
  END (*ENTRY*);
```

U(pdate and R(un the program again. Enter names and scores
for one or more students, then enter the name STOPLER.
Did the program terminate? No, it requested three more
scores, since the Boolean evaluation uses all of the characters in the NAME string, not just the first four. Now enter
the name STOP for the next student. The COMMAND
prompt should reappear at the top of the screen, indicating
that the program has come to an end. We now have a program that will allow the teacher to enter names and grades,
and then perform the necessary calculations and outputting
functions until instructed to stop.

8.2 IF..THEN..ELSE

Return to the Editor and change the name of this program to
GRADER1. Then change the IF NAME ( ) 'STOP' THEN statement to IF NAME = 'STOP' THEN and add the following lines
immediately after the IF..THEN

```
IF NAME = 'STOP' THEN
  BEGIN
    WRITELN;
    WRITELN ('END OF GRADER PROGRAM')
  END
ELSE
```

When this is done, use A(djust to indent the block

```
BEGIN
  CALCULATE;
  WRITEOUT
END
```

under the ELSE line. This section of the program should now look like

```
IF NAME = 'STOP' THEN
  BEGIN (* IF..THEN *)
    WRITELN;
    WRITELN ('END OF GRADER PROGRAM')
  END (* IF..THEN *)
ELSE
  BEGIN (* ELSE *)
    CALCULATE;
    WRITEOUT
  END; (* ELSE *)
```

U(pdate and R(un the program. It should work exactly as it did before, but now when you enter the name STOP, the END OF GRADER PROGRAM message appears on the screen as well as the COMMAND prompt.

We have changed the IF..THEN statement into an IF..THEN..ELSE statement. This statement takes the form

IF *Boolean expression* THEN *statement1* ELSE *statement2;*

Figure 8–2 shows its syntax diagram. The initial part of the statement works in exactly the same manner as the original IF..THEN. If the Boolean expression evaluates as TRUE, *statement1* following the THEN is executed. However, if the expression evaluates as FALSE, *statement2* following the ELSE will be executed. Thus, we have built a branching routine into the program. If the expression is TRUE, the statements on the first (TRUE) branch are executed; if it is FALSE, the statements on the second (FALSE) branch are executed. This gives us a great deal of control within the program.

Figure 8–2. IF..THEN.. ELSE Syntax Diagram

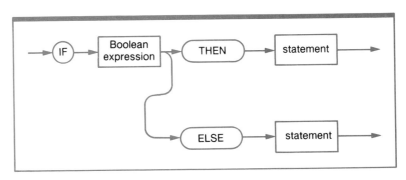

Notice how the IF..THEN..ELSE works in conjunction with the REPEAT..UNTIL statement. When NAME equals STOP, the ending message is written to the screen and the ELSE statement is ignored. This takes the program to the UNTIL line, and since this line now evaluates as TRUE, the loop is terminated and the program comes to an end.

Return to the Editor, then Q(uit by W(riting this program to the STORAGE disk under the name (STORAGE:GRADER1. TEXT). E(xit and move to Filer, clear the workfile, then return to the Editor.

8.3 USING NESTED IF..THEN STATEMENTS FOR GREATER CONTROL

It is possible to use one IF..THEN statement **nested** within another IF..THEN. For example, consider the following set of statements

```
BEGIN (*EXAMPLE1*)
  WRITELN('ENTER A VALUE BETWEEN 1 AND 1
  0);
  READLN (VALUE);
  IF VALUE > 0 THEN
    IF VALUE < 11 THEN
      WRITELN ('THE VALUE IS ',VALUE)
    ELSE
      WRITELN ('THAT VALUE IS NOT BETWEE
      N 1 AND 10')
END. (*EXAMPLE1*)
```

Follow the logic in this program. Suppose we input a value of 6. The first expression (VALUE > 0) evaluates as TRUE, and so does the second expression (VALUE < 11). Thus, the line THE VALUE IS 6 is printed on the screen and the program ends. If we input a value of 15, the first expression still evaluates as TRUE, but the second expression evaluates as FALSE, since 15 is not less than 11. Thus, the message THAT VALUE IS NOT BETWEEN 1 AND 10 will be printed on the screen.

Now consider the following example.

```
BEGIN (*EXAMPLE2*)
  WRITELN('ENTER A VALUE BETWEEN 1 AND 1
  0);
  READLN (VALUE);
  IF VALUE > 0 THEN
    IF VALUE < 11 THEN
      WRITELN ('VALUE IS ',VALUE)
  ELSE
    WRITELN ('THAT VALUE IS NOT BETWEEN
    1 AND 10')
END. (*EXAMPLE2*)
```

Again suppose that the value read is 6. Since the value is greater than zero and less than 11, the message THE VALUE IS 6 will appear. And if we input a value of 15, the second IF..THEN expression (VALUE (11) will evaluate as FALSE and the message THAT VALUE IS NOT BETWEEN 1 AND 10 will appear again. This program segment works exactly the same way as the one shown in EXAMPLE1. But the ELSE statement is now associated with the first IF..THEN statement rather than the second, right? Wrong! Since the spacing and indentation mean nothing to the computer, both of these examples are exactly the same.

How can you tell which IF..THEN statement the ELSE will work with? The ELSE is always associated with the immediately preceding IF..THEN statement, unless that statement has been ended or closed before the ELSE.

How do you end the IF..THEN statement? There are two ways to do it. The first is to use BEGIN and END statements to let the computer know where the statement begins and ends. For example, suppose we want to associate the ELSE statement with the first IF..THEN statement (as it appeared to be in EXAMPLE2)—we could enclose the second IF..THEN statement between a BEGIN and an END:

```
BEGIN (*EXAMPLE3*)
  WRITELN('ENTER A VALUE BETWEEN 1 AND 1
  0);
READLN (VALUE);
IF VALUE > 0 THEN
  BEGIN
    IF VALUE < 11 THEN
      WRITELN ('VALUE IS ',VALUE)
  END (*OF FIRST IF..THEN*)
ELSE
  WRITELN ('THAT VALUE IS NOT BETWEEN
  1 AND 10')
END. (*EXAMPLE3*)
```

In this case, the BEGIN and END statements identify the limits of the compound statement associated with the first IF..THEN (*statement1*). Since the second IF..THEN is within this compound statement, any ELSE associated with this statement must also be within the compound statement. Because the ELSE follows the END, it must be associated with the first IF..THEN.

8.4 THE NULL STATEMENT

The second method used to end an IF..THEN is to use an ELSE with a null *statement2*. A null statement, like a null string, is one that does not really exist. Thus, we could rewrite the preceding example as

```
BEGIN (*EXAMPLE4*)
  WRITELN('ENTER A VALUE BETWEEN 1 AND 1
  0);
  READLN (VALUE);
  IF VALUE > 0 THEN
    IF VALUE < 11 THEN
      WRITELN ('VALUE IS ',VALUE)
    ELSE (*NULL STATEMENT*)
  ELSE
    WRITELN ('THAT VALUE IS NOT BETWEEN
    1 AND 10')
END. (*EXAMPLE4*)
```

Since the first ELSE statement is followed by the null statement, if the VALUE is not less than 11, the program will move to the first ELSE and the null statement will be executed. The program will then terminate. The first ELSE is only included to end the preceding IF..THEN.

Have you ever wondered what would happen if you included a semicolon where one was not needed, for example, preceding an END statement?

```
  WRITELN;
END.
```

In most cases the program would still work fine. Why? Because the computer encounters the semicolon and expects another statement. If the next line is an END line, the computer simply treats the semicolon as if it preceded a null statement and continues.

Now that we have seen how the IF..THEN and ELSE statements match up, let's return to the original example, EXAMPLE1. Add the necessary lines above the program block

```
PROGRAM EXAMPLE1;

VAR
  VALUE:INTEGER;

BEGIN
  WRITELN('ENTER A VALUE BETWEEN 1 AND 1
  0);
  READLN (VALUE);
  IF VALUE > 0 THEN
    IF VALUE < 11 THEN
      WRITELN ('VALUE IS ',VALUE)
    ELSE
      WRITELN ('THAT VALUE IS NOT BETWEE
      N 1 AND 10')
END.
```

U(pdate, and R(un the program. When you are prompted for a value, enter 6(RET). The program should work as expected.

Type R again, and this time enter 15(RET). Still working as expected. Type R one more time and then enter −8(RET). Oops. No message at all. That is because there is no ELSE statement associated with a value less than 1. Would EXAMPLE4 work? EXAMPLE4 would give you the "not between" message with a value of −8, but not with a value of 15. To get the correct message for all values, we would have to add the "not between" message after both ELSE lines (this is not too much of a problem using D(elete, ESC, CTRL-0, and C(opy Buffer, and perhaps an A(djust here and there). Make the necessary changes so that the end of the program looks like this

```
    ELSE
       WRITELN ('THAT VALUE IS NOT BETWEE
       N 1 AND 10')
    ELSE
       WRITELN ('THAT VALUE IS NOT BETWEEN
       1 AND 10')
    END. (*EXAMPLE5*)
```

and R(un it again. This time, all values less than 1, between 1 and 10, or greater than 10, should produce the correct messages. We could even improve the program a little more with the following alterations

```
    ELSE
       WRITELN ('THAT VALUE IS ABOVE 10')
    ELSE
       WRITELN ('THAT VALUE IS BELOW 1')
    END. (*EXAMPLE5*)
```

This program not only identifies values that are outside the range, it also tells the user why the value is outside the range.

8.5 THE NOT, AND, AND OR OPERATORS

The IF..THEN..ELSE statement's power can be increased even further through the use of three operators, NOT, AND, and OR. These operators can be used with combinations of Boolean expressions or variables to create more complex controls within a single statement. In EXAMPLE4, for instance, we used two IF.. THEN statements to determine the acceptable range of input values. We could have used the AND operator to do this with only one statement

```
    IF (VALUE > 0) AND (VALUE < 11) THEN
```

The AND operator links the two Boolean expressions and returns one result, either TRUE or FALSE. With the AND operator, both expressions in the combined expression must evaluate as TRUE for the combined expression to be TRUE. (When more than two expressions are joined by ANDs, all expressions in the combination must be TRUE for the combination to be TRUE.)

Notice that when we use more than one Boolean expression with an operator, we place the expressions in parentheses.

With the OR operator, on the other hand, the combined expression will evaluate as TRUE if either of the expressions in the combination evaluates as TRUE. Thus, the statement

```
IF (VALUE > 9) OR (VALUE < 11) THEN
```

would always evaluate as TRUE, since there is no single value that would make both of the expressions FALSE. When evaluating any number of Boolean expressions linked by ORs, the combination will evaluate as TRUE if any expression in the combination is TRUE.

The NOT operator operates literally on the expression. It reverses the value of the expression. For example, if VALUE = 5, we would evaluate the expression

```
IF NOT (VALUE = 5) THEN
```

by first evaluating VALUE = 5 as TRUE and therefore evaluating NOT (VALUE = 5) as NOT TRUE or FALSE. The operators here are used with the IF..THEN statement, but they can be used equally well with the REPEAT..UNTIL and the WHILE.. DO statements.

8.6 PRECEDENCE USING OPERATORS

Just as there is a precedence in the evaluation of mathematical symbols (multiplication and division are evaluated before addition and subtraction), there is a precedence in the evaluation of the NOT, AND, and OR operators. The NOT operators are evaluated first, the ANDs second, and the ORs last, with the evaluation proceeding from left to right. As with mathematical symbols, parentheses can be used to force certain combinations, since expressions in parentheses are evaluated first. Thus, if we had Boolean variables A, B, and C, the expression

```
NOT A OR B AND C
```

would evaluate NOT A first, then B AND C, and finally (NOT A) OR (B AND C). Sometimes evaluation of these expressions gets a little tricky for us humans (the computer has no problems).

Evaluate the following expressions when A = TRUE, B = FALSE, and C = TRUE:

1. NOT A OR B AND C
2. (NOT A OR B) AND C
3. NOT (A OR B) AND C
4. NOT A OR (B AND C)

Now let's see how you made out. In expression 1, NOT A = FALSE, B AND C = FALSE (since B is FALSE), and therefore,

Exhibit 8–2. Evaluating the AND, OR, NOT Operators

Expression 1	Expression 2	Operator	Result
TRUE	TRUE	AND	TRUE
TRUE	FALSE	AND	FALSE
FALSE	TRUE	AND	FALSE
FALSE	FALSE	AND	FALSE
TRUE	TRUE	OR	TRUE
TRUE	FALSE	OR	TRUE
FALSE	TRUE	OR	TRUE
FALSE	FALSE	OR	FALSE
TRUE		NOT	FALSE
FALSE		NOT	TRUE

FALSE OR FALSE results in FALSE. Expression 2 is also FALSE since (NOT A OR B) is FALSE (FALSE OR FALSE), and FALSE AND TRUE will result in FALSE. In expression 3, (A OR B) = TRUE, making NOT (A OR B) = FALSE, and therefore the expression 1 with a set of unnecessary parentheses thrown in.

If you find the evaluation of these combined expressions somewhat difficult or confusing, you have plenty of company. Just remember that with AND, all expressions must be TRUE for the combination to produce a TRUE, while with OR, any TRUE expression will give a combination that is TRUE. NOT simply reverses the evaluation, i.e., NOT TRUE is FALSE and NOT FALSE is TRUE. The summary in exhibit 8–2 should be helpful.

As exhibit 8–2 shows, there are four possible AND or OR results with two expressions. If you had three expressions in combination, there would be eight possible results. Four expressions would produce sixteen possible results and so on. The more expressions you combine, the greater the number of possible results you must anticipate when writing your program.

8.7 THE KEYPRESS FUNCTION IS ALIVE AND WELL IN APPLESTUFF

Let's try a new graphics program. Clear your workfile and then enter the program in exhibit 8–3. Take a careful look at this program. What does it do? It places the Turtle at coordinates X = 15 and Y = 10, turns on the pen, adds 5 (the value of DISTANCE) to X and moves to the new X,Y coordinate. It continues to move across the screen in units of 5 until KEYPRESS, whatever that is. U(pdate and R(un the program. After the Turtle moves off the right side of the screen, press (RET). Now R(un the program again, but this time press the space bar when the Turtle is about two-thirds of the way across the screen. The Turtle should stop in its tracks when you press the space bar.

Exhibit 8–3. Program
ZIGZAG

```
PROGRAM ZIGZAG;

USES TURTLEGRAPHICS,APPLESTUFF;

VAR
   DISTANCE,X,Y:INTEGER;

BEGIN (*ZIGZAG *)
   INITTURTLE;
   X:= 15;
   Y:= 10;
   DISTANCE:= 5;
   MOVETO (X,Y);
   PENCOLOR(WHITE);
   REPEAT
     X: = X + DISTANCE;
     MOVETO (X,Y)
   UNTIL KEYPRESS;
   READLN;
   TEXTMODE
END. (* ZIGZAG *)
```

Why? Because the REPEAT..UNTIL loop is repeated until the
Boolean expression KEYPRESS is TRUE. KEYPRESS is FALSE
until a key on the keyboard is pressed (it can be any key, not
just the space bar); then KEYPRESS becomes TRUE and the loop
terminates.

But we did not declare KEYPRESS as a variable in the program. How does the computer know what KEYPRESS stands for,
let alone whether it is TRUE or FALSE? If you refer back to the
beginning of the program, you will see that we have added a
second library routine (APPLESTUFF) on the USES line. This
routine defines the Boolean function KEYPRESS. KEYPRESS is
FALSE until one of the Apple's keys is pressed. Once it becomes TRUE, it will remain TRUE until the next READ or
READLN statement. Either of these statements will change
KEYPRESS back to FALSE.

What would happen if you had pressed the (RET) key to
activate KEYPRESS? Pressing (RET) turns KEYPRESS to TRUE
and the loop is terminated. The next statement in the program
is the READLN statement. The (RET) also causes this line to be
executed, since any READLN is terminated by the (RET) character. The reason the same (RET) works for both statements is
that the KEYPRESS function checks the keyboard to see if any
key has been pressed, but it does not clear the keyboard buffer
(the part of memory that stores information about which keys
have been pressed). Thus, when the READLN statement
searches the keyboard buffer for a (RET), it finds one and the
statement is executed. If we had used a READ rather than a

READLN before the TEXTMODE statement, pressing any key would have satisfied both the KEYPRESS and READ statements and the program would have returned the text image to the screen immediately.

8.8 PUTTING IT ALL TOGETHER

Let's combine what we have learned about IF..THEN..ELSE, REPEAT..UNTIL, and KEYPRESS. Modify the ZIGZAG program to the form shown in exhibit 8–4. Can you tell what effect these modifications wil have? The first IF..THEN statement permits the Turtle to move as long as it is on the screen (between the X coordinates 10 and 273). Once the Turtle moves out of the acceptable range, the ELSE part of the statement is executed, changing the distance moved from $+5$ to -5 and moving the Turtle up five units on the Y coordinate. Note, however, that if the Y coordinate becomes greater than 186, the Turtle is moved back down 191 units. Because the Turtle started at $Y = 10$ and moved upward in 5-unit steps (to a

Exhibit 8–4. Modified Program ZIGZAG

```
PROGRAM ZIGZAG;

USES TURTLEGRAPHICS,APPLESTUFF;

VAR
  DISTANCE,X,Y:INTEGER;

BEGIN (* ZIGZAG *)
  INITTURTLE;
  X:= 15;
  Y:= 10;
  DISTANCE:= 5;
  MOVETO (X,Y);
  PENCOLOR(WHITE);
  REPEAT
    X:= X + DISTANCE;
    IF (X > 10) AND (X < 273) THEN
      MOVETO (X,Y)
    ELSE
      BEGIN (* ELSE *)
        DISTANCE:= DISTANCE * (- 1);
        (*CHANGES DIRECTION OF TURTLE*)
        Y:= Y + 5;
        IF (Y > 186) THEN
          Y:= Y - 191
      END; (* ELSE *)
  UNTIL KEYPRESS;
  READLN;
  TEXTMODE
END. (* ZIGZAG *)
```

maximum of Y = 190), moving down 191 units will ensure that the Turtle's new trail does not overlap its previous trail.

When the loop is repeated, the X: = X + DISTANCE (now − 5) will move the Turtle back into the 10 to 273 range and the first part of the IF..THEN will now be executed again, moving the Turtle from right to left across the screen until it reaches X = 10. At that point, the ELSE part of the statement is entered again, reversing the direction and moving the Turtle upwards.

U(pdate and R(un the program. You can halt the execution at any time by pressing a key; you can return to the text screen and COMMAND mode by pressing **(RET)**. If you let the Turtle go long enough, it will eventually color a large rectangle on the screen, one line at a time. It will then begin to move over its previous trail, becoming invisible as it draws white over white.

This program used an IF..THEN statement to keep the Turtle on the screen and also demonstrated a technique to turn the Turtle around (DISTANCE: = DISTANCE*(− 1)). Now S(ave the ZIGZAG program and G(et GRADER.

FOCUS
On Problem
Solving

Now that the GRADER problem is working so well, Mr. Matthews would like the program to determine the letter grade for each student rather than just a numerical average. He is using a fairly standard grading distribution—95 and above is an A, 85 to 94 a B, and so on, with an F for any grade below 65. Write a procedure named ASSIGN that will do this for him, and then add a line in the WRITEOUT procedure to output the result (call it LETTERGRADE).

The algorithm for this procedure is fairly straightforward:

Procedure to assign lettergrade:
a. if grade is between 95 and 100 lettergrade is A;
b. if grade is between 85 and 94 then lettergrade is B;
c. if grade is between 75 and 84 then lettergrade is C;
d. if grade is between 65 and 74 then lettergrade is D;
e. if grade is less than 65 then lettergrade is F.

Once you have the program written, compiled, and running, enter the following data to see if it works as expected.

Student	Scores
Andrew	97 95 98
Alice	100 100 100
Bill	79 92 88
Carol	75 75 75
Dave	67 56 74
Fran	32 61 53
Stop	

Each student should receive a letter grade that is the same as the first letter in his or her name. If your program did this, you have made Mr. Matthews very happy (for the time being). If you had problems, let's look at a solution. The program should add a variable declaration

```
LETTERGRADE:CHAR;
```

and an ASSIGN procedure containing a number of IF..THEN statements

```
PROCEDURE ASSIGN;
  BEGIN
    IF (GRADE <= 100) AND (GRADE >= 95)
    THEN
       LETTERGRADE := 'A';
    IF (GRADE < 95) AND (GRADE >= 85) TH
    EN
       LETTERGRADE := 'B';
    IF (GRADE < 85) AND (GRADE >= 75) TH
    EN
       LETTERGRADE := 'C';
    IF (GRADE < 75) AND (GRADE >= 65) TH
    EN
       LETTERGRADE := 'D';
    IF (GRADE < 65) THEN
       LETTERGRADE :='F'
  END;
```

You also have to insert the line

```
WRITELN (NAME, '''S LETTERGRADE ,LETTE
RGRADE)
```

just before the end of the WRITEOUT procedure (be sure to add a semicolon at the end of the previous WRITELN statement), and then insert ASSIGN; between CALCULATE; and WRITE-OUT; in the main program.

Could you have used a string variable instead of a CHAR variable for LETTERGRADE? Yes, but since only one character will be assigned to this variable, the CHAR variable is preferable. S(ave this program again as GRADER and clear your workfile. ■

8.9 THE CASE..OF STATEMENT

If we wanted to write a graphics program that would allow us to control the Turtle's direction from the keyboard, we could probably do it with a combination of KEYPRESS, READ, and IF..THEN statements. For example, the segment

```
BEGIN
  READ(KEY);
  IF KEY = 'L' THEN
    TURNTO (0);
```

```
       IF KEY = 'T' THEN
          TURNTO (90);
       IF KEY = 'K' THEN
          TURNTO (180);
       IF KEY = 'G' THEN
          TURNTO (270)
    END; (* IF KEYPRESS *)
```

would allow us to press the T key to turn the Turtle up, K to turn it left, L to turn it right, and G for down. If this segment was placed in a loop that caused the Turtle to move, we could change the Turtle's direction each time we pressed one of these keys.

Although this program segment would work fine, there is another statement, the CASE..OF statement, that would achieve the same results more efficiently. CASE..OF takes the following form

```
CASE expression OF
   case constant list
END;
```

The expression between the reserved words CASE and OF must take an ordinal value (Integer, Boolean, or Char). The case constant list is a list of values and action statements separated by colons:

```
value1:statement 1;
value2:statement2;
        .

        .

        .
value n:statement n;
```

The syntax diagram for the CASE..OF statement is shown in figure 8–3. We could use a CASE..OF statement to rewrite the Turtle-directing segment as

```
IF KEYPRESS THEN
   BEGIN
      READ (KEY);
      CASE KEY OF
         'L':TURNTO (0);
         'T':TURNTO (90);
         'K':TURNTO (180);
         'G':TURNTO (270)
      END (* CASE..OF *)
   END; (* IF KEYPRESS *)
```

The variable KEY is evaluated in the CASE statement, then its value is used in the case constant list to select the appropriate statement to be executed. In many versions of Pascal, the case

Figure 8–3. CASE..OF
Syntax Diagram

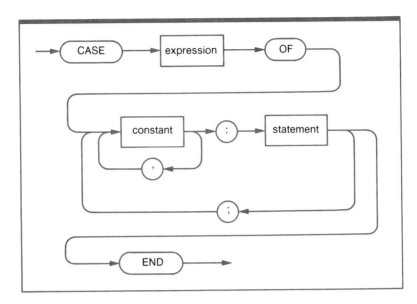

constant list must contain all potential values of KEY or an error will result. Fortunately, Apple Pascal is more forgiving—if you press a key not contained in the case constant list, it is simply ignored.

A complete graphics program using CASE..OF to control the movement of the Turtle is shown in exhibit 8–5.

The pause loop is included to slow the Turtle down to a point where those of us with slower reflexes have a chance to turn the Turtle before it disappears off the screen (although it is possible to let it move off, then do a U-turn and bring it back on again). C(ompile and run the program and try it. Remember, K and L move left and right, T and G move up and down, and Q quits the loop. The **(RET)** key returns to the text screen. If you find the movement too slow, you can shorten the pause loop to speed up the Turtle's movement. When you are through playing (excuse me, experimenting) with this program, save it as DRAWGAME.

8.10 SUMMARY

In this chapter you have learned about some Pascal control structures, i.e., structures that allow the computer to make a decision about which set of statements it will execute. The computer evaluates a Boolean expression in the IF..THEN structure and executes the following statement if the expression is true. Adding the ELSE condition to IF..THEN causes the computer to execute one set of statements if the expression is true and another set if the expression is false. The CASE..OF statement allows you to use a multiple branching structure based upon the value of an ordinal variable.

Exhibit 8–5. Program
MAKEDESIGN

```
PROGRAM MAKEDESIGN;

USES TURTLEGRAPHICS,APPLESTUFF;

VAR
    PAUSE:INTEGER;
    KEY:CHAR;

BEGIN
    INITTURTLE;
    PENCOLOR(WHITE);
    REPEAT
        MOVE (4);
        FOR PAUSE:= 1 TO 500 DO
            BEGIN
            END;
        IF KEYPRESS THEN
            BEGIN
                READ (KEY);
                CASE KEY OF
                    'L':TURNTO (0);
                    'T':TURNTO (90);
                    'K':TURNTO (180);
                    'G':TURNTO (270);
                    'Q': ;
                END (*CASE..OF *)
            END; (* IF KEYPRESS *)
    UNTIL KEY = 'Q';
    READLN;
    TEXTMODE
END. (* MAKEDESIGN *)
```

The Boolean operators AND, OR, and NOT further expanded
our ability to control the execution of statements in the program. The chapter also introduced you to KEYPRESS, a routine
contained in APPLESTUFF, which tells the computer to check
to see if a key on the keyboard has been pressed.

**Review
Questions**

1. How does the IF..THEN statement differ from the FOR..DO statement?

2. Explain how the IF..THEN statement uses a Boolean expression to
determine whether or not to execute the following statement.

3. How does ELSE modify the IF..THEN statement?

4. What is meant by nested IF..THEN statements? Give an example.

5. If a statement contains two IF..THEN statements, but only one
ELSE, which IF..THEN will the ELSE be associated with?

SUMMARY of Pascal Syntax

Reserved Words	Built-in Procedures	Built-in Functions	Library Units
PROGRAM	WRITE		TURTLEGRAPHICS
USES	WRITELN		APPLESTUFF
CONST	READ		
VAR	READLN		
PROCEDURE	INITTURTLE		
FOR..DO	PENCOLOR		
TO	MOVE		
DOWNTO	TURN		
REPEAT	MOVETO		
UNTIL	TURNTO		
WHILE..DO	TEXTMODE		
IF	GRAFMODE		
THEN			*Boolean Constants*
ELSE			
CASE..OF			FALSE
BEGIN			TRUE
END			
DIV			
MOD			
NIL			
AND			
OR			
NOT			*Integer Constants*

6. What is meant by the null statement?

7. Explain the meaning of the Boolean operators NOT, AND, and OR. Give an example of their use.

8. What precedence is used with the NOT, AND, and OR operators?

9. Can you use more than one Boolean operator in an expression? Explain.

10. What is KEYPRESS? How does it work?

11. Is it possible to create a repetitive loop with the IF..THEN statement (without using any of the other repetitive statements)?

12. How is the CASE..OF statement similar to the IF..THEN statement? How do they differ?

13. What is the form of the CASE..OF statement?

14. What is the case constant list? What form does it take?

15. When would the CASE..OF statement be preferable to the IF.. THEN statement?

16. Can we use expressions in the CASE..OF list, e.g., X **)** 9 : Y = 6; ?

17. What happens if the actual value of the CASE..OF expression is not contained in the CASE constant list?

<table>
<tr><td>

Programming Exercises

</td><td>

1. Write a statement that outputs the value of X only when X exceeds the value of Y.

2. Write a statement that compares the values of X and Y and outputs either X IS GREATER or Y IS GREATER (assume they will not be equal).

3. B is a Boolean variable. Write a statement that outputs B IS FALSE when (and only when) B is actually FALSE.

4. Write a statement using CASE..OF which, given the variables X and Y, both 0 or 1 Integer values, outputs either X IS GREATER, Y IS GREATER, or X AND Y ARE EQUAL.

5. Write a statement using CASE..OF that sets X = 3 if I = 1, X = 7 if I = 2, and X = 14 if I = 3.

</td></tr>
</table>

<table>
<tr><td>

Diagnostic Exercises

</td><td>

6. Evaluate the following expressions:
a. 12 **)** 5
b. 4 **(** 3
c. 7 = 5
d. 6 **()** 8

</td></tr>
</table>

7. Write statements to declare FLAG a Boolean variable and make it TRUE.

8. Evaluate the following expressions if VAL = 6.
   a. VAL > 5 AND VAL < 10
   b. (VAL < 5) OR (VAL > 3)
   c. NOT (VAL =)
   d. (VAL <> 6) OR (VAL = 6)

9. If A = TRUE, B = TRUE, C = FALSE, and D = FALSE, evaluate:
   a. A AND C
   b. NOT A OR B
   c. A OR NOT D
   d. A AND NOT B OR C

10. If A = TRUE, B = TRUE, C = FALSE, and D = FALSE, evaluate:
   a. A AND (B OR C)
   b. NOT (A OR C) AND B
   c. (A OR C) AND (B OR D)
   d. (A OR B) AND NOT (B AND C)

Problems

11. A 60 average is passing in a particular course. Write a program that declares the Boolean variable PASS and assigns it the correct value (TRUE or FALSE) based upon an input average.

12. A store offers a 10% discount on any purchase over $100. Write a program that allows the purchase price to be entered, then outputs the cash price.

13. Write a program that prompts DO YOU WANT TO STOP (Y/N)? and continues prompting until either a Y or N is entered.

14. Rewrite the ASSIGN procedure in section 8.9 using IF..THEN.. ELSE statements.

15. A chemical process continues to increase in temperature until it is finished, then the temperature begins to fall. Write an algorithm for a program that will allow a worker to enter temperature readings and output either PROCESS CONTINUING if the temperature is still rising or PROCESS COMPLETED if the temperature falls.

16. Code and test the program developed in problem 15.

17. A store has the following special:

Number of Boxes	Price per box
1–3	$5.00
4	4.45
5	4.20
6*	$4.00
(*maximum purchase = 6 boxes)	

Write a program that will read the number of boxes purchased and output the total price.

18. Modify the program in problem 17 to alert the clerk when someone attempts to purchase more than 6 boxes.

19. A clothing store is having a tag sale where the color of the price tag indicates the discount on the item.

Color	Code	Discount
green	G	25%
red	R	20%
blue	B	15%
yellow	Y	10%

Write a program that allows a clerk to enter the list price and the color code and then outputs the correct selling (discounted) price.

9

Procedures and Parameters

In past chapters, the variables we used in our procedures were the same variables we used in the main body of our program. There will be times when we will want to write procedures that will function correctly regardless of the variable identifiers used in the body of the program. We can accomplish this through the use of **parameters**, which are special values or variables that are used by both procedures and their calling programs. Parameters allow us to pass values from the main body of the program to procedures and/or back to the main program, even when the variable identifiers are not the same. In this chapter, we will explore the use of parameters and refine our ability to use procedures correctly.

9.1 ACTUAL AND FORMAL PARAMETERS

Different parameters are given different names, depending on their purpose in a program. To clarify the distinctions between different types of parameters and to understand their purpose better, let's look at the example program in exhibit 9–1.

In this program there are two procedures, ONE and TWO. Procedure ONE works exactly like the other procedures we have used. The values of variables X, Y, N, and I are assigned in the body of the program. When procedure ONE is called, it uses those values to evaluate Z and to write output to the screen. After the procedure is completed, the main program again writes the value of the variables to the screen for comparison. As you would expect, they are the same.

The string N is then changed to 'TWO' and procedure TWO is called. In the calling statement for procedure TWO, however, the variables are listed in parentheses following the procedure name:

```
TWO (X,Y,N,I)
```

These variables are called **actual parameters**; their current values are **passed** from the program to the procedure.

In the procedure declaration statement, four new variables (A, B, M, and H) and their respective data types are listed:

```
PROCEDURE TWO(A,B:REAL;M:STRING;H:INTEGE
R);
```

These variables are the parameters that will be used in the procedure—they are called **formal parameters**. They are defined in the procedure declaration statement in the **formal parameter list**.

Formal parameters must always have their data types defined, and those data types must match the data types of the values being passed from the actual parameters to the formal parameters. Look at the calling statement and the procedure declaration statement together:

```
TWO(X,Y,N,I);
PROCEDURE TWO(A,B:REAL;M:STRING;H:INTEGE
R);
```

Exhibit 9-1. Program
PARAMETERS

```
PROGRAM PARAMETERS;

VAR
   X,Y,Z:REAL;
   N:STRING;
   I:INTEGER;

PROCEDURE ONE;
   BEGIN
      Z :=2.0 * X - 3.0 * Y;
      WRITELN(X:6,Y:6,Z:6);
      WRITELN(N,I:6)
   END;

PROCEDURE TWO(A,B:REAL;M:STRING;H:INTEGER);
   VAR
      X:REAL;
      I:INTEGER;
   BEGIN
      X := 2.0 * A - 3.0 * B;
      WRITELN(A:6,B:6,X:6);
      I := 9;
      WRITELN(M,H:6)
   END;

BEGIN
   X := 8.0;
   Y := 3.0;
   N := 'ONE';
   I := 1;
   ONE;
   WRITELN(X:6,Y:6,N:10,I:6);
   WRITELN;
   N := 'TWO';
   TWO(X,Y,N,I);
   WRITELN(X:6,Y:6,N:10,I:6);
   WRITELN;
   TWO(2.0,5.0,'TWOPLUS',3)
END.
```

You can see that the actual and formal parameters have matching data types. This is essential. When values are passed between parameters, they are passed from the actual parameter to the formal parameter in the order in which they are listed. Thus, the value of X is passed to A, the value of Y is passed to B, and so on. Since X is a real data type, A must also be a real data type. If the data types do not match, an error will occur.

9.2 GLOBAL AND LOCAL VARIABLES

In a program that does not use parameters (and that includes all of the programs we have written up to this point), all of the variables are **global variables**. Whenever global variables are referenced by the program or a procedure, the computer uses the same memory locations to find their values. Thus, whenever the variable X is used, the same memory location is used and X has the same value everywhere within the program, even in procedures. Thus these variables are called global variables because they have the same value throughout the program. In procedure ONE, for example, the variables in the procedure were the same variables with the same values as those in the main program.

Procedure TWO performs the same calculation as procedure ONE, and again the results are output. When the procedure is completed, the main program outputs the values of the variables for comparison. Again, they match. This may surprise you, because in the procedure we assigned the value of the expression to X and we assigned I a value of 9. But when we return to the main program and output the values, X is still 8 and I is still 1.

This can be understood by looking at the way Pascal identifies variables. Whenever variables are defined in a procedure, they are known as **local variables**; their values only apply locally, i.e., within the procedure that defined them. What happens when local variables are given the same identifier names as variables defined by the main program? In that case, the local identifiers apply within the procedure and the variables are treated as local variables. Returning to procedure TWO, you can see that two variables, X and I, were defined within the procedure. Since these variables also exist in the main program, they will be treated as distinct local variables in the procedure, and separate memory locations will be set aside for them. Thus, when the expression $X := 2*A - 3*B$ is evaluated and the result is assigned to X, the local variable X is used. The value of X in the body of the program remains 8. What about parameters that use the same identifier? Formal parameters are treated the same as local variables. With the exception of variable parameters (which will be discussed later), any parameters defined in the procedure declaration statement are also treated as local variables.

9.3 VALUE PARAMETERS

Any formal parameter that is used to pass a value to a procedure is called a **value parameter**. Thus, the parameters in the formal parameter list for procedure TWO are all value parameters. Although value parameters are used to pass values to procedures, they cannot pass values back to the actual parameters.

Moving down the main program in exhibit 9–1, procedure TWO is called again by the last statement in the program

```
TWO(2.0,5.0,'TWOPLUS',3);
```

In this case, the actual parameters are values rather than variables. (But they are *not* value parameters. Only formal parameters that can receive values from actual parameters (but cannot pass values back) are known as value parameters.) A takes a value of 2.0, B a value of 5.0, M becomes 'TWOPLUS', and H takes the value 3. Again, the values passed by the parameters must match the data types that have been defined for the formal parameters.

Actual parameters can also be expressions. For example, it would have been possible to use the following statement to call procedure TWO:

```
TWO(3*X-5,Y-2/X,'STILLMORE',4*I);
```

The expression $(3*X - 5)$ would be evaluated as 19 $(3*8 - 5)$, and the value 19 would be passed to parameter A. Parameter B would be passed the value 2.75 (3–2/8), and H would become 4 $(4*1)$. Notice that these values still match the data types for the formal parameters.

9.4 VARIABLE PARAMETERS

In each of the examples we have discussed, we passed values from the main program to the procedure through actual and formal parameters. But the values calculated in the procedure only applied within that procedure, because the variables were local in nature. Does this mean that we must use global variables in order to use values calculated in a procedure elsewhere in the program? The answer is no. It is possible to identify certain parameters as **variable parameters** rather than value parameters. While a value parameter can pass data only to the procedure and not back to the program, a variable parameter can pass values back to the actual parameter. We identify variable parameters by placing the word VAR before any variable parameters in the formal parameter list.

For example, if we used the following calling and procedure declaration statements

```
THREE(X,Y,Z,N,I);
PROCEDURE THREE(A,B:REAL;VAR C:REAL;M:ST
RING;VAR H:INTEGER);
```

the values of the actual parameters X, Y, Z, N, and I would be passed to the formal parameters A, B, C, M, and H. But in this case, the parameters C and H are variable parameters. This means that if the values of C and/or H are changed within the procedure, those new values will be passed back to variables Z and I. This has the same effect as using global variables, but it does not confine us to using the same identifier names in the procedure that we used in the program.

The rules of agreement between actual and formal parameters still apply, i.e., both must be of the same data type. In addition, since the formal parameter is now a variable that can pass results back to the main program (or another procedure), the actual parameter must also be a variable—it would be impossible to pass results back to a value or an expression.

9.5 WHY USE PARAMETERS?

One of the first questions that may come to mind as you go through this chapter is, why bother to use parameters at all when global variables seem to work so well? The answer is a matter of correctness and style. Why do we bother to indent subsections of a Pascal program as we write it? It is not necessary for the program to compile or run correctly—we do it because it makes the program easier to read, correct, or update, especially if the program is large.

The case for using parameters is similar. Global variables work well in small programs, but as programs become larger and more complex, the use of parameters offers several advantages. When a procedure is written using parameters, it can be called several times from different points in the program and used with different variables each time. Using global variables can also cause problems if a variable value is accidentally changed in a procedure. For example, if a FOR..DO loop uses the variable I as a counter and the value of I is altered by a procedure called from within the loop, it could have a serious effect on the results of the program. An unintentional change in the value of a variable in a procedure is called a **side effect**. Side effects are usually undesirable, so it is best to avoid them whenever possible by using parameters rather than global variables. Another problem can arise if a large program has several procedures that are called not only by the main program, but by several other procedures as well. If the value of a global variable is changed incorrectly in one procedure, it may be extremely difficult to find the error, since that incorrect value will then be passed to all of the remaining procedures (and the main body of the program) as well. If parameters are used, the procedure causing the error is much easier to isolate and correct, since the remaining procedures should remain unaffected.

Thus we can conclude that it is a matter of good programming practice to use parameters rather than global variables whenever possible. Obviously, if you are writing a short program with few procedures, this practice will slow you down slightly. But if you get used to using parameters whenever you write a program, you will develop a consistent programming style that should benefit you in the long run.

9.6 USING PARAMETERS IN A GRAPHICS PROGRAM

In chapter 6 we used a graphics program to draw a square (we named it SQUARE and even saved it). You can G(et or T(ransfer it back to the SYSTEM.WRK file and then move to the Editor and modify it as shown in exhibit 9–2, or you can simply enter the program in exhibit 9–2 (this might be faster).

In procedure DRAW there are three formal parameters, SIZE, ANGLE, and SIDES, all integers. We have also defined an integer variable I as a local variable in the procedure. What does the procedure DRAW do? It uses a loop to move the Turtle a distance equal to SIZE and then turn it ANGLE degrees a number of times equal to SIDES. The local variable I is used as the counter in the FOR..DO loop.

The first time DRAW is called, the value parameters are 50, 90, and 4. This sets the SIZE to 50, sets the ANGLE to 90, and informs the procedure that the shape has 4 SIDES—thus a square is drawn. The second call passes values of 40, 60, and 6 to the parameters, and a hexagon is the result. The third call passes values of 60, 120, and 3, resulting in a triangle.

Exhibit 9–2. Program SHAPES2

```
PROGRAM SHAPES2;

USES TURTLEGRAPHICS;

PROCEDURE DRAW(SIZE,ANGLE,SIDES:INTEGER);
   VAR
     I:INTEGER;
   BEGIN (* DRAW *)
     FOR I:= 1 TO SIDES DO
        BEGIN  (* FOR..DO *)
           MOVE(SIZE);
           TURN(ANGLE)
        END  (* FOR..DO *)
   END; (* DRAW *)

BEGIN  (* SHAPES2 *)
   INITTURTLE;
   PENCOLOR (WHITE);
   DRAW (50,90,4);
   PENCOLOR (NONE);
   MOVETO (30,30);
   PENCOLOR (WHITE);
   DRAW (40,60,6);
   PENCOLOR (NONE);
   MOVETO (200, 130);
   PENCOLOR (WHITE);
   DRAW (60,120,3);
   READLN
END.  (* SHAPES2 *)
```

<table>
<tr><td>

FOCUS
On Problem
Solving

</td><td>

The program SHAPES2 draws closed shapes, i.e., shapes that end where they begin. Modify the program so that: (1) only two parameters are passed to the procedure; (2) the program allows us to input the necessary values from the keyboard and then draws the specified figure; (3) the program draws a total of five figures; and (4) it only draws one figure at a time on the screen, beginning at location (130,40). Try your hand at this before proceeding with the text. Once you have a program that meets the above requirements, you may continue.

</td></tr>
</table>

In developing the algorithm for this problem, we can state the problem as: (1) given two input values for a closed shape, draw it beginning at point (130,40); and (2) repeat this process four more times. Clearly step 1 is the key to the problem, so we could write our algorithm as:

SHAPES5;
  1. procedure to draw shape;
  2. do the following steps 5 times:
     a. input values;
     b. initialize screen;
     c. call procedure to draw shape.

Refining part 2 of the algorithm somewhat might give us

  2. do the following steps 5 times:
     a. input values:
       (1) prompt for values;
       (2) input SIZE and SIDES values;
     b. initialize screen:
       (1) clear screen;
       (2) move Turtle to (130,40);
       (3) put pen down;
     c. call DRAW procedure;
     d. pause before proceeding.

The key to using only two inputs is to recognize that for a closed shape the Turtle will always turn through 360°. Since the angles are all equal, the program can calculate ANGLE from the number of sides. Refining part of the algorithm might then give us:

  1. procedure to draw shape:
     a. calculate angle size;
     b. for each side:
       (1) move a distance = size of side;
       (2) turn the proper angle;

and still further refinement might produce:

SHAPES5;
  1. procedure to draw shape:
     a. ANGLE = 360 / number of sides;

  b. for each SIDE
     (1) MOVE distance = SIZE;
     (2) TURN ANGLE degrees;
  2. (* would remain basically unchanged from the previous refinement *)

Moving from the algorithm to the program, our procedure would look like this

```
DRAW (SIZE,SIDES:INTEGER);
  VAR
    ANGLE,I:INTEGER;
  BEGIN
    ANGLE := 360 DIV SIDES;
    FOR I := 1 TO SIDES DO
      BEGIN
        MOVE (SIZE);
        TURN (ANGLE)
      END
  END;
```

Since the program is to accept input from the keyboard for two variables, we would define the variables at the beginning of the program and include a READLN statement to input them, for example:

```
VAR
  DISTANCE,NUMBER:INTEGER;

BEGIN
  WRITELN('INPUT SIZE AND THE NUMBER OF
  SIDES');
  READLN(DISTANCE,NUMBER);
```

The third requirement, that the program draw exactly five figures, can be accomplished through the use of a FOR..DO loop. We can add another VAR (J) as a counter and then place the main body of the program in the following loop:

```
BEGIN
  FOR J := 1 TO 5
    BEGIN
      .
      .
      .
    END
END.
```

The last requirement (drawing one figure at a time beginning at (130,40) can be accomplished by including the INIT-TURTLE statement in the loop. This will clear the screen prior to drawing the next shape. We can start at the location (130,40)

by using a MOVETO statement prior to setting PENCOLOR (WHITE). Since we want to be able to see the shapes once they are drawn, we added a pause loop to slow things down. And finally, we would probably want to switch back to TEXTMODE each time we prompted for the next input. Following the algorithm and combining the program segments we have developed would give us a program something like the one shown in exhibit 9–3. Test the program with a triangle, pentagon, hexagon, octagon, and a figure with a size of 5 and 72 sides. What figure did you get in the last case? It should resemble a circle. ■

Drawing the "Perfect" Circle

Run the program again, varying the distance and number. What combination seems to give the best circle (and still fit on the screen)? As you experiment, you may find that numbers that

Exhibit 9–3. Program SHAPES

```
PROGRAM SHAPES5;

USES TURTLEGRAPHICS;

VAR
  DISTANCE,NUMBER,J,P:INTEGER;

PROCEDURE DRAW(SIZE,SIDES:INTEGER);
  VAR
    ANGLE,I:INTEGER;
  BEGIN (* DRAW *)
    ANGLE := 360 DIV SIDES;
    FOR I:= 1 TO SIDES DO
      BEGIN (* FOR..DO *)
        MOVE(SIZE);
        TURN(ANGLE)
      END (* FOR..DO *)
  END; (* DRAW *)

BEGIN (* SHAPES5 *)
  FOR J := 1 TO 5 DO
    BEGIN (* FOR..DO *)
      WRITELN('INPUT SIZE AND THE NUMBER
        OF SIDES');
      READLN(DISTANCE,NUMBER);
      INITTURTLE;
      MOVETO (130,40);
      PENCOLOR (WHITE);
      DRAW (DISTANCE,NUMBER);
      FOR P := 1 TO 4000 DO; (*PAUSE*)
      TEXTMODE
    END; (* FOR..DO *)
END. (* SHAPES5 *)
```

divide evenly into 360 work best, since they make a complete circle. If you aren't convinced, try something like 7 and 55. You'll notice that the Turtle stops short of completing the circle. That's because 360/55 is 6.54545, but 360 DIV 55 is 6; thus, the Turtle turns 55° 6 times for a total of 330°, leaving the circle short of completion.

Some obvious values to try would be 30, 45, 60, 72, 90, 120, 180, and 360. You might feel that a small distance with a large number of sides might give the best result, e.g., 1 & 360. Do they? Obviously not. Nor do 2 & 180 or 4 & 120. In theory, these seem like logical choices, but they don't work well in practice because we are trying to draw curved lines on a rectangular grid. Remember, the pixels on your monitor screen are the intersect points of a large grid. If we looked at an expanded picture of several adjacent pixels, they would look something like figure 9–1. Assume the Turtle is located at the darker pixel facing right. If we tell the Turtle to move one space to the right, it has no trouble. But what if we tell it to turn 1° and move one space? Let's expand the darkened pixel and three of its adjacent neighbors (see figure 9–2). If the Turtle is to move one space, it must move to pixel A, B, or C. Pixel A would involve a turn of 0°, B a turn of 45°, and C a turn of 90°. Thus, if we tell the Turtle to turn 1°, it will come as close as it can, a turn of 0°. Twenty-two such instructions should turn the Turtle a total of 22°, but the visual result will be twenty-two horizontal moves. Thus, small distances and small turns (resulting from the use of a large number of sides) do not work well on the screen to produce curved lines. If we expand our view of the screen slightly as in figure 9–3, we can see that enlarging the distance the Turtle moves give us the same choices of 0°, 45°, and 90° turns to A, C, and E and also adds turns of approximately 27° to point B and 63° to point D. Thus, larger distances and larger turns give more choices, from which a better selection can be made.

Figure 9–1. Adjacent Pixels on the Screen

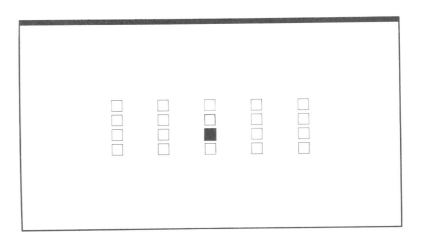

Figure 9–2. Adjacent
Pixels—Close-Up View

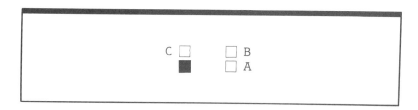

Figure 9–3. Adjacent
Pixels—Expanded View

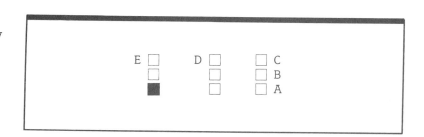

As you may have already discovered, the following combinations (among others) seem to give fairly good results:

Distance	Number (of sides)
15	30
10	45
7	60
6	72
5	90

The point of this whole exercise is *not* drawing the "perfect" circle but thinking through the method (and therefore the program) used to produce a circle, given the constraints imposed by the graphics screen. S(ave this program to your storage disk under the name SHAPE5 and then clear your workfile.

9.7 PASSING PARAMETERS TO PROCEDURES

Let's write a program that allows us to input the height and width of a rectangle and then calculates its perimeter and area. We will input data in the main program and create separate procedures for the two calculations. Each procedure must perform the necessary calculations and output the appropriate results. The program would then look something like this

```
PROGRAM RECTANGLE;

PROCEDURE PERIMETER;
  BEGIN
  END;

PROCEDURE AREA;
  BEGIN
  END;
```

```
BEGIN
  PERIMETER;
  AREA
END.
```

before we write the variable declarations or the input, calculation, or output statements. Would this program compile and
run? Try it and see.

The answer is clearly yes, although the output leaves something to be desired. One of the advantages of programming in
Pascal is that the language allows us to conceptualize a program and its various parts and, if we are careful, to even create
a program outline that will actually compile and run before we
have completed the program. As the programs you write become
longer, this advantage will become more obvious.

Let's begin fleshing this program out a bit. We'll start by
declaring our variables for the main program and writing the
necessary input statements (with appropriate prompts, of
course). The prompts will request the input of two variables,
height and width, so we will use those as the variable names.
Since we do not know whether fractional input values might
be entered, we will use Real data types instead of Integers:

```
VAR
  HEIGHT,WIDTH:REAL;
```

Our input statements might look something like this:

```
BEGIN
  WRITE ('INPUT HEIGHT ');
  READLN (HEIGHT);
  WRITELN;
  WRITE ('INPUT WIDTH ');
  READLN (WIDTH);
  PERIMETER;
  AREA
END.
```

If this program segment was added to our program it would
still compile and run, although we would get no output. But
we could run it to find out if the input statements were working properly. And just to be sure, we could temporarily add an
extra statement to output the values for HEIGHT and WIDTH:

```
WRITELN ('HEIGHT = ',HEIGHT:6:2,'     W
IDTH = ',WIDTH:6:2);
```

just prior to the calling statement for the procedure PER-
IMETER. This would allow us to test the inputing segment before moving on to the procedures.

Once the input segment is correct, we can add parameters
to the first calling statement

```
   PERIMETER(HEIGHT,WIDTH);
```

and then complete the PERIMETER procedure

```
PROCEDURE PERIMETER (TALL,WIDE:REAL);
  VAR
    AROUND:REAL;
  BEGIN
    AROUND := 2*TALL + 2*WIDE;
    WRITELN;
    WRITELN ('PERIMETER = ',AROUND:8:2)
  END; (* PERIMETER *)
```

The extra WRITELN statement should make the output easier to read. When you have correctly entered the above lines or your own version of them, compile and run the program. You should now have a program that allows the user to input the height and width of a rectangle and then calculates and outputs the value of the perimeter. We now have a working program that provides us with some results even though we have not completed the programming.

Before we proceed to AREA, let's take a look at what we have so far. Our program has two global variables, HEIGHT and WIDTH. They are used as actual parameters and their values are passed to the formal value parameters TALL and WIDE. A third variable, AROUND, is declared in PERIMETER, so it is a local variable with meaning only within the procedure.

Now let's finish up the program by completing the AREA calling statement and procedure. They will be very similar to the last calling statement and procedure and might look like this

```
AREA (HEIGHT,WIDTH);
```

and

```
PROCEDURE AREA (UP,ACROSS:REAL);
  VAR
    SURFACE:REAL;
  BEGIN
    SURFACE := UP*ACROSS;
    WRITELN;
    WRITELN ('AREA = ',SURFACE:8:2)
  END; (* AREA *)
```

This second procedure also has two formal parameters, UP and ACROSS, and a local variable named SURFACE. Add these statements and make any necessary changes, remove the temporary WRITELN statement we used to check the input statements, and run the program. The program is now complete and (barring typing errors) both procedures should be working correctly.

Although we don't want to belabor the point, it is important to realize that the variables HEIGHT and WIDTH can be used anywhere in the main program or in either of the procedures. The variables TALL, WIDE, and AROUND have meaning only within PERIMETER, and the variables UP, ACROSS, and SURFACE have meaning only within AREA. If you attempt to refer to the variable AROUND in the AREA procedure or in the main program, you will get an undefined variable error.

9.8 USING VARIABLE PARAMETERS

Now that our program is working well, we'll modify it. Our modified program will find the perimeter and area for five rectangles and then find the average perimeter and area for the group of five rectangles. To find the average for each measurement, we will have to add the results we obtain and then divide the totals by 5. To calculate five perimeters and areas, we can simply put a loop in the main body of the program. To obtain the necessary totals, we will have to add a variable to keep a running total of our results for each measurement. To calculate the averages, we will add another procedure:

```
PROCEDURE AVERAGE (SUM,NUMBER:REAL;ID:ST
RING);
  VAR
    MEAN:REAL;
  BEGIN
    MEAN := SUM/NUMBER;
    WRITELN;
    WRITELN ('AVERAGE ',ID,' = ',MEAN:8:2)
  END; (* AVERAGE *)
```

The string variable ID has been added so that we can pass a parameter identifying which measurement we are averaging. Thus, our calling statement might look like

```
AVERAGE (SUMAREA,5,'AREA');
```

We will also add two new variables, SUMPMTR and SUMAREA, to the main program; they will keep our running totals. The next question is where are we going to calculate these totals? For the sake of the example, we'll perform the calculations still another procedure, called ADDER:

```
PROCEDURE ADDER (INPUT:REAL;VAR TOTAL:RE
AL);
  BEGIN
    TOTAL := TOTAL + INPUT
  END; (* ADDER *)
```

This procedure will be called with statements from the PERIMETER and AREA procedures such as

ADDER (AROUND,SUM); and ADDER (SURFACE,SUM):

Notice that the formal parameter list for the procedure ADDER is somewhat different from our other parameter lists so far. We have declared not only the parameter INPUT, but a variable parameter, TOTAL, as well. The variable parameter is preceded by the prefix VAR to identify it as a variable parameter. The difference between the formal parameter INPUT and the variable parameter TOTAL is that the computer allocates a separate memory location for the value of INPUT. It does not allocate a separate memory location for TOTAL; it simply uses a **pointer** to point to the memory location of the actual variable. Remember, TOTAL will be passed the value of the actual parameter, but that when the value of TOTAL changes, the value of the actual parameter will also be changed, i.e., the resulting value of TOTAL will be passed back to the actual parameter.

We will also add variable parameters to the PERIMETER and AREA procedures so that the sums can be passed back to the main body of the program. When these modifications are all made, our program might look something like the one shown in exhibit 9–4.

Exhibit 9–4. Program RECTANGLE2

```
PROGRAM RECTANGLE2;

VAR
   HEIGHT,WIDTH,SUMPMTR,SUMAREA:REAL;
   I:INTEGER;

PROCEDURE PERIMETER (TALL,WIDE:REAL;VAR
SUM:REAL);
   VAR
      AROUND:REAL;
   BEGIN (* PERIMETER *)
   AROUND := 2*TALL + 2*WIDE;
      WRITELN;
      WRITELN ('PERIMETER = ',AROUND:8:2);
      ADDER (AROUND,SUM)
   END; (* PERIMETER *)

PROCEDURE AREA (UP,ACROSS:REAL;VAR SUM:R
EAL);
   VAR
      SURFACE:REAL;
   BEGIN (* AREA *)
      SURFACE := UP*ACROSS;
      WRITELN;
      WRITELN ('AREA = ',SURFACE:8:2);
      ADDER (SURFACE,SUM)
   END; (* AREA *)
```

```
PROCEDURE ADDER (INPUT:REAL;VAR TOTAL:RE
AL);
  BEGIN (* ADDER *)
    TOTAL := TOTAL + INPUT
  END; (* ADDER *)

PROCEDURE AVERAGE (SUM,NUMBER:REAL;ID:ST
RING);
  VAR
    MEAN:REAL;
  BEGIN (* AVERAGE *)
    MEAN := SUM/NUMBER;
    WRITELN;
    WRITELN ('AVERAGE ',ID,' = ',MEAN:8:2)
  END; (* AVERAGE *)

BEGIN (* RECTANGLE2 *)
  SUMPMTR := 0.0; (* INITIALIZE AT ZERO *)
  SUMAREA := 0.0; (* INITIALIZE AT ZERO *)
  FOR I := 1 TO 5 DO
    BEGIN (* FOR..DO *)
      WRITE ('INPUT HEIGHT ');
      READLN (HEIGHT);
      WRITELN;
      WRITE ('INPUT WIDTH ');
      READLN (WIDTH);
      PERIMETER (HEIGHT,WIDTH,SUMPMTR);
      AREA (HEIGHT,WIDTH,SUMAREA)
    END; (* FOR..DO *)
  AVERAGE (SUMPMTR,5,'PERIMETER');
  AVERAGE (SUMAREA,5,'AREA')
END. (* RECTANGLE2 *)
```

Check your program to make sure there are no errors, but do not attempt to compile and run it yet.

9.9 FORWARD REFERENCES FOR PROCEDURES

If you tried to run RECTANGLE2, you would get an "undeclared identifier" error when the compiler reached the ADDER (AROUND,SUM) line in the PERIMETER procedure. This error occurs because this line is calling procedure ADDER, but the procedure is not declared until after the PERIMETER procedure, so it is still unknown to the Pascal compiler. We could avoid this problem by moving ADDER so that it is declared before the procedures that call it. This solution would work in some cases (this is one) but not necessarily in all cases. Therefore, we will use another approach, the **forward declaration** or **forward reference**. This is done by adding a statement declaring the procedure and its parameters followed by the word FOR-

WARD; this statement must be placed prior to the first procedure that calls this undeclared procedure. For example,

```
PROCEDURE ADDER (INPUT:REAL;VAR TOTAL:RE
AL); FORWARD;
```

would be added just prior to the statement that declares the PERIMETER procedure. The FORWARD statement tells the compiler that a procedure named ADDER is going to be declared later in the program listing and includes any parameters that will be included in ADDER. When ADDER is declared later in the program, it is not necessary to list the parameters again. In fact, a duplicate listing is acceptable in Standard Pascal, but it will cause an error in Apple Pascal. Thus, the formal parameter list must be included in the forward declaration statement and excluded from the later procedure declaration. Notice that the word FORWARD is preceded and followed by semicolons.

Once you have added the forward declaration and removed the parameter list from the procedure statement, compile and run the program. Try entering the same data each time to make it easy to check the program's performance when calculating the averages. If the program runs properly, you can S(ave it as RECTANGLE2. If it does not run properly, find the mistakes, correct them, and then save the program.

9.10 NESTED PROCEDURES

When we wrote the LOOP program in chapter 7 to help Mr. Matthews with his grades, we used three procedures, ENTRY, CALCULATE, and WRITEOUT, with global variables throughout. This practice was convenient at the time to illustrate how a larger program could be divided into smaller modules that were both logical and distinct. Let's return to that program and see how it might have been written differently. We will retain the three distinct parts of the program, i.e., the procedures that input, process, and output the data, but now we will use **nested procedures**, that is, one procedure within another. Thus, a skeleton of the program (now called NEST) might look like this:

```
PROGRAM NEST;

PROCEDURE ENTRY;

  PROCEDURE CALCULATE;

    PROCEDURE WRITEOUT;

BEGIN (* NEST *)
END. (* NEST *)
```

The procedure ENTRY contains another procedure named CAL-
CULATE, which contains a third procedure named WRITEOUT.
Adding the parameters and calling statements, the program
would look something like exhibit 9–5. Notice that in each
case, the subprocedure is declared before the statement block
of the procedure containing it. This is necessary because a
procedure cannot be called before it is declared. Because the
procedures are nested, however, we do not have to use forward
declaration.

Exhibit 9–5. Program
NEST

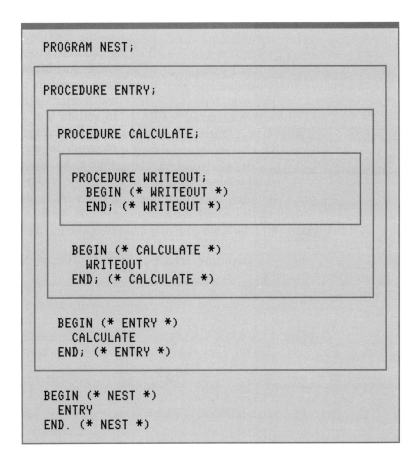

```
PROGRAM NEST;

  PROCEDURE ENTRY;

    PROCEDURE CALCULATE;

      PROCEDURE WRITEOUT;
        BEGIN (* WRITEOUT *)
        END; (* WRITEOUT *)

      BEGIN (* CALCULATE *)
        WRITEOUT
      END; (* CALCULATE *)

    BEGIN (* ENTRY *)
      CALCULATE
    END; (* ENTRY *)

  BEGIN (* NEST *)
    ENTRY
  END. (* NEST *)
```

Exhibit 9–6 shows the program with the variable declarations and other statements added (the ENTRY prompt
statements have been omitted to save space). Notice that no parameters are passed from one procedure to another. The variables declared in ENTRY are considered **nonlocal** in nature;
although they are not global, they are accessible by any procedures nested within ENTRY. Thus, CALCULATE and WRITE-
OUT recognize the variables declared in ENTRY, and WRITE-
OUT recognizes any variables declared in CALCULATE. On the
other hand, variables declared in WRITEOUT are local and not

Exhibit 9–6. Program NEST

```
PROGRAM NEST;

CONST
   WGTNOTES = 0.20;
   WGTPROJ = 0.30;
   WGTFINAL = 0.50;

PROCEDURE ENTRY;
   VAR
      NOTES,PROJECT,FINAL:REAL;
      NAME:STRING;

   PROCEDURE CALCULATE;
   VAR
      GRADE:REAL;

      PROCEDURE WRITEOUT;
         BEGIN (* WRITEOUT *)
            WRITELN;
            WRITELN (NAME,'''S FINAL GRADE =
               ',GRADE:8:2);
            WRITELN
         END; (* WRITEOUT *)

      BEGIN (* CALCULATE *)
         GRADE := WGTNOTES*NOTES + WGTPROJ
            *PROJECT + WGTFINAL*FINAL;
         WRITEOUT
      END; (* CALCULATE *)

   BEGIN (* ENTRY *)
      (* PROMPT STATEMENTS WOULD GO HERE *)
      READLN (NOTES,PROJECT,FINAL);
      (* MORE PROMPT STATEMENTS HERE *)
      READLN (NAME);
      CALCULATE
   END; (*ENTRY *)

BEGIN (* NEST *)
   ENTRY
END. (* NEST *)
```

recognized by ENTRY or CALCULATE, and variables declared in CALCULATE are not recognized by ENTRY.

One last point on nested procedures must be made: CALCULATE and WRITEOUT cannot be accessed directly from the main body of the program. They are considered **local** to ENTRY. Thus, procedures that are meant to be used only within other procedures of a more general nature that might be called from other parts of the program should stand alone.

9.11 SUMMARY

In this chapter we have examined Pascal's ways of passing parameters from the main body of the program to procedures or from one procedure to another. You have learned the difference between actual parameters and formal parameters, value parameters and variable parameters, and local and global variables. Remember that whenever using parameters, the actual and formal parameters must be of the same data type.

When calling procedures that have not yet been declared, you must use a forward declaration statement, which must include the formal parameter list for the procedure. The procedure declaration statement, however, cannot contain a formal parameter list if the procedure has been declared in a FORWARD statement.

In addition, procedures can be nested within one another, and when this is done, variables declared in an outer procedure can be referenced by inner procedures. But variables declared in the inner procedures are local in nature and cannot be referenced by the outer procedure. Procedures nested in another procedure cannot be called from outside of the procedure they are nested in.

Finally, when writing programs with procedures, it may be easier to use only global variables, but it is better programming style (and a good habit) to use parameters to pass values to those procedures. This will avoid side effects that can compound errors and make debugging difficult.

Review Questions

1. **a.** What is a parameter?
   b. What is a parameter list?

2. Explain the difference between an actual and a formal parameter.

3. What form does a formal parameter list take?

4. Explain the difference between a local and a global variable.

5. Explain the difference between value and variable parameters.

6. What is a side effect?

7. The main program declares an Integer variable XDO and a procedure in the program declares a Real variable XDO. Is this possible? Explain.

8. What is a forward declaration? When would it be used?

9. What is meant by **nested** procedures? If procedure B is nested in procedure A, can it be called from the main program?

10. Explain why procedures with parameters are more consistent with top-down program design than procedures using global variables.

SUMMARY of Pascal Syntax

Reserved Words	Built-in Procedures	Built-in Functions	Library Units
PROGRAM	WRITE		TURTLEGRAPHICS
USES	WRITELN		APPLESTUFF
CONST	READ		
VAR	READLN		
FORWARD			
PROCEDURE	INITTURTLE		
	PENCOLOR		
FOR..DO	MOVE		
DOWN..TO	TURN		
	MOVETO		
REPEAT	TURNTO		
UNTIL	TEXTMODE		*Boolean Constants*
	GRAFMODE		
WHILE..DO			
			FALSE
IF			TRUE
THEN			
ELSE			
DIV			
MOD			
NIL			
AND			
OR			
NOT			*Integer Constants*

1. Write a procedure that will sum all consecutive integer values beginning with I and ending with J and output the result. (Do *not* use global variables.)

2. Write the call statement for the procedure in exercise 1.

3. Modify the procedure in exercise 1 so that the result is output by a second procedure.

4. How would the procedure declaration and call statements change if the value of the sum in exercise 1 was returned to the main program (without using a global variable).

5. Write a procedure that prompts for and reads two values and a nested procedure that determines the product of those two values.

6. Identify which parameter lists are correct and which are incorrect in terms of syntax. If incorrect, explain why.
   a. `(X;Y:REAL)`
   b. `(X:REAL;Y:REAL)`
   c. `(X,Y:REAL,I:INTEGER)`
   d. `(VAR; X:REAL; Y:REAL)`
   e. `(X:REAL;VAR Y:REAL)`

7. Given the following procedure declaration and call statements:

```
PROGRAM MAIN;
VAR
   F,G,X:INTEGER;
PROCEDURE ONE(A,B:INTEGER);
   VAR
      M,N:INTEGER;

      .
      .
      .
ONE(X,8);

   .
   .
   .
```

   a. Identify the actual parameters.
   b. Identify the formal parameters.
   c. Identify the value parameters.
   d. Identify the variable parameters.
   e. Identify the global variables.
   f. Identify the local variables.

8. In the following program segment:

```
PROGRAM MAIN;
VAR
   A,B:INTEGER;
PROCEDURE ONE;
   VAR
      C,D:INTEGER;
```

```
PROCEDURE TWO;
  VAR
    E,F:INTEGER;
      .
      .
```

a. Is variable A known by MAIN?
b. Is variable A known by ONE?
c. Is variable A known by TWO?
d. Is variable D known by MAIN?
e. Is variable D known by TWO?
f. Is variable E known by MAIN?
g. Is variable F known by ONE?

9. Given

```
VAR
  A,B,C:REAL;
  D,E:INTEGER;
PROCEDURE ONE (L,M:REAL;VAR N:INTEGER);
  VAR
    S:INTEGER;
      .
      .
ONE(4.0,3*A,E);
```

a. Identify the actual parameters.
b. Identify the formal parameters.
c. Identify the value parameters.
d. Identify the variable parameters.

Diagnostic Exercises

10. Given

```
PROGRAM MAIN;
VAR
  X,Y,Z:INTEGER;
PROCEDURE SUB(A,B,C:INTEGER);
  VAR
    M,N:INTEGER;
  BEGIN
    FOR M:= 1 TO C DO
      B:=B+A;
  END;
BEGIN
  X:=5;
  Y:=0;
  Z:=3;
  SUB (X,Y,Z);
  WRITELN(X,Y,Z)
END.
```

What will be output by this program?

11. Given

```
PROCEDURE ONE(X,Y,Z:REAL);
   BEGIN
      Z:= 3*XY;
   END;
BEGIN
   A:=4.0;
   B:=9.0;
   ONE(A,10,C)
END.
```

What are the final values of:

a. A   **d.** Y

b. C   **e.** Z

c. X

12. Given

```
PROCEDURE SUB(X:INTEGER; VAR Y,Z:INTEGER);
   BEGIN
      Z:= 5*X + 2*Y
   END;
BEGIN
   A:= 1;
   B:= 4;
   C:= 8;
   SUB(*A,B,C)
END.
```

What are the final values of:

a. X   **d.** A

b. Y   **e.** C

c. Z

Problems

13. Write a procedure that reads 10 values input from the keyboard.

14. Write a procedure that determines whether a value is positive or negative and increments the counter POS or NEG based on the result.

15. Write a program that uses the procedure from problem 13 to enter values and the procedure from problem 14 to tally the positive and negative entries. Output the results (POS and NEG) from the main program.

16. Develop an algorithm for a procedure that determines the largest and smallest (maximum and minimum) values entered and outputs the results. (Use the input procedure from problem 13 to input the values.)

17. Code and test the program for the algorithm developed in problem 16.

10

Functions

In this chapter you will learn about Pascal functions, which are similar to procedures. The difference between procedures and functions is that procedures are subprograms that can be called and executed by either the main program or procedures, while functions are subprograms that calculate a single value and return that value to the calling statement. Some arithmetic functions already exist in an Apple Pascal system library unit. We can define other functions ourselves to meet our needs.

10.1 FUNCTIONS

Like procedures, functions must be called. The **function call** consists of the function name or identifier followed by the actual parameter or parameters (within parentheses) that are being passed to the function:

FNAME *(actual parameter list)*

There is no semicolon after a function call because a function call is not a complete statement.

Unlike the calling statement for a procedure, a function call can appear in an expression or as an actual parameter being passed to a procedure or another function. A function cannot appear on the left-hand side of an assignment statement, however, any more than a value could. The statement

FNAME := 15*(X-8)/4;

would be no more acceptable than

12 := 15*(X-8)/4;

There are no restrictions on the identifiers used as names for functions. You can use any name that meets the general rules for identifiers. Apple Pascal also has some **intrinsic** or built-in functions, and these functions have identifiers that are considered reserved words.

10.2 BUILT-IN ARITHMETIC FUNCTIONS

As we have mentioned, there are a number of previously defined arithmetic functions that already exist in the Pascal language. Some of these functions can be called simply by using the function's reserved word identifier. Other intrinsic arithmetic and trigonometric functions reside in TRANSCEND, one of Apple Pascal's system library units. TRANSCEND is contained in the file SYSTEM.LIBRARY, which you probably noticed when you listed the contents of your system disk. If you want to use any of the functions in TRANSCEND, you must specify TRANSCEND in a USES statement, just as you specified TURTLEGRAPHICS when you wanted to use the Apple graphics commands.

The built-in arithmetic functions are ABS, SQR, SQRT, ROUND, TRUNC, EXP, LN, LOG, PWPROFTEN, ATAN, COS, and SIN. (Note: Some of these functions may not be available in some of the earlier versions of Apple Pascal.) Of these functions, ABS, SQR, ROUND, TRUNC, and PWROFTEN are available directly in Apple Pascal. The remainder require the USES TRANSCEND; statement.

Let's take a brief look at exhibit 10–1, which lists each of these functions. The X in parentheses following the function name represents the argument or parameter passed to the function. In most cases, the function is of the same data type as X, i.e., if X is Real, the function will return a Real value and if X is Integer, the function will return an Integer value. Occasionally, however, it is possible to have a Real argument and an Integer function or an Integer argument and a Real function. If we state that the function and argument can be Real or Integer, it means that a Real argument will produce a Real function and an Integer argument will produce an Integer function. In most cases, an Integer argument can also be used to produce a Real function.

It is sometimes possible to use these arithmetic functions in combination to produce desired results. For example, if you want to raise X to the fourth power, you could use the expression

```
Y := SQR(SQR(X));
```

If X = 2, this expression will evaluate SQR(X) and return the value of 4. It will then evaluate SQR(4) and return 16. If you want to raise X to the fifth power, you could simply expand the above expression to

```
Y := SQR(SQR(X))*X;
```

A slight variation of this format would give you X raised to the sixth power

```
Y := SQR(SQR(X)*X);
```

Another useful combination would be ABS and SQRT. You cannot take the square root of a negative number, so you might use the following combination to insure the desired result

```
Y := SQRT(ABS(X));
```

The ABS function will convert any negative value to a positive one before the square root is taken.

While there is no exponential operator in Apple Pascal, we can make one by combining some of the existing functions.

Exhibit 10–1. Built-in Apple Pascal Functions

Function	Explanation
ABS(X)	returns the absolute value of X. Both X and ABS(X) can be Real or Integer values. If X is -4, then ABS(X) will equal 4.
SQR(X)	returns the value of X squared. Both X and SQR(X) can be Real or Integer values. If X is 2, then SQR(X) will be 4.
SQRT(X)	returns the value of the square root of X. X can be Real or Integer, but SQRT(X) must be Real. X must be greater than zero. If X is 16, then SQRT(X) will equal 4.
ROUND(X)	returns the value of X rounded to the nearest integer value. X must be Real, since there is no need to round an Integer, but ROUND(X) can be Real or Integer. If X is 12.64, then ROUND(X) will equal 13; if X is 12.44, then ROUND(X) will equal 12.
TRUNC(X)	returns the value of X truncated to the nearest Integer value. X must be Real (you cannot truncate an Integer value), but TRUNC (X) can be Real or Integer. If X is 9.86, then TRUNC(X) will equal 9.
EXP(X)	returns the value of e (2.71828) raised to the X power. X can be Real or Integer, but EXP(X) must be Real. If X is 3, EXP(X) will equal 20.0855 (or 2.00855E1).
LN(X)	returns the value of the natural logarithm (the logarithm to the base e) of X. X can be Real or Integer, but LN(X) must be Real. If X is 8, then LN(X) will equal 2.07944.
LOG(X)	returns the value of the logarithm (to the base 10) of X. X can be Real or Integer, but LOG(X) must be Real. If X is 8, then LOG(X) will equal 0.90309 (or 9.03090E-1).
PWROFTEN(X)	returns the value of ten raised to the X power. X can be Real or Integer, but it really should be Integer since a Real argument is treated as if it were an Integer, i.e., if X is 2.4, it would be treated as if it were 2. In addition, X must be positive; negative values produce a program-terminating error. If X is 2, then PWROFTEN(X) will equal 100.
SIN(X)	returns the value of the sine of X. X must be in radians, not degrees. (The relationship between degrees and radians can be expressed by: 2π (**pi**) radians $= 360°$, where $\pi = 3.14159$.) X can be Real or Integer, but SIN(X) must be Real. If X $= 2$, SIN(X) will be 0.909297 (or 9.09297E-1).
COS(X)	returns the value of the cosine of X. X is assumed to be in radians and can be Real or Integer, but COS(X) will be Real. If X $= 3$, COS(X) wil be -0.989992 (or $-9.89992E-1$).
ATAN(X)	returns the value of the arctangent of X. X is assumed to be in radians and can be Real or Integer, but ATAN(X) must be Real. If X is 2, then ATAN(X) will equal 1.10715.

Thus, if we want to raise X to the power n, we could use the expression

$$X^n = \exp\,(n^*\ln(X))$$

or, as an assignment statement:

```
Y := EXP(N*LN(X));
```

Thus, if X = 4 and we want to raise X to the third power (X cubed), the expression would evaluate LN(X) as 1.38629, then evaluate 3*LN(X) as 4.15888, and finally evaluate EXP(4.15888) as 64.

Similarly, there is no function for the trigonometric functions tangent, arcsine, and arccosine, but these functions can be calculated using the sine, cosine, and arctangent functions. For example, the tangent is simply the sine divided by the cosine (tan(x) = (sin(x)/cos(x)). We can not use this equation as an assignment statement, however, since TAN(X) would be interpreted as an identifier, TAN, with an actual parameter. TAN is *not* a Pascal function, but remember that no function name can appear on the left-hand side of an assignment statement (it represents a value and you cannot make an assignment to a value). We could use

```
TANGENT := SIN(X)/COS(X);
```

where TANGENT is an identifier of type Real.

Using ROUND and TRUNC

Up to this point, we have been very careful not to mix data types within an expression or assignment statement. Mixing data types often produces "type conflict" error messages when we try to compile the program. While mixing Real and Integer data types is still not a good practice, there are times when it may be necessary. It is possible to assign Integer values to Real variables through normal assignment statements or to use Integer values in a Real expression, but you cannot assign Real values to Integer variables or use Real values in an Integer expression in the same manner.

This problem can be overcome, however, through the use of the two functions ROUND and TRUNC. These functions are sometimes referred to as **transfer functions** because they provide a method for transferring a Real value (actually the integer portion of a Real value) to an Integer variable. Thus, if R is a Real variable and we wish to use its value in an Integer expression, we could write

```
J := I*ROUND(R)+K;
```

We can achieve the same effect by using

```
J := I*TRUNC(R + 0.5) + K;
```

since adding 0.5 to the value of R before truncating would increment any decimal part of R larger than .5 to the next whole number. Note that if the value of R is negative, the proper truncating statement would be

```
J := I*TRUNC(R - 0.5) + K;
```

since negative numbers round down, i.e., away from zero. Thus, − 12.86 would round to − 13. Fortunately, the availability of ROUND saves us the effort of writing a program segment that branches to the first truncation statement when R is positive and the second when R is negative.

You can also use ROUND to round values to any decimal place you select. For example, if you want to round the value of X to the nearest two decimal places, you could use the following statement

```
Y := (ROUND(X*100)/100);
```

If X is equal to 89.3762, X would first be multiplied by 100 to produce 8937.62. This product would then be rounded to 8938, and finally, that result would be divided by 100 to give the desired result of 89.38. Of course, the same result could be achieved in output by simply formatting to two decimal places, e.g., WRITELN(Y:8:2).

Before leaving this section, let's restate that in general, it is not a wise practice to mix Real and Integer data types, but when you must do so, the ROUND and TRUNCATE functions allow you to accomplish the transfer without data type errors.

10.3 A BOOLEAN FUNCTION THAT'S ODD

In addition to the arithmetic functions available in Apple Pascal, there is a special Boolean function named ODD. The function takes the form ODD(X) and returns the value TRUE when X is odd and FALSE when X is even. X must be an Integer value, and ODD(X) will always be of type Boolean.

Can you think of an algorithm that would produce the same results as this function? A basic test for even numbers would be, are they evenly divisible by two? We could test that with DIV 2, but we are really more interested in whether there is a remainder. Therefore, we could use MOD 2; if the result was equal to 0, we would know we had an even number. We could test our algorithm by writing a program and comparing its results with those of the ODD function. If you want to try

Exhibit 10–2. Program ODDCHECK

```
PROGRAM ODDCHECK;

VAR
  FUNCHK,ALGCHK:BOOLEAN;
  DATAIN,CHK:INTEGER;
  STR:STRING;

PROCEDURE OUTPUT (RESULT:BOOLEAN;VAR STG:
STRING);
  (* CREATES STRING EQUAL TO BOOLEAN VAL
  UE *)
  BEGIN
    IF RESULT THEN
      STG := 'TRUE'
    ELSE
      STG :='FALSE'
  END; (* OUTPUT *)

PROCEDURE CHECK(RESULT:INTEGER;VAR BLN:B
OOLEAN);
  (* SETS BOOLEAN VALUE BASED UPON MOD 2*)
  BEGIN
    IF RESULT = 0 THEN
      BLN := FALSE
    ELSE
      BLN := TRUE
  END; (* CHECK *)

BEGIN (* ODDCHECK *)
  WRITE('ENTER AN INTEGER ->');
  READLN(DATAIN);
  FUNCHK := ODD(DATAIN);
  OUTPUT (FUNCHK,STR);
  WRITELN ('FUNCTION RESULT = ',STR);
  CHK := DATAIN MOD 2;
  CHECK(CHK,ALGCHK);
  OUTPUT(ALGCHK,STR);
  WRITELN('CALCULATION RESULT = ',STR)
END. (* ODDCHECK *)
```

this on your own, do so before proceeding. When you are finished, see if your program resembles the one shown in exhibit 10–2. The program has to include the OUTPUT procedure to create strings that are equivalent to the Boolean values, since Pascal cannot WRITE a Boolean value.

10.4 SOME FUNCTIONS BRING ORDER TO PASCAL

There are other intrinsic functions in Pascal that are sometimes referred to as **ordinal** or ordering functions, because they refer to the order or sequence that the computer uses with regard to its character set. The Apple computer uses what is known as an ASCII character set, which assigns each letter on the keyboard a specific ordinal value. The ASCII number for the capital letter A is 65, the number for B is 66, and so on. In Pascal, therefore, the letter A is not only considered not equal to the letter B, it is also considered less than the letter B, since its ordinal value (65) is less than the ordinal value of B (66). The ordinal functions shown in exhibit 10–3 are based on this numbering sequence and the computer's ability to make comparisons between these ordinal values. The arguments passed to the functions may be values or variables.

Obviously, the values returned by these ordinal functions depend on the character set used by the computer. The ASCII character set used by the Apple is shown in appendix B. If you are using an Apple IIe or have upper and lower display capabilities, you will be able to see lowercase letters on your screen. If you are using the normal Apple II +, or a IIc with a television screen, only uppercase letters will be displayed, although upper- and lowercase letters have different ordinal values.

One possible use of the ORD function might be to convert a numeric character into the same Integer value. If you look at

Exhibit 10–3. Apple Pascal Ordinal Functions

Function	Explanation
ORD(X)	returns the ordinal value of X. If X is a character, ORD(X) will be an Integer value. For example, if X is 'R', then ORD(X) would equal 82.
CHR(X)	returns the Char value represented by the ordinal value of X. X must be an Integer value and CHR(X) will be a Char. If X is 68, the value of CHR(X) will be 'D'.
PRED(X)	returns the value of the **predecessor** of X. X must be an ordinal data type and PRED(X) will return an ordinal value. The most common usage of this function will be with Char data types. If X is 'N', the value of PRED(X) will be 'M'. If X is 8, PRED(X) will be 7.
SUCC(X)	returns the value of the **successor** of X. X must be an ordinal data type and SUCC(X) will return an ordinal value. As with PRED, the most common use of this function will be with Char data types. If X = 'M', then SUCC(X) will be 'N'.

the ASCII code, however, you will note that the code for the character '6' is 54, not 6. Thus, a statement such as

```
VAL := ORD('6');
```

would not give us the desired result. Does this mean that we cannot make the conversion? No, it simply means we have to modify our approach. If you look at the ASCII characters, you will note that the alphabetic and numeric characters are still in their normal order, so their ordinal values are also in order. Therefore, the following statement would accomplish our purpose:

```
VAL := ORD('6') - ORD('0');
```

Since the value of ORD('6') is 54 and ORD('0') is 48, VAL will equal 6, i.e., (54 − 48). This algorithm works equally well with alphabetic characters.

Write a program that will allow the user to input a letter, then determine and output the ordinal value of the letter in the character set (its ASCII value) and its position in the alphabet. The program should repeat this process until the space bar is pressed. Your program might look something like this:

```
PROGRAM POSITION;

VAR
  CH:CHAR;
  VAL:INTEGER;

BEGIN
  REPEAT
    WRITE(CHR(13),'INPUT A CHARACTER ->');
    READ(CH);
    WRITE(CHR(13),'ORDINAL VALUE OF',CH
      ,' = ',ORD(CH));
    VAL := ORD(CH) - PRED(ORD('A'));
    WRITE(CHR(13), 'POSITION IN ALPHABET
      = ',VAL,CHR(13))
  UNTIL CH = ' '
END.
```

Notice that no WRITELN statements were used in this program. They were omitted for illustrative purposes. What does writing a CHR(13) do? Since CHR(13) is the ASCII value for the carriage return, it issues a (RET) every time it is encountered in a WRITE statement. The READ statement was used rather than READLN because we are only inputting a single character; using READLN would require an extra (and unnecessary) keystroke each time.

There are a number of algorithms we could have used in the expression for VAL. We obviously want VAL to be 1 when the variable CH is the character 'A'. The expression ORD(CH)-ORD('A') would not work, because it would return a value of 0 for 'A'. We could modify this expression by adding 1 to the resulting value, i.e., (ORD(CH)-ORD('A')) + 1. Or we could have looked up the character just prior to 'A' in the ASCII character set (it is the character '@') and used the expression ORD(CH)-ORD('@'). This is essentially what we did, but we didn't look up the ordinal value preceding the character 'A', we let the computer do it by using the function PRED.

FOCUS On Problem Solving	We know that if you want to input a number (digit) from the keyboard and accidentally enter a nonnumeric character, you will cause a program-terminating error. But if you were writing a program that required new users to input a simple value, e.g., a digit between 1 and 9, you might want to avoid this potential error by reading the entry as a character and then converting it into an Integer value. Write a program that will accomplish this, using a procedure to make the actual conversion. Include a message that informs the user an error has been made if any character other than a digit (1–9) is entered; a re-entry should then be allowed.

The algorithm for this problem might take the form:

1. Enter a character;
2. Convert the character to a digit;
3. If the digit is not between 1 and 9 inclusive, then
   a. Output an error message;
   b. Repeat steps 1 through 3a;
4. Indicate a good entry.

Because step 3b calls for the possible repetition of steps 1–3, we will modify the order of these steps to:

1. Repeat the following process until the proper entry is made:
   a. Enter a character;
   b. Convert to a digit;
   c. If the digit is not between 1 and 9 inclusive:
      (1) Indicate an error has been made;
2. Indicate a good entry.

We could then refine this algorithm further, perhaps producing something like:

1. Repeat the following process until the proper entry is made:
   a. Entry:
      (1) Prompt for a digit entry;
      (2) Accept character entry;
   b. Call CONVERT procedure;

c. If the digit is less than 1 or greater than 9, then:
   (1) Output an error message;
   (2) Return to step 1;
2. Output a message indicating a good entry has been made.

The CONVERT procedure listed in Step 1b can be refined as 1b)
CONVERT

   (1) Determine the input character's ASCII value;
   (2) Subtract the ASCII value of the character 0 from the input character's ASCII value to determine the ordinal value of the digit.

Coding the program might then produce a program similar to the one shown in exhibit 10–4.

As usual, your program may vary. In this case, the Boolean variable BAD was used to illustrate that a Boolean variable rather than a Boolean expression can be used to control the program flow. Enter and test this program. Once you are satisfied that it is correct, S(ave it as NOERROR. ■

Exhibit 10–4. Problem Solving Program NOERROR

```
PROGRAM NOERROR;

VAR
  ANY:CHAR;
  DIGIT:INTEGER;
  BAD:BOOLEAN;

PROCEDURE CONVERT (CH:CHAR;VAR X:INTEGER
);
  BEGIN
    X := ORD(CH) - ORD('0')
  END; (* CONVERT *)

BEGIN (* NOERROR *)
  REPEAT
    WRITELN;
    WRITE ('ENTER A NUMBER BETWEEN 1 & 9
      :');
    READ (ANY);
    WRITELN;
    CONVERT (ANY,DIGIT);
    BAD := (DIGIT < 1) OR (DIGIT > 9);
    IF BAD THEN
      WRITELN (ANY,' IS NOT BETWEEN 1 &
        9!');
  UNTIL NOT BAD;
  WRITELN (DIGIT, ' IS OK')
END. (* NOERROR *)
```

10.5 CREATING YOUR OWN FUNCTIONS

Up until now, we have been working with predefined Pascal functions. We can also create our own functions. Like procedures, functions must be declared before they can be called. The function declaration is similar to the procedure declaration, with one exception. Since the function represents a value, the function's data type must be declared in the first statement of the function declaration. The declaration statement would take the form

FUNCTION *fname (parameter list):data type;*

where *fname* is the function identifier, the formal parameter list includes the value parameters (and their data types) being passed to the function, and the data type defines the type of result that will be returned by the function (Real, Integer, Boolean,…). The syntax diagram for function declarations is shown in Figure 10–1. The function declaration takes the same form as a procedure declaration; local constants can be defined, local variables can be declared, local procedures or functions can be declared, and the processes to be carried out by the function are included in a compound statement.

As with intrinsic functions (but not procedures), the function call does not have to be a separate statement. The function name (followed by a list of actual parameters) can be used anywhere in an expression.

Because functions and procedures are so similar, you may wonder when you should use a function and when you should use a procedure. The answer to that depends on what the function or procedure is supposed to accomplish. If we want a value calculated and nothing more, then a function should be used. If, on the other hand, we want data input or output or several calculations performed, a procedure should be used. The LOOP program we used in chapter 7 provides an excellent example of this. In that program we had a procedure CALCULATE:

```
PROCEDURE CALCULATE;
  BEGIN
    GRADE := WGTNOTES*NOTES + WGTPROJ*PR
    OJECT + WGTFINAL*FINAL
  END (*ENTRY*);
```

Figure 10–1. Function Syntax Diagram

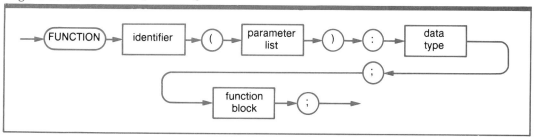

This procedure only performs one calculation and returns a value for GRADE. Thus, we could use a function in its place:

```
FUNCTION GRADE (N,P,F:REAL):REAL;
  BEGIN
    GRADE := WGTNOTES*N + WGTPROJ*P + WG
    TFINAL*F
  END; (* GRADE *)
```

We could then eliminate the calling statement for CALCULATE and simply include the actual parameters passed to the function after the function call

```
WRITELN (NAME,'''S FINAL GRADE = ',GRADE
(NOTES,PROJECT,FINAL):8:2);
```

Could we have done the same thing in the RECTANGLE2 program in chapter 9, i.e., could we have replaced some (or all) of the procedures with functions? The answer is yes. The program RECTFUNCT (exhibit 10–5) illustrates the change.

We might even say this program is more efficient, since it was eight program lines shorter. Because function calls return values directly, four of the calls are included in the WRITELN statements rather than in assignment statements. Remember, however, that this program is used to illustrate the use of func-

Exhibit 10–5. Program RECTFUNCT

```
PROGRAM RECTFUNCT;

VAR
  HEIGHT,WIDTH,SUMP,SUMA:REAL;
  I:INTEGER;

FUNCTION PERIMETER (TALL,WIDE:REAL):REAL;
  BEGIN
  PERIMETER := 2*(TALL + WIDE)
  END; (* PERIMETER *)

FUNCTION AREA (UP,ACROSS:REAL):REAL;
  BEGIN
    AREA := UP * ACROSS
  END; (* AREA *)

FUNCTION ADDER (INPUT,SUM:REAL):REAL;
  BEGIN
    ADDER := INPUT + SUM
  END; (* ADDER *)

FUNCTION AVERAGE (SUM,N:REAL):REAL;
  BEGIN
    AVERAGE := SUM/N
  END; (* AVERAGE *)
```

```
BEGIN (* RECTFUNCT *)
   SUMP := 0;
   SUMA := 0;
   FOR I := TO 5 DO
      BEGIN (* FOR..DO *)
         WRITELN;
         WRITE('INPUT HEIGHT ->)');
         READLN(HEIGHT);
         WRITELN;
         WRITE('INPUT WIDTH -->)');
         READLN(WIDTH);
         WRITELN;
         WRITELN('PERIMETER = ',PERIMETER(H
EIGHT,WIDTH):8:2);
         WRITELN;
         WRITELN('AREA =',AREA(HEIGHT,WIDT
H):8:2);
         WRITELN;
         SUMP := ADDER(PERIMETER(HEIGHT,WID
TH),SUMP);
         SUMA := ADDER(AREA(HEIGHT,WIDTH),S
UMA)
      END; (* FOR..DO *)
   WRITELN('AVERAGE PERIMETER = ',AVERAGE
(SUMP,5):8:2);
   WRITELN('AVERAGE AREA = ',AVERAGE(SUMA
,5):8:2)
END. (*RECTFUNCT *)
```

tions, not necessarily as an example of the most efficient programming techniques. For example, we used function calls to sum the perimeters and areas, but the following lines would have accomplished the same purpose without using the ADDER function.

```
SUMP := SUMP + PERIMETER(HEIGHT,WIDTH);
SUMA := SUMA + AREA(HEIGHT,WIDTH)
```

10.6 LOOKING AHEAD FOR FUNCTIONS

In chapter 9, we encountered a situation where a procedure was called before it was declared. Since this would have produced a compiler error, we used a FORWARD statement to alert the compiler that the procedure would be declared at a later point in the program. Does this also work with functions that are called before they have been declared? The answer is yes, as exhibit 10–6 demonstrates.

Exhibit 10-6. Program
AHEAD

```
PROGRAM AHEAD;

VAR
  A,B:REAL;

FUNCTION TWO (X,Y:REAL):REAL; FORWARD;

PROCEDURE ONE (X,Y:REAL);
  VAR
    C:REAL;
  BEGIN
    C := 3.0*TWO(X,Y)-5.0;
    WRITELN('C = ',C:8:2)
  END; (* ONE *)

FUNCTION TWO;
  BEGIN
    TWO := SQR(X)*ABS(Y)
  END; (* TWO *)

BEGIN (* AHEAD *)
  A := 2.0;
  B : = -3.0;
  ONE (A,B)
END. (* AHEAD *)
```

Let's take a moment to consider the program in exhibit
10–6 further. It illustrates not only a FORWARD reference for a
function, but also (1) a function call within an expression; (2)
intrinsic functions within a user-defined function; (3) a function
call from a procedure; and (4) a procedure with parameters.
That's a lot of material in one short program. This program
was provided to illustrate specific points, *not* to be an example
of good programming. Let's disregard the fact that the program
was primarily for illustration purposes and assume it was
written to accomplish a purpose, the calculation and output of
the value of C. If this were the case, would a function be necessary at all? No. We could have written the assignment statement

```
C := 3.0*(SQR(X)*ABS(Y)) - 5.0;
```

And we can carry the analysis one step further and ask, was the
procedure necessary? Again, the answer is no. The program
would have produced the same results if it were written

```
PROGRAM AHEAD;

BEGIN
  WRITELN('C = ',3.0*(SQR(2.0)*ABS(-3.0))-5.0)
END.
```

(Of course, from an even more practical point, it would have been even more efficient to calculate the result with a pencil and paper.)

This raises the question, when should we write functions and when shouldn't we? The primary use of a function should be to save us (or the computer) time. If we have a program that calls for the same calculation repeatedly with differing input values, then a function is probably best. If, on the other hand, we are only performing the calculation once or twice (with different values), then we can simply use the expression.

Despite this reasoning, there may be times when you want to use functions, even when they will only be called once or twice. If the program is long and there is a chance that you may wish to modify the function in the future, it will be easier to find the proper program line if it is located in a function declaration statement at the beginning of the program.

10.7 A RANDOM FUNCTION WITHOUT PARAMETERS

Apple Pascal also has intrinsic functions that do not use any parameters. KEYPRESS, which we used in chapter 8, was one of them. There is another one named RANDOM, which is used to produce random numbers. (Because the sequence of numbers produced by the function is predictable and repeatable, the purist would argue that the numbers produced by this function are only pseudo-random numbers, rather than true random numbers. While the purist would be correct, the term *pseudo-random numbers* is more cumbersome and perhaps pretentious as well. Therefore, we will refer to the numbers produced by the function RANDOM as *random numbers* and leave it to you to some day explain patiently to a friend that the numbers are, in fact, only pseudo-random numbers.) Returning to the point, this Pascal function produces random numbers that are Integer values between 0 and 32,767.

The function RANDOM is contained in the library unit APPLESTUFF, so you must add USES APPLESTUFF; to your program when you wish to call RANDOM. Let's take a quick look at some of these random numbers. S(ave your current program if you haven't already and enter

```
PROGRAM RNTEST;

USES APLESTUFF;

VAR
  I:INTEGER;

BEGIN
  FOR I := 1 TO 10 DO
    WRITELN(RANDOM);
END.
```

When you compile and run this program, you should get results that look like this

```
9305
22934
3922
10796
32327
13781
9407
20898
32338
6184
```

Run the program again. You should get the same results, because the computer uses a formula to produce the numbers, and the numbers produced depend on the first number the formula uses. This first number is called a **seed**. When the computer uses the same seed each time it begins producing random numbers, it will generate the same sequence each time. Does that mean that every time we use the function RANDOM in a program, we will get the same sequence? No, no more than we got the same number in the above program where we called RANDOM ten times in the loop. It only means that if the same seed is used, the *sequence will begin* at the same point each time we run a new program. In some cases, this is a desirable feature; it allows us to replicate results achieved with random numbers when we wish to do so.

RANDOMIZE

There are times, however, when getting the same results each time we run the program is not desirable. In those cases, it is possible to tell the computer to generate a unique sequence each time the program is run. We do this through an intrinsic procedure called RANDOMIZE, which is also found in APPLE-STUFF. When this procedure is called, it uses a chance physical event to produce a new seed for the random number generator (the formula). Modify the RNTEST program by inserting the procedure call RANDOMIZE; just before the FOR..DO statement. When you compile and run this program, you should see a different sequence of random numbers. Each time you run this program, it should produce a different set of random numbers. You should understand, however, that we have not changed the formula that produces the random numbers, but only the seed number that determines the beginning point in the sequence.

How would this function be used? We can use it whenever we want to simulate events that occur randomly, such as flipping a coin or rolling a die. Let's do that now. We'll begin with the flip of a coin. The possible results are heads and tails. How often would you expect each result to occur? Normally, we would expect heads about half of the time and tails the other half. Given this 50–50 distribution, we could divide the total number of possible random numbers (32,768) in half, and say that anytime a number between 0 and 16,383 was generated, we would call it a "head." When a number between 16,384 and 32,767 was generated, we would call it a "tail." This would give us half "heads" and half "tails," produced in a random fashion. Or we could divide the distribution by splitting the random numbers into odds and evens, since there are an equal number of each (and since it gives us a chance to try out the ODD function we covered earlier in the chapter).

The program in exhibit 10–7 simulates 10 flips of a coin. This program uses RANDOMIZE to ensure a unique distribution of random numbers and then uses the Boolean function ODD with the function RANDOM as its parameter. Thus, any time the random number is odd, the function will be TRUE and the WRITELN('TAILS') statement will be executed. When the random number is even, the function will evaluate as FALSE and the ELSE portion of the statement, WRITELN ('HEADS'), will execute. When you compile and run this program, you should get approximately five heads and five tails. But because the results are being generated in a random fashion, you will not always get exactly five heads and five tails. If you ran the program a large number of times, you might even find cases where you got all heads or tails, but the *average* number of heads and tails should be approximately five.

That was easy enough. Now let's try the roll of a die. In this case our results can be 1, 2, 3, 4, 5, or 6. We could again divide up our distribution of random numbers, this time into sixths rather than halves. (While 32,768 does not divide evenly by 6, it would come close enough for our purposes; a random

Exhibit 10–7. Program COINFLIP

```
PROGRAM COINFLIP;

USES APPLESTUFF;

VAR
  I:INTEGER;

BEGIN
  RANDOMIZE;
  FOR I := 1 TO 10 DO
    IF ODD(RANDOM) THEN
      WRITELN('TAILS')
    ELSE
      WRITELN('HEADS');
END.
```

number between 0 and 5,460 would represent a 1, a number between 5,461 and 10,923 would represent a 2, and soon.) Alternatively, while we could not use ODD as we did in the last example, we could use the same approach by letting every sixth value represent one side of the die. This can be done through integer arithmetic: if we use RANDOM MOD 6, the result will be 0, 1, 2, 3, 4, or 5, since we are asking for the remainder of a random number divided by 6. While the results clearly divide themselves into six distinct categories, they are not exactly what we wanted—they are off by one. But we can modify or expression as follows

```
RANDOM MOD 6 + 1;
```

and obtain the desired results.

Instead of writing out the results from each roll of the die, we'll let our program tabulate the results so that we can see whether or not we get a fairly even distribution of outcomes. Since the more rolls we simulate, the more likely we are to get an even distribution, we'll let the computer roll the die 6,000 times. If the function works correctly, we should get approximately 1,000 occurrences of each outcome. To test this, we will have to set up six variables to store the sums for each outcome. Then, when one of the outcomes occurs, the sum for that particular outcome can be incremented by one. Can you remember a statement that would be very useful for tabulating the outcomes? You should remember the CASE..OF statement, which is used in the program in exhibit 10–8.

Enter, compile, and run the program. Be patient, it can take the Apple as long as 20 seconds to generate and tabulate those 6,000 numbers! Do your results suggest that the program works fairly well at simulating the roll of a die? If all the totals lie between 900 and 1,100 you probably have a fairly good random distribution.

The expression (RAMDOM MOD 6 + 1) seems to work fairly well for the tossing of a die, so we'll take the time to modify it into a more generalized function that will return a random number falling within any defined range. To generalize this, we want to generate a set of random numbers over a range specified by two boundary points, B1 and B2. In the example, we had a range of 6 with a lower boundary (B1) of 1 and an upper boundary (B2) of 6. If we had wanted a range from 1 to 9, we would have used the expression RANDOM MOD 9 + 1, since RANDOM MOD 9 would return integers between 0 and 8. But what if we wanted a range from 4 to 9? Because we want the integers 4, 5, 6, 7, 8 and 9, we would use RANDOM MOD 6 to produce the six integers from 0 to 5 and then add what value? If you said 4, you're correct. We will always add the lower boundary (B1) of the desired range to the results produced by integer division of the random value. The divisor in the

Exhibit 10–8. Program
TOSSDIE

```
    PROGRAM TOSSDIE;

    USES APPLESTUFF;

    VAR
      SUM1,SUM2,SUM3,SUM4,SUM5,SUM6,I:INTEGE
      R;

    BEGIN (* TOSSDIE *)
      (*INITIALIZE ALL SUMS*)
      SUM1 := 0; SUM2 := 0; SUM3 := 0;
      SUM4 := 0; SUM5 := 0; SUM6 := 0;
      RANDOMIZE;
      FOR I := 1 TO 6000 DO
        CASE RANDOM MOD 6 + OF
          1: SUM1 := SUM1 + 1;
          2: SUM2 := SUM2 + 1;
          3: SUM3 := SUM3 + 1;
          4: SUM4 := SUM4 + 1;
          5: SUM5 := SUM5 + 1;
          6: SUM6 := SUM6 + 1
        END; (* CASE..OF *)
      WRITELN('SUM1 = ',SUM1:6,' SUM2 =
      ',SUM2:6);
      WRITELN('SUM3 = ',SUM3:6,' SUM4 =
      ',SUM4:6);
      WRITELN('SUM5 = ',SUM5:6,' SUM6 =
      ',SUM6:6)
    END. (* TOSSDIE *)
```

expression is equal to the width of the range we want, and
that range can be expressed as $(B2 - (B1 - 1))$ or $(B2 - B1 + 1)$.
In our previous examples, $[6 - (1 - 1)] = 6$ and $[9 - (4 - 1)] =$
6. Thus, we can rewrite our expression in the generalized form

```
RANDOM MOD (B2-B1+1) + B1
```

We can now take this generalized expression and use it to
create our own modified random number function

```
FUNCTION RND (B1,B2:INTEGER):INTEGER;
  BEGIN
    RND := RANDOM MOD (B2-B1+1) + B1
  END;
```

We can do a quick check on this function by including it in the
program in exhibit 10–9, which outputs five sets of 20 random
numbers between the sets of values we supply for B1 and B2.

Exhibit 10–9. Program CHECKRND

```
PROGRAM CHECKRND;

USES APPLESTUFF;

VAR
   LOWER,UPPER,I,J:INTEGER;

FUNCTION RND (B1,B2:INTEGER):INTEGER;
   BEGIN
      RND := RANDOM MOD (B2-B1+1) + B1
   END; (* RND *)

BEGIN (* CHECKRND *)
   RANDOMIZE;
   FOR I := 1 TO 5 DO
     BEGIN
       WRITE('LOWER BOUND ->');
       READLN(LOWER);
       WRITE('UPPER BOUND ->');
       READLN(UPPER);
       FOR J := 1 TO 20 DO
         WRITELN(RND(LOWER,UPPER));
     END;
END.
```

Random Numbers Make Games More Fun

It is the random number generating ability of the computer that allows programmers to produce many of the interesting games that have somewhat unpredictable results when you play them. We can use the new RND function we created to create a simple game of our own. Write a program that generates a random number between 1 and 10 and allows the player to guess what the number is. The program should also keep track of the number of trys it takes the player to guess correctly, give prompts such as "high" or "low," and stop the game and reveal the correct answer if the player has not been successful in five guesses. This program should give you practice with some of the control statements introduced in chapter 8.

When you have completed this practice exercise, see exhibit 10–10 for an example program.

This program provides a good review of the use of conditional transfers. It contains an IF..THEN..ELSE statement nested within another IF..THEN..ELSE, which is used in a REPEAT.. UNTIL statement.

10.8 GAME PADDLE FUNCTIONS

Apple Pascal also includes special intrinsic functions that can be used if your Apple has game paddles attached. These functions, which are contained in APPLESTUFF, are named PADDLE and BUTTON. The Apple game paddles are typically labeled 0

Exhibit 10–10. Program GUESSNUMBER

```
PROGRAM GUESSNUMBER;


USES APPLESTUFF;

VAR
   A,B,I,J,K:INTEGER;

FUNCTION RND (B1,B2:INTEGER):INTEGER;
   BEGIN
      RND := RANDOM MOD (B2-B1+1) + B1
   END; (* RND *)

BEGIN  (* GUESSNUMBER *)
   RANDOMIZE;
   A := 1;  (* LOWER BOUND *)
   B := 10;  (* UPPER BOUND *)
   J := 0;  (* INITIALIZES COUNTER *)
   K := RND(A,B);  (* SETS NUMBER *)
   REPEAT  (* GUESSING PROCESS *)
      J := J + 1;  (* INDEX COUNTER *)
      WRITE('YOUR GUESS —>');
      READLN(I);  (* INPUT GUESS *)
      IF (I = K) THEN  (* RIGHT GUESS *)
         WRITELN('YOU''RE RIGHT! YOU GUESSE
         D CORRECTLY ON TRY #',J)
      ELSE  (* WRONG GUESS *)
         BEGIN  (* PROMPTING *)
            WRITELN('WRONG');
            IF (I)K) THEN
               WRITELN('TOO HIGH')
            ELSE
               WRITELN('TOO LOW')
         END;  (* WRONG GUESS *)
   UNTIL (I=K) OR (J=5);  (* RIGHT GUESS
   OR LIMIT *)
   IF NOT (I=K) THEN (* LIMIT EXCEEDED *)
      WRITELN('TOO BAD.  THE CORRECT ANSWE
      R WAS ',K)
END.
```

and 1; both functions require the paddle number as a parameter in the function call. Thus, PADDLE(0) reads a value for paddle 0 and PADDLE(1) reads a value for paddle 1.

The PADDLE function returns an Integer value between 0 and 255. This value changes as the knob on the paddle is turned. Turning the knob to the left lowers the value and turning it to the right raises the value. The value returned by the function is the value read at the instant the function is called.

The BUTTON functions return a Boolean value, i.e., TRUE or FALSE. If the button is being pressed, the value TRUE is returned, otherwise the value is FALSE.

The program in exhibit 10–11 gives you an opportunity to test these functions if you have game paddles attached to your Apple. Let's look more closely at this program. We include the statement USES APPLESTUFF; because we want to use the PADDLE and BUTTON functions. Within loop 2 (the inner loop) we let the computer read and output a value for paddle 0. This will let you turn the knob on that paddle and observe the results. You may notice that some values are skipped as you turn the knob or that the values still change slightly from reading to reading when you make no adjustment at all. These results are caused by the amount that you turn the knob and the Apple's ability (or inability) to measure these electrical impulses precisely. Pause 1 is included to slow things down a bit and make the values appearing on the screen easier to read. (Note that if you are reading values from both paddles in succession, it is necessary to put in a slight delay in order to give the computer time to keep up.)

The IF..THEN statement allows you to test the button function on paddle 1. If the button is being pressed when that point in the program is reached, the message "BUTTON 1 PRESSED" will appear between the continuing PADDLE(0) outputs. When you tire of turning the knob and pressing the PADDLE(1) button, you can press the button on paddle 0 to exit loop 2. This will produce the message "OUT OF LOOP 2". Pause 2 again slows things down to give you a chance to react before the

Exhibit 10–11. Program PADLTEST

```
PROGRAM PADLTEST;

USES APPLESTUFF;

VAR
  P:INTEGER;

BEGIN
  REPEAT  (* LOOP 1 *)
    REPEAT  (* LOOP 2 *)
      WRITELN(PADDLE(0));
      FOR P := 1 TO 300 DO; (* PAUSE 1 *)
      IF BUTTON(1) THEN
        WRITELN('BUTTON 1 PRESSED')
      UNTIL BUTTON(0);  (* END LOOP 2 *)
      WRITELN('OUT OF LOOP 2');
      FOR P := 1 TO 2000 DO; (* PAUSE 2 *)
  UNTIL BUTTON(0)  (* END LOOP 1 *)
END.  (* PADLTEST *)
```

computer proceeds. If you release the button as soon as the "OUT OF..." message appears, loop 1 will continue and move you back into loop 2. When you are ready to end the program, press the button on paddle 0 to exit loop 2 and then continue to press it until you exit loop 1. Notice that unlike KEYPRESS, which is set equal to TRUE when a key is pressed and remains TRUE until the next READ or READLN statement, BUTTON is FALSE unless the button is being pressed at the time the function is executed. BUTTON is only TRUE when the button is being pressed; when it is released, the value of BUTTON immediately becomes FALSE again.

10.9 SUMMARY

In this chapter, you have learned about a number of intrinsic functions, some arithmetic or trigonometric, some Boolean, and some related to the game paddles. Some of these functions required parameters, others did not. In all cases, however, the functions represented a value of a particular data type. A **function call**, which can be included in an expression, was used to return the value of the function. You also learned how to create your own functions through the use of **function declarations** and function calls. One of the functions we designed raises numbers to a power, an ability excluded from Pascal's normal arithmetic operators.

We examined the use of RANDOM to generate random numbers and developed a special function called RND designed to generate random numbers over a specified range. And finally, in programs using some of these functions, you reviewed the use of loops and conditional transfers.

Apple Pascal has additional intrinsic functions that relate to string handling capabilities and creating sounds with the Apple. Discussion of these functions will be deferred to those chapters dealing with strings and sound.

Exhibit 10–12 summarizes the intrinsic functions covered by the chapter and, where appropriate, the system library unit in which the functions are declared.

Exhibit 10–12. Apple Pascal Built-in Functions

General Functions	*TRANSCEND Functions*	*APPLESTUFF Functions*
ABS(X)	ATAN(X)	BUTTON(X)
CHR(X)	COS(X)	PADDLE(X)
ODD(X)	EXP(X)	RANDOM
ORD(X)	LN(X)	RANDOMIZE
PRED(X)	LOG(X)	
PWROFTEN(X)	SIN(X)	
ROUND(X)	SQRT(X)	
SQR(X)		
SUCC(X)		
TRUNC(X)		

SUMMARY of Pascal Syntax

Reserved Words	Built-in Procedures	Built-in Functions	Library Units
PROGRAM	WRITE	ABS	TURTLEGRAPHICS
USES	WRITELN	SQR	APPLESTUFF
CONST	READ	SQRT	TRANSCEND
VAR	READLN	ROUND	
FUNCTION	INITTURTLE	TRUNC	
FORWARD	PENCOLOR	EXP	
PROCEDURE	MOVE	LN	
FOR..DO	TURN	LOG	
TO	MOVETO	PWROFTEN	
DOWNTO	TURNTO	ATAN	
REPEAT	TEXTMODE	SIN	
UNTIL	GRAFMODE	COS	
WHILE..DO		ORD	*Boolean Constants*
IF		CHR	
THEN		PRED	
ELSE		SUCC	FALSE
CASE..OF			TRUE
BEGIN			
END			
DIV			
MOD			
NIL			
AND			
OR			*Integer Constants*
NOT			

Review Questions	1. What is a built-in function?

Review Questions

1. What is a built-in function?

2. Explain the use of the following functions: ABS, SQR, SQRT.

3. How do the functions ROUND and TRUNC differ?

4. List Apple Pascal's built-in ordinal functions. Explain the purpose or use of each.

5. The ordinal value of the character 8 is 56. Explain what this means.

6. What is the form of the function declaration statement?

7. What is the basic difference between user-defined functions and procedures? When is a function preferable to a procedure?

8. Why must the data type of a function be declared?

9. How do function calls differ from procedure calls?

10. **a.** In what library unit does the SORT function reside?
    b. The CHR function?
    c. The RANDOM function?

11. What does the RANDOM function do? How does it differ from most other built-in functions?

12. What does the RANDOMIZE function do?

13. What are the game paddle functions and how do they work?

Programming Exercises

1. Write a statement that will output the square root of 793.

2. Write a statement that will output the value of 6^3.

3. Write a statement that will output the tangent of an angle of 3 radians.

4. Write a function MULT that sums the Real variables A, B, and C and returns a Real value.

5. Modify the MULT function in exercise 4 so that it returns the nearest Integer value.

Diagnostic Exercises

6. What is the value of each of the following functions?
   a. SQR(5)
   b. PWROFTEN(3)
   c. SQRT(9)
   d. SQRT(ABS(−20+4))

7. What is the value of each of the following functions?
   a. ROUND(193.68)
   b. ROUND(247.39*10)/10
   c. TRUNC(651.829)
   d. TRUNC(SQRT(5))

8. What is the value of each of the following functions?
   a. ATAN(3.5)
   b. 1SIN(5.2)
   c. COS(4.6)
   d. SIN(3)/COS(3)

9. What is the value of each of the following functions?
   a. EXP(4)
   b. LN(12)
   c. LOG(8)
   d. EXP(2*LN(5))

10. Identify the error(s), if any, in the following function declarations:
   a. FUNCTION TWO;
   b. FUNCTION FOUR(A,B:REAL);
   c. FUNCTION SIX(A,B:REAL;VAR C:INTEGER);REAL;
   d. FUNCTION TEN(A;B:REAL):INTEGER;

11. If function ONE is declared in procedure A, are the variables declared in ONE known to A?

12. Given

```
FUNCTION ADD(A,B:INTEGER):INTEGER;
  BEGIN
    ADD:= A + B
  END;
BEGIN
  C:= ADD(5,6)*2
END.
```

What is the value of A? B? C?

Problems

13. Write a function ABIGGER that compares two values, A and B, and returns the value TRUE if A is larger than B.

14. Write a function PAY that uses RATE times HOURS to determine PAY, but pays time-and-one-half for any hours over 40.

15. A charge account service determines the monthly balance due by subtracting any payments from the existing balance and then adding new charges. Write a function to perform this calculation.

16. Modify the function in problem 15 to add a 1.5% service charge on the total balance if the previous existing balance is not paid off.

17. Test your function (problem 16) with the following data:

Existing Balance	Payment	New Charges
$100	$100	$ 50
150	200	50
200	100	0
300	200	100

18. A simple game called *Horse Race* moves two markers (horses) around a 50 space "race track" based on the roll of a die, i.e., if player 1 rolls a 5, he/she moves 5 spaces. An algorithm for this game might look like:

    1. Initialize game;
    2. Determine player's turn;
    3. Move piece;
    4. Check for winner;
    5. If no winner, repeat steps 2–4.

Develop an algorithm for a function RUN that determines the number of spaces moved each turn.

19. Referring back to problem 18, develop an algorithm that determines whether it is player 1's turn or player 2's. (Player 1 always goes first.)

20. Referring to problem 18 again, develop an algorithm for a function WINNER that checks to see if either horse has crossed the finish line and returns a Boolean winner.

21. Using the functions developed in 19 and 20, refine the total algorithm for the game.

22. Code and test the algorithm developed in problem 21.

11

Scalar Data Types and Sets

So far you have worked with five data types: Real, Integer, Char, String, and Boolean. Three of these data types (Integer, Char, and Boolean) are **scalar data types**. In this chapter you will learn about scalar data types, declaring your own data types, and subranges of types. You will also learn how to define sets and how to perform operations on those sets.

11.1 SCALAR DATA TYPES

In the last chapter, we learned that some functions require ordinal values, i.e., values that occur in a certain order. The letters of the alphabet (Char data type) have ordinal values, and so do Integers—you can always tell what comes before and after a letter of the alphabet or an Integer. Boolean values are also ordinal (FALSE = 0 and TRUE = 1). What about Real or String types? Obviously, these are not ordinal values, since they do not have predictable predecessors or successors (3. comes before 4., but so does 3.1, 3.9, 3.99, 3.9999, and so forth). Since ordinal data types must be used in FOR..DO loops or CASE..OF statements, we could use characters rather than Integers for example,

```
FOR CH := 'A' TO 'Z' DO
  BEGIN
    .
    .
  END;
```

will pass through the body of the loop 26 times, as the variable CH indexes from 'A' to 'Z'. In this example the counter variable CH must be of type Char.

We can divide data types into two broad classifications, **simple** and **structured**. A simple data type is one in which a variable has only one value, e.g., 4, 'A', 3.64, TRUE. Real, Integer, Char, and Boolean are all simple data types. A String, however, can be thought of as a group of characters "strung" together. A String is therefore a structured data type because it contains a number of character values arranged in a specific order (i.e., a structured order).

Simple data types can be divided further into ordinal or **scalar** data types, which include Integer, Char, and Boolean types, and nonordinal, or Real, data types. A **scalar data type** is any data type whose values can be enumerated (listed) in a particular order. Scalar data types have ordinal values similar to the ordinal values of Char data types and can therefore be used in FOR..DO loops, CASE..OF statements, and logical comparisons. Pascal also permits one more scalar data type—the **user-defined** data type.

11.2 USING THE TYPE STATEMENT
TO DEFINE SCALAR DATA TYPES

In Pascal, you can define your own scalar data types by inserting a TYPE declaration statement between the constant and variable declaration statements. For example, the following set of statements creates a scalar variable of type DIGIT:

```
TYPE
   DIGIT = INTEGER;

VAR
   X:DIGIT;
```

What type of variable is X? It is a DIGIT type variable, and we have defined DIGIT as Integer. Thus, X can be considered to be a variable of the Integer data type. Since we could have simply used X:Integer;, there is little advantage to creating this new data type.

There are times, however, when it may be desirable to create our own scalar data types. For example, remember our teacher's program for determining his students' final grades. Suppose Mr. Matthews wants to use this program to determine grades for three different science classes (biology, chemistry and physics), where he uses the same grading scheme. He could accomplish this by adding a FOR CLASS := 1 TO 3 DO loop where

   1 = biology
   2 = chemistry
   3 = physics

He could even create a different grade function PHYS-GRADE for physics and use the program segment

```
WRITE (NAME,'''S FINAL GRADE = ');
IF CLASS = THEN
   WRITELN (PHYSGRADE (NOTES,PROJECT,FINA
   L):8:2);
ELSE
   WRITELN (GRADE (NOTES,PROJECT,FINALQ:8:2)
```

But if he (or anyone else) were to review the program listing at a later date, it would not be obvious that 3 was the code for physics. That's where user-defined scalar data types can be useful. We can use the TYPE statement to declare a new data type and define the scalar values contained in that type. For example

```
TYPE
   CLASS = (BIOLOGY, CHEMISTRY, PHYSICS);
```

establishes the scalar data type CLASS, which contains the three scalar values BIOLOGY, CHEMISTRY, and PHYSICS.

Figure 11–1. TYPE
Statement Syntax
Diagram

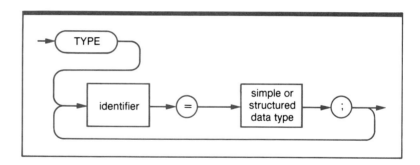

Note that while these identifiers have an implied meaning for
us, the computer sees them only as three distinct identifiers
that specify a particular order.

The TYPE statement has the general form

```
TYPE
   sname = (sv₁,sv₂,...,svₙ)
```

where *sname* is the name given to the scalar data type; *sname*
is equal to the constant block of **scalar values**. Each scalar value
(*sv*) must be specified by an identifier in the parentheses. The
names given to the scalar values can be anything you choose,
but they must meet the normal requirements for identifiers. The
syntax diagram for the TYPE statement is shown in figure 11–1.

Let's look at another example to make this idea of order
clearer.

```
TYPE
   NUMBERS = (ONE,TWO,THREE,FOUR,FIVE);
```

establishes the scalar data type NUMBERS, which contains five
scalar values identified as ONE, TWO, and so forth. ONE is the
first value, TWO the second, and so on. If we had used

```
NUMBERS = (THREE,FIVE,ONE,FOUR,TWO);
```

the computer would recognize THREE as the first value in the
data type NUMBERS and TWO as the fifth value. (This wouldn't
confuse the computer, but we might have problems keeping
things straight!)

11.3 DECLARING VARIABLES TO BE OF SCALAR DATA TYPES

Once we have declared a scalar type, we can then declare variables to be of that type. For example, we might use

```
TYPE
   CLASS = (BIOLOGY, CHEMISTRY, PHYSICS);

VAR
   SUBJECT:CLASS;
```

```
BEGIN
  FOR SUBJECT := BIOLOGY TO PHYSICS DO
    .
    .
    .
  IF SUBJECT = PHYSICS THEN
    .
    .
    .
```

There are no cryptic codes to remember in this program segment; the program will be much clearer to anyone using it or to the programmer at a later date.

Returning to the second example in the preceding section, we could write the following program

```
PROGRAM SCALAR;

TYPE
  NUMBERS = (ONE,TWO,THREE,FOUR,FIVE);

VAR
  COUNTER,LIMIT:NUMBERS;

BEGIN
  LIMIT := FOUR;
  FOR COUNTER := TWO TO LIMIT DO
    WRITELN('*')
END.
```

If we ran this program, the loop would repeat three times as the variable COUNTER indexed from TWO to LIMIT (which was assigned the ordinal value associated with FOUR). Note that this variable is of type NUMBERS and cannot, therefore, be mixed with other data types. Any of the values defined in the type statement can be assigned to any variable of type NUMBERS.

While scalar values can be assigned to a variable or used in a FOR..DO loop, CASE..OF statement, or logical comparison, they have no value other than their ordinal value within the type NUMBERS. Thus, the following statements would be incorrect.

```
COUNTER := THREE + ONE;
COUNTER := THREE + 1;
```

Both of these statements would cause error messages during an attempt to compile. They both attempt to add a value to a scalar value, which cannot be done. The second statement is also in error because it attempts to mix a user-defined scalar type with an Integer data type.

What would happen if you used the following statements in a program?

```
COUNTER := ONE;
COUNTER := PRED(COUNTER);
```

You might have answered that an error would result in the second statement, since ONE was the first scalar value declared and would not, therefore, have a predecessor. While this would be true in Standard Pascal, Apple Pascal is more tolerant. Let's see why. Enter the following program

```
PROGRAM SCALARCHK;

TYPE
  NUMBERS = (ONE,TWO,THREE,FOUR,FIVE);

VAR
  COUNTER:NUMBERS;

BEGIN
  FOR COUNTER := ONE TO FIVE DO
    WRITELN(ORD(COUNTER));
  WRITELN;
  COUNTER := ONE;
  WRITELN('PREDECESSOR OF ONE ',ORD(PRED
  (COUNTER)));
  COUNTER := FIVE;
  WRITELN('SUCCESSOR OF FIVE ',ORD(SUCC(
  COUNTER)))
END.
```

As you can see from the use of ORD, PRED, and SUCC, scalar data types can be used as parameters and passed to functions or procedures. In fact, you have already used a scalar data type as a parameter—remember the statements PENCOLOR (WHITE) and PENCOLOR (NONE) in chapter 6? TURTLEGRAPHICS has intrinsically defined scalar values with the following values of type SCREENCOLOR:

NONE	BLACK1	BLACK2
WHITE	GREEN	ORANGE
BLACK	VIOLET	BLUE
REVERSE	WHITE1	WHITE2
RADAR		

Each of these values is an intrinsic constant rather than a variable. The colors are listed in order of their ordinal values (by column).

Now run the program SCALARCHK. The results show you the ordinal values the computer assigns to each type of NUMBERS. Note that the computer begins with the ordinal value 0 (zero) and increments by one (a logical indexing system for ordinal values). Thus, the values ONE through FIVE are assigned ordinal values of 0 through 4. To the computer, the ordinal value that precedes 0 is −1, even though there is no value preceding ONE, and the value that succeeds 4 is 5. While Apple Pascal tolerates this, you should be cautious with this practice.

There are no values of type NUMBERS that correspond to the ordinal values of − 1 or 5, and using these ordinal values could produce logical errors in a program.

Remember that although these scalar values can be assigned or used in a FOR..DO loop, they have no values other than their ordinal values within the type NUMBERS. They can be neither input with a READ or READLN statement or output with WRITE or WRITELN. What use are they if they cannot be input or output or mixed with other data types? Basically, they are used for control purposes in FOR..DO, CASE..OF, and logical comparison statements. Can't we do these same things with Integer variables? Yes, we can. The primary advantage of using our own scalar values is that we can declare types with identifiers that have a clear meaning (such as the CLASS values in Mr. Matthews' program). If we make ONE the first scalar value in a user-defined type, there is no question as to how many times a loop indexing from ONE to THREE will be repeated. (In contrast, the Integer variable ONE can have any value from − 32,768 to 32,767, and we would have to search through the program for the most recent assignment statement to find its value.)

Without referring to the TYPE statements at the beginning of a program, however, it is impossible to distinguish scalar data types from any other type in a program. For example, in the program segment below, are FRED and MARY Integer or scalar variables or constants?

```
BEGIN
  FOR I:= FRED TO MARY DO
    BEGIN
      :
      :
    END
END.
```

There is no way to tell without looking at the declaration portion of the program.

We have stated that scalar values defined in the TYPE statement can be assigned to variable of the appropriate type. What about constants? Can we se scalar variables as constants? The question almost answers itself—can a variable be a constant? The answer is obviously no.

We also know that we cannot mix scalar values with data of other types (Integer, Real, and so forth), but can we mix scalar data types as is done in the following program?

```
TYPE
  NUMBER = (ONE,TWO,THREE,FOUR,FIVE);
  ORDER = (FIRST,SECOND,THIRD);

VAR
  COUNTER:NUMBER;
  INDEX:ORDER;
```

```
BEGIN
  COUNTER := ONE;
  INDEX := THIRD;
  FOR COUNTER := ONE TO THIRD DO
    WRITE('*');
  WRITELN
END.
```

The answer is no. We will get a type conflict error if we attempt to compile this program (even with a PROGRAM statement). Nor could we use INDEX := TWO. In order to assign the value of one scalar variable to another scalar variable, they must be **compatible**, i.e., of the same data type. If we want to use two different scalar values as limits for a loop, we would have to take the following approach:

```
PROGRAM MIXED;

TYPE
  NUMBER = (ONE,TWO,THREE,FOUR,FIVE);
  ORDER = (FIRST,SECOND,THIRD);

VAR
  COUNTER:NUMBER;
  INDEX:ORDER;
  I:INTEGER;

BEGIN
  COUNTER := FIVE;
  INDEX := SECOND;
  FOR I := ORD(INDEX) TO ORD(COUNTER) DO
    WRITE ('*');
  WRITELN;
END.
```

When you compile and run this program, four asterisks will be printed out. In this program we use an Integer value (I) as the FOR..DO counter, and use the ordinal values of two different scalar variables (INDEX and COUNTER) as the lower and upper limits for the loop. Because the ORD function returns an Integer, there is no type conflict. The ordinal value of INDEX is 1 and that of COUNTER is 4, so the loop is repeated four times.

11.4 CREATING SUBRANGES OF DATA TYPES

We can also use the TYPE statement to create **subranges** of ordinal data types. We occasionally have a problem where our data should fall only within a given range. We can create and use a subrange to ensure that it does. For example, suppose we have a scalar data type declared as

```
TYPE
  NUMBERS = (SEVEN,EIGHT,NINE,TEN,ELEVEN
    ,TWELVE);
```

and we want to use a scalar variable of this type that can take only the values of the single-digit numbers, i.e., SEVEN, EIGHT, or NINE (recognizing that the distinction between single- and double-digit numbers exists only in our minds, not to the computer). Could we set up another scalar type

```
DIGIT = SEVEN,EIGHT,NINE);
```

and then define our single-digit variable to be of type DIGIT? The answer is no, because we have already used these scalar values in NUMBERS; we would get an "identifier declared twice" error when we tried to compile.

We could, however, create a subrange of NUMBERS named DIGIT:

```
TYPE
  NUMBERS = SEVEN,EIGHT,NINE,TEN,ELEVEN
  ,TWELVE);
  DIGIT = SEVEN..NINE;
```

The second line creates a subrange of type NUMBERS that contains only the scalar values between SEVEN and NINE inclusive. The subrange statement has the form

srname = firstvalue..lastvalue;

where *srname* is the identifier used to name the subrange, and *firstvalue* and *lastvalue* are the names of the first and last values in the range. These value names are separated by two periods. The names used for *firstvalue* and *lastvalue* must have been defined in a type statement (if they are user-defined values) and the ordinal value of *firstvalue* must precede (be less than) the ordinal value of *lastvalue*. The syntax diagram for declaring subranges is shown in figure 11–2.

Consider the program shown in exhibit 11–1. The scalar data type NUMBERS is declared with a subrange DIGIT. The variable ANY is declared to be of type NUMBERS and the variable SINGLE is declared of type DIGIT. ANY is assigned the value EIGHT and the IF..THEN..ELSE statement is used to test whether or not the value of ANY is between SEVEN and NINE and output that result. The variable SINGLE is then assigned the value of ANY (EIGHT). Although ANY is of type NUMBERS and SINGLE is of type DIGIT, we can assign the value of ANY

Figure 11–2. Subrange Syntax Diagram

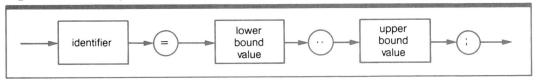

Exhibit 11–1. Program
SUBRANGE

```
PROGRAM SUBRANGE;

TYPE
  NUMBERS = (SEVEN,EIGHT,NINE,TEN,ELEVEN
  ,TWELVE);
  DIGIT = SEVEN..NINE;

VAR
  ANY:NUMBERS;
  SINGLE:DIGIT;

BEGIN
  ANY := EIGHT;
  IF (ANY)=SEVEN) AND (ANY<=NINE) THEN
    WRITELN('SINGLE DIGIT NUMBER')
  ELSE
    WRITELN('DOUBLE DIGIT NUMBER');
  WRITELN;
  SINGLE := ANY;
  IF (SINGLE)=SEVEN) AND (SINGLE<=NINE)
  THEN
    WRITELN('SINGLE DIGIT NUMBER')
  ELSE
    WRITELN('DOUBLE DIGIT NUMBER')
END.
```

to SINGLE because DIGIT is a subrange of NUMBERS. The test is then repeated with SINGLE. Enter, compile, and run the program.

Testing the program this way provides visual output that assures us that the program runs without error. As you can see from the output, both tests give the message "SINGLE DIGIT NUMBER". Now let's see how we can use subrange is to ensure that undectable errors do not result from accidentally using a value outside of an acceptable range. Return to the program, change the first assignment statement to ANY : = ELEVEN; and run the program again. This time the output will look like this

```
RUNNING...
DOUBLE DIGIT NUMBER


VALUE RANGE ERROR
S# 1, P# 1, I# 97
TYPE (SPACE) TO CONTINUE
```

Pressing the space bar will cause the system to reinitialize. As you can see, the first test result tells us that ELEVEN is indeed a double-digit number. The program never reaches the second test, however. When it attempts to assign the value of ANY to SINGLE, the program encounters a terminal error. This happens because ELEVEN is not in the subrange DIGIT. While it may seem to be an extreme measure to include a subrange that can cause the program to crash (terminate), it is better to do this than to have a program that produces erroneous results without comment. (Our test would have caught this double-digit value if the program had not terminated, but most programs include loops or comparisons that are more practical than test segments.)

Subranges are not limited solely to user-defined scalar data types. The following examples show how subranges of other ordinal data types (Integer and Char) could be used.

```
TYPE
   SMALL = 1..99;
   HALF = 'A'..'M';

VAR
   TINY:SMALL;
   FRONT:HALF;
```

The variable TINY would be an Integer data type between 1 and 99; the variable FRONT would be a Char data type between the letters 'A' and 'M'.

It is also possible to declare overlapping ranges of the same data type, for example

```
TYPE
   SMALL = 1..99;
   MEDIUM = 50..149;
   LARGE = 100..199;

VAR
   LITTLE:SMALL;
   MIDDLE:MEDIUM;
   BIG:LARGE;
```

All of these variables are Integer (and therefore compatible), and each range overlaps the preceding range. Thus, within the program, LITTLE could be assigned a value in the subrange MEDIUM and MIDDLE could be assigned the value of BIG, *provided* the values are in the overlapping section of the ranges. LITTLE could *not* be assigned the value of BIG, however, since these ranges do not overlap. Overlapping ranges can also be declared for user-declared types, for example

```
TYPE
   NUMBERS = (ONE, TWO, THREE, FOUR, FIVE
   , SIX, SEVEN);
   LOWER = ONE..FIVE;
   UPPER = THREE..SEVEN;
```

To repeat, the primary purpose of the use of subranges is to prevent the program from using an erroneous value. For example, suppose we have a complex program that includes a variable representing the temperature of water, where the temperature could vary anywhere from freezing to boiling, and suppose we made a programming mistake. If we used an Integer data type for the temperature variable, it could take the value −9, 12, 400, or any other value within the usual range for Integer. But if we declared a subrange

```
TYPE
   DEGREES = 32..212;
```

and

```
VAR
   TEMP:DEGREES;
```

(Since we know water freezes at 32° and boils at 212° F.) the program would terminate with an error message if a value outside of the DEGREES range was ever assigned to TEMP. This provides an extra safeguard against programming errors. Notice that the statement

```
TEMP := TEMP + 100;
```

may or may not cause an error. If the current value of TEMP is less than 113, no error will occur. But if the current value of TEMP is greater than 112, adding 100 will result in an error.

You should also note that since we are declaring ranges of Integer and Char values, values of these types can be input with READ or READLN and output with WRITE or WRITELN. Furthermore, values that are outside the range can be read in and written out without causing an error, that is,

```
READLN (TEMP);
WRITELN (TEMP);
```

would accept and write out a value equal to −26 or 400 with no problem. (Apparently the Apple assumes you know what you're doing when you input values!) It is only when a value outside the range is assigned to the variable within the program that the terminating error occurs. Even the TEMP := TEMP + 100 statement would execute properly if an initial (unacceptable) value of −50 was read in, since TEMP would then become +50, a value within the appropriate range.

11.5 DECLARING SET STRUCTURES AND ASSIGNING VALUES TO SETS

Pascal also allows users to define specific **set structures**, which are similar to subranges, except that they do not have to be inclusive. Sets also differ from subranges in that we can use operators on sets. Before we can use sets, we must declare them

Figure 11–3. Set
Syntax Diagram

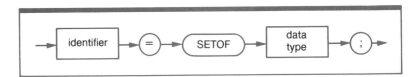

in a TYPE statement and then assign values to the set. The set declaration statement takes the form

set name = SET OF *data type;*

where *set name* is the identifier used to name the set and the *data type* must be ordinal (scalar). Figure 11–3 shows the set syntax diagram.

Let's look at some examples of data sets.

```
TYPE
   NUMBERS = (ONE,TWO,THREE,FOUR,FIVE,SIX);   [1]
   EVEN = SET OF NUMBERS;                      [2]
   VOWELS = SET OF CHAR;                       [3]
   LOWNUM = 1..25;                             [4]
   SMALL = SET OF LOWNUM;                      [5]
   TINY = SET OF 1..5;                         [6]
```

Line [1] declares scalar type NUMBERS and line [2] defines EVEN as a set of NUMBERS. Line [3] defines VOWELS as a set of characters. Line [4] declares a subrange of integers named LOWNUM and line [5] defines SMALL as a set of LOWNUM (integers in the range of 1 to 25). Line [6] defines TINY as a set of integers in the range 1 to 5; notice that this line defines a set directly without first naming a subrange.

Once we have defined a set, we can declare a **set variable** (a variable that belongs to that particular set) and then assign values to that set variable with a **set assignment** statement. This statement takes the form

set var name := [*set expression*];

where *set var name* is the identifier used to name the set variable and the *set expression* in the square brackets (CTRL-K and Shift-M for those of you without Apple IIe's) represents the values assigned to the set. The syntax diagram for the set assignment statement is shown in figure 11–4.

For example, if DIGIT has been declared a variable of set EVEN (which is a set of type NUMBERS), we would use the program statement

```
DIGIT := [TWO,FOUR,SIX];
```

to assign the scalar values TWO, FOUR, and SIX to the set DIGIT. The values in a set are frequently referred to as the set's

Figure 11–4. Set Assignment Statement Syntax Diagram

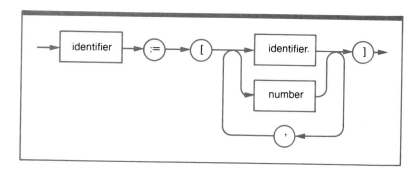

elements. Thus, the above set has three elements. Because a set can contain more than one value, it is a structured data type.

Let's look at another example. What does the program segment below do?

```
TYPE
   LETTERS = SET OF CHAR;

VAR
   VOWELS:LETTERS;

BEGIN
   VOWELS := ['A', 'E', 'I', 'O', 'U'];
```

It declares a set named LETTERS to be a set of characters, then declares a variable VOWELS of type LETTERS (and therefore a set of characters), and finally assigns the vowel characters to the set. This set has five elements.

We can also use two periods in a set assignment statement to indicate an inclusive series of elements. For example

```
VALUES := [1..5,11..15,21..25];
```

assigns fifteen elements to the set VALUES—the integers 1 through 5, 11 through 15, and 21 through 25.

11.6 PERFORMING OPERATIONS ON SETS

One advantage of sets is that you can perform operations on them. You can define an empty or "null" set, find the union, intersection, or difference of two sets, or use them with relational operators to return Boolean values.

An **empty** or **null** set is one that contains no values. You can define a null set using a normal assignment statement such as

```
EMPTY := [];
```

Just as we initialized variables that were to be used to sum values, we can use an empty set assignment to initialize a set that we are going to add values to later in the program.

The **union** of two sets contains any elements that are found in either or both sets. The set operator for a union is the plus sign (+). In the following examples, assume X is a set variable. The first line of each example will show an assignment statement using a set operator, and the following line, enclosed in brackets, {}, will show the result of the set operation.

```
X := ['A', 'B', 'C'] + ['B','C', 'D'];
{X = ['A', 'B', 'C', 'D']}

X := [1, 3, 5] +[2, 4, 6];
{X = [1, 2, 3, 4, 5, 6]}
```

The **intersection** of two sets contains any elements that are common to both sets. The set operator for an intersection is the asterisk (*).

```
X := ['A', 'B', 'C'] * ['B', 'C', 'D',];
{X: = ['B', 'C']}

X := [1..10] * [2, 4, 8..14]
{X = [2, 4, 8..10]}
```

The **difference** between two sets contains any elements that are found in the first set but not in the second set. The set operator for difference is the minus sign (−).

```
X :=['A', 'B', 'C'] − ['B', 'C', 'D'];
{X = ['A']}

X := [1..10] − [2, 4, 8..14];
{X = [1, 3, 5..7]}
```

We can use these set operators to perform operations on sets and to create new sets. For example

```
TYPE
  WHOLE = SET OF 1..100;

VAR
  ALL, SINGLE, DOUBLE:WHOLE;

BEGIN
  ALL := [1..100];
  SINGLE := [1..9];
  DOUBLE := ALL − SINGLE;
    :
    :
```

defines three sets of type WHOLE, which is itself a set of integers from 1 to 100. The first set, ALL, is assigned all of the elements from 1 to 100, and the second set, SINGLE, is assigned the single-digit integers 1 to 9. The set DOUBLE is then assigned the difference between ALL and SINGLE. Does this give us all the two-digit values in the set? The answer might be "sort of." It gives us all the double-digit elements and the three-digit element (100) as well. To set only the two-digit elements, we'll modify the assignment statement to

```
DOUBLE := ALL - SINGLE - [100];
```

This modification removes all of the elements of SINGLE from the set ALL and then removes the value 100 as well. The single value 100 can be thought of as a one-element set or a **unit set**. As the example shows, we can add a single element to or delete one from any existing set by using a set operation with the unit set.

Again, this example was for illustrative purposes only. We could have accomplished the same result with the assignment

```
DOUBLE := [10..99];
```

and saved ourselves some typing, too. We'll look at a better example shortly.

In addition to the set operators we have discussed, the Boolean relational operators can be applied to sets. A summary of these operators is shown in exhibit 11–2. Notice the new addition to our relational operators, the **IN** operator. The IN operator implies membership in a specified set. For example,

```
IF X IN Y THEN DO
```

tells the computer to see whether the variable (or set variable) X is contained in the set Y. If it is, the Boolean value TRUE is returned; if not, the value is FALSE. Remember, all of the results of these operators (comparisons) will be Boolean (TRUE or FALSE).

What does it mean for one set to be greater than or less than another set? It is a question of whether one set is a **subset** or **superset** of another set. Consider two sets, A and B. A is said to be a subset of B if all the elements in A are also contained in B. A is said to be a superset of B if all the elements of B are also contained in A. As you can see, these descriptions are

Exhibit 11–2.
Relational Operators

Sign	Operation
=	equals
< >	not equals
>	greater than
> =	greater than or equals
<	less than
< =	less than or equals
IN	membership

complementary, i.e., if A is a superset of B, then B must be a subset of A. The summary in exhibit 11–3 explains the relational operators in terms of sets.

The examples in exhbit 11–4 may help to clarify the results of such operations; it shows the Boolean values that will be returned from various operations. While the empty set would always be less than (and less than or equal to) a set with one or more elements, Apple Pascal does not allow the use of the empty set in these operations.

Exhibit 11–3. Pascal
Set Operators

Example	Explanation
A = B	The two sets contain exactly the same elements.
A < > B	The two sets do not contain the same elements.
A > B	A contains all the elements in B and at least one more.
A > = B	A contains all the elements in B (and may contain more).
A < = B	B contains all the elements in A (and may contain more).
A IN B	All of the elements in set A are in set B.

Exhibit 11–4. Boolean
Values Using
Set Operators

[1,2,3] = [1,2,3]	TRUE
[1,2,3] = [3,1,2]	TRUE (order is not important)
[1,2,3] = [2,3,4]	FALSE
[1,2,3] < > [2,3,4]	TRUE
[1,2,3] < > [2,3,1]	FALSE
[1,2,3] > [1,2]	TRUE
[1,2,3] > [1,2,3]	FALSE
[1,2,3] > [1,4]	FALSE
[1,2,3] > = [1,2]	TRUE
[1,2,3] > = [1,2,3]	TRUE
[1,2,3] > = [1,4]	FALSE
[1,2] < [1,2,3]	TRUE
[1,2,3] < [1,2,3]	FALSE
[1,4] < [1,2,3]	FASLE
[1,2] < = [1,2,3]	TRUE
[1,2,3] < = [1,2,3]	TRUE
[1,4] < = [1,2,3]	FALSE
[1,2] IN [1,2,3]	TRUE
[1,2,3] IN [1,2,3]	TRUE
[1,4] IN [1,2,3]	FALSE

11.7 USING SET STRUCTURES IN PROGRAMS

We could use the IN operator to test our earlier example with set operators. Enter, compile, and run the following program. If you want to stop the screen from scrolling temporarily so that you can read the output, hold down the CTRL key and press the S key. This will stop the output. When you want to start again, just CTRL-S to resume.

```
PROGRAM DIGITSETS;

TYPE
  WHOLE = SET OF 1..100;

VAR
  ALL,SINGLE,DOUBLE:WHOLE;
  I:INTEGER;

BEGIN
  ALL := [1..100];
  SINGLE := [1..9];
  DOUBLE := ALL - SINGLE - [100];
  FOR I := 1 TO 150 DO
    IF I IN DOUBLE THEN
      WRITELN (I,' IS DOUBLE DIGIT')
    ELSE
      IF I IN SINGLE THEN
        WRITELN(I,' IS SINGLE DIGIT')
      ELSE
        WRITELN(I,' IS TRIPLEDIGIT')
END.
```

FOCUS
On Problem
Solving

Once you have made sure this program works, let's try another. This time we'll start out with a set containing one value and add values to it. A **prime number** is an integer that is greater than one and is divisible only by itself and 1 (1 is generally not considered a prime). Thus, 2 and 3 are prime numbers, but 4 is not because it is exactly divisible by 2. Five and 7 are prime numbers, but 6, 8, 9, and 10 are not. We would like to write a program that will look at all numbers from 2 to 100 and tell us which numbers are prime. We could do this by writing a program that starts at two and attempts to divide each succeeding value by all of the previously identified prime numbers. This program is a little tricky, since we will have to use a loop with a changing upper limit for our division attempts.

We will develop the algorithm first. Our problem statement would be "find and output all the prime numbers between 2 and 100 (inclusive)." The next step might look like this

1. identify 2 as a prime number;
2. check all numbers from 3 to 100 to see if they are primes;
3. output all prime numbers.

Refining the above algorithm, we might move to:

1. identify 2 as a prime number;
2. for all values from 3 to 100:
    a. check to see if it is a prime number;
    b. if it is, add it to the set of primes;
3. output all prime numbers.

Further refinement would concentrate on step (2):

1. identify 2 as a prime number;
2. for all values from 3 to 100, is the value exactly divisible by a prime number?
    a. for every number from 2 to 100:
        (1) if this number is a prime then divide the value by the prime; if exactly divisible then value is not a prime; continue divisions until all primes have been tried;
        (2) if not divisible by any primes then add the number to the list of primes;
3. output all prime numbers:
    a. when all values have been checked
        (1) for every number from 2 to 100:
        (2) if the number is a prime number then output it.

The algorithm is not in Pascal code, but it should be fairly easy to convert to code; the result is shown in exhibit 11–5. Since we cannot assume a number is a prime simply because it is not evenly divisible by one prime number, we use a Boolean value as a check. If the number is evenly divisible by any prime number, then the check is set equal to FALSE (not a prime); otherwise it remains TURE and tells the computer to add the number to its list of primes and then change the limit value (last prime number) to reflect this fact. ■

11.8 SUMMARY

In this chapter you learned more about scalar data types. You also learned that you can declare your own scalar data types through the use of the TYPE statement. Although these types cannot be used for input or output, they can be used for control purposes in loops or relational operations, and the identifiers assigned to them often make it easier for the programmer to follow the process in a logical fashion. You also learned how to define subranges of scalar values and use them to avoid possible errors that might otherwise be difficult to detect. Finally, you learned how to define sets (structured data types), how to assign values to sets, and how to perform set operations.

Exhibit 11–5. Program
PRIME

```
PROGRAM PRIME;

TYPE
  ALL = SET OF 2..100;

VAR
  I,J,LAST:INTEGER;
  PRIMES:ALL;
  CHECK:BOOLEAN;

BEGIN (* PRIME *)
  PRIMES := [2];
  LAST := 2;
  FOR I := 3 TO 100 DO
    BEGIN (* FOR..DO *)
      J := 1;
      CHECK := TRUE;
      REPEAT
        J := J + 1;
        IF J IN PRIMES THEN
          IF I MOD J = 0 THEN
            CHECK := FALSE;
      UNTIL J = LAST;
      IF CHECK = TRUE THEN
        BEGIN (* IF..THEN *)
          PRIMES := PRIMES + [I];
          LAST := I
        END; (* IF..THEN *)
    END; (* FOR..DO *)
  WRITELN ('HESE NUMBERS ARE PRIME NUMB
ERS:');
  FOR I := 1 TO 100 DO
    IF I IN PRIMES THEN
      WRITELN (I);
END. (* PRIME *)
```

**Review
Questions**

1. What is a scalar data type?

2. How can we create a user-defined scalar data type?

3. How can we create a subrange of a scalar data type? Give an example.

4. If a value is outside of the declared subrange for a particular type of variable, what will happen if we try to assign that value to the variable?

5. How can we define variables as belonging to a set? How can we assign specific values to a set?

6. What is the difference between a subrange and a set?

SUMMARY of Pascal Syntax

Reserved Words	Built-in Procedures	Built-in Functions	Library Units
PROGRAM	WRITE	ABS	TURTLEGRAPHICS
USES	WRITELN	SQR	APPLESTUFF
CONST	READ	SQRT	TRANSCEND
TYPE	READLN	ROUND	
SET OF	INITTURTLE	TRUNC	
VAR	PENCOLOR	EXP	
FUNCTION	MOVE	LN	
FORWARD	TURN	LOG	
PROCEDURE	MOVETO	PWROFTEN	
FOR..DO	TURNTO	ATAN	
TO	TEXTMODE	SIN	
DOWNTO	GRAFMODE	COS	
REPEAT		ORD	*Boolean Constants*
UNTIL		CHR	
WHILE..DO		PRED	FALSE
IF		SUCC	TRUE
THEN			
ELSE			
CASE..OF			
BEGIN			
END			
DIV			
MOD			
NIL			
AND			
OR			
NOT			*Integer Constants*
IN			

7. What is the empty set?

8. What are the Apple Pascal set operators? Give an example of the use of each.

9. Can the Boolean operators be used with sets? Explain.

10. If set A is greater than set B (A > B), what does this mean?

11. What is the purpose of the IN operator?

12. What is the difference between a superset and a subset?

Programming Exercises

1. Write a program that outputs the letters from A to M.

2. Write a statement that declares a data type WEEK containing the seven days of the week. Begin with Sunday.

3. Write a statement that declares the subrange WEEKDAY to be the days MONDAY through FRIDAY.

4. Write a variable declaration statement declaring a variable DAY to be of type WEEK.

5. Write a statement declaring a subrange of integers from 5 to 35 and a variable declaration creating a variable SOME that contains values within that subrange.

6. What will happen if we make the following assignment

```
SOME := 8 * 20;
```

where SOME is the variable declared in exercise 5?

7. Write a statement declaring a set of integers between 5 and 35. Declare the variable LOW to be of this type.

8. Write a statement placing the values 10 through 20, 25, and 30 in the set declared in exercise 7.

9. If A and B are both sets of the same data type, write a statement that will assign all the elements that occur in both of these sets to a new set, C.

Diagnostic Exercises

Given
```
TYPE
   COLOR = (RED,BLUE,ORANGE,YELLOW);

VAR
   BRIGHT:COLOR;
```

10. What would be the value of ORD(RED)?

11. How many times would the loop FOR BRIGHT: = RED TO ORANGE be repeated?

12. Is the statement COLOR := YELLOW an acceptable statement? Why or why not?

13. Is the statement FLAG = RED..BLUE a valid TYPE statement? Why or why not?

14. If X := [1..10] and Y := [2,4,8,16], what will be the contents of set Z if:
a. Z := X − Y
b. Z := X * Y
c. Z := X + Y

15. If X := [1..5] and Y := [3,4,2], evaluate the expressions:
a. Y = X
b. X <> Y
c. Y <= X
d. Y IN X

16. If X := [1..20], Y := [3,5,7,9], and Z := [16], what will set A contain if:
a. A := X − Y − Z
b. A := Y + Z
c. A := X * Y
d. A := Y * Z

Problems

17. Write a program that declares a data type MONTHS containing the twelve months of the year. Then use a FOR..DO loop to index through the months and an IF..THEN statement to output the message IT'S THE 4TH! when the month is July.

18. Write a program that asks the user to input a letter of the alphabet from the keyboard and identify whether it is a consonant or a vowel. The program should then check to ensure that (1) the character entered is a letter, and (2) the letter was correctly identified.

19. Modify the program from exercise 18 so that the program randomly selects a letter and lets the user identify it as a consonant or vowel, still checking for correct responses.

12

Arrays

In previous chapters we have worked primarily with simple variables. In this chapter we will look at a structured data type, the **array**. An array allows us to store a number of values in the computer's memory under the same variable name. An array is different from a set, a structured data type that was introduced in chapter 11; a variable of type set can contain any one of a range of values, but the variable could still only have one value at a time. Strings, another structured data type will also be discussed in this chapter; a string is simply a number of characters (Char data type) strung together.

12.1 DECLARING ONE-DIMENSIONAL ARRAY

Pascal permits us to declare a structured data type called an **array**, which allows us to store and use a list of different values under one variable name. For example, if we have a string variable equal to the word FIRST, we could think of the string as a list of five variables of type Char. The first variable would be the letter F, the second the letter I, and so on. To place these five characters in an array, we must first tell the computer how long the list will (or might) be so that it can allocate enough memory to hold each value in the array. We can do this either through a TYPE statement

```
TYPE
    WORD = ARRAY [1..5] OF CHAR;

VAR
    LIST:WORD;
```

or directly through the variable declaration

```
VAR
    LIST:ARRAY [1..5] OF CHAR;
```

The syntax diagram for the array declaration is shown in figure 12–1; the array declaration has the form

array name = ARRAY [*limit1..limit2*] OF *data type;*

where an identifier is set equal to ARRAY [*limit1..limit2*]. ARRAY is a reserved word that tells the computer that this variable is structured and contains more than one value. *Limit1* and *limit2* define the size of the array and must have ordinal values, and *limit1* must be less than *limit2*. OF *data type* declares the type of data that will be contained in the array. An array can contain elements of any of the data types we have worked with thus far, but all elements must be of the same

Figure 12–1. Array Declaration Syntax Diagram

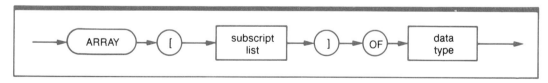

type, i.e., if we declare an array OF Real, each element must be a Real value.

Since the limits must have ordinal values, we can also use characters to define the limits of an array, for example

```
LIST2 = ARRAY['A'..'T'] OF REAL;
```

defines an array of 20 elements, each element a Real value.

An array can also be defined with the statement

array type = ARRAY [*sname*] OF *data type;*

where *sname* is the identifier used to name a predefined scalar data type or subrange. In this case, the number of elements in the array is defined by the number of scalar values or the number of values in the subrange. The following segment declares an array named MIXED that contains 6 elements.

```
TYPE
   NUTS = (WALNUTS, PECANS, FILBERTS, PEA
   NUTS, ALMONDS, CASHEWS);
   MIXED = ARRAY[NUTS] OF INTEGER;
```

12.2 ASSIGNING VALUES TO AN ARRAY

When we declare an ARRAY [1..5] OF CHAR, we are telling the computer that we have a structured variable (LIST) that will contain up to five elements and that each element is a character. The variable LIST, therefore, is a structured data type that can contain up to five characters (elements) simultaneously. Each element is differentiated from the others by its location within LIST. You can think of the first character as element 1, the second as element 2, and so forth. Typically, we refer to each specific element in the array by using **subscripts** that identify the position of the element in the array. If we were writing down the elements of LIST, we might write

$list_1$, $list_2$, $list_3$, $list_4$, $list_5$

Since we cannot enter subscripts from the keyboard, Pascal represents subscripts with numbers enclosed in square brackets (CTRL-K for [and SHIFT-M for]) following the array name, for example

```
LIST[1], LIST[2], LIST[3], LIST[4], LIST[5]
```

We can assign the characters in the string FIRST to the elements of the array LIST through normal assignment statements:

```
LIST[1] := 'F';
      .
      .
      .
LIST[5] := 'T';
```

The program in exhibit 12–1 compares using a string variable to using an array of characters. Enter, compile and run the program. Now let's take a careful look at it. On line 1 we declare a data type (WORD) that is an array of 5 characters. Line 2 defines the variable LIST of type word, i.e. an array. The segment beginning with line 3 reads a five-character string and then writes it to the screen. The segment beginning with line 4 uses a loop to read and output five separate characters. On line 5 (within the loop) each character is read into a subscripted variable. Notice that the subscript is an Integer variable. The

Exhibit 12–1. Program STRINGS

```
PROGRAM STRINGS;

TYPE
   WORD = ARRAY[1..5] OF CHAR;                  {1}

VAR
   LIST:WORD;                                    {2}
   STR:STRING;
   I:INTEGER;

BEGIN  (* STRINGS *)
   WRITE('ENTER A 5 CHARACTER STRING & <R       {3}
ET>');
   READLN(STR);
   WRITELN('STRING = ',STR);
   WRITELN;
   WRITELN('ENTER 5 CHARACTERS (NO RETURN       {4}
) ');
   WRITELN;
   FOR I:= 1 TO 5 DO
     BEGIN  (* FOR..DO *)
       READ(LIST[I]);                           {5}
       WRITELN;
       WRITELN('CHARACTER ',I,' = ',LIST[
       I]);
     END;  (* FOR..DO *)
   WRITELN;
   FOR I:= 1 TO 5 DO                             {6}
     WRITE(LIST[I]);
   WRITELN;
   WRITELN;
   FOR I := 5 DOWNTO 1 DO                        {7}
     WRITE(LIST[I]);
   WRITELN('     (BACKWARDS)');
   WRITELN;
   FOR I := 1 TO 5 DO                            {8}
     WRITELN(I,'  ',LIST[I],'        ',6-I       {9}
     ,'   ',LIST[6-I]);
END.  (* STRINGS *)
```

loop beginning at line 6 writes out the five characters using a
WRITE statement; this should produce output that is identical
to the string output (if the same five characters are entered).
The loop that begins with line 7 uses DOWNTO to write the
characters beginning with the fifth character and proceeding
backwards (down) to the first. Line 8 then creates a loop that
will use WRITELN to write each character preceded by its corresponding array subscript on a separate line. Line 9 shows that
we can reverse the subscript order by using the expression (6-I),
and that we can use an expression (6-I) as a subscript (as long
as it returns an Integer value). Notice that the array of characters offers much more flexibility than the string.

12.3 USING ARRAYS

We frequently write programs that allow us to use the same
variable name over and over again, because we output our results immediately and then reuse the same variable name, for
example

```
FOR I := 1 TO 50 DO
  BEGIN
    READLN (DATA);
    DATA := DATA * 5 / 9;
    WRITELN (DATA)
  END;
```

In this example, the variable DATA is used to enter 50 values
(one at a time), calculate a new value that is five-ninths of the
input value, and then output the result.

There are times, however, when we must retain all of the
input values in memory before we can output any results. This
requires that each value be assigned to a variable with a unique
name. Rather than declare 50 different names, we can use an
array of 50 elements. Suppose we want to input 10 values, sum
them, and output the percentage of the total represented by
each value. In this case, we cannot determine the output values
until we have input all ten values and summed them, so we
will store the input values in an array:

```
PROGRAM PERCENT;

VAR
  DATA: ARRAY [1..10] OF REAL;
  I: INTEGER;
  SUM: REAL;

BEGIN  (* PERCENT *)
  SUM := 0.0;
  WRITELN ('INPUT TEN VALUES');
```

```
FOR I := 1 TO 10 DO
  BEGIN  (* FOR..DO *)
    WRITE (I:4,' --> ');
    READLN (DATA[I]);
    SUM := SUM + DATA[I]
  END;  (* FOR..DO *)
WRITELN;
WRITELN (' VALUE    PER CENT');
FOR I := 1 TO 10 DO
  WRITELN (DATA[I]:6,(DATA[I]/SUM)*100
  :10:2,'%');
END.  (* PERCENT *)
```

The first FOR..DO loop reads the values into the elements of the array DATA and sums the values. The second FOR..DO loop outputs a list of the original data values and the percent values.

Another useful application of arrays is in counting. For example, suppose we wished to use a random number generator to simulate 500 rolls of a pair of dice and to count the number of times each sum of the dice occurred. Assuming a function (ROLL) which will return the sum of the dice (two random values between 1 and 6), we could declare a variable SUM to be

```
SUM:ARRAY[2..12] OF INTEGER;
```

and then use the segment

```
FOR I:= 1 TO 500 DO
  SUM(ROLL):= SUM(ROLL) + 1;
```

to accumulate the number of times each result occurred. Remember that the value of each element in the array had to be initialized to zero before beginning.

12.4 MULTIDIMENSIONAL ARRAYS

Our previous examples used one-dimensional arrays, which are equivalent to lists. We can also define **multidimensional arrays**. You can picture a two-dimensional array as a table with rows and columns; a two-dimensional array is often called a **matrix**. Its elements have two subscripts, one to indicate the row in the matrix (table) and the second to indicate the column.

Consider figure 12–2, which shows a matrix (array) with three rows and five columns. If we named this array TABLE, we could use an ARRAY statement to tell the computer its size. We could say this is an array of three rows and that each row is an array of five columns (lists) by using the declaration

```
VAR
  TABLE: ARRAY [1..3] OF ARRAY [1..5] OF REAL;
```

Figure 12–2. A Three-by-Five Matrix

	Columns				
	1	2	3	4	5
Rows 1	A		B		
2	C				
3					D

but we can abbreviate this ARRAY..OF ARRAY statement by simply using the declaration

```
VAR
   TABLE: ARRAY [1..3,1..5] OF REAL;
```

Thus we establish a two-dimensional array by specifying the number of rows and columns it contains.

We refer to elements of this array by identifying their rows and columns (using subscripts). Thus, element A in the array would be TABLE[1,1] (first row and first column), element B would be TABLE[1,3] (first row, third column), element C is TABLE[2,1] (second row, first column), and D is TABLE[3,5]. Normal assignment statements are used with elements of multidimensional arrays, for example

```
TABLE[3,5] := 6.25
```

Is it possible in Pascal to have an array of more than two dimensions? The answer is yes. The statement

```
CUBE: ARRAY [1..5,1..4,1..4] OF REAL;
```

creates a three-dimensional array. You might picture this as a table with five rows of values. Each row contains four values (corresponding to four columns), but each of those values is structured rather than simple, i.e., each of those values is a list of four items.

The following statement would also be acceptable.

```
BIG: ARRAY [1..5,1..5,1..5,1..5,1..5] OF CHAR;
```

This array is five-dimensional, and it is a little harder to visualize. You could think of this as an array of five elements, where each element is an array of five elements, where each of those elements is an array of five elements...It's usually a good idea to limit your arrays to one, two, or three dimensions since you will have an easier time conceptualizing the location of each value you wish to place in an array.

While it is not necessarily a good programming idea, Pascal is generally tolerant of ordinal array dimensions. For example, the following statement defines a three-dimensional array DIFFER.

```
DIFFER: ARRAY [1..5,0..3,3..8] OF CHAR;
```

The array DIFFER has five rows, each with four columns that contain six elements each. When you assign values to the elements, the subscripts *must* be within the defined range. Although there are only six fields for the third dimension of this array, the subscripts must be in the range of 3 to 8. This example is provided only to show you what Apple Pascal will accept, not to illustrate a particularly desirable programming practice. The general rule for programming is to keep things simple and understandable, so that additions or modifications are not difficult to accomplish. It is also more logical and practical to number a list of six items from 1 to 6.

12.5 DEFINING ARRAYS OF VARYING SIZE

Pascal is somewhat more flexible than many languages when it comes to dimensioning arrays. The following set of statements illustrates that we can define a constant (MAXSIZE) and then use this constant as a limit when we dimension an array.

```
CONST
  MAXSIZE = 10;

VAR
  LIST: ARRAY[1..MAXSIZE] OF REAL;
```

While not often used, this feature can be helpful in situations where we know that we will be redefining the size of an array from time to time. If we have a large number of arrays, it is easier to find and alter a constant such as MAXSIZE.

12.6 USING LOOPS TO INITIALIZE ARRAYS AND ASSIGN VALUES

In the past, when we used variables that held sums or served as counters, we initialized them to zero. When we initialize an array, we must initialize each element of the array. The easiest way to accomplish this is with a FOR..DO loop, for example

```
FOR I := 1 TO 10 DO
  LIST[I] := 0;
```

or

```
FOR I := 1 TO 10 DO
  FOR J := 1 TO 10 DO
    TABLE[I,J] := 0;
```

We can also use loops to assign values to an array. The program in exhibit 12–2: (1) defines an array TABLE as a two-dimensional array with five rows and five columns; (2) outputs the row and column numbers for each element using a procedure named ELEMENTS; (3) initializes all matrix values to zero and outputs the matrix (using the procedure WRITEMAT); and (4) assigns each element a value (beginning with 1 and ending with 25) and then outputs that matrix. Enter and run the program. Notice that by using a WRITE statement in the J loop and a WRITELN statement in the I loop, we output the result in a traditional matrix format.

12.7 PACKED ARRAYS

When you declare an array, Pascal sets aside enough memory space to store the values of each element. On some occasions, however, it is possible to store the values using less memory space. Characters and Boolean values can clearly be represented in less space than would be required for Integer, Real, or String values. To economize on the use of memory space, UCSD Pascal allows us to declare **packed arrays**. The declaration statement is the same as the normal array declaration, except that the word PACKED is added. For example, the TYPE statement

```
PACTIGHT = PACKED ARRAY [1..9] OF CHAR;
```

declares PACTIGHT to be a packed array of nine characters. A packed array differs from a normal array in that a packed array of type Char must be input through an assignment statement that treats the array more like a string than an array of characters. Thus, if TIGHT is a variable of TYPE PACTIGHT, the statement

```
TIGHT := 'NINE CHAR';
```

would be perfectly legal even though TIGHT is an array (packed) of characters. Packed arrays of type Char can also be output like a string rather than character by character, for example

```
WRITELN(TIGHT)
```

We can also change any of the nine characters in the array through specific assignments to the element of the array we want to change, for example

```
TIGHT[3] := 'C';
```

If we then used WRITELN(TIGHT), the output would be NICE CHAR, reflecting the change of the third character to a C.

Exhibit 12–2. Program
TABLVAL

```
PROGRAM TABLVAL;

VAR
  TABLE: ARRAY [1..5,1..5] OF INTEGER;
  I,J,K:INTEGER;

PROCEDURE ELEMENTS;  (* WRITES ROW & COL
VALUES *)
  BEGIN
    FOR I := 1 TO 5 DO
      BEGIN
        FOR J := 1 TO 5 DO
          WRITE(I:4,',',J);
        WRITELN;
      END;
  END; (* ELEMENTS *)

PROCEDURE WRITEMAT;  (* WRITE MATRIX TO
SCREEN *)
  BEGIN
    FOR I := 1 TO 5 DO
      BEGIN
        FOR J := 1 TO 5 DO
          WRITE(TABLE[I,J]:6);
        WRITELN;
      END;
  END; (* WRITEMAT *)

BEGIN (* TABLVAL *)
  WRITELN ('ELEMENTS - ROW & COL NOS:');
  ELEMENTS;
  WRITELN ('INITIALIZED MATRIX');
  FOR I := 1 TO 5 DO    (* INITIALIZE TO
  ZERO *)
    FOR J := 1 TO 5 DO
      TABLE[I,J] := 0; (* END INITIALIZE *)
  WRITEMAT;
  WRITELN;
  WRITELN ('ELEMENTS EQUAL TO COUNTER');
  K := 0;  (* K IS THE COUNTER VARIABLE *)
  FOR I := 1 TO 5 DO (* SET ELEMENTS =
  COUNTER *)
    FOR J := 1 TO 5 DO
      BEGIN
        K := K + 1;
        TABLE[I,J] := K
      END;  (* END ELEMENT = COUNTER LOOP *)
  WRITEMAT
END.  (* TABLVAL *)
```

UCSD Pascal supports String variables, but let's assume for a moment that it does not. In that case, we might attempt to create our own form of strings through packed arrays of type Char. Let's try it. A problem statement might be "Design a procedure that will allow us to input a string of characters and have that string be treated like a String data type." The input would be a number of characters (we will establish an upper limit of 80, which is the normal Apple Pascal String limit) and the output would be those same characters in string form. Since outputting a packed array of characters is identical to outputting a string, our procedure need only deal with inputting. Our Level 0 algorithm would be to design a procedure that allows us to input a variable number of characters (up to 80) into a packed array. A Level 1 refinement might then be

1. Define the array (within the main program);
2. Call the procedure (from the body of the program);
3. Procedure:
    a. Until the end of the line is reached, repeat the process of:
    (1) Reading a character;
    (2) Adding the character to the "string";

Whenever we tell the computer to read a string, we use a READLN statement because the string contains all the characters up to the **(RET)**. Pascal has a special function called **EOLN**, which stands for end-of-line. EOLN returns a Boolean value of TRUE or FALSE. We can use this function in our procedure to determine whether or not the **(RET)** has been entered, i.e., the end of the line has been reached. We will include EOLN in our Level 2 refinement:

1. Declare the array:
    a. Declare STRG to be of TYPE packed array with up to 80 characters;
    b. Declare a VAR STR of TYPE STRG;
2. Call READSTG (STR);
3. READSTRG:
    a. Declare VAR parameter ST of TYPE STRG (packed array);
    b. Declare VAR for character to be read, CH;
    c. Declare an Integer VAR (I) as a counter;
    d. Initialize the counter to zero;
    e. Until the end of the line (EOLN) is reached, repeat:
    (1) Increment the counter (I) by 1;
    (2) Read a character (CH);
    (3) If not the end of the line (EOLN) then
        (a) Add the character to the array as element I;

Normally, this would be sufficient refinement to proceed to the coding of the program. In this case, however, we must address one additional item. We created a packed array of 80 characters because, as we stated earlier, Apple Pascal String types normally contain up to 80 characters. When we use a WRITELN statement to output this array, it will output 80 characters. But what if we only input 10 or 20 characters? Unfortunately, if we input less than 80 characters and then output the contents of memory for the entire 80-character array, we are likely to get some very strange results, for example, a screen with some of the prompts or displays highlighted (inverse video—dark letters on a light background). While this can be corrected by pressing RESET (or CTRL-RESET) to reinitialize the system, it is a nuisance best avoided. Therefore, we will add a step that initializes the array by assigning a blank space (i.e., a space, not a null character) to each element:

> do the following (loop)
>   assign a space to the next array element;
> 80 times;

before we begin reading characters.

The program in exhibit 12–3 (see p. 282) will approximate the UCSD built-in string-handling procedure following the algorithm we just defined. Note that we use a special READ statement named READSTRG (which is actually a parameter call) to read a string variable. And, since we cannot read data directly into the array element, we will read it into a character variable first and then assign the character value to the element.

Fortunately, UCSD Pascal normally supports Strings and we do not have to go through this process. Standard Pascal does not support Strings variables, however, and users of standard Pascal must create procedures like this one to handle strings. There would be a subtle difference in such a program, however, because Standard Pascal does not allow the user to declare a packed array (although it has provisions for packing and then later unpacking an array through PACK and UNPACK commands). ■

12.8 VARYING THE LENGTH OF STRINGS

Apple Pascal normally allows strings to be from 1 to 80 characters in length, but we can specify the length we want a string to have when we declare it. For example, the declaration

```
VAR
  SHORT:STRING[10];
  NORMAL:STRING;
  LONG:STRING[255];
```

declares a String variable SHORT of 10 characters, a variable NORMAL of 80 characters (the default length of a String data type), and a variable LONG of 255 characters. Apple Pascal is

Exhibit 12–3. Program
BUILDSTRING

```
PROGRAM BUILDSTRING;

TYPE
  STRG = PACKED ARRAY [1..80] OF CHAR;

VAR
  STR:STRG;

PROCEDURE READSTRG (VAR ST:STRG);
  VAR
    CH:CHAR;
    I:INTEGER;
  BEGIN  (* READSTRG *)
    FOR I := 1 TO 80 DO        (* BLANKS
    ARRAY *)
      ST[I] := ' ';           (* INITIALIZE
      COUNTER *)
    I := 0;
    REPEAT
      READ (CH);
      IF NOT EOLN THEN
        BEGIN (* ADD CHAR TO STRING *)
          I := I + 1;
          ST[I] := CH
        END;  (* ADD CHAR TO STRING *)
    UNTIL EOLN;
  END;  (* READSTRG *)

BEGIN  (* BUILDSTRING *)
  READSTRG (STR);
  WRITELN (STR)
END.  (* BUILDSTRING *)
```

limited to a maximum length of 255; you cannot declare a string longer than 255 without an error. Since the default length is 80, strings of up to 80 characters do not have to have any length specified.

The advantage of declaring a string to be less than 80 characters long is that it saves computer memory space, since the computer does not have to allocate enough memory to store 80 characters. The disadvantage is that Pascal will not allow you to assign a string longer than you have declared to the variable, i.e., you cannot assign an 11-character string to SHORT. The 11th character would cause program termination with a STRING OVERFLOW message. If you use a READLN statement to enter SHORT, however, you would not get an error message. The first 10 characters would be read into SHORT and the remainder discarded.

12.9 MIXING STRINGS AND CHAR DATA TYPES

As we have seen in the past, String and Char data types are different and cannot, therefore, be mixed. There is one situation, however, where this is not true. Remember, a string is nothing more than an array of characters. Since each element of the array is a character, it is possible to assign a Char data type to a single element of a string variable. The program in exhibit 12–4 illustrates this, as well as the creation of a short string, which was discussed in the preceding section.

Enter, compile, and run the program. When you are asked to input a string, enter NOW IS THE TIME. The string will be truncated to NOW IS THE. Then enter 8(RET) N, 9(RET) 0, and 10(RET) T. This will alter the string to NOW IS NOT.

Exhibit 12–4. Program ALTER

```
PROGRAM ALTER;

VAR
  SHORT:STRING[10];
  I:INTEGER;
  CH:CHAR;

PROCEDURE OUT;
  BEGIN  (* OUT *)
    WRITELN;
    WRITELN('STRING = ',SHORT);
    WRITELN
  END;  (* OUT *)

BEGIN  (* ALTER *)
  WRITELN('ENTER A STRING ( 11 CHARACTER
  S LONG');
  READLN(SHORT);
  OUT;
  REPEAT
    WRITE('NUMBER OF CHARACTER TO ALTER
    ->');
    READLN(I);
    IF I < 11 THEN
      BEGIN  (* IF..THEN *)
        WRITE('NEW CHARACTER ->');
        READ(CH);
        WRITELN;
        PAGE (OUTPUT);
        SHORT[I] := CH;
        OUT
      END  (* IF..THEN *)
    ELSE
      WRITELN('ALTERATION FINISHED');
  UNTIL I > 10;
END.  (* ALTER *)
```

Note the PAGE (OUTPUT) statement on the 12th line of the main program. This statement clears the text page (screen) and places the cursor in the upper left-hand corner. Enter 12 as the character to alter to exit the program. Now run the program again and enter the string NOW(RET). Change character 1 to H, to make the string HOW. Then alter character 5 to E. When you make this entry, you should find yourself looking at a message similar to

```
VALUE RANGE ERROR
S# 1, P# 1, I# 203
TYPE (SPACE) TO CONTINUE□
```

Even though we declared the string to be 10 characters long, we originally entered only three characters (NOW), so we can only alter the first three characters in the string. Any attempt to alter a character beyond the length of the original string will result in an error.

12.10 ASSIGNING ARRAY VALUES TO ANOTHER ARRAY

Assume you have two similar arrays, X and Y. If you want to assign the values in array X to the elements in array Y, you could use a loop or set of loops to make the assignments, element by element:

```
FOR I := 1 TO 5 DO
  FOR J := 1 TO 5 DO
    Y[I,J] := X[I,J];
```

There is an easier way to accomplish this. The following statement does the same thing without any loops:

```
Y := X;
```

This statement assigns the value of every element in array X to the corresponding element in array Y.

The program in exhibit 12–5 is a modification of the program named TABLVAL in section 12.6. See if you can figure out what it will do, then modify TABLVAL and run it to see if you were right.

As you could see when you ran the program, the value of K is first assigned to each element in the array so that the elements are numbered from 1 to 25 (just as in TABLVAL). The program then assigns the values in TABLE to the matrix SAME and outputs the results. Finally, it performs an element-by-element assignment, assigning the values in reverse order, i.e., the last element in TABLE to the first element in FLIPPED, and so forth.

Exhibit 12–5. Program
FLIPMAT

```
PROGRAM FLIPMAT;

TYPE
  MATRIX = ARRAY [1..5,1..5] OF INTEGER;

VAR
  TABLE,SAME,FLIPPED: MATRIX;
  I,J,K:INTEGER;

PROCEDURE WRITEMAT (OUTER:MATRIX);
(*WRITE MATRIX TO SCREEN *)
  BEGIN  (* WRITEMAT *)
    FOR I := 1 TO 5 DO
      BEGIN  (* FOR..DO *)
        FOR J := 1 TO 5 DO
          WRITE(OUTER[I,J]:6);
        WRITELN
      END;  (* FOR..DO *)
  END; (* WRITEMAT *)

BEGIN (* FLIPMAT *)
  WRITELN;
  K := 0;  (* K IS THE COUNTER VARIABLE *)
  FOR I := 1 TO 5 DO (* SET ELEMENTS =
  COUNTER *)
    FOR J := 1 TO 5 DO
      BEGIN  (* FOR J DO *)
        K := K + 1;
        TABLE[I,J] := K
      END;  (* FOR J DO (ELEMENT = COUNT
      ER) *)
  WRITELN ('MATRIX TABLE');
  WRITEMAT(TABLE);
  WRITELN;
  WRITELN;
  WRITELN ('MATRIX SAME');
  SAME := TABLE;  (* DUPLICATES MATRIX *)
  WRITEMAT(SAME);
  WRITELN;
  WRITELN;
  FOR I := 1 TO 5 DO
    FOR J := 1 TO 5 DO
      FLIPPED[I,J] := TABLE[6-I,6-J];
  WRITELN ('MATRIX FLIPPED');
  WRITEMAT (FLIPPED)
END. (* FLIPMAT *)
```

12.11 USING ARRAYS IN A PROBLEM

Matrices can be useful when we want to save a number of entries to use later in the program. For example, in the program we have been developing for Mr. Matthews, we input the student's name and three grades. We then calculated the student's average and repeated the process for the next student. Because we used the same variable names, the first set of data was erased (overwritten) when the second set was input. If we were to establish a list of names and a table of grades using arrays, we could refer to this data again later in the program; for example, we could use it to calculate averages. Our list and table could be in the form shown in exhibit 12–6. The first column is a list of names (a one-dimensional array of type (String) and the remaining columns form the table of grades (a two-dimensional array of type Real).

Mr. Matthews has decided that our abilities have expanded greatly since we worked on his first grading program, so he has a list of "minor" changes he would like to see incorporated into a new version of the grading program:

1. a listing of all students' names and grades in a format similar to the one in exhibit 12–6;
2. a revised input routine that asks for each component by name (he could never get the hang of lining up the grades under the column headings);
3. a further revision of the input routine to allow him to end his input without having to type STOP as a name entry (a simple **(RET)** should do);
4. average scores for notes, projects, and final exams for each class; and
5. a routine that allows him to correct some of his many typing mistakes, since he cannot backspace/erase to change a mistyped grade.

Before we begin, we should review where we are (or might be). Program REVGRDR in exhibit 12–7 is a modified program

Exhibit 12–6. Name List and Grade Table

Student Name	Notebook Grade	Project Grade	Final Grade	Course Grade
Sara	84	94	82	86.0
Rachel	92	86	90	89.2
.	.	.	.	.
.	.	.	.	.
.	.	.	.	.
Total	?	?	?	?
Average	?	?	?	?
(Names)	(	Grades		)

that incorporates the changes made in chapters 10 and 11. (We did not include the altered physics grading scheme that we discussed in chapter 11; it was there for illustration only.) Review the program now, then we will consider each of the requested changes individually.

Exhibit 12–7. Program REVGRDR

```
PROGRAM REVGRDR;

CONST
  WGTNOTES = 0.20;
  WGTPROJ = 0.30;
  WGTFINAL = 0.50;

TYPE
  SUBJECT = (BIOLOGY,CHEMISTRY,PHYSICS);

VAR
  NOTES,PROJECT,FINAL,SUM,AVE:REAL;
  NUM:INTEGER;
  NAME,CNAME:STRING;
  CLASS:SUBJECT;

FUNCTION GRADE (N,P,F:REAL):REAL;
  BEGIN
    GRADE := WGTNOTES * N + WGTPROJ * P
    + WGTFINAL * F;
  END; (* GRADE FUNCTION *)

PROCEDURE ENTRY;
(* READS 3 SCORES AND A NAME FROM KEYBOA
RD *)
  BEGIN
    WRITELN;
    WRITE ('ENTER NAME AND TYPE RETURN:');
    READLN (NAME);
    IF NAME()'STOP'THEN
      BEGIN  (* IF..THEN *)
        WRITELN;
        WRITELN ('ENTER GRADES UNDER THE');
        WRITELN ('APPROPRIATE COMPONENT
        WITH SPACES');
        WRITELN ('BETWEEN THEM, THEN HIT
         RETURN');
        WRITELN;
        WRITELN ('  COMPONENTS');
        WRITELN ('NOTE PROJ FINAL');
        WRITELN ('---- ---- -----');
        READLN (NOTES,PROJECT,FINAL);
        WRITELN
      END  (* IF..THEN *)
    END; (* ENTRY *)
```

```
PROCEDURE WRITEOUT;
  BEGIN
    WRITELN;
    WRITELN (NAME,'''S FINAL GRADE = ',G
RADE(NOTES,PROJECT, FINAL):8:2);
    WRITELN
  END; (* WRITEOUT *)

BEGIN
  FOR CLASS := BIOLOGY TO PHYSICS DO
    BEGIN  (* FOR..DO *)
      CASE CLASS OF
        BIOLOGY: CNAME := 'BIOLOGY';
        CHEMISTRY: CNAME := 'CHEMISTRY';
        PHYSICS: CNAME := 'PHYSICS'
      END; (* CASE..OF *)
      WRITELN;
      SUM := 0;
      NUM := 0;
      REPEAT
        ENTRY;
        IF NAME = 'STOP' THEN
          BEGIN  (* IF..THEN *)
            WRITELN;
            WRITELN ('END OF GRADES FOR
            ',CNAME)
          END  (* IF..THEN *)
        ELSE
          BEGIN  (* ELSE *)
            NUM := NUM + 1;
            SUM := SUM + GRADE(NOTES,PRO
JECT,FINAL);
            WRITEOUT
          END;  (* ELSE *)
      UNTIL NAME = 'STOP';
      IF NUM <> 0 THEN
        AVE := SUM/NUM
      ELSE
        AVE := 0;
      WRITELN;
      WRITELN ('AVERAGE FOR ALL ',CNAME,
      'STUDENTS = ',AVE:6:2)
    END  (* FOR..DO *)
END.  (* REVGRDR *)
```

First, Mr. Matthews wants a listing of all the students'
names and grades in tabular format. We can do this using the
two arrays already discussed. We'll keep the identifiers NAMES
and GRADES for the arrays. Notice that when we set up the
table, we used the last column to hold each student's grade and
the last two rows to hold the sum and average for each grade

component (these will be determined when we consider item 4). The size of these arrays will be a function of the number of students in each of Mr. Matthews' classes. Because this may change over time, we will declare a constant called CLASSSIZE and set it equal to the expected class size plus two (two extra rows set aside for the sums and averages). We will begin our modifications, therefore, by including the following declarations

```
CONST
  :
  :
  CLASSSIZE = 25; (* EXPECTED SIZE PLUS
  TWO *)

VAR
  NAMES: ARRAY [1..CLASSSIZE] OF STRING;
  GRADES: ARRAY [1..CLASSSIZE,1..4] OF R
  EAL;
```

We will then let each row of the array represent a particular student and input the grade components for that student into the first three columns of the GRADES array. Normally, we would work on the input segment of the program before the output segment, but we will continue with the output now and complete the input later (remember that Pascal lends itself to segmentation and independent work on each segment). We will have to make some assumptions about the form the data will be in: we will assume that the arrays NAMES and GRADES contain the data in the form described above; we will further assume that class sizes will vary (up to a limit of CLASSSIZE–2) and that the limit will be passed to the output procedure as a parameter.

With these assumptions we can begin our new output procedure. Since it will be in tabular form, we'll even put in column headings.

```
PROCEDURE WRITEOUT (LIMIT:INTEGER);
  VAR
    S:INTEGER;
  BEGIN  (* WRITEOUT *)
    WRITELN;
    WRITELN ('   NAME      NOTES PROJECT
    FINAL  GRADE');
    WRITELN ('   ----      ----- -------
    ----- ----- ');
    FOR S := 1 TO LIMIT DO
      WRITELN (NAMES[S]:10,GRADES[S,1]:7
      :1,GRADES[S,2]:7:1,GRADES[S,3]:7:1
        ,GRADES[S,4]:7:1);
  WRITELN;
```

```
WRITELN ('  AVERAGE ',GRADES[25,1]:7
:1,GRADES[25,2]:7:1,GRADES[25,3]:7:1
  ,GRADES[25,4]:7:1)
END; (* WRITEOUT *)
```

Notice that the two WRITELN statements that write the individual student grades and the average scores are very similar. If we assigned the string 'AVERAGE' to NAMES[25], we could use the same statement. And if we used the same statement, we could substitute a procedure call for each of the statements. Notice too that the only difference between each of the GRADES elements specified in the statement is the column number. Looping for each column using a WRITE statement within a loop would give us the same output. With these changes, our WRITEOUT procedure would take the following form:

```
PROCEDURE WRITEOUT (LIMIT:INTEGER);
  VAR
    S:INTEGER;

  PROCEDURE OUTPUT;
    BEGIN
      WRITE (NAMES[S]:10);
      FOR J := 1 TO 4 DO
        WRITE (GRADES[S,J]:7:1):
      WRITELN
    END; (* OUTPUT *)

  BEGIN (* WRITEOUT* )
    WRITELN;
    WRITELN ('   NAME      NOTES PROJECT
    FINAL  GRADE');
    WRITELN ('   ----      ----- -------
    ----  -----');
    FOR S := 1 TO LIMIT DO
      OUTPUT;
    WRITELN;
    S := 25;
    NAMES[S] := '  AVERAGE ';
    OUTPUT;
  END; (* WRITEOUT *)
```

But since this is much longer than the first version, we will regard it only as an illustration of an alternative approach and use the first version. This segment should satisfy the first requirement (and part of the fourth as well).

The second requirement was for a revised input routine requesting each component by name. In the input procedure, we will include a counter called CNTR that will increment by 1 each time we add a new student name. One form of this procedure is shown on the following page.

```
PROCEDURE ENTRY (VAR CNTR:INTEGER);
  BEGIN
    WRITELN;
    CNTR := CNTR + 1;
    WRITE ('ENTER A NAME AND TYPE RETURN:');
    READLN (NAMES[CNTR]);
    IF NAMES[CNTR] <> 'STOP' THEN
      BEGIN  (* IF..THEN *)
        WRITELN;
        WRITE ('NOTES ->');  READLN (GRA
        DES[CNTR,1]);
        WRITE ('PROJECT ->');  READLN (G
        RADES[CNTR,2]);
        WRITE ('FINAL ->');  READLN (GRA
        DES[CNTR,3]);
        WRITELN
      END;  (* IF..THEN *)
END;  (* ENTRY *)
```

The counter CNTR is declared as a variable in the parameter list so that its value will be passed back to the program. This is necessary, since we just wrote an output procedure that uses this value (the parameter LIMIT). We have also made our input consistent with our output in terms of the global arrays we are using.

The third requirement was to make input termination easier than having to enter the name STOP. We'll substitute a null string for the word STOP, then Mr. Matthews will only have to hit the RETURN key to terminate the input procedure. The IF statement in the ENTRY procedure would now be

```
IF NAMES[CNTR] <> '' THEN
```

We will also have to change the IF and UNTIL statements in the main program to be consistent with this change. If we use the variable NUM as the counter in the main program body, we would then add the following statement to the main program

```
NUM := 0; (* INITIALIZE COUNTER TO ZERO *)
```

immediately after the CASE..OF statement (as shown in Exhibit 12–7). Then the UNTIL statement in the main program would have to be altered to be consistent with our new termination flag (the null string instead of STOP):

```
REPEAT
  ENTRY
UNTIL NAMES[NUM] = '';
```

and the following statement would be added immediately after the UNTIL statement

```
NUM := NUM - 1;
```

What is the purpose of this statement? If you said that it corrects the counter so that it corresponds to the number of students excluding the null string, you were right. The counter was incremented before the null string was entered, but we don't want to count this (null) string as part of our class list. We decrement our counter by one, therefore, making NUM correspond to the actual number of students entered.

The fourth requirement was to average the scores for the notes, projects, and final exams for each class. This can be accomplished by summing the scores in each column into the 24th row location (which we set aside just for such a purpose) and then dividing those sums by the number of students in the class (which we counted into NUM). We will place the result in the 25th row location, which we again set aside for that purpose. We already have a function named GRADE to calculate each student's grade, so we will simply add a procedure to sum and then average each column. This procedure is shown below.

```
PROCEDURE CALCULATE (LIMIT:INTEGER);
  BEGIN
    FOR I := 1 TO LIMIT DO
      BEGIN  (* FOR LOOP *)
        (* COMPUTES STUDENT GRADES USING
        GRADE FUNCTION *)
        GRADES[I,4] := GRADE(GRADES[I,1]
        ,GRADES[I,2],GRADES]I,3]);
        FOR J := 1 TO 4 DO  (* SUMS EACH
        COLUMN *)
          GRADES[24,J] := GRADES[24,J] +
          GRADES[I,J];
      END;  (* FOR LOOP *)
    FOR I := 1 TO 4 DO  (* COMPUTES AVER
    AGES *)
      IF LIMIT <> 0 THEN
        GRADES[25,I] := GRADES[24,I]/LIM
        IT
      ELSE
        GRADES[25,I] := 0
  END;  (* CALCULATE *)
```

Why is the IF..THEN..ELSE loop included? If Mr. Matthews decides he doesn't want to calculate grades for a particular class, he can simply hit the (RET) at the first name inquiry. But this will set the LIMIT (NUM) value equal to zero and the computer cannot divide by zero. The IF..THEN..ELSE loop, therefore, prevents the computer from attempting to divide when LIMIT = 0. Because we are summing values into GRADES[24,I], we will include the following loop in the main program body after the NUM := 0; statement to initialize these matrix values to zero as well:

```
FOR I := 1 TO 4 DO
  GRADES[24,I] := 0;
```

Why don't we initialize the entire matrix? There is no need to. All of the array element values are assigned directly except for row 24, which contains values being summed. Because the assignment statement for row 24 adds values to the existing elements, we must first make sure those values are zero.

Our fifth and final task is to include a routine that allows Mr. Matthews to correct typing mistakes. We will do this with a new procedure called ERROR. It would be logical to call this procedure from the ENTRY procedure. Since this is the only place the ERROR procedure will be used, it would also make sense to place it in ENTRY. (This does not allow us to place it after the other procedures and practice our FORWARD statements, but we'll go with the logical approach.) Thus, the following procedure will be declared in ENTRY. (You might want to see if you can write the algorithm for this procedure before proceeding.)

```
PROCEDURE ERROR;
  VAR
    ANS:CHAR;
  BEGIN (* ERROR *)
    WRITE('ERRORS (Y/N)?');
    READ (ANS);  WRITELN;
    IF ANS = 'Y' THEN
      BEGIN  (* IF..THEN *)
        WRITELN ('[N] NOTES  [P] PROJE
        CT [F] FINAL',CHR(13),
        'ENTER LETTER  (N, P OR F)';
        REPEAT
          READ(ANS)
        UNTIL ANS IN['N','P','F'];
        WRITELN;
        CASE ANS OF
          'N': I := 1;
          'P': I := 2;
          'F': I := 3
        END;  (* CASE..OF *)
        WRITE ('ENTER CORRECT VALUE -)');
        READLN (GRADES[CNTR,I]);
        ERROR
      END  (* IF..THEN *)
  END;  (* ERROR *)
```

The first two statements below will be inserted at the end of the ENTRY procedure.

```
      WRITELN;
      ERROR;
      WRITELN
    END
END; (* ENTRY *)
```

There are some features in the ERROR procedure we should make note of. Because the WRITELN statement for the prompt would produce a prompt longer than 40 characters, CHR(13) was included to split the prompt. (If you have an 80-column display, this is obviously not necessary.) Also note the use of the beginning letters of each component as a response (N, P, and F) and the use of a CASE..OF statement to convert these letters into integer values. Couldn't we have simply used 1, 2, and 3 as the responses, i.e., [1] NOTES [2] PROJECT [3] FINAL? The answer is yes, and this method would probably work fine. Always remember, however, that the more logical or natural the response requested, the fewer mistakes the user is likely to make. And since it would be possible to accidently hit some key other than one of the three specified (N, P or F), the RE-PEAT..UNTIL ANS IN ['N', 'P', 'F'] is included. The last feature in this procedure is of special importance; it is the ERROR call immediately after the last READLN statement in the ERROR procedure. What does this statement (call) do? It calls the ERROR procedure, that is, it calls itself. This is known as **recursion**, and it is perfectly allowable in Pascal. While allowing a procedure to call itself could throw the computer into an endless loop, this call does not, since it is only executed when the user responds with a Y to the question ERRORS (Y/N)? This allows the user to correct more than one error, e.g., if errors were made in two components, or it allows the user to correct an error made when entering his or her correction!

What happens when the user responds with an answer other than Y? Since the comparison is only made with Y, any other response will exit the procedure. If Mr. Matthews wants to shortcut the response, he can simply press **(RET)** rather than N **(RET)**.

We now have the ENTRY procedure shown in exhibit 12–8. The variables now declared in the program are

```
VAR
  NAMES: ARRAY [1..CLASSSIZE] OF STRING;
  CNAME: STRING;
  CH: CHAR;
  I,J,NUM: INTEGER;
  CLASS: SUBJECT;
  GRADES: ARRAY [1..CLASSSIZE,1..4] OF R
  EAL;
```

and the main body of the program should look like exhibit 12–9.

Putting it all together, a skeleton of the program is shown on page 296. Since each procedure and the main body of the program have already been illustrated, they will not be repeated. The skeleton will show the order of the various program segments.

Exhibit 12–8.
Procedure ENTRY

```
PROCEDURE ENTRY (VAR CNTR:INTEGER);

   PROCEDURE ERROR;
     VAR
       ANS:CHAR;
     BEGIN  (* ERROR *)
       WRITE('ERRORS (Y/N)?'Q;
       READ (ANS);  WRITELN;
       IF ANS = 'Y' THEN
         BEGIN  (* IF..THEN *)
           WRITELN ('[N] NOTES  [P] PROJE
           CT  [F] FINAL',CHR(13),
           'ENTER LETTER  (N, P
           OR F)';
           REPEAT
             READ(ANS)
           UNTIL ANS IN ['N','P','F'];
           WRITELN;
           CASE ANS OF
             'N': I := 1;
             'P': I := 2;
             'F': I := 3
           END;  (* CASE..OF *)
           WRITE ('ENTER CORRECT VALUE ->');
           READLN (GRADES[CNTR,I]);
           ERROR
         END  (* IF..THEN *)
     END;  (* ERROR *)

   BEGIN  (* ENTRY *)
     WRITELN;
     CNTR := CNTR + 1;
     WRITE ('ENTER A NAME AND TYPE RETURN:');
     READLN (NAMES[CNTR]);
     IF NAMES[CNTR] <> '' THEN
       BEGIN  (*IF..THEN *)
         WRITELN;
         WRITE ('NOTES ->');  READLN (GRA
         DES[CNTR,1];
         WRITE ('PROJECT ->');  READLN (G
         RADES[CNTR,2];
         WRITE ('FINAL ->');  READLN (GRA
         DES[CNTR,3]);
         WRITELN;
         ERROR;
         WRITELN
       END  (* IF..THEN *)
   END; (* ENTRY *)
```

Exhibit 12-9. Main
Body of Program

```
BEGIN  (* GRADEMAT *)
  FOR CLASS := BIOLOGY TO PHYSICS DO
    BEGIN  (* FOR..DO *)
      CASE CLASS OF
        BIOLOGY: CNAME := 'BIOLOGY';
        CHEMISTRY: CNAME := 'CHEMISTRY';
        PHYSICS: CNAME := 'PHYSICS'
      END;  (* CASE.OF *)
      NUM := 0;
      FOR I := 1 TO 4 DO
        GRADES[24,I] := 0;
      WRITELN;
      WRITELN ('GRADES FOR ',CNAME,' CLASS');
      WRITELN;
      REPEAT
        ENTRY(NUM)
      UNTIL NAMES[NUM] = '';
      NUM := NUM - 1;
      CALCULATE(NUM);
      PAGE(OUTPUT);
      WRITELN;
      WRITELN ('GRADES FOR ',CNAME);
      WRITEOUT(NUM)
    END;  (* FOR..DO *)
END.  (* GRADEMAT *)
```

```
PROGRAM GRADEMAT;

CONST

VAR

FUNCTION GRADE(N,P,F:REAL):REAL;

PROCEDURE ENTRY (CNTR:INTEGER);
  PROCEDURE ERROR;

PROCEDURE CALCULATE (LIMIT:INTEGER);

PROCEDURE WRITEOUT;

BEGIN

END.
```

Enter, compile, and run the program. Mr. Matthews should
now have a program that will calculate student grades and
component and class averages for all three classes. And with
an error correcting routine, no less! When you are done, save
the program under the name GRADEMAT.

12.12 SUMMARY

In this chapter we explored the structured data type known as an array. The array data type allows us to create lists or tables of values under one variable name or identifier. We can assign values to particular points in the list or table by using subscripts to tell the computer which location in the matrix is being referenced. Before we actually use an array, however, we must declare it with an ARRAY..OF statement, which tells the computer how much space to set aside for the matrix values.

We also learned about packed arrays, which are similar to normal arrays, but which allow the computer to store the values in less space. Packed arrays are most frequently used with arrays of characters or Boolean values. Packed arrays of characters can also be written out in total (much like a string) by simply referencing the array name rather than specific elements.

While assignments are normally made to a specific element of an array, designated by its subscript, we also saw that we could assign the values of all of the elements of one array to the elements of another array of equal size by using the array identifiers without subscripts in the assignment statement. This has the same effect as an element-by-element assignment made using nested loops.

Finally, we learned about the EOLN function, which returns a Boolean value of TRUE whenever the last character read is a (RET). This function can be used in conjunction with REPEAT..UNTIL or WHILE..DO statements to read character arrays and locate the end of the line.

Review Questions

1. What is an array?

2. There are two methods of declaring arrays. What are they?

3. How do we designate the size of an array?

4. How would you initialize the 200 elements of a one-dimensional array LIST to zero?

5. What is the major advantage of using arrays?

6. Would the variable declaration LIST:ARRAY[LETTER] OF CHAR; be acceptable? Explain.

7. What is a packed array? How do packed arrays of characters differ from normal arrays of characters?

8. Strings can be declared to be of varying length. What is:
   a. the default length?
   b. the minimum length?
   c. the maximum length?

SUMMARY of Pascal Syntax

Reserved Words	Built-in Procedures	Built-in Functions	Library Units
PROGRAM	WRITE	ABS	TURTLEGRAPHICS
USES	WRITELN	SQR	APLESTUFF
CONST	READ	SQRT	TRANSCEND
TYPE	READLN	ROUND	
SET..OF		TRUNC	
PACKED		EXP	
ARRAY[..]OF	INITTURTLE	LN	
	PENCOLOR	LOG	
VAR	MOVE	PWROFTEN	
FUNCTION	TURN	ATAN	
FORWARD		SIN	
PROCEDURE	MOVETO	COS	
	TURNTO	ORD	*Boolean Constants*
BEGIN	TEXTMODE	CHR	
	GRAFMODE	PRED	
FOR..DO	PAGE(OUTPUT)	SUCC	FALSE
TO		EOLN	TRUE
DOWNTO			
REPEAT			
UNTIL			
WHILE..DO			
IF			
THEN			
ELSE			
CASE..OF			
END			
DIV			*Integer Constants*
MOD			
NIL			
AND			
OR			
NOT			
IN			

9. In Pascal there is a very simple method for assigning the values of the elements of one array to the elements of a second array. Explain.

10. We can alter parts of existing strings without reentering the entire string. Explain how.

11. Why did we use two arrays rather than one in the grading problem?

12. What is meant by *recursion*?

13. How can recursion be used? Are there any dangers associated with the use of recursion?

14. What does the EOLN function do?

Programming Exercises

1. Write a statement that declares a data type LIST to be a one-dimensional array with 30 elements.

2. Write a statement that declares a variable A to be of type LIST (see exercise 1) and a variable B to be a one-dimensional array of 40 elements.

3. Declare a scalar data type with five values in it and then declare an array of Integer using your new data type to indicate the size of the array.

4. Write a program that declares an array to be a 5 by 5 matrix of Integer and then initializes each element to zero.

5. Write a program segment to sum the contents of the 20-element array LIST.

6. Declare a packed array of 20 characters and then write a program segment to change the odd numbered elements (1,3,5,...) to asterisks (*) and output the result.

7. Assuming we have a string variable ST that contains a string, write a program segment illustrating the use of the EOLN function.

Diagnostic Exercises

8. What will the following program segments do? Write out the resulting arrays.
```
a. FOR I := 1 TO 10 DO
      A[I] := 11 - I;
b. FOR I := 1 TO 10 DO
      FOR J := 1 TO DO
         A[J,I] := J;
c. FOR I := 'A' TO 'J' DO
      A[I] := I;
```

d. FOR I := 1 TO 10 DO
   A[I] := I;
  I; = 6;
  J := 2;
  FOR J := 1 TO 10 DO
   B[J] := A[I];

e. ST := 'ARRAY';
  ST[2] := ST[1];
  ST[3] := ST[1];
  ST[5] := ST[2];
  WRITELN(ST);

9. If array A contains the elements 1,3,5,7 and array B contains the elements 1,3,4,8, what will be the result of the expression A = B?

10. If A is a packed array of 10 Char and B is a String[10], are the following statements acceptable?
a. A := B;
b. B[5] := A[5];
c. S[10] := 'S';
d. WRITELN (A);
e. WRITELN (B:8);

Problems

11. Write a program that creates a 5 by 5 matrix with the following values:

1	0	0	0	0
0	1	0	0	0
0	0	1	0	0
0	0	0	1	0
0	0	0	0	1

12. Write a procedure to output the matrix from exercise 11 in the form shown above.

13. Write the algorithm for a procedure to create a 5 by 5 matrix with the following values:

1	1	1	1	1
1	0	0	0	1
1	0	0	0	1
1	1	1	1	1

14. Code and test the algorithm developed in exercise 13.

15. Write a procedure that creates the packed array of Char shown below and outputs it to the screen.

```
        *
      *   *
    *   *   *   *
        *
        *
```

16. Write a procedure that will convert the asterisks in a packed array to spaces and convert the spaces to asterisks. Test the procedure on the array created by problem 15.

17. Write a procedure that randomly generates the numbers from 1 to 52 and places them in an array DECK. (Note: none of the numbers may be repeated; every number between 1 and 52 must appear once and only once.) Output the result.

18. The procedure created in problem 17 has the same effect as shuffling a deck of cards. Write a second procedure that takes the 52 Integer values from the array DECK and converts them into two-character representations of specific cards, i.e., the first character will represent the suit (S,H,D,C for spades, hearts, diamonds, and clubs), and the second character will represent rank (A (ace), 2–10, J (jack), Q (queen), K (king). These card representations should also be stored in an array. Output the results of the two procedures side by side.

13

Records

In chapter 12, you were introduced to the array, a structured data type that allows you to create lists or tables of data using one variable name. We could not, however, include elements of different data types in one array. In this chapter, we will begin to explore the real ability of Pascal to deal with items of related data, even when those items are of different data types. Through the use of a new structured data type, the **record**, we will be able to link related data together. We will also discover how to create records that can vary in size and type, depending on the results of assignments or calculations performed within the program.

13.1 RECORDS

In the last chapter, we saw that we could use arrays to store lists or tables of data. When we wanted to store information pertaining to Mr. Matthews' classes, however, we had to use one array for names and a second array for grades, because we had two different data types.

Pascal, unlike many other languages, has a special structured data type called a **record**, which allows us to store different types of data together. For example, if we want to keep track of student information consisting of a student's name, numerical average, and letter grade, we might use a String variable for the name, a Real variable for the numerical average, and a Char variable for the letter grade. It's obvious that these three items are related to one another. Pascal allows us to store these three different types of data together through the new data type mentioned above, the record. A record is a single data structure that lets us combine data of different types.

Declaring Records

We declare a record through the TYPE statement. The record declaration statement takes the form

> *record name* = `RECORD`
> > *field identifier : data type;*
> > *field identifier : data type;*
>
> > .
> > .
> > .
>
> > *field identifier : data type*
> `END`;

where *record name* is the identifier used to name the record. RECORD is a reserved word that tells the computer this is a structured data type. The list of field identifiers declares each component or **field** of the record. Figure 13–1 shows the RECORD syntax diagram.

Figure 13–1. RECORD
Syntax Diagram

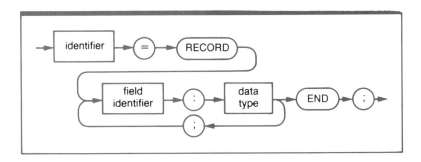

Thus, we could declare our student information to be of TYPE RECORD as shown below:

```
TYPE
  INFO = RECORD
            NAME: STRING;
            AVE: REAL;
            LETTER: CHAR
         END;  (* RECORD *)
```

All three of these items would then be part of the record INFO. We could then declare a variable STUDENT to be of TYPE INFO:

```
VAR
    STUDENT: INFO;
```

When we refer to a particular field of this record, we do so by stating the variable name, STUDENT, followed by a period (.) and the suffix that represents (names) the particular record field, e.g., STUDENT.NAME would refer to the NAME field.

Assigning Values to Record Variables

We can assign values to the record elements just as we did before with other structured data types. For example, the statements

```
STUDENT.NAME := 'MARY';

STUDENT.AVE := 88.2;

STUDENT.LETTER := 'B';
```

would assign the name MARY to the NAME field, 88.2 to the AVE field, and B to the LETTER field.

13.2 ARRAYS AS RECORD FIELDS

In the preceding example, we used the field AVE for the student's average. But we might have wanted to use the student's original test scores to determine the average instead. If we had five test scores, we could use a five-element array for the scores by making SCORES a record field:

```
INFO = RECORD
              :
              :
          SCORES: ARRAY [1..5] OF REAL;
              :
              :
       END;  (* RECORD *)
```

Since SCORES is an array, we have to include a subscript when accessing this record field. For example, if we want to refer to the second test score, we would use

```
STUDENT.SCORE[2]
```

The program in exhibit 13–1 (see p. 308) illustrates the use of an array as a record field.

13.3 RECORD HIERARCHIES—NESTED RECORDS

It is also possible to declare records which have a field of TYPE RECORD. This produces nested records, or records within records. For example,

```
TYPE
  DATA = RECORD
            AGE: INTEGER;
            SEX: CHAR;
          END;  (* RECORD DATA *)

  INFO = RECORD
            NAME: STRING;
            SCORES: ARRAY [1..5] OF REAL;
            AVE: REAL;
            LETTER: CHAR;
            OTHER: DATA
          END;  (* RECORD INFO *)

  VAR
    STUDENT:INFO;
```

declares a variable STUDENT of TYPE INFO, where INFO is a record with five fields. The fifth field, OTHER, is a record of TYPE DATA, which contains the fields AGE and SEX.

Exhibit 13–1. Program
RECDINFO

```
PROGRAM RECDINFO;

TYPE
  INFO = RECORD
              NAME: STRING;
              SCORES: ARRAY [1..5] OF REAL;
              AVE: REAL;
              LETTER: CHAR
          END;  (* RECORD *)

VAR
  STUDENT: INFO;
  I: INTEGER;
  SUM: REAL;

BEGIN  (* RECDINFO *)
  SUM := 0.0;
  WRITE ('NAME --> ');
  READLN (STUDENT.NAME);
  FOR I:= 1 TO 5 DO
    BEGIN  (* FOR..DO *)
      WRITE ('TEST ',I,'  ');
      READLN (STUDENT.SCORES[I]);
      SUM := SUM + STUDENT.SCORES[I]
    END;  (* FOR..DO *)
  STUDENT.AVE := SUM/5.0;
  WRITE ('AVE = ',STUDENT.AVE:8:2,'     G
  RADE = ');
  READ (STUDENT.LETTER);
  WRITELN;
  WRITELN;
  WRITELN (STUDENT.NAME:15,STUDENT.AVE:1
  0:2,        STUDENT.LETTER:5)
END.  (* RECDINFO *)
```

To specify a student's age, we would have to use both
suffixes

```
STUDENT.OTHER.AGE := 16;
```

It is possible to have several levels of hierarchial records, although some thought should go into the design of such records
to ensure ease of use.

13.4 ARRAYS OF RECORDS

Let's expand this example to include an entire class of students. We'll use the INFO record (name, test scores, average,
and letter grade) for each student and then declare a CLASS

record with information for twenty-five students in the class. We'll also declare a scalar data type SCIENCE containing BIOLOGY, CHEMISTRY, and PHYSICS. And finally, we'll declare a variable TERM to be an array of records (CLASS).

```
TYPE
  INFO = RECORD
            NAME: STRING;
            SCORES: ARRAY [1..5] OF REAL;
            AVE: REAL;
            LETTER: CHAR
         END;  (* RECORD INFO *)

  SCIENCE = (BIOLOGY,CHEMISTRY,PHSYICS);

  CLASS = RECORD
            SUBJECT: SCIENCE;
            STUDENT: ARRAY [1..25] OF INFO
         END;  (* RECORD CLASS *)

VAR
  TERM: ARRAY [SCIENCE] OF CLASS;
```

This means that TERM contains information on three classes, and that each class contains information on 25 students.

To refer to the records for a specific course, we would use a subscript identifying the appropriate course, for example

```
TERM[CHEMISTRY]
```

Similarly, information on the fifth student in the chemistry course could be referred to with

```
TERM[CHEMISTRY].STUDENT[5]
```

and the name of that student could be obtained through the somewhat lengthy identifier

```
TERM[CHEMISTRY].STUDENT[5].NAME
```

If we want to refer to this student's score on the second test we could use

```
TERM[CHEMISTRY].STUDENT[5].SCORES[2]
```

In this example, we have used not only an array of records, but also nested records and records with fields of arrays. As you can see, the record is a very powerful data type, since it allows us to combine many different data types into logical units.

Let's consider another example. Suppose we own a small repair shop with an inventory of ten different parts, each with a part name, a part number, a cost, and a quantity-on-hand figure. We want to (1) establish a record that will contain this information and (2) write a procedure that will give us the dollar value of our current inventory. We will concentrate on these two points and ignore the remainder of the program in this example.

Our inventory record will have four parts: a part name, a part number, a cost, and the quantity on hand. The part name will be a String, the part number and quantity on hand will both be Integer values, and the cost will be a Real value. We could declare this record with the following statement:

```
TYPE
   INVENTORY = RECORD
                 NAME : STRING;
                 PARTNO,QUANTITY : INTEGER;
                 COST : REAL
               END;
```

As in our previous example, this record would store all of the required data for one part, but not for all ten parts. We have two options: we could make each field an array of ten items, or we could use an array of records. We will use the second approach and declare PARTS to be

```
PARTS = ARRAY [1..10] OF INVENTORY;
```

To determine the value of our current inventory, we could simply sum the total investment in each part (the quantity on hand of each type of part multiplied by the cost per part). Our algorithm is fairly straightforward:

1. initialize sum to zero;
2. for each part: determine the value of those parts; add the value to the sum.

Refining the algorithm

1. initialize SUM = 0;
2. FOR each part:

```
VALUE := QUANTITY * COST;
SUM := SUM + VALUE.
```

We can then code the procedure itself.

```
PROCEDURE VALUATION (PTS:PARTS;VAR VAL:R
EAL);
   VAR
     I : INTEGER;
     PTVAL : REAL;
```

```
BEGIN  (* VALUATION *)
  VAL := 0.0;
  FOR I := 1 TO 10 DO
    BEGIN  (* FOR..DO *)
      PTVAL := PTS.QUANTITY[I] * PTS.COST[I];
      VAL := VAL + PTVAL
    END  (* FOR..DO *)
END;  (* VALUATION *)
```

Thus, PTS.QUANTITY[I] is the quantity of part I and PTS. COST[I] is the cost of part I. The array of records is passed to the procedure as a parameter, and the total inventory value, VAL, is returned to the main program as a variable parameter.

Could we have used a function rather than a procedure in this example? Yes, we could have, since we are returning only one value to the main program. In fact, using a function would be preferable to using a parameter (for purposes of form), although a parameter would work equally well. We could make this change by changing the procedure declaration statement to the function declaration

```
FUNCTION VALUE (PTS:PARTS):REAL;
```

and including the statement VALUE:= VAL immediately after END (* FOR..DO *).

13.5 THE WITH RECORD DO STATEMENT

As you may have noted in the previous examples, providing the proper record suffixes, e.g., TERM[CHEMISTRY].STUDENT[5]. SCORES[2] can be a tedious task, especially if you have numerous references to the record. Pascal gives us a way around this problem through the WITH..DO statement. The statement takes the form

```
WITH record name DO
  BEGIN
    field name ...
  END;
```

where *record name* is the identifier used as the record name and *field name* is the record field identifier (suffix). The WITH..DO Syntax Diagram is shown in figure 13–2. Any reference to the record within the WITH..DO statement omits the record name from the prefix.

Figure 13–2. WITH.. DO Syntax Diagram

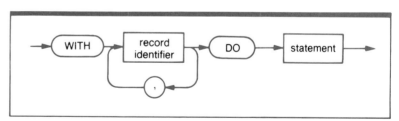

Returning to our example, the statement

```
TERM[CHEMISTRY].STUDENT[5].SCORE[2]
```

would take the form

```
WITH TERM[CHEMISTRY] DO
  BEGIN
    STUDENT[5].SCORES[2] := ...
  END;
```

You can see that this would be very useful if this variable was referred to frequently in a program segment. In this example, since the statement following the WITH..DO is not a compound statement, the BEGIN and END could be omitted.

WITH..DO Hierarchies—Nested WITH..DO Statements

Just as we can nest records within other records, we can nest WITH..DO statements within other WITH..DO statements to handle those nested records. We could alter the preceding example to include both prefixes in WITH..DO statement:

```
WITH TERM[CHEMISTRY] DO
  WITH STUDENT[I] DO
    BEGIN
      SCORES[J] := ...
    END;
```

It is even possible to shorten this statement further. Nested WITH..DO statements can be combined into a single statement. For example, the preceding statements could be rewritten as

```
WITH TERM[CHEM].STUDENT[I] DO
  BEGIN

    .
    .

  END;
```

or as

```
WITH TERM[CHEMISTRY],STUDENT[I] DO
  BEGIN

    .
    .

  END;
```

The only difference between these two forms is in the punctuation of the first line. The first form specifies that the prefix TERM[CHEMISTRY].STUDENT[I] will be used for each record field. The second form adds the prefixes TERM[CHEMISTRY] and STUDENT[I] to field identifiers as necessary, e.g., if we were referring to the field SUBJECT, only the prefix TERM [CHEMISTRY] would be added; if we were referring to the NAME field, however, both prefixes would be added. The second form can also be useful when we want to prefix two or more unique records. If we had two different record names, e.g., ONE and TWO, and each of these records contained a field named EXTENSION, which one would be referred to by the following nested WITH..DO statement? In this case it would be the second record (TWO).

```
WITH ONE, TWO DO
  BEGIN
    EXTENSION := 65
  END;
```

The value 65 would be assigned to the record TWO.EXTENTION. Whenever there are two or more records with the same field name, the record named last in the WITH..DO statement will be used. ■

13.6 BOOLEAN OPERATORS AND RECORDS

While logical (Boolean) comparisons can be made between elements of different records, it is also possible to compare complete records using the Boolean operators. If we have two records of identical type, e.g., ONE and TWO, we could use the statement

```
IF ONE = TWO THEN
```

to compare the complete records. If every value in every field of ONE is identical to the corresponding elements of TWO, this expression will evaluate to TRUE, otherwise it will evaluate to FALSE.

13.7 RECORD VARIANTS

When Niklaus Wirth designed Pascal, he also built in the ability to define **record variants**. A record variant allows a user to declare a record in such a manner that the number of fields and the data types of those fields can change during the execution of a program. Records can actually have two parts, a **fixed** part and a **variant** part. The fixed part does not change during execution of the program. The records we have used as examples thus far have all had only fixed parts, i.e., fields that did not change. While records can have both fixed and variant parts, we will first consider an example where a record has only variant parts.

Record variants are created by including a CASE..OF statement within the record declaration statement. The following TYPE and variable declaration statements illustrate the creation of a record variant:

```
TYPE
  SIZE = (SMALL, MEDIUM, LARGE);
  AMOUNT = RECORD
              CASE MARK:SIZE OF         (*
              TAG FIELD *)
                SMALL: (TINY:ARRAY [1..5]
                OF INTEGER);
                MEDIUM: (MID:ARRAY [1..20
                ] OF INTEGER);
                LARGE: (BIG:ARRAY [1..100
                ] OF REAL)
              END;

VAR
  MEASURE : AMOUNT;
```

In this example the field MARK (of type SIZE) is known as a **tag** field. It is used to tag the correct variant field. Thus, if MEASURE.MARK := SMALL, the record field TINY, an array of five elements, will be tagged, and we could make assignments such as MEASURE.TINY[2] := 4; If MEASURE.MARK := MEDIUM, then the MID field would be tagged, and we might make the assignment MEASURE.MID[18] := 21. And finally, if MEASURE.MARK := LARGE, then the BIG field would be tagged and the assignment MEASURE.BIG[87] := 3.27 could be made. Note that not only are the fields of different size, but they are of different type as well; TINY and MID are Integer and BIG is a Real type.

You should also note that there is not a separate END for the CASE..OF, as there would normally be. The END that marks the end of the RECORD..OF statement also marks the end of the CASE..OF. Thus, the variant part of a record must be the last field declared. Fixed fields are always listed first, followed by the variant fields. Pascal allows only one variant field in a record.

Because the size and type of the record field is determined during the program execution, a value must be assigned to the tag field. And care must be taken to insure that no assignments are made to a variant record field that has not been tagged.

13.8 PACKED RECORDS

Apple Pascal allows us to create **packed records** to save memory space, just as we did with arrays. The declaration is similar to that of the packed array; instead of declaring an identifier to be a record, we declare it to be a packed record, for example

```
TYPE
  ONE = PACKED RECORD
                  FIRST : BOOLEAN;
                  SECOND : BOOLEAN;
                  THIRD : PACKED ARRAY [1
                  ..5] OF CHAR
                END;
```

Whenever a field of a packed record is an array or a record, however, it begins at the next word in memory. (A **word**, like the terms bit and byte, is a unit of measurement. A byte is made up of eight bits, and a word contains two bytes or 16 bits of memory.) Thus, even though the Boolean values in fields FIRST and SECOND occupy only two bits, THIRD will begin at the next word, leaving 14 bits unoccupied.

When using Pascal, memory space should **not** be your primary concern, i.e., it is not normally necessary to pack arrays or records whenever possible. This topic was introduced simply to inform you that you have the option, should you ever need it.

13.9 MODIFYING THE GRADING PROGRAM—AGAIN

We can now include records in the program we have been developing for Mr. Matthews. Mr. Matthews noticed that one of our examples had a record field with letter grades, so he would now like his program to incorporate that feature as well, along with the function or procedure necessary to determine the letter grade. We'll work on this procedure or function first.

In chapter 8 we developed a program that assigned letter grades using a number of IF..THEN loops. Although that approach is probably the easiest one for this problem, we will illustrate an alternative method here. The alternative is effective in this problem because of the manner in which Mr. Matthews determines his grades: 95 and up is an A, 85 and up a B, and so on. If we do not use IF..THEN statements, the logical alternative is the CASE..OF statement. Although we could use

```
CASE GRADES[4] OF
  100,99,98,97,96,95 : LETTER := 'A';
  94,93,92,91,90,89,88,87,86,85 : LETTER := 'B'
        (* AND SO ON *)
```

we'll modify this statement slightly. Notice that each grade break occurs in the middle of the 90s, 80s, and so forth. Thus, if we were to round each value to the nearest tens value (e.g., round 78 to 80, 93 to 90, and so on), we could use the CASE statement with the rounded values. Or we could divide each value by ten and use the values 10, 9, 8, 7, and below 7 to determine the letter grades. We can actually simplify the process by dividing the grade values by ten first and then rounding the results to the nearest integer value. We'll create a new variable TEMP (temporary) and make the assignment

```
TEMP := ROUND (GRADES[4] / 10);
```

We can then use the CASE..OF statement

```
CASE TEMP OF
   10 : LETTER := 'A';
    9 : LETTER := 'B';
      (* AND SO ON *)
```

But instead of using the statement

```
0,1,2,3,4,5,6 : LETTER := 'F'
```

we will make the assignment LETTER := 'F'; prior to the CASE statement and then just end the CASE..OF after the D grade:

```
    7 : LETTER := 'D'
END;
```

Thus we are now assigning every student an F grade initially, and then using the CASE statement to alter that grade for each student with a numerical grade above 65.

As we have said before, this solution is not the only approach, nor is it necessarily the best one. But it is a slightly different approach, and it therefore provides another example that you may find useful in the future.

Now let's go on to the actual program (we S(aved it under the name GRADEMAT in chapter 12). We'll change the name of the program from GRADEMAT to GRADEREC. We will again take a slightly different approach from the example used earlier in the chapter, where we declared an array of records that contained all the records for three classes, BIOLOGY, CHEMISTRY, and PHYSICS. We will now create a record for each student; each record will contain the student's name, grades, and letter grade. We will then create an array of student records for each class. This time, instead of using an array with one record for each class, we will use only one record. When we have finished the calculations for one class, we will use the same record for the next class (since we have no need to save the data for all three classes).

As you review the new program, you will notice that we added the same WITH..DO statement to many of the procedures. You may wonder why we didn't just use one WITH..DO statement in the body of the main program before calling the procedures; we cannot do this, because the compiler would not recognize the field identifiers in the procedures without their prefixes (remember that the procedures are compiled first). You will also note that we have changed some of the record and variable identifiers from the previous examples. The modified program is shown in exhibit 13–2 in its entirety.

Exhibit 13–2. Program GRADEREC

```
PROGRAM GRADEREC;

CONST
  WGTNOTES = 0.20;
  WGTPROJ  = 0.30;
  WGTFINAL = 0.50;
  CLASSSIZE = 25;   (* TWO ROWS INCLUDED
FOR SUMS *)

TYPE
  SCIENCE = (BIOLOGY, CHEMISTRY, PHYSICS);

  STUDENT = RECORD
              NAME: STRING;
              GRADES: ARRAY [1..4] OF RE
AL;
              LETTER: CHAR
            END;

  GRADEBOOK = RECORD
                CLASS: ARRAY[1..CLASSIZE]
                  OF STUDENT
                END;

VAR
  RECDS: GRADEBOOK;
  CNAME: STRING;
  CH: CHAR;
  I, J, NUM, TEMP: INTEGER;
  COURSE: SCIENCE;

FUNCTION GRADE (N,P,F:REAL):REAL;
  BEGIN
    GRADE := WGTNOTES * N + WGTPROJ * P
      + WGTFINAL * F;
  END; (* GRADE FUNCTION *)
```

Exhibit 13–2.
Continued

```
PROCEDURE ENTRY (VAR CNTR:INTEGER);

  PROCEDURE ERROR;
    VAR
      ANS:CHAR;
    BEGIN  (* ERROR *)
      WRITE('ERRORS (Y/N)?');
      READ (ANS);  WRITELN;
      IF ANS = 'Y' THEN
        BEGIN (* CORRECTION *)
          WRITELN ('[N] NOTES  [P] PROJE
          CT  [F] FINAL', CHR(13),
              'ENTER LETTER  (N, P OR F)');
          READ (ANS);
          WRITELN;
          CASE ANS OF
            'N': I := 1;
            'P': I := 2;
            'F': I := 3
          END;
          WRITE ('ENTER CORRECT VALUE ->');
          READLN (RECDS.CLASS[CNTR].GRAD
          ES[I]);
          ERROR
        END (* CORRECTION *)
    END; (* ERROR *)

  BEGIN  (* ENTRY *)
    WRITELN;
    CNTR := CNTR + 1;
    WRITE ('ENTER A NAME AND TYPE RETURN
    :');
    WITH RECDS.CLASS[CNTR] DO
      BEGIN
        READLN (NAME);
        IF NAME () '' THEN
          BEGIN  (* IF..THEN *)
            WRITELN;
            WRITE ('NOTES ->');
            READLN (GRADES[1]);
            WRITE ('PROJECT ->');
            READLN (GRADES[2]);
            WRITE ('FINAL ->');
            READLN (GRADES[3]);
            WRITELN
          END  (* IF .. THEN *)
      END; (* WITH .. DO *)
    ERROR
  END; (* ENTRY *)
```

Exhibit 13–2.
Continued

```
PROCEDURE CALCULATE (LIMIT:INTEGER);
  BEGIN
    WITH RECDS DO
      BEGIN  (* WITH..DO *)
        FOR I := 1 TO LIMIT DO
          BEGIN  (* FOR LOOP *)
            WITH CLASS[I] DO
              GRADES[4] := GRADE(GRADES[
              1],GRADES[2],GRADES[3]);
              FOR J := 1 TO 4 DO  (* SUMS
              EACH COLUMN *)
                CLASS[24].GRADES[J]:=CLASS
                [24] GRADES[J]+CLASS[I].GR
                ADES[J];
          END;  (* FOR LOOP *)
        FOR I := 1 TO 4 DO  (* COMPUTES
        AVERAGES *)
          IF LIMIT = 0 THEN
            CLASS[25].GRADES[I] := CLASS
            [24].GRADES[I]/LIMIT
          ELSE
            CLASS[25].GRADES[I] := 0
      END  (* WITH .. DO *)
  END;  (* CALCULATE *)

PROCEDURE WRITEOUT (LIMIT:INTEGER);
  VAR
    S:INTEGER;
  BEGIN  (* WRITEOUT *)
    WRITELN;
    WRITELN ('   NAME      NOTES PROJECT
    FINAL  GRADE');
    WRITELN ('     ----       ----- -------
    -----  -----');
    WITH RECDS DO
      BEGIN
        FOR S := 1 TO LIMIT DO
          WITH CLASS[S] DO
            WRITELN (NAME:10,GRADES[1]:7
            :1,GRADES[2]:7:1,GRADES[3]:7
            :1,GRADES[4]:7:1,LETTER:2);
        WRITELN;
        WITH CLASS[25] DO
          WRITELN ('  AVERAGE ',GRADES
          [1]:7:1,GRADES[27]:7:1,GRAD
          ES[3]:7:1,GRADES[4]:7:1);
      END  (* WITH RECDS.. DO *)
  END;  (* WRITEOUT *)
```

Exhibit 13–2.
Continued

```
PROCEDURE ABCDF;
  BEGIN
    WITH RECDS.SUBJECT[COURSE] DO
      BEGIN  (* WITH..DO *)
        FOR I := 1 TO NUM DO
          BEGIN  (* FOR..DO *)
            WITH CLASS[I] DO
              BEGIN  (* WITH..DO *)
                LETTER := 'F';
                TEMP := ROUND (GRADES[4]
                /10);
                CASE TEMP OF
                  10: LETTER := 'A';
                   9: LETTER := 'B';
                   8: LETTER := 'C';
                   7: LETTER := 'D'
                END  (* CASE *)
              END  (* WITH CLASS[] DO*)
          END  (* FOR..DO *)
      END  (* WITH RECDS DO *)
  END;  (* ABCDF *)

BEGIN  (* GRADEREC *)
  FOR COURSE := BIOLOGY TO PHYSICS DO
    BEGIN  (* FOR..DO *)
      CASE COURSE OF
        BIOLOGY: CNAME := 'BIOLOGY';
        CHEMISTRY: CNAME := 'CHEMISTRY';
        PHYSICS: CNAME := 'PHYSICS'
      END;  (* CASE..OF *)
      NUM := 0;
      FOR I := 1 TO 4 DO
        RECDS.CLASS[24].GRADES[I] := 0;
      WRITELN;
      WRITELN ('GRADES FOR ',CNAME,' CLA
SS');
      WRITELN;
      REPEAT
        ENTRY(NUM)
      UNTIL RECDS.CLASS[NUM].NAME = '';
      NUM := NUM - 1;
      CALCULATE(NUM);
      PAGE(OUTPUT);
      WRITELN;
      WRITELN ('GRADES FOR ',CNAME);
      WRITEOUT(NUM)
    END  (* FOR..DO *)
END.  (* GRADEREC *)
```

Make the necessary changes to the GRADEMAT program and then compile, run, and test it. Once you have it running properly, save it under the name GRADEREC.

13.10 SUMMARY

In this chapter, we have learned about a new structured data type, the record, which allows us to combine or group different data types together. Each component of a record is called a field. We declare records and their fields through the TYPE statement. We also learned that records can have fixed or variant fields; the variant part of a record, declared using the CASE..OF, allows the record to vary in size depending on a value that can be determined during execution of the program.

Records are referred to in a program by using the record variable identifier and the field name separated by a period. Since it is possible to have a record within a record (a field of one record is declared to have the type of another record), it may be necessary to specify more than one field suffix to refer to a particular component of a record. It is also possible to have arrays as record fields, or even arrays of records. In these cases, a subscript is also required to reference the proper element of the array. We saw, however, that the Pascal WITH..DO statement allows us to drop common record or field prefixes when we refer to records. When prefixes are included in the WITH.. DO, Pascal automatically adds them to any field identifiers used in the body of the statement.

Review Questions

1. What is a record?

2. What advantage does the record offer over other data types?

3. What is the form of the record declaration?

4. Can a record have a structured field? Explain.

5. What is a nested record? Give an example.

6. Explain the difference between an array of records and a record of arrays.

7. How do we assign values to record variables? Give an example.

8. What is the purpose of the WITH..DO statement? Give an example of its use.

9. Can records be used in Boolean expressions? Explain.

10. What is a record variant?

11. What is a tag field?

12. What is a packed record?

SUMMARY of Pascal Syntax

Reserved Words	Built-in Procedures	Built-in Functions	Library Units
PROGRAM	WRITE	ABS	TURTLEGRAPHICS
USES	WRITELN	SQR	APLESTUFF
CONST	READ	SQRT	TRANSCEND
TYPE	READLN	ROUND	
SET..OF		TRUNC	
PACKED		EXP	
ARRAY[..]OF	INITTURTLE	LN	
RECORD	PENCOLOR	LOG	
VAR	MOVE	PWROFTEN	
FUNCTION	TURN	ATAN	
FORWARD		SIN	
PROCEDURE	MOVETO	COS	
	TURNTO	ORD	*Boolean*
BEGIN	TEXTMODE	CHR	*Constants*
	GRAFMODE	PRED	
FOR..DO	PAGE(OUTPUT)	SUCC	FALSE
TO		EOLN	TRUE
DOWNTO			
REPEAT			
UNTIL			
WHILE..DO			
IF			
THEN			
ELSE			
CASE..OF			
WITH..DO			
END			
DIV			*Integer*
MOD			*Constants*
NIL			
AND			
OR			
NOT			
IN			

1. Declare a record ONE with an Integer field and a Boolean field.

2. Declare a record TWO with two fields, one Integer and one an array of ten Real numbers.

3. Declare a record DATA that will contain an individual's name, city address, age, sex, and rate of pay.

4. Declare a record PLAYER which will contain a baseball player's name, team, age, and batting average for each of the past five seasons.

5. Declare a record DEPT that will contain the department name and number (4 digits) and DATA records (see exercise 3) for twenty people.

6. Declare a variable WORK to be of type DEPT (see exercise 5), and then write the necessary statements to assign the department number 1234 to the department and an age of 35 to the second worker in the department.

7. Modify the assignment statements in exercise 6 to show the proper use of a WITH..DO statement.

8. Write a record declaration with a variant field SIZE of type Integer. When SIZE is 1, declare a field ONE (Integer) and when SIZE is 2, declare a field TWO (Real).

9. Some of the following declarations are correct and some are incorrect. If a statement(s) is incorrect, correct it. Then explain or describe the variable REC.

a. ```
TYPE
   NAME = RECORD
             LNAME: STRING;
             INITIAL: CHAR
             END;
 VAR
    REC: LNAME;
```

b. ```
TYPE
   DATA = RECORD
             ITEM: STRING;
             INSTOCK: BOOLEAN;
             QUANTITY: INTEGER
             END;
 VAR
    REC: ARRAY[1..10] OF DATA;
```

```
c. TYPE
     SUBJECT = (MATH, HISTORY, ENGLISH);
     DATA = RECORD
               CLASS: SUBJECT;
               SUPPLIES = RECORD
                               BOOKS: INTEGER;
                               EXAMS: ARRAY[1..
                               5] OF INTEGER
                          END;
               TEACHER:STRING
            END;
   VAR
     REC: DATA;


d. TYPE
     DATA = RECORD
               ITEM: STRING;
               QUANTITY: ARRAY[1..10] OF INTEGER
            END;
   VAR
     REC: ARRAY[1..5] OF DATA;


e. TYPE
     CATEGORY = (FICTION,NONFICT);
     BOOK = RECORD
               AUTHOR: STRING[20];
               TITLE: STRING;
               CASE CATEGORY OF
                  FICTION: ADVENTURE:BOOLEAN;
                  NONFICT: (BIOG:BOOLEAN;
                            SUBJ:PACKED ARRAY
                            [1..20] OF CHAR)
            END;
     SHELF: ARRAY[1..50] OF BOOK;
   VAR
     CAT:CATEGORY;
     REC: SHELF;
```

10. Is the following declaration acceptable? Why or why not?

```
TYPE
  PART1 = RECORD
             ITEM,
             QUANTITY: INTEGER
          END;
  PART2 = RECORD
             ITEM,
             QUANTITY: INTEGER
             PRICE: REAL
          END;
VAR
  REC1:PART1;
  REC2:PART2;
```

11. Given the declaration in exercise 10, is each of these segments correct? If not, why not?
a. (1) `PART1.ITEM := 43;`
   (2) `REC1: QUANTITY := 37.0;`
   (3) `REC2.ITEM := 56;`
   (4) `REC2.PART2.PRICE := 12.95;`
b. (1) `WITH REC1. DO`
       `ITEM := 14;`
   (2) `WITH REC2.ITEM DO`
       `ITEM := 26;`
   (3) `WITH REC1,REC2 DO`
       `QUANTITY := 108;`
   (4) `WITH REC1,REC2 DO`
       `PRICE := 14.50;`
   (5) `REC1.PRICE := 8.95;`
   (6) `REC2.QUANTITY := REC1.QUANTITY;`

12. Given the declarations in exercise 9(e), are the following statements correct? If so, what do they do?
a. `REC.AUTHOR := 'DANIELS, G.B.';`
b. `REC.SHELF[12].FICTION := TRUE;`
c. `CAT := FICTION;`
   `REC.SHELF[50].CATEGORY := TRUE;`
d. `CAT := NONFICT;`
   `REC.[2].SUBJ := 'BIOGRAPHY';`
e. `WITH REC DO`
      `TITLE := 'REPAIRING YOUR OWN COMPUTER';`
f. `WITH SHELF[I] DO`
      `AUTHOR := 'MERTZ, JAMES L.';`
g. `WITH REC[I] DO`
      `AUTHOR := 'ANON';`
h. `CAT := FICTION;`
   `WITH REC.SHELF[I] DO`
      `ADVENTURE := TRUE;`
i. `CAT := FICTION;`
   `WITH REC, SHELF[I] DO`
      `SUBJ[6] := 'G';`

Problems

13. A trucking company has a fleet of trucks consisting of 9 five ton trucks, 15 ten ton trucks, and 4 twenty ton trucks. The company wishes to have the following information available on each truck: its license number, weight capacity, and the hours on the road since the last service work was performed. Declare the necessary record and variable(s) to store this information.

14. Write a procedure which provides the license number of each truck, and then reads the number of hours on the road this week and adds it to the total hours since service. If the total number of hours exceeds 750, a warning message should be issued.

15. In chapter 5 we calculated the floor area of square and round rooms so that we could determine carpet costs. We now wish to use the following information on three types of carpeted rooms: shape (square, round, or rectangular), dimensions (side, radius, or length and width), area, and carpet cost. Declare a record which would contain the necessary information for one room.

16. Declare a variable FLOOR which will contain the data from problem 15 for ten rooms.

17. Write a program segment using a WITH..DO statement which will calculate the area of all rectangular rooms.

14 Files

In the last chapter, we learned how to create structured data types called records. Records allow us to combine any quantity or type of data we want into logical units. But we cannot store records permanently; when we turn the computer off, all the information stored in records is erased from the computer's memory. In this chapter, we will learn how to save data in **files** on our disks. Then we will learn how to retrieve the data from the files so that our programs can use it.

14.1 FILES

Whenever we save programs using the S(ave or W(rite option, they are saved in **files** on the disk. Those files are given the suffixes TEXT or CODE. We can also create a third type of file, the **DATA** file, to store data we want to use in a program.

Declaring a File Variable

To save data to a file, however, we must first declare a **file variable**. We do this by declaring a variable in a FILE OF statement. This declaration statement takes the form

file identifier : `FILE OF` *data type;*

where *file identifier* is the name given to the file, the reserved words FILE OF declare this variable to be a file, and *data type* tells the computer what type of data will be stored in the file. The FILE OF syntax diagram appears in Figure 14–1.

File Buffer

Whenever we declare a variable using the FILE OF statement, the computer creates a variable called a **file buffer** variable. This variable serves as a transfer point between the values in the computer's memory and the disk file. The file buffer is simply a memory buffer that is used for temporary storage of information that is being written to or read from a disk. Thus, when we read data from a disk file to memory, the data goes first to the file buffer, and when we write data to a file on a disk, the data is taken from the file buffer. The file buffer variable is distinguished from other variables by a circumflex (^) immediately after the variable identifier, e.g., X represents a normal variable, while X^ represents a file buffer variable.

Figure 14–1. FILE OF
Syntax Diagram

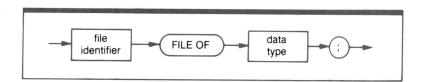

We have referred to writing data to and reading it from a file. These actions, while similar, are distinct and will be introduced separately in the following sections.

14.2 WRITING DATA TO A FILE

Let's look at a simple example. This program uses a FOR..DO loop to input 5 values:

```
PROGRAM PUTFILE;

VAR
  NUMBER,I: INTEGER;

BEGIN  (* PUTFILE *)
  FOR I:= 1 TO 5 DO
    BEGIN  (* FOR..DO *)
      WRITE ('ENTER NUMBER ');
      READLN (NUMBER)
    END  (* FOR..DO *)
END.  (* PUTFILE *)
```

As you can see, this program simply prompts for and then reads five values. There is nothing fancy about it; it doesn't even write the numbers back to the screen. We will modify this simple example so that it will write data (the five values) to a file on the system disk. We will begin our modifications by adding the variable declaration

```
DF: FILE OF INTEGER;
```

This statement tells the computer that we are declaring DF to be a variable of type file containing Integer values. We will then add the statement

```
REWRITE (DF, 'DFILE.DATA');
```

This line tells the computer to open a file on the disk named DFILE.DATA, and that this file will be associated with the variable DF. REWRITE tells the computer that data will be written to this file. Since we did not specify a disk volume name, the system disk (Apple0: or Apple1:) is used as the default. If we wanted to have our file written to some other disk, we would specify the disk name as well, e.g. 'STORAGE:DFILE. DATA'.

We will now add the lines

```
DF^ := NUMBER;
PUT(DF)
```

The first line assigns the value of variable NUMBER to the file buffer variable DF. Remember, the arrow pointing upward (^)

after the identifier DF is called a circumflex and is used to tell the computer that the identifier (DF) refers to the file buffer variable for the file variable DF. Thus, the value of NUMBER is placed in the file buffer DF^. The second line tells the computer to PUT the value currently contained in the file buffer onto the disk file. PUT is a reserved word that is similar to WRITELN; but PUT writes the file buffer variable to the disk.

The final line we will add to the program is

```
CLOSE (DF,LOCK)
```

This line closes the file referenced by file variable DF, which was opened by REWRITE. The word **LOCK** tells the computer this is a permanent file that should be saved at the termination of the program. If the word LOCK is not included, the file will be treated as a temporary or "scratch" file and deleted when it is closed. The entire program should now look like this:

```
PROGRAM PUTFILE;

VAR
  NUMBER,I: INTEGER;
  DF: FILE OF INTEGER;

BEGIN  (* PUTFILE *)
  REWRITE (DF,'DFILE.DATA');
  FOR I:= 1 TO 5 DO
    BEGIN  (* FOR..DO *)
      WRITE ('ENTER NUMBER ');
      READLN (NUMBER);
      DF^  := NUMBER;
      PUT (DF)
    END;  (* FOR..DO *)
  CLOSE (DF,LOCK)
END.  (* PUTFILE *)
```

Enter, compile, and run the program. When you are prompted for the five values, enter 101, 102, 103, 104, and 105. You may have noticed that when you ran the program and input the numbers, the computer did not write to the disk between each entry. The computer was simply being efficient; the five entries did not begin to fill the file buffer, so the computer waited until the CLOSE instruction and then wrote all five entries onto the disk at one time. If you now move to the Filer and L(ist the directory for the system disk, you will see the file DFILE.DATA, which occupies 1 block of disk space.

14.3 READING DATA FROM A FILE ▬▬▬▬▬▬▬▬▬

Once we have entered data into a file, we want to be able to access it later. We'll now modify our program to access the five integer values stored in DFILE. Make the necessary changes so that the program matches the one shown in exhibit 14–1:

Exhibit 14–1. Program
GETFILE

```
PROGRAM GETFILE;

VAR
  I,J: INTEGER;
  DF: FILE OF INTEGER;

BEGIN  (* GETFILE *)
  RESET (DF, 'DFILE.DATA');
  FOR I := 1 TO 5 DO
    BEGIN  (* FOR..DO *)
      J := DF^ ;
      GET (DF);
      WRITELN (J)
    END;  (* FOR..DO *)
  CLOSE (DF)
END.  (* GETFILE *)
```

In addition to changing the name of the program from PUTFILE to GETFILE, we substituted the word RESET for REWRITE. Just as REWRITE opens a file so that we can write data to it, RESET opens a file so that we can read data from it. We then reversed the assignment statement so that the variable J was assigned the value of the file buffer variable. GET replaced PUT and does exactly what you might expect it to do; it gets the next value from the disk and moves it to the buffer variable. The CLOSE statement was modified to remove the LOCK parameter. Since the file is already a permanent file, all we have to do is close it; LOCK is unnecessary when we use RESET and GET data from a file.

Compile and run the program. If you made no errors, you should see the numbers 101, 102, 103, 104, and 105 appear on the screen. Let's take a closer look at how the program works. After using RESET to open the file, we assigned J the value of the buffer variable and then used GET to move the next value into DF^. Notice that although we did not use GET before assigning the value of DF^ to J, the correct value (101) was output. How did this happen? It happens because two things actually occur when we use RESET to open the file. First, the file is opened, and second, a GET is performed to move the first value in the file into the buffer (DF^). Thus RESET opened the file and put the value 101 in DF^. The assignment statement then assigned J the value 101. When the GET(DF) statement was then executed, the next value (102) was moved to DF^. The loop was then repeated, J was assigned the value 102 and GET moved the third value (103) into DF^. The process is easy to follow up until the last execution of the loop: J is assigned the value 105, but what value is moved to DF^ when the last GET is executed? The answer is the EOF (end of file) marker.

14.4 EOF

When you were learning to enter program lines in the Editor, you learned that there was an EOLN (end of line) character at the end of every line, even though we could not see it. There is a similar character (marker) called the EOF marker at the end of every file. Although we cannot see it, the computer can. We will see how to use this feature in a moment.

If we modify the GETFILE program to the form shown in exhibit 14–2, will it still work? The answer is yes. The basic difference between this program and the original one is that the loop is only repeated four times, so only four GET statements are executed. But since the RESET also did a GET, we will retrieve a total of five values from the disk.

This program will work, but its control structure is a little clumsy and very dependent upon our remembering how many numbers we entered originally. You may remember from chapter 7 that we can enter a dummy value, e.g., 9999, as our last value and then repeat a loop until this value is read. We can do the same sort of thing here, but we don't have to enter a dummy value to mark the end of our real data. The EOF mark can be used for that purpose. And since we don't want to read any data past the EOF mark, we will use the WHILE..DO rather than the REPEAT..UNTIL. Modify the program again to the form shown in exhibit 14–3 and try running it. Becuase the RESET moves the first value to DF^, the WHILE statement will evaluate NOT EOF(DF). If the value in DF^ is not the EOF marker, the loop will be executed. Note that whenever we use the file buffer variable as a parameter, we do *not* include the circumflex.

Exhibit 14–2. Program GETFILE

```
PROGRAM GETFILE;

VAR
  I,J: INTEGER;
  DF: FILE OF INTEGER;

BEGIN  (* GETFILE *)
  RESET (DF, 'DFILE.DATA');
  FOR I := 1 TO 4 DO
    BEGIN  (* FOR..DO *)
      J := DF^ ;
      GET (DF);
      WRITELN (J)
    END;  (* FOR..DO *)
    J := DF^ ;
    WRITELN (J)
  CLOSE (DF)
END.  (* GETFILE *)
```

Exhibit 14–3. Program
GETFILE

```
PROGRAM GETFILE;

VAR
  I,J: INTEGER;
  DF: FILE OF INTEGER;

BEGIN  (* GETFILE *)
  RESET (DF, 'DFILE.DATA');
  WHILE NOT EOF(DF) DO
    BEGIN  (* WHILE..DO *)
      J := DF^ ;
      GET (DF);
      WRITELN (J)
    END;  (* WHILE..DO *)
  CLOSE (DF)
END.  (* GETFILE *)
```

14.5 FILES WITH ARRAYS AND RECORDS

When we save data to a disk, we usually save the values associated with a declared variable. If we declare our file buffer variable to be a FILE OF a structured data type, e.g., an array, set, or record, all elements of the data type can be assigned to the file buffer and then PUT to the disk at one time. The following program illustrates this with an array.

```
PROGRAM PUTARRAY;

TYPE
  TABLE = ARRAY [1..5,1..5] OF INTEGER;

VAR
  I,J: INTEGER;
  MAT: TABLE;
  DA: FILE OF TABLE;

BEGIN  (* PUTARRAY *)
  REWRITE (DA,'DARRAY.DATA');
  FOR I:= 1 TO 5 DO
    FOR J:= 1 TO 5 DO
      MAT[I,J] := I * 10 + J;
  DA^ := MAT;
  PUT (DA);
  CLOSE (DA,LOCK)
END.  (* PUTARRAY *)
```

The program first creates a 5 by 5 matrix and assigns values to each element. It then assigns all of the values in the array to the file buffer DA^ a, and PUTs them to the disk.

To recover the matrix values saved by this program, we could simply change the main body of the program as follows:

```
BEGIN  (* PUTARRAY *)
  RESET (DA,'DARRAY.DATA');
  MAT := DA^ ;
  FOR I:= 1 TO 5 DO
    BEGIN          (* LOOP TO WRITE MATRIX
    ELEMENTS *)
      FOR J := 1 TO 5 DO
        WRITE (MAT[I,J]:6);
      WRITELN
    END;           (* LOOP WRITING MATRIX
    ELEMENTS *)
  CLOSE (DA,LOCK)
END.  (* PUTARRAY *)
```

Enter, compile, and run each of these programs to verify that the data is saved by the first program and recovered by the second.

Now let's look at a set of programs that deal with records. In this example, we will use a record containing Integer, Real, and String values. The program that creates the file is shown in exhibit 14–4. The program is fairly straightforward. We declare a record (MIXED) containing the three different data types and then declare the variable ONE to be an array of MIXED. We also declare the file buffer variable TWO to be a FILE OF an ARRAY [1..5] OF MIXED. After all of the elements of ONE are entered, they are read through a series of READLN statements, then we assign the values contained in the array ONE to the file buffer array TWO^ and PUT those values to the file.

When you have entered this program, compile it and run it with the following data

```
11   12.12FILE
22   22.22OF AN
33   32.32ARRAY
44   42.42 OF
55   52.52RECORDS
```

S(ave the program (if you wish) under the name PUT-RECORD, then return to the Editor and change it to the program in exhibit 14–5. In the program GETRECORD, we use RESET to open the file and then assign all of the array elements from the file buffer to the array ONE. Compile and run this program to ensure that it reads all of the records back out

Exhibit 14–4. Program
PUTRECORD

```
PROGRAM PUTRECORD;

TYPE
  MIXED = RECORD
             I:INTEGER;
             R:REAL;
             S:STRING
           END;

VAR
  ONE: ARRAY[1..5] OF MIXED;
  TWO: FILE OF ARRAY[1..5] OF MIXED;
  J:INTEGER;

BEGIN  (* PUTRECORD *)
  REWRITE(TWO,'FREC.DATA');
  WRITELN ('ENTER INTEGER,  REAL & STRING
VALUES');
  FOR J := 1 TO 5 DO
    READLN (ONE[J].I,ONE[J].R,ONE[J].S);
  TWO^ := ONE;
  PUT(TWO);
  CLOSE (TWO,LOCK)
END.  (* PUTRECORD *)
```

Exhibit 14–5. Program
GETRECORD

```
PROGRAM GETRECORD;

TYPE
  MIXED = RECORD
             I:INTEGER;
             R:REAL;
             S:STRING
           END;

VAR
  ONE: ARRAY[1..5] OF MIXED;
  TWO: FILE OF ARRAY[1..5] OF MIXED;
  J:INTEGER;

BEGIN  (* GETRECORD *)
  RESET(TWO,'FREC.DATA');
  ONE := TWO^ ;
  FOR J := 1 TO 5 DO
    WRITELN(ONE[J].I,ONE[J].R,ONE[J].S);
  CLOSE (TWO)
END  (* GETRECORD *)
```

of the file correctly. You can then S(ave it under the name GETRECORD. (You may want to check the available space on your system disk and T(ransfer some of these files to your STORAGE: disk if you are running out of space on your system disk. You should use K(runch from time to time to ensure that you have the maximum number of adjacent free blocks on the disk.)

14.6 THE SEEK OPTION

In all of the data files we have created, the data has been stored in those files in **sequential** order. That means that the first item sent to the disk is stored in position 1 in the file, the second item in position 2, and so on. When data is read back out of the file, it is also read in sequential order. Thus, when we use RESET to open a file and it does a GET, it gets the first item in the file. Then, whenever another GET is performed, the next item in the file is read, i.e., the second, and then the third, and so on. If we want to use the data stored in the fifth position in the file, we must read the data in the first four positions first (the fourth GET would access the data we want). So that we don't have to loop through a series of GET statements to reach the data we want, UCSD Pascal provides us with a special command, the SEEK statement, which can be used to move the file buffer variable to the appropriate position in the file. The SEEK statement has the form:

SEEK *(filename, fileposition)*;

where *filename* is the file variable identifier and *fileposition* refers to the sequential position of the data we want. When you use the SEEK statement, you must remember that the first data set in the file is considered to be at position 0 (zero). Thus, if you want to access the data in the tenth position, you would use 9 for the *fileposition*. We can use our DFILE.DATA file to test this. Enter, compile, and run the program in exhibit 14–6.

Notice that we do GET immediately after we do a SEEK. This is because SEEK moves the file buffer to the correct position, but it does *not* get the data. Therefore, we must include a GET statement after each SEEK. Because an entire element of a file is transferred to the file buffer each time the computer does a GET, the SEEK statement can be extremely useful when dealing with data stored in records.

Since the values in the data file we are using are numbered sequentially, i.e., 101, ... 105, it should be fairly easy to test the program to make sure it works properly. Once you have run the program and made sure it works to your satisfaction, you can S(ave it or simply clear the workfile.

Exhibit 14–6. Program
SEEKER

```
PROGRAM SEEKER;

VAR
   I,J,K: INTEGER;
   DF: FILE OF INTEGER;

BEGIN  (* SEEKER *)
   RESET (DF,'DFILE.DATA');
   WHILE NOT EOF(DF) DO
     BEGIN  (* VERIFICATION LOOP *)
       J := DF^ ;
       WRITELN (J);
       GET (DF)
     END;  (* VERIFICATION LOOP *)
   FOR I := 1 TO 5 DO
     BEGIN  (* SEEKING LOOP *)
       WRITE ('ENTER POSITION NUMBER -> ');
       READLN (J);
       SEEK (DF,J);
       GET (DF);
       K := DF^ ;
       WRITELN ('POSITION ',J,' DATA = ',K)
     END;  (* SEEKING LOOP *)
   CLOSE (DF)
END.  (* SEEKER *)
```

Because SEEK merely specifies the next position in the file to be accessed, SEEK can also be used before a PUT statement, e.g., if you want to replace one element in the file with new data, you could use SEEK to move to the correct position and then use PUT to overwrite the old values with new ones. Thus you can retrieve or alter any data in the file without having to read or rewrite the entire file (but you must know the sequential location of the data involved).

While the SEEK statement gives you flexibility when working with data stored in files, you should remember that SEEK only locates the proper sequential element in the file. You should never use two consecutive SEEK statements without a GET or PUT between them. Doing so would produce unpredictable results.

14.7 TEXT FILES

In all of the preceding examples, we used DATA files to store our data; these files were declared through the FILE OF statement. If we declared a FILE OF INTEGER, the values stored in the file were Integer values, but the only way we could enter data into this file was by writing a program to do so using

PUT statements. Pascal also allows us to declare files of type TEXT, the same type of file that we use to store our Pascal programs.

When we declare files to be of type TEXT, we can omit FILE OF and simply use the word TEXT, for example

```
DA: TEXT;
```

TEXT files are different from data files, however, in that we do not use GET or PUT commands or normal assignment statements with the file buffer variable. Instead we use READ and WRITE statements with the file identifier as the first item in the READ or WRITE list.

Writing to a TEXT File

Let's look at an example program that writes data to a text file. The program in exhibit 14–7 is exactly the same as the PUTARRAY program in section 14.5, except that the appropriate changes have been made for a TEXT file.
Notice that the

```
WRITE(DA,MAT[I,J])
```

statement replaces the two statements

Exhibit 14–7. Program WRITEARRAY

```
PROGRAM WRITEARRAY;

TYPE
  TABLE = ARRAY [1..5,1..5] OF INTEGER;

VAR
  I,J: INTEGER;
  MAT: TABLE;
  DA: TEXT;

BEGIN  (* WRITEARRAY *)
  REWRITE (DA,'WARRAY.TEXT');
  FOR I:= 1 TO 5 DO
    BEGIN  (* I LOOP *)
      FOR J:= 1 TO 5 DO
        BEGIN  (* J LOOP *)
          MAT[I,J] := I * 10 + J;
          WRITE(DA,MAT[I,J])
        END;  (* J LOOP *)
      WRITELN (DA)
    END;  (* I LOOP *)
  CLOSE (DA,LOCK)
END.  (* WRITEARRAY *)
```

```
DA^ := MAT[I,J];
PUT(DA)
```

(although in the second case, we could have assigned the entire array to the file buffer variable at one time (DA^ := MAT) rather than element by element). What is the purpose of the WRITELN (DA) statement in the FOR I..DO loop? It writes an EOLN mark after every five entries. The program segment

```
FOR J:= 1 TO 5 DO
  BEGIN  (* J LOOP *)
    MAT[I,J] := I * 10 + J;
    WRITE(DA,MAT[I,J])
  END;  (* J LOOP *)
WRITELN (DA)
```

is equivalent to the segment

```
FOR J:= 1 TO 5 DO
  MAT[I,J] := I * 10 + J;
WRITELN (DA,MAT[I,1],MAT[1,2],MAT[I,3],M
AT[I,4],MAT[I,5]);
```

Make the necessary changes (in the complete program), and compile and run this program. Then move to the Filer and press T for T(ransfer. When prompted, T(ransfer the file WARRAY. TEXT to CONSOLE:. This will write the contents of the file onto the screen. The file should look something like

```
1112131415
2122232425
3132333435
4142434445
5152535455
```

Because this file is a TEXT file, we can treat it like any other TEXT file. If we were to attempt to use a READ statement on this file, however, we would have some difficulty. Just as we have some trouble knowing where one value ends and the next begins, a READ statement looking for Integer values would be unable to differentiate the five values. Reading entries from a file is similar to reading entries from the keyboard; they must be separated by a space or a (RET) so that the computer can tell where one value ends and the next begins. Using WRITELN instead of WRITE for each element would solve this problem, but there is another solution. Return to the Editor and change the output line to

```
WRITE(DA,MAT[I,J]:6)
```

This formats the output, and since each value is only two digits long, it will add four spaces between values. Compile and run the program again. Use T(ransfer (to the CONSOLE:) to check

the file. We should now have the spaces necessary to differentiate between the numbers. S(ave the program under the name
WRARRAY.

Reading data from a TEXT File

We can now create a second program to read the data back out
of the WARRAY.TEXT file. The READ statement will be similar
to the WRITE statement in that it will include the file buffer
variable to be used and the variable to be read. And just as the
WRITE statement replaced both the assignment and PUT statements, the READ replaces the assignment and GET statements,
i.e.

```
READ (DA,MAT[I,J]);
```

will replace

```
MAT[I,J] := DA^ ;
GET (DA);
```

You can now G(et GETARRAY and modify it or just enter the
program in exhibit 14–8.

Exhibit 14–8. Program
READARRAY

```
PROGRAM READARRAY;

TYPE
   TABLE = ARRAY [1..5,1..5] OF INTEGER;

VAR
   I,J: INTEGER;
   MAT: TABLE;
   DA: TEXT;
   FNAME: STRING;

BEGIN  (* READARRAY *)
   FNAME := 'WARRAY.TEXT';
   RESET (DA,FNAME);
   FOR I:= 1 TO 5 DO
     BEGIN  (* I LOOP *)
       FOR J := 1 TO 5 DO
         BEGIN  (* J LOOP *)
           READ (DA,MAT[I,J]);
           WRITE (MAT[I,J]:7)
         END;  (* J LOOP *)
       WRITELN
     END;          (* I LOOP *)
   CLOSE (DA)
END.  (* READARRAY *)
```

Note that in addition to the changes you might have expected in modifying this program to read a text file, we also added a String variable FNAME. We then assigned the string WARRAY.TEXT to FNAME and used the string variable in the RESET statement. The purpose of these changes was simply to illustrate that the file name used in the REWRITE and RESET statements is nothing more than a string. Thus, we could write programs where REWRITE, RESET, and CLOSE statements are included in procedures, and the value of FNAME could be changed between procedure calls or read from the keyboard.

Once you have entered or modified the program, compile and run it to ensure that it works properly. You should see the matrix element values spaced out across the screen.

Even though the file was of type TEXT and the variable MAT of type TABLE (an ARRAY of INTEGER), it was possible to read the values for MAT from the file. This is because the value that is being read from the TEXT file will attempt to take the form of the data type of the named variable (e.g., MAT). However, if the variable was of Integer data type and the value being read from the file was Real (or String, Char, or Boolean), an error would result.

14.8 CREATING DATA FILES FROM THE EDITOR

S(ave the last program under the name READARRAY, clear the workfile, and then move to the Editor. Press **(RET)** to create a new file and I(nsert the following numbers:

101	102	103	104	105
201	202	203	204	205
301	302	303	304	305
401	402	403	404	405
501	502	503	504	505

CTRL-C to accept the entries, then Q(uit the Editor and W(rite the file to EDATA. Move to the Filer, L(ist to make sure a file named EDATA.TEXT exists, then G(et READARRAY, and go to the Editor and change the FNAME assignment to EDATA.TEXT (i.e., FNAME := 'EDATA.TEXT';). Once the change is made, Q(uit, U(pdate, and R(un the program. You should see the values you entered written to the screen. Thus, you can create data files by using the Editor instead of writing a program to do so, as long as you use TEXT files. You can also modify existing TEXT files (e.g., WARRAY.TEXT) by moving them to the Editor and using I(nsert or D(elete (or any of the other Editor options) to make changes.

Because data written to a TEXT file is written as a String, however, you must be careful not to write more than a total of 255 characters on one "line"—this could happen if you use a series of WRITE statements. If you are not sure how many characters of data will be included, you can always use a WRITELN statement to avoid this problem. You may remember that when we used a WRITE statement to write the MAT values to the file, we also included a WRITELN statement (WRITELN(DA)) in the outer (I) loop to place an EOLN character after each set of 5 values. It wasn't really necessary in this case since the 25 Integer values in MAT only occupied 150 characters of space (we used a six-space format for each value), but it illustrates one method of ensuring that data does not exceed the 255-character limit.

When we enter data into a file using the Editor, we may not want to stop and count the number of lines. By using the EOF marker when we read the data back out, we don't have to know how many lines of data are in the file. We still must know the number of data items per line, however. For example, to read the data stored in the EDATA.TEXT file, we could use the following program segment:

```
BEGIN  (* PROGRAM BLOCK *)
  I := 0;
  RESET(DA,'EDATA.TEXT');
  WHILE NOT EOF(DA) DO
    BEGIN  (* WHILE..DO *)
      I := I + 1;
      READLN(DA,MAT[I,1],MAT[I,2],MAT[I,
      3],MAT[I,4],MAT[I,5]);
      WRITELN(MAT[I,1]:7,MAT[I,2]:7,MAT[
      I,3]:7,MAT[I,4]:7,MAT[I,5]:7)
    END;  (* WHILE..DO *)
  CLOSE(DA)
END.  (* PROGRAM BLOCK *)
```

We could have used a second loop to shorten the READLN and WRITELN statements:

```
          :
          :
I := I + 1;
FOR J := 1 TO 5 DO
  BEGIN  (* FOR..DO *)
    READ (DA,MAT[I,J]);
    WRITE (MAT[I,J]:7)
  END;  (* FOR..DO *)
READLN (DA);
WRITELN
          :
          :
```

Use G(et to reload GETARRAY, make the necessary changes, and run the program. You should see the data you entered through the Editor in the EDATA file listed on your screen. When you are finished you can S(ave this modified program as GETARRAY or give it a new name.

For an example, let's look at a problem similar to the grading program we have been refining for Mr. Matthews. Ms. Smith bases the final average for her students on the results of four exams. The exams also determine each of the term grades, i.e., grades for the first term are based on the first test, grades for the second term are based on the second test, and so on. Ms. Smith would like a program (or programs) that will: (1) allow her to record grades for her class at the end of each term, (2) determine the year-to-date average based on the term tests taken thus far, and (3) keep a file (or files) of student names and grades for her records. The last (fourth) year-to-date average will also be the final average.

To save some time and programming effort, let's assume that Ms. Smith will create a file in the Editor containing the course name and a list of the students' names for that course. Use the Editor now to create a file containing the following information:

```
HISTORY 324
SUE ALLISON
JILL BARKER
TOM PARKER
MARY SMITHE
BILL WILLIAMS
```

(The normal class list would probably be much longer, but this will do for our illustrative purposes.) When you have finished, Write this information to a file named HIST324N (which stands for History 324 Names).

Now let's design a program for Ms. Smith. We can divide the problem into three areas, input or data entry, calculation of YTD grades, and output. The input section should allow Ms. Smith to input the course name, the term, and the term grades for each student. It will also read previous term grades (where appropriate) from a grade file. The YTD grade calculation section will simply average the grades for the completed terms. The output section will output current YTD results to the screen and all term grades to the grade file.

Let's begin with the data entry section of the program. The program should allow current term grades to be entered from the keyboard and read previous term grades from a grade file. Since we already have a list of the students in each course, it would be a nice feature to have the computer prompt Ms. Smith with each student's name prior to the grade entry. This will involve reading the names file, which was created using the Editor. Because we could have a different file of names for each course, we will require the user (Ms. Smith) to input the appropriate course name. For consistency, we will use a seven-character name for each course. The first four characters will designate the course and the last three characters will be the course number, e.g., HIST324. Our file HIST324N follows this form and uses the eighth character (N) to identify if as a name file. We can then use an identical file name with a G for the eighth character to designate the grade file for the course.

An algorithm for this section (procedure) might look like this:

1. Entering necessary data:
   a. Prompt for course name;
   b. Prompt for term number;
   c. Read student names from course file;
   d. Input current term grades for all students;
   e. Input previous term grades for all students;

Refinement of this algorithm might produce:

PROCEDURE ENTER
1. Prompt user for and then get:
   a. Course name;
   b. Term number;
2. Get student names from the course name file:
   a. Open names file;
   b. Get course name;
   c. Get names of all students;
   d. Close the file;
3. Get current term grades:
   a. For each student:
      (1) Prompt with student's name;
      (2) Get student's current term grade;
4. Get prior term grades:
   a. If this is not term 1:
      (1) Open grades file;
      (2) Get prior grades for each student;
      (3) Close the file;

Because we will want to use the course name, term number, student names, and grades elsewhere in the program, we will make these all variable parameters. We will use a two-dimensional array for grades, with each row representing a different student and each column representing a different term grade. We will use a 7-character course identifier plus an N or a G for the file name. Since the actual file name must have the .TEXT suffix, we will declare a 13-character string (including the 5-character suffix) when the string is initialized. Converting the algorithm to Pascal code will produce a procedure similar to the one shown in exhibit 14–9.

Exhibit 14–9.
Procedure ENTER

```
PROCEDURE ENTER (VAR FNAME:COURSE; VAR T
ERM, NO:INTEGER; VAR LIST:NAMES;
                  VAR GRADE:GRADES);
  VAR
    I,J: INTEGER;
    CNAME, CID: STRING;
    DN: TEXT;
  BEGIN  (* ENTER *)
    FNAME := '        .TEXT';
    WRITE ('ENTER COURSE IDENTIFIER ');
    READLN (CID);
    FOR I := 1 TO 7 DO
      FNAME[I] := CID[I];
    FNAME[8] := 'N';
    WRITE ('WHAT IS THE TERM NUMBER (1-4
) ? ');
    READLN (TERM);
    RESET (DN,FNAME);
    READLN (DN,CNAME);
    I := 0;
    WHILE NOT EOF(DN) DO
      BEGIN  (* READ NAMES LOOP *)
        I := I + 1;
        READLN(DN,LIST[I])
      END;  (* READ NAMES LOOP *)
    CLOSE(DN);
    NO := I;
    PAGE (OUTPUT);
    WRITELN ('ENTER CURRENT TERM GRADE F
OLLOWING NAME');
    WRITELN;
    FOR I := 1 TO NO DO
      BEGIN  (* GET CURRENT GRADES LOOP *)
        WRITE (LIST[I],'   ');
        READLN (GRADE[I,TERM])
      END;  (* GET CURRENT GRADES LOOP *)
    IF TERM > 1 THEN
      BEGIN  (* IF..THEN BRANCH *)
        FNAME[8] := 'G';
        RESET (DN,FNAME);
        FOR I := 1 TO NO DO
          BEGIN  (* READ GRADE LOOP *)
            FOR J := 1 TO (TERM-1) DO
              READ (GRADE[I,J];
            READLN (DN)
          END  (* READ GRADE LOOP *)
      END  (* IF..THEN BRANCH *)
  END;  (* ENTER *)
```

Now that the term grades have been entered, we can go on to the second part of our program, calculating the YTD grades. This will be a fairly straightforward function (since we are only calculating a value). The algorithm would be something like this:

1. Calculate grades for each student:
a. Sum term grades;
b. Divide the sum by the number of terms;

Since the YTD grade will be determined from the sum of the term grades for each student, we will have to pass the student number, the term number, and the array of grades to this function. When coded, the function might look like the one in exhibit 14–10.

Now we need a procedure to output the results. As we have previously specified, this procedure should output the YTD grades to the screen and the existing term grades to a grade file. The algorithm might be:

1. For each student:
a. Output student name and YTD average;
2. Save grade file:
a. Open the grade file;
b. For each student:
(1) For each term:
(a) Write grade to the file;
c. Close the file;

When we save the grades to the grade file, we will simply replace the old grades with the new updated array. The file identifiers will remain unchanged from the entry procedure. Thus, the output procedure might look like exhibit 14–11 when the algorithm is coded.

Exhibit 14–10.
Function YTD

```
FUNCTION YTD (I,TERM: INTEGER; GRADE: GR
ADES):REAL;
   VAR
      J: INTEGER;
        SUM: REAL;
   BEGIN  (* YTD *)
      SUM := 0;
      FOR J := 1 TO TERM DO
         SUM := SUM + GRADE[I,J];
      YTD : SUM/TERM
   END;  (* YTD *)
```

Exhibit 14–11.
Procedure RESULTS

```
PROCEDURE RESULTS (FNAME:COURSE; NO, TER
M:INTEGER; LIST:NAMES; GRADE:GRADES);
   VAR
     I,J: INTEGER;
     GF: TEXT;
   BEGIN  (* RESULT *)
     PAGE (OUTPUT);
     WRITELN ('CURRENT AVERAGES FOR ',FNA
ME:7);
     WRITELN;
     FOR I := 1 TO NO DO
       WRITELN (LIST[I]:20,YTD(I,TERM,GRA
DE):8:2);
     REWRITE (GF,FNAME);
     FOR I := 1 TO NO DO
       BEGIN  (* GRADES TO FILE LOOP *)
         FOR J := 1 TO TERM DO
           WRITE (GF, GRADE[I,J]:8);
         WRITELN (GF)
       END;  (* GRADES TO FILE LOOP *)
     CLOSE (GF,LOCK)
   END;  (* RESULT *)
```

The first loop outputs the list of names and YTD grades. The grade file is then opened and all the term grades for each student are written to the file.

We can now complete the program by combining our function and two procedures with the main body of the program (exhibit 14–12). (To save space, the procedures and function are not repeated.)

Enter the complete program and then test it using the following grades:

		Term			
Name	1	2	3	4	Results
Sue Allison	90	60	90	80	80.0
Jill Barker	80	60	90	80	77.5
Tom Parker	70	70	70	70	70.0
Mary Smithe	60	60	90	80	72.5
Bill Williams	50	80	90	80	75.0

Be sure you take the terms in order, i.e., you must run the program with term 1, then term 2, and so on. Once you have successfully tested the program, S(ave it as YTDGRADES,

Exhibit 14–12.
Program YTDGRADES

```
PROGRAM YTDGRADES;

TYPE
   COURSE = STRING[13];
   NAMES = ARRAY[1..25] OF STRING;
   GRADES = ARRAY[1..25],1..4] OF INTEGER;

VAR
   ID: COURSE;
   NUM, TERM: INTEGER;
   GRADE: GRADES;
   LIST: NAMES;

FUNCTION YTD...

PROCEDURE ENTER...

PROCEDURE RESULTS...

BEGIN  (* YTDGRADES *)
   ENTER (ID, TERM, NUM, LIST, GRADE);
   RESULTS (ID, NUM, TERM, LIST, GRADE)
END.  (* YTDGRADES *)
```

clear the workfile, then G(et HIST234G and move to the Editor to make sure the grades have been stored properly. ■

14.9 SUMMARY

In this chapter, we have learned how to create files to store our data in. These files can be either DATA files or TEXT files. When we want to write to a file, we open it by using REWRITE (*file identifier*, *file name*), and we close it using CLOSE(*file identifier*, LOCK). The LOCK parameter ensures that the file is saved. When we want to read from a file, we open it by using RESET(*file identifier*, *file name*) and close it using CLOSE(*file identifier*). The LOCK parameter is not necessary when closing a file that already exists.

Once we have opened a DATA file, data elements that are being written to the file or read from the file are transferred to the file buffer variable, identified by the circumflex (ˆ) following the variable identifier. We move data from the file to the file buffer variable with the GET statement or from the file buffer variable to the file with the PUT statement. (Whenever a file is opened using RESET, a GET is performed automatically so that the first element in the file is moved to the file buffer.) When writing a value to a file we must first assign the value to the file buffer and then PUT it to the file; when reading a value from a file, we must first GET the value (moving it to the file buffer), and then assign it to a normal variable.

While data files are ordered sequentially, it is possible to read a value from or write a value to a specific file location by using the SEEK statement, which allows us to specify the particular sequential location of the data we want to use. We must remember, however, that the sequential locations are numbered beginning with 0 rather than 1 and that the SEEK only moves to the designated location in the file; it does not GET or PUT the value. Thus, we must always use a GET or PUT after a SEEK statement.

We also saw that we could use the Editor to enter data directly into TEXT files. We can write values to or read them from TEXT files using normal READ and WRITE statements, as long as we identified (declared) the TEXT file and included the file identifier as the first item in the READ or WRITE list. TEXT files contain EOLN markers at the end of each line and an EOF marker at the end of the file, and we saw that we could use this EOF marker to read all of the data between the beginning of the file and the EOF marker.

| **Review Questions** | 1. There are three types of Pascal files that are stored on disks. Identify them. |

1. There are three types of Pascal files that are stored on disks. Identify them.

2. What is a file buffer?

3. How do we declare a DATA file? What types of data can be stored in a DATA file? How do we distinguish a file buffer variable?

4. How do we open a file for output? How would we output a value to the file?

5. How do we tell the computer that we have finished using a file? How do we tell the computer that we want to keep the file we created?

6. How do we open a file for input? How would we read information from a DATA file?

7. What is the EOF function? What data type is it?

8. Is it possible to have a DATA file that is a structured data type? Explain.

9. What does the SEEK procedure do? Explain.

10. Data can be stored in TEXT files rather than DATA file. How do TEXT files differ from DATA files?

SUMMARY of Pascal Syntax

Reserved Words	Built-in Procedures	Built-in Functions	Library Units
PROGRAM	WRITE	**EOF**	TURTLEGRAPHICS
USES	WRITELN		APPLESTUFF
CONST	READ	ABS	TRANSCEND
TYPE	READLN	SQR	
SET..OF		SQRT	
PACKED	**RESET**	ROUND	
ARRAY[..]OF	**REWRITE**	TRUNC	
RECORD	**PUT**	EXP	
FILE..OF	**GET**	LN	
VAR	**SEEK**	LOG	
FUNCTION	**CLOSE**	PWROFTEN	
FORWARD	**LOCK**	ATAN	
PROCEDURE	INITTURTLE	SIN	*Boolean Constants*
BEGIN	PENCOLOR	COS	
FOR..DO	MOVE	ORP	
TO	TURN	CHR	FALSE
DOWNTO	MOVETO	PREP	TRUE
REPEAT	TURNTO	SUCC	
UNTIL	TEXTMODE	EOLN	
WHILE..DO	GRAFMODE		
IF	PAGE(OUTPUT)		
THEN			
ELSE			
CASE..OF			
WITH..DO			*Integer Constants*
END			
DIV			
MOD			
NIL			
AND			
OR			
NOT			
IN			

11. How do we put data into TEXT files or get data from them? How does this differ from DATA files?

12. When we use TEXT files to store data, we do not need a special program or procedure to create the files. Explain.

Programming Exercises

1. Declare a variable INFO to be a file containing Real values.

2. Write a statement that opens a file named TEST.DATA to store information on the variable INFO.

3. Write the necessary statement(s) to store the value 23.56 in the file referred to in exercises 1 and 2.

4. Write the necessary statement(s) to retrieve the value of INFO that we stored in a file in exercise 3.

5. Modify the program segment in exercise 4 so that all of the data points stored in the file would be read from the file and output to the screen.

6. Assume we only want to read the fifth data value from a file and output it to the screen. Write a program segment that would do this for us.

7. We wish to store information containing people's names, addresses, and ZIP codes on a disk. How would we declare the file to store this information?

8. Create a TEXT file containing the following data:

11	22	33
44	55	66
77	88	99

9. Write a procedure that would read the data from the file created in exercise 8 and divide each value by eleven.

Diagnostic Exercises

The declaration DFILE: FILE OF INTEGER; has been made. If the following statements are incorrect, correct them. Then explain what the result of the statement(s) would be.

10.
```
REWRITE (DF,'DFILE.DATA');
DF^   := 64;
PUT (DF);
```

11.
```
REWRITE (DFILE,ONE.DATA);
DFILE := 56;
PUT (DFILE);
```

12. REWRITE (DFILE,'ONE.DATA');
    DFILE^ := 87.2;
    PUT (DFILE);

13. REWRITE (DFILE,'ONE.DATA');
    DFILE^ := 202;
    PUT (DFILE);
    PUT (DFILE);

14. REWRITE (DFILE,'ONE.DATA');
    DFILE^ := 341;
    PUT (DFILE);
    CLOSE ('ONE.DATA');

15. RESET (DFILE,'ONE.DATA');
    NV := DFILE;
    WRITE (NV);

16. RESET (DFIE, 'ONE.DATA');
    GET (DFILE);
    NV := DFILE^ ;
    WRITE (NV);

17. RESET (DFILE,'ONE.DATA');
    SEEK(DFILE,4);
    NV := DFILE^ ;
    WRITE (NV);

18. RESET (DFILE,'ONE.DATA');
    NV := DFILE^ ;
    GET (DFILE);
    NV := DFILE^ ;
    WRITE (NV);
    CLOSE(DFILE,LOCK);

Problems

19. Write a procedure that will read Integer values from the keyboard and then output them to a file named TRIAL.DATA. We do not know how many values there are before we begin.

20. Write a procedure that will open a file of Integer values and then find the fifth value in the file and replace it with the value 76.

21. Suppose you have two files, FILE1 and FILE2, each containing twenty values. Develop the algorithm for a procedure that would read the contents of these files and output any values that are common to both files.

22. Code and test the algorithm developed in problem 21 using TEXT files for FILE1 and FILE2.

23. A file contains records of names and addresses. Write a procedure that allows the user to input a name, finds that person in the file, and then allows the address to be changed.

15

Pointers and Linked Lists

In chapter 12 we learned about arrays, which let us establish lists or matrices of values. Arrays are very useful, but they suffer from one limitation: they are **static** in nature, i.e., their size is fixed and cannot change. Once we declare an array to be of a certain size (and that size must be a constant), the computer sets aside enough memory for an array of that size. If we declare an array that is too small, we must go back to the Editor, change the declaration, and recompile the program before proceeding. If we declare an array that is too large (which is the normal procedure when we don't know the number of values to be assigned to the array), we use memory needlessly.

Pascal allows us to declare variables that are **dynamic** in nature, i.e., their size can change while the program is running. We do this through the use of a **pointer**, which points to the memory location where a variable value is stored. By using pointers, we can use as many or as few memory locations as we need to store our list of values, and we do not have to know the number of values in the list before we run the program.

15.1 POINTERS

A **pointer** or **pointer variable** describes a predefined Pascal data type. The value of the pointer variable is the address of one of the computer's memory locations. For example, suppose memory location 2036 has the Integer value 9 stored in it (see the following figure).

Figure 15–1. Memory Representation

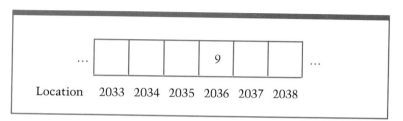

A pointer value of 2036 would tell the computer to go to location 2036 to find the value stored there (9). The pointer is thus similar to a variable name or identifier. Fortunately, we do not have to know the addresses of the Apple's memory locations to be able to use pointer variables. The address is assigned automatically every time we declare a new pointer variable, i.e., a memory unit is automatically allocated for the value to be stored and the pointer variable is assigned the correct memory address.

Declaring a Pointer Variable

Pointer variables are declared in the normal manner, i.e., through the VAR declaration statement. When a pointer variable is declared, a circumflex (^) precedes the data type, for example

```
VAR
    POINTER: ^INTEGER;
```

declares a pointer variable named POINTER (the word pointer is *not* a reserved word in Pascal) that will point to an Integer value. Remember, the value of POINTER is the memory location of the value being pointed to. We cannot assign a value to POINTER or output its value.

Referenced Variables

The values (variables) pointed to by the pointer variables are known as **referenced variables**. In figure 15–1, the pointer value (2036) pointed to a referenced variable with a value of 9. The referenced variable takes its name from the pointer variable name, but the referenced variable identifier is followed by a circumflex (^). Thus,

```
POINTER^ := 15;
```

assigns the value of 15 (an Integer) to the memory location pointed to by POINTER. Pointer variables are no different than other variables in terms of their data types. They can point to simple or structured data types, but the referenced variable must have a value that corresponds to the declared type. Since POINTER was declared to be Integer, POINTER^ can only be assigned Integer values.

Creating NEW Pointer Variables

Declaring the variable POINTER to be a pointer variable simply told the computer that we intended to use pointers in the program. It did not cause the computer to allocate any memory space for referenced variables. To allocate memory space, we use the built-in procedure NEW with the pointer variable as a parameter. For example,

```
NEW (POINTER);
```

creates a pointer variable that points to a specific memory location. Each time we use the NEW statement, another memory location is set aside for a referenced variable with a pointer pointing to it. The following program creates a pointer variable POINTER, reads a value into the referenced variable, doubles it, and then outputs the resulting value:

```
PROGRAM POINT;

VAR
  POINTER: ^INTEGER;

BEGIN
  NEW (POINTER);
  WRITE('ENTER INTEGER VALUE -->');
  READLN (POINTER^);
  POINTER^ := POINTER^ * 2;
  WRITELN;
  WRITELN (POINTER^:8)
END.
```

In this program the pointer really has no advantage over a normal variable name. Consider the following modified version of the program:

```
PROGRAM POINT;.

VAR
   POINTER,POINTER2: ^INTEGER;

BEGIN
   NEW (POINTER);
   WRITE('ENTER INTEGER VALUE -->');
   READLN (POINTER^);
   POINTER^ := POINTER^ * 2;
   WRITELN;
   WRITELN (POINTER^:8);
   NEW (POINTER2);
   POINTER2^ := 14;
   POINTER2 := POINTER;
   WRITELN;
   WRITELN (POINTER2^:8)
END.
```

If we input a value of 3 when prompted by the program, what will be output? The value 3 is multiplied by 2 and the result (6) is output. A new variable, POINTER2, is then created, and the referenced variable is assigned a value of 14. POINTER2 is then assigned the value of POINTER and the value of POINTER2^ is then output. What value will be output now? If you said the second value output (POINTER2^) would also be 6, you were correct. The program allocated two memory locations for referenced variables, one containing a value of 6 and the other a value of 14, but when the assignment statement POINTER2 : = POINTER was executed, the pointer variable for the second variable was assigned the memory location of the first variable (6). What happened to the 14? It's still in the computer's memory, but now there is no pointer pointing to that memory location. In effect, the 14 is still in memory (somewhere), but it has been lost to us, since we no longer have any means of accessing it. We could have omitted the lines

```
NEW (POINTER2);
POINTER2^ := 14;
```

completely with no effect on the output, since NEW allocates a new memory location for a referenced variable and we let POINTER 2 point to an existing referenced variable.

This example simply illustrates the difference between the pointer variables (POINTER or POINTER 2) and the referenced variables (POINTER^ or POINTER 2^). The important point to remember is that the referenced variables cannot be accessed except through a pointer variable, which provides the referenced variable's location in the computer's memory. We can now take the concept of the pointer variable and see how we can build a dynamic variable list.

15.2 LINKED LISTS

Using a pointer variable for a single data element is of little or no value. We want to be able to create a list of undeclared size. If we were to create a unique pointer variable for each item in the list, it would still have no advantage over an array, since we would need to know the number of pointers to create. What we want is a group of items with one common identifier that are linked together in some manner; this structure is known as a **linked list**, and the pointer variable will allow us to create such a list.

Creating a Linked List

To create a dynamic, linked list, we will begin by creating a record with two fields. The first field will contain the value of the data we want to store in our list. The second field will contain a pointer that points to the next item in the list. The record and variable declarations would take the following form:

```
TYPE
  POINTER = ^LIST;
  LIST = RECORD
           VALUE: INTEGER;
           NEXT: POINTER
         END;

VAR
  P,S: POINTER;
```

Here we have declared POINTER to be a pointer variable that points to the record LIST. LIST has two fields: VALUE, which holds the referenced variable; and NEXT, which holds the pointer variable. We have also declared the variables P and S to be of type POINTER, i.e., pointers to the record LIST. In this case POINTER was declared as a pointer variable in the TYPE statement (instead of in the variable declarations), so we do *not* include the circumflex before the type identifier POINTER. We will use P as the pointer variable for our list and S as the pointer that points to the beginning of the list.

At this time, we shall reintroduce the Pascal constant NIL, which means none or nothing. The last item in our list will not have a following item to point to, so NIL will designate the end of our list. The program shown in exhibit 15–1 creates a linked list using the procedure CREATE. Let's follow the logic of this procedure. The first line sets the pointer variable S to NIL. We then enter a REPEAT..UNTIL loop. The third line uses NEW (P) to allocate memory for a record of type LIST and to set the value of the pointer P so that it points to this location (the record LIST). These variables are shown in figure 15–2.

Exhibit 15–1. Program LINKED

```
PROGRAM LINKED;

TYPE
  POINTER = ^LIST;
  LIST = RECORD
           VALUE: INTEGER;
           NEXT: POINTER
         END;

VAR
  P,S: POINTER;

PROCEDURE CREATE (VAR P,S:POINTER);
  BEGIN  (* CREATE *)
    S := NIL;
    REPEAT
      NEW (P);
      WRITE ('ENTER AN INTEGER VALUE --> ');
      READLN (P^.VALUE);
      P^.NEXT := S;
      S := P;
    UNTIL P^.VALUE = 0
  END;  (* CREATE *)

BEGIN  (* LINKED *)
  CREATE(P,S);
  WRITELN;
  WRITELN ('ALL DONE ')
END.  (* LINKED *)
```

Figure 15–2.

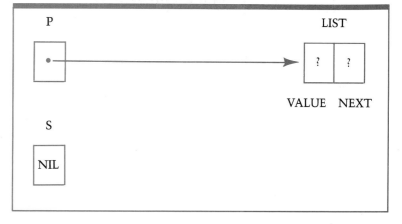

The fifth line reads a value (assume it's 23) into the VALUE field of the referenced record P^ and the sixth line assigns the value of S (NIL) to the NEXT field. The seventh line then assigns the value of P (the pointer) to S. Thus, pointers S and P now both point to variable P^, and P^.NEXT is now equal to NIL, as shown in figure 15–3.

Figure 15–3.

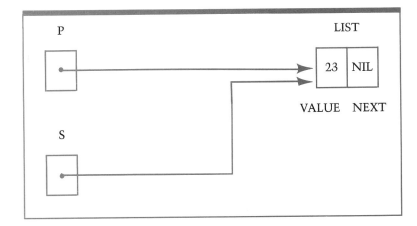

Since P^.VALUE is 23, the UNTIL expression evaluates as FALSE and the loop is repeated. The NEW (P) statement creates a new LIST variable with P pointing to it, so the value of the pointer P is changed to point to the new memory location. The new P^.VALUE is then read (assume a value of 35), P^.NEXT is assigned the value of S (pointing at the first LIST record), and then S is assigned the value of P (pointing at the new (second) LIST record). This is illustrated in figure 15–4.

Figure 15–4.

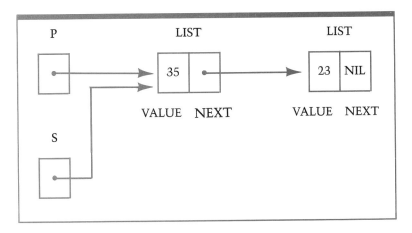

This process will be repeated until we enter a flag value of 0. At that point, we will return to the main program and terminate the program with the ALL DONE message.

Reading Data from Linked Lists

We can use the program LINKED to create a linked list of any length (within the available memory constraints). But pointer variables, being dynamic, exist only in the computer's memory. We'll make sure the list is stored in the computer's memory, by adding a procedure to our program to output the linked list. Since the P^.NEXT value for the last item in the list (our first entry) is NIL, we can add the following procedure to our program:

```
PROCEDURE DISPLAY(P:POINTER);
  BEGIN  (* DISPLAY *)
    WHILE P <> NIL DO
      BEGIN  (* WHILE..DO *)
        WRITELN (P^.VALUE);
        P := P^.NEXT
      END  (* WHILE..DO *)
  END;  (* DISPLAY *)
```

While the pointer variable P is not equal to NIL, this procedure will output the value of VALUE for the current referenced variable and then set the pointer to the value of NEXT, so that it points to the previous entry. The complete program is shown exhibit 15–2 (see page 364).

Enter, compile, and run this program using the following data values as entries: 2, 4, 6, 8, and 0. This program should first create and then output a linked list. The only problem is that the output is in reverse order from the input. This could be a serious problem in some cases, so we'll look at a modification that will allow us to keep the list in the proper sequence.

15.3 ORDERED LINKED LISTS

In the previous example, our pointer S moved each time we added a new variable so that it was always pointing at the last variable in the list. To correct this problem, we will add a local pointer variable named E (S for Start and E for End) that we will use in the REPEAT loop. But we will read the first variable in the list (and only the first variable) using S. The modified program is shown in exhibit 15–3. Note that we changed the DISPLAY parameter from P to S.

We begin CREATE by creating a new LIST variable with S pointing to it and then entering a VALUE (again, assume 23). We then set P equal to S (both P and S now point to the first value in LIST). This is shown in figure 15–5. Notice that the NEXT field value is not yet defined. We then create a new LIST

Exhibit 15–2. Program
LINKED

```
PROGRAM LINKED;

TYPE
  POINTER = ^LIST;
  LIST = RECORD
            VALUE: INTEGER;
            NEXT: POINTER
          END;

VAR
  P,S: POINTER;

PROCEDURE CREATE (VAR S,P:POINTER);
  BEGIN  (* CREATE *)
    S := NIL;
    REPEAT
      NEW (P);
      WRITE ('ENTER AN INTEGER VALUE -->');
      READLN (P^.VALUE);
      P^.NEXT := S;
      S := P;
    UNTIL P^.VALUE = 0
  END;  (* CREATE *)

PROCEDURE DISPLAY(P:POINTER);
  BEGIN  (* DISPLAY *)
    WHILE P <> NIL DO
      BEGIN  (* WHILE..DO *)
        WRITELN (P^.VALUE);
        P := P^.NEXT
      END  (* WHILE..DO *)
  END;  (* DISPLAY *)

BEGIN  (* LINKED *)
  CREATE(S,P);
  WRITELN;
  WRITELN ('ALL DONE ');
  WRITELN;
  DISPLAY(P)
END.  (* LINKED *)
```

record (NEW(E)) and read in a value (assume 35). Pointer E is now pointing at the second record in the list. We then assign the value of E to P^.NEXT; since pointer P is pointing to the first record in the list, this sets the NEXT value for the first record equal to (pointing to) E. This is shown in figure 15–6.

Exhibit 15–3. Program
ORDERED

```
PROGRAM ORDERED;

TYPE
  POINTER = ^LIST;
  LIST = RECORD
            VALUE: INTEGER;
            NEXT: POINTER
          END;

VAR
  S,P:POINTER;

PROCEDURE CREATE(VAR S,P:POINTER);
  VAR
    E:POINTER;
  BEGIN   (* CREATE *)
    NEW (S);
    WRITE ('ENTER AN INTEGER VALUE -->');
    READLN (S^.VALUE);
    P := S;
    REPEAT
      NEW (E);
      WRITE ('ENTER AN INTEGER VALUE -->');
      READLN (E^.VALUE);
      P^.NEXT := E;
      P := E;
    UNTIL E^.VALUE = 0;
    P^.NEXT := NIL
  END;  (* CREATE *)

PROCEDURE DISPLAY(S:POINTER);
  VAR
    P:POINTER;
  BEGIN  (* DISPLAY *)
    P := S;
    WHILE P <> NIL DO
      BEGIN  (* WHILE..DO *)
        WRITELN (P^.VALUE);
        P := P^.NEXT
      END  (* WHILE..DO *)
  END;  (* DISPLAY *)

BEGIN  (* ORDERED *)
  CREATE(S,P);
  WRITELN;
  WRITELN ('ALL DONE ');
  WRITELN;
  DISPLAY(S)
END.  (* ORDERED *)
```

Figure 15–5.

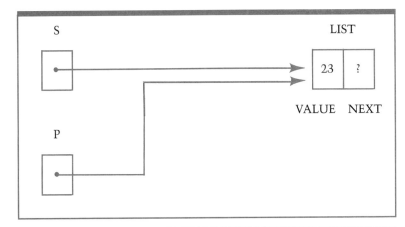

Figure 15–6.

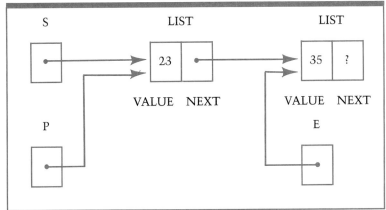

The value of E is then assigned to P, so that P now also points at the second record (see figure 15–7).

Figure 15–7.

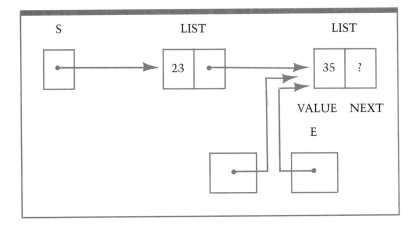

This process is repeated, adding a new record with E pointing to it, assigning P^.NEXT (the pointer value from the previous record) the value of E, and then changing P so that it points to the last record. When the flag value of zero is entered, the loop terminates and P^.NEXT is assigned the value NIL. Thus the last record does not point to another record.

When we want to output the list (Procedure DISPLAY), we first assign local pointer variable P the value of parameter S (which is still pointing to the first record in the list) (see figure 15–8) and then enter the same WHILE..DO loop we used before.

Figure 15–8.

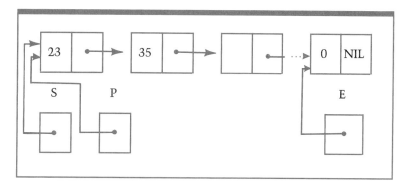

If we wished to exclude the record with the flag value from the list, we could use

```
WHILE P^.VALUE <> 0 DO
```

to output the list, or we could prevent it from being added to the list in the first place by modifying the repeat loop to:

```
REPEAT
  NEW (E);
  WRITELN ('ENTER AN INTEGER VALUE -->');
  READLN E^.VALUE);
  IF E^.VALUE <> 0 THEN
    BEGIN  (* IF..THEN *)
      P^.NEXT := E;
      P := E
    END  (* IF..THEN *)
UNTIL E^.VALUE = 0;
```

This excludes the last record from the list by not setting the value of P^.NEXT equal to E, i.e., when the repeat loop is completed and P^.NEXT is set equal to NIL, the record containing the zero value will not be part of the list (see figure 15–9).

Figure 15–9.

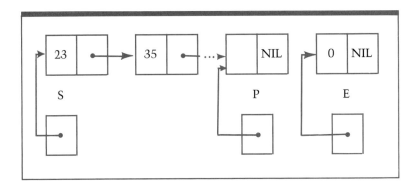

15.4 INSERTING RECORDS INTO A LINKED LIST

Once we have a linked list, there may be times when we want to insert another record into the list. We could do this with the segment:

```
NEW (E);
WRITELN ('ENTER AN INTEGER VALUE -->');
READLN (E^.VALUE);
P^.NEXT := E;
P := E;
P^.NEXT := NIL;
```

This segment would add the record at the end of the list. But what if we had entered our list in numerical order and wanted to insert the record in the proper sequential location in the list? To do this, we would have to locate the correct position in list (let's assume it's the third position) and then insert the record by changing the P^.NEXT value on the second record so that it pointed to our new record and letting the P^.NEXT value of our new record point to the previous third (now the fourth) record. This process is illustrated in figure 15–10.

Figure 15–10.

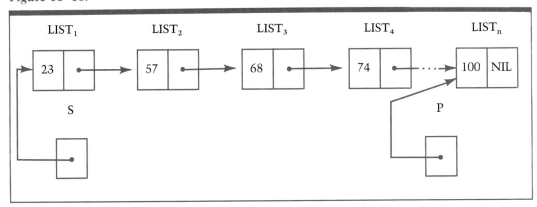

3

3

FOCUS
On Problem
Solving

Before proceeding, see if you can develop an algorithm for a procedure to accomplish this task (insertion of a new value into a linked list at the proper sequential position). Your algorithm might begin with:

1. Enter a new value;
2. Set the pointer to the beginning of the list;
3. Compare the new value with the current list value:
   a. If the new value is less than or equal to the current list value, then:
      (1) Insert the new value at this position;
   b. Otherwise go to the next value in the list;
   c. Until the end of the list is reached;
4. If the end of the list is reached without inserting the new value, insert the new value at the end of the list.

Refining the algorithm further might give us:
1. Enter a new value:
   a. Prompt for a new value;
   b. Input the value;
2. Set the pointer to the beginning of the list;
3. Compare the new value with the current list value:
   a. If the new value is less than or equal to the current list value, then:
      (1) Insert the new value at this position;
         (a) Set the new record pointer equal to the previous record's pointer;
         (b) Set the previous record's pointer so that it points to the new record;
   b. Otherwise go to the next value in the list;
   c. Until the end of the list is reached (the record points to NIL);
4. If the end of the list is reached without inserting the new value, insert the new value at the end of the list:
   a. Set last record's pointer equal to the new pointer;
   b. Set the new record's pointer equal to NIL;

This refinement would insert the new record between any two existing records or at the end of the list, but what if the new record has a value that is less than that of the first record in the list? In that case, there is no previous record and we cannot set our new record's pointer equal to that of the previous record. We have to add a refinement to handle this situation, so we'll refine step 2 to be:

2. Set the pointer to the beginning of the list;
   a. If the new value is less than or equal to the first value in the list:
      (1) Set the pointer variable field for the new record equal to the pointer that points to the beginning of the list;
      (2) Set the pointer that points to the beginning of the

Exhibit 15–4.
Procedure INSERTION

```
PROCEDURE INSERTION (VAR S:POINTER);
  VAR
    NP,P:POINTER;
  BEGIN (* INSERTION *)
    P := S;
    NEW (NP);
    WRITE ('ENTER AN INTEGER VALUE -->');
    READLN (NP^.VALUE);
    IF NP^.VALUE <= S^.VALUE THEN
      BEGIN  (* IF..THEN *)
        NP^.NEXT := S;
        S := NP
      END  (* IF..THEN *)
    ELSE
      BEGIN  (* ELSE *)
        WHILE (P^.NEXT^.VALUE < NP^.VALU
          E) AND (P^.NEXT <> NIL) DO
          P := P^.NEXT;
        IF (P^.NEXT = NIL ) THEN
          BEGIN  (* IF..THEN *)
            P^.NEXT := NP;
            NP^.NEXT := NIL
          END  (* IF..THEN *)
        ELSE
          BEGIN (* ELSE *)
            NP^.NEXT := P^.NEXT;
            P^.NEXT := NP
          END  (* ELSE *)
      END  (* ELSE *)
  END; (* INSERTION *)
```

list equal to the new pointer;

b. Otherwise proceed to Steps 3 and 4;

The coded procedure for this insertion is shown in exibit 15–4.

The first IF..THEN loop (IF (NP^.VALUE...) deals with the situation where NP^.VALUE is less than the first LIST value. In that case, the new record is inserted before the first record, the value of S is assigned to NP^.NEXT, and the value of NP is assigned to S (see figure 15–11).

If the new value is not less than or equal to the first value in the list, we move to the ELSE branch and the WHILE..DO statement. Note that in the first WHILE expression, P^.NEXT^. VALUE gives us the value of the field VALUE in the *next* record in the list. P^ is the current (referenced) record and NEXT^ is the value of the pointer that points to the next record. Thus, the WHILE..DO simply moves us from record to record in the list until we either find the insertion point prior to an existing record or come to the end of the list.

The IF (P^.NEXT = NIL) THEN .... loop deals with the situation where NP^.VALUE is greater than the last (*n*th) record in the list. Remember, the last record always has a pointer value of NIL. In this case, P^.NEXT is assigned the value of NP (see figure 15–12). ■

Figure 15–11.

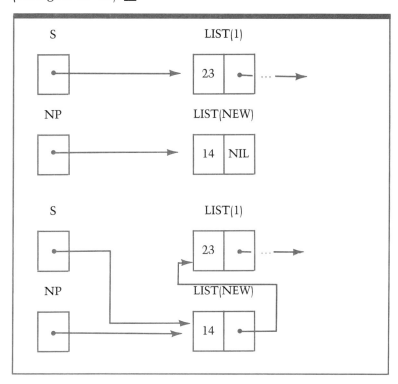

Figure 15–12.

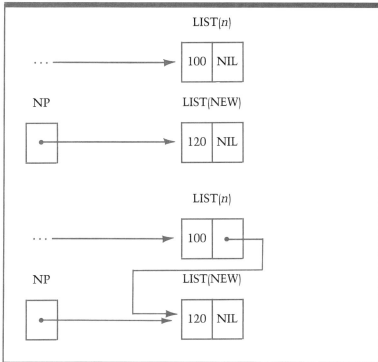

15.5 DELETING A RECORD FROM A LINKED LIST

To delete a record, we must first locate it, and then change the pointers so that they no longer point to the record we want to delete. Remember, the record won't actually be deleted, since it will still be in memory. But with no pointer pointing to it, it will have been removed from the linked list. Exhibit 15–15 contains a procedure that will delete a record from a linked list.

We begin this procedure by entering the value we want to delete from the list. We then set P equal to S and compare the value in our first record with OUT. If they are the same, we assign S the value of S^.NEXT, so that S will point to the second record in the list (see figure 15–13).

If OUT is not equal to the first record value, we enter the ELSE loop. This compares the value of OUT to the value of the next record. If there is no match *and* if the value of the next record pointer (NEXT) is not NIL (which would indicate the end of the list), we move the pointer P to the next record. We continue this process until either the value of the next record is equal to OUT or the next pointer is equal to NIL; at that point we exit the loop. We then deal with these conditions separately. If the next record has a pointer value of NIL, the end of the list was reached without locating a value equal to OUT and the message VALUE TO BE DELETED NOT IN LIST is output. If the value of the next record is equal to OUT, we change the

Exhibit 15–5.
Procedure DELETION

```
PROCEDURE DELETION (VAR S:POINTER);
  VAR
    P:POINTER;
    OUT:INTEGER;
  BEGIN  (* DELETION *)
    WRITE ('ENTER VALUE TO BE DELETED --)');
    READLN (OUT);
    P := S;
    IF P^.VALUE = OUT THEN
      S := S^.NEXT
    ELSE
      BEGIN  (* ELSE *)
        WHILE (P^.NEXT^.VALUE <> OUT) AN
        D (P^.NEXT <> NIL) DO
          P := P^.NEXT;
        IF P^.NEXT = NIL THEN
          WRITELN ('VALUE TO BE DELETED
          NOT IN LIST')
      END;  (* ELSE *)
    IF P^.NEXT^.VALUE = OUT THEN
      P^.NEXT := P^.NEXT^.NEXT
  END;  (* DELETION *)
```

Figure 15–13.

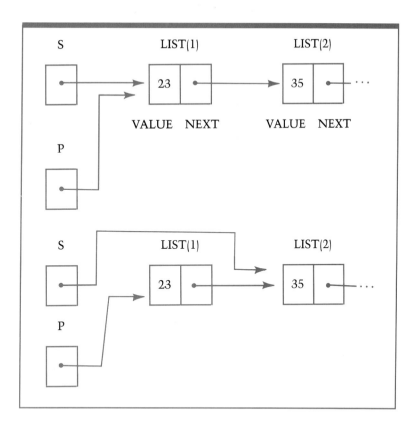

pointer value of the current record (P^.NEXT) to the pointer value of the next or matching record (P^.NEXT^.NEXT), thus bypassing the record to be deleted. This is illustrated in figure 15–14 (see p. 374).

15.6 SAVING A LINKED LIST IN A DATA FILE

Because the linked list is dynamic, it only exists while the program is running. If we want to save the values contained in a linked list, we can do so by writing them to a file. We'll declare a file of type TEXT and use a procedure similar to DISPLAY to write the values into the file. Remember, we cannot output the pointer values. The procedure would look like this:

```
PROCEDURE SAVELIST(S:POINTER);
  VAR
    P:POINTER;
    LF:TEXT;
  BEGIN  (* SAVELIST *)
    REWRITE (LF,'LINKLIST.TEXT');
    P := S;
```

Figure 15–14.

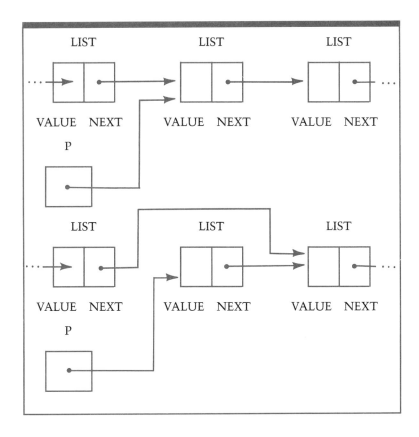

```
WHILE P <> NIL DO
   BEGIN  (* WHILE..DO *)
      WRITELN (LF,P^.VALUE);
      P := P^.NEXT
   END;  (* WHILE..DO *
   CLOSE (LF,LOCK)
END;  (* SAVELIST *)
```

In this example, we declared a file variable LF to be a TEXT file and gave the file the name LINKLIST.TEXT.

15.7 PUTTING IT ALL TOGETHER

Now that we have covered the creation of, insertion into, and deletion from linked lists (as well as the output of these lists to the screen or a file), let's enter and test a program that will include all of the topics covered in this chapter. The program LLTEST is shown in exhibit 15–6. Enter, compile, and test the program. When it runs successfully, you can S(ave it under the name LINKLIST.

Exhibit 15–6. Program
LLTEST

```
PROGRAM LLTEST;

TYPE
  POINTER = ^LIST;
  LIST = RECORD
            VALUE: INTEGER;
            NEXT: POINTER
         END;

VAR
  S,P:POINTER;

PROCEDURE CREATE(VAR S,P:POINTER);
  VAR
    E:POINTER;
  BEGIN  (* CREATE *)
    NEW (S);
    WRITE ('ENTER AN INTEGER VALUE -->');
    READLN (S^.VALUE);
    P := S;
    REPEAT
      NEW (E);
      WRITE ('ENTER AN INTEGER VALUE -->');
      READLN (E^.VALUE);
      IF E^.VALUE () 0 THEN
        BEGIN  (* IF..THEN *)
          P^.NEXT := E;
          P := E
        END  (* IF..THEN *)
    UNTIL E^.VALUE = 0;
    P^.NEXT := NIL
  END;  (* CREATE *)

PROCEDURE DISPLAY(S:POINTER);
  VAR
    P:POINTER;
  BEGIN  (* DISPLAY *)
    P := S;
    WHILE P () NIL DO
      BEGIN  (* WHILE..DO *)
        WRITELN (P^.VALUE);
        P := P^.NEXT
      END  (* WHILE..DO *)
END  (* DISPLAY *)
```

Exhibit 15–6.
Continued

```
PROCEDURE INSERTION (VAR S:POINTER);
  VAR
    NP,P:POINTER;
  BEGIN (* INSERTION *)
    P := S;
    NEW (NP);
    WRITE ('ENTER AN INTEGER VALUE -->');
    ;
    READLN (NP^.VALUE);
    IF NP^.VALUE <= S^.VALUE THEN
      BEGIN  (* IF..THEN *)
        NP^.NEXT := S;
        S := NP
      END  (* IF..THEN *)
    ELSE
      BEGIN  (* ELSE *)
        WHILE (P^.NEXT^.VALUE < NP^.VALU
        E) AND (P^.NEXT <> NIL) DO
          P := P^.NEXT;
        IF (P^.NEXT = NIL ) THEN
          BEGIN  (* IF..THEN *)
            P^.NEXT := NP;
            NP^.NEXT := NIL
          END  (* IF..THEN *)
        ELSE
          BEGIN (* ELSE *)
            NP^.NEXT := P^.NEXT;
            P^.NEXT := NP
          END  (* ELSE *)
      END  (* ELSE *)
  END; (* INSERTION *)

PROCEDURE DELETION (VAR S:POINTER);

  VAR
    P:POINTER;
    OUT:INTEGER;

  BEGIN  (* DELETION *)
    WRITE ('ENTER VALUE TO BE DELETED -->');
    READLN (OUT);
    P := S;
    IF P^.VALUE = OUT THEN
      S := S^.NEXT
    ELSE
```

Exhibit 15–6.
Continued

```
        BEGIN  (* ELSE *)
          WHILE (P^.NEXT^.VALUE <> OUT) AN
          D(P^.NEXT <> NIL) DO
            P := P^.NEXT;
          IF P^.NEXT = NIL THEN
            WRITELN ('VALUE TO BE DELETED
            NOT IN LIST')
        END;  (* ELSE *)
      IF P^.NEXT^.VALUE = OUT THEN
        P^.NEXT := P^.NEXT^.NEXT
    END;  (* DELETION *)

PROCEDURE SAVELIST(S:POINTER);
  VAR
    P:POINTER;
    LF:TEXT;
  BEGIN  (* SAVELIST *)
    REWRITE (LF,'LINKLIST.TEXT');
    P := S;
    WHILE P <> NIL DO
      BEGIN  (* WHILE..DO *)
        WRITELN (LF,P^.VALUE);
        P := P^.NEXT
      END;  (* WHILE..DO *)
    CLOSE (LF,LOCK)
  END;  (* SAVELIST *)

BEGIN  (* LLTEST *)
  CREATE(S,P);
  WRITELN;
  WRITELN ('CREATE DONE ');
  WRITELN;
  DISPLAY(S);
  INSERTION(S);
  WRITELN;
  WRITELN ('INSERTION DONE');
  WRITELN;
  DISPLAY(S);
  DELETION(S);
  WRITELN;
  WRITELN ('DELETION DONE');
  WRITELN;
  DISPLAY(S);
  SAVELIST(S);
  WRITELN;
  WRITELN ('SAVELIST DONE')
END.  (* LLTEST *)
```

15.8 SUMMARY

In this chapter we have learned about a new variable type, the pointer variable. Pointer variables allow us to create new data variables within memory without declaring each variable first. The pointer variable simply points to the location of the referenced variable, i.e., the data variable.

We also learned how to use pointer variables to create linked lists, which are dynamic lists of data, and we learned how to insert values into and delete values from these lists. While the linked list is a very powerful tool, we have to remember that the linked list exists only while the program is running (unless we save it as a file before ending the program).

Review Questions

1. What is the difference between a static variable and a dynamic variable?

2. What is a pointer variable?

3. What is the form of a pointer variable declaration?

4. Can we assign a value to a pointer variable? Explain.

5. What is a referenced variable?

6. Referenced variables are not declared in the same manner as other variables. Explain.

7. What is the effect of assigning the value of one pointer to another pointer?

8. What is the purpose of the NEW procedure?

9. What is a linked list?

10. What is the maximum length of a linked list?

11. How is the constant NIL used in linked lists?

12. Can records used in linked lists have more than two fields? Explain.

13. Use a diagram to show a linked list containing four values (102, 142, 238, and 589).

14. The value of a referenced variable that has been deleted from a linked list is still in memory. Explain.

15. Is it possible to use the value of a referenced variable that has been deleted from a linked list? Explain.

16. Explain how new records are added to a linked list.

17. Explain how records are deleted from a linked list.

SUMMARY of Pascal Syntax

Reserved Words	Built-in Procedures	Built-in Functions	Library Units
PROGRAM	WRITE	EOF	TURTLEGRAPHICS
USES	WRITELN		APPLESTUFF
CONST	READ	ABS	TRANSCEND
TYPE	READLN	SQR	
SET..OF	NEW	SQRT	
PACKED	RESET	ROUND	
ARRAY[..]OF	REWRITE	TRUNC	
RECORD	PUT	EXP	
FILE..OF	GET	LN	
VAR	SEEK	LOG	
FUNCTION	CLOSE	PWROFTEN	
FORWARD	LOCK	ATAN	*Boolean*
PROCEDURE	INITTURTLE	SIN	*Constants*
BEGIN	PENCOLOR	COS	
FOR..DO	MOVE	ORD	
TO	TURN	CHR	FALSE
DOWNTO	MOVETO	PRED	TRUE
REPEAT	TURNTO	SUCC	
UNTIL	TEXTMODE	EOLN	
WHILE..DO	GRAFMODE		
IF	PAGE(OUTPUT)		
THEN			
ELSE			
CASE..OF			
WITH..DO			
END			
DIV			*Integer*
MOD			*Constants*
NIL			
AND			
OR			
NOT			
IN			

1. Write a statement that declares a pointer variable PNTR.

2. Write a program segment that assigns the value 43 to the variable referenced by pointer PNTR.

3. Write a statement that outputs the value of the referenced variable created in exercise 2.

4. Write a program segment that assigns 12 to A^ and 33 to B^. Then swap the pointers so that A points to 33 and B points to 12. (You may want to use a third pointer.)

5. Write the necessary statement(s) to declare a record DATA that will be used in a linked list of names.

6. Write the necessary statement(s) to declare a record DATA that will be used in a linked list; DATA contains names, numerical grades, and letter grades.

7. Write a procedure that would assign values (input or calculated elsewhere) to the record declared in exercise 6.

8. Explain what will be output by each of the following segments:
   a. ```
      NEW(A);
      A^.VALUE := 12;
      NEW(A);
      A^.VALUE := 14;
      WRITELN (A^.VALUE)
      ```
   b. ```
      NEW(A);
      A^.VALUE := 10;
      NEW(B);
      B^.VALUE := 57;
      B := A;
      WRITELN (A^.VALUE,B^.VALUE)
      ```
   c. ```
      NEW(A);
      A^.VALUE := 43;
      NEW(B);
      B^.VALUE := 24;
      A := B;
      A^.VAL := 36;
      WRITELN (A^.VALUE,B^.VALUE)
      ```

9. Explain what the following program segments will do:
   a. ```
      NEW(A);
      A^.VALUE := 31;
      A^.NEXT := NIL
      ```
   b. ```
      NEW(A);
      A^.VALUE := 31;
      A^.NEXT := NIL;
      NEW(B);
      B^.VALUE := 9;
      B^.NEXT := A
      ```
      ```

```
c. NEW(A);
   A^.VALUE := 31;
   A^.NEXT := NIL;
   NEW(B);
   B^.VALUE := 9;
   B^.NEXT := A;
   B^.NEXT^.VALUE := B^.
    VALUE;
   B^.NEXT := B^.NEXT^.
   NEXT
```

10. Given the following declarations:

```
TYPE
   POINTER = ^LIST;
   LIST = RECORD
              VALUE: INTEGER;
              NEXT: POINTER
          END;
VAR
   A,B,C:POINTER;
```

Use the diagrams below to show each of the following statements or program segments does.

a. A := B;

b. A^.NEXT := B;

c. A^.VALUE := 9;

d. C := A^.NEXT;

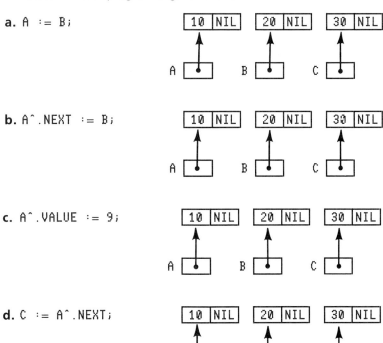

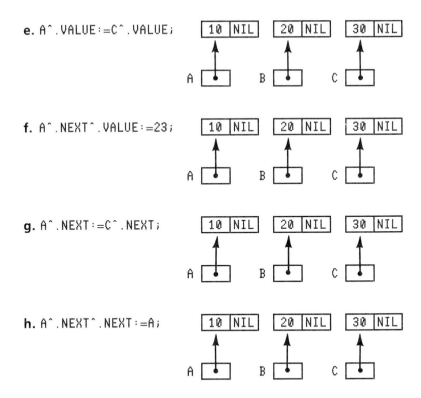

e. A^.VALUE:=C^.VALUE;

f. A^.NEXT^.VALUE:=23;

g. A^.NEXT:=C^.NEXT;

h. A^.NEXT^.NEXT:=A;

Problems

11. In section 15–7 you were asked to test program LLTEST. What data did you use? Explain why this data was appropriate for the test.

12. Develop a procedure that will create a linked list by reading the data from a file rather than from the keyboard.

13. The program LLTEST allows us to create a linked list, output it, add one item to it, delete one item from it, and write it to a file. Develop an algorithm for a procedure that gives the user a choice (via a menu) from among these options and one additional one, Quit, which leaves the list as is.

14. Code and test the algorithm you developed in problem 13.

16

Strings and String Handling Functions

Some times we want to alter String values in a program, as we did in the last program in chapter 14. In this chapter we will explore UCSD Pascal's special built-in functions and procedures that allow us to manipulate String variables. You will learn how to find the length of a string, how to combine two or more strings, how to determine the relative position of a substring within a longer string, how to copy or extract part of a string, how to delete a portion of an existing string, and how to insert one string into another.

This chapter will also introduce you to a special variable, the **long integer**. You will learn how to use long integers for greater numerical accuracy in calculations and how to use another built-in procedure to convert a long integer into a String variable.

16.1 BUILT-IN STRING FUNCTIONS AND PROCEDURES

Pascal has seven built-in string handling functions or procedures. Six of these functions and procedures are listed in exhibit 16–1 (the seventh one will be introduced in section 16.10). The exact meaning or use of each of these functions and procedures will be clarified by examples in the following sections.

16.2 LENGTH

The LENGTH function returns the length (number of characters) of the parameter string as an Integer value. For example, in the following program segment

Exhibit 16–1. String Functions and Procedures

Function or Procedure	Parameters
LENGTH (S)	S = a String variable
CONCAT (S1,S2...)	S1,S2... = String variables
POS (S1,S)	S1 = Substring S = String variable
COPY (S,B,N)	S = String variable B = Position of starting point in the String S N = Number of characters to be copied
DELETE (S,B,N)	S = String variable B = Position of starting point in the String S N = Number of characters to be deleted
INSERT (S1,S,P)	S1 = Substring to be inserted S = String variable P = Position in the String S where the substring S1 is to begin

```
S := 'THIS IS A STRING';
L := LENGTH (S);
```

the variable L would take an Integer value of 16, since there are 16 characters in the String S.

The program in exhibit 16–2 breaks the string into its individual characters and writes each character to the screen. Enter the program, compile it, and run it.

The results should look like this (these are the results referred to in exhibit 16–2):

```
LENGTH OF STRING = 16 CHARACTERS
THIS IS A STRING
T
H
I
S

I
S

A

S
T
R
I
N
G
```

S(ave this program under the name TAKEAPART and clear your workspace.

Exhibit 16–2. Program TAKEAPART

```
PROGRAM TAKEAPART;

VAR
  I,L: INTEGER;
  S: STRING;
  CH:CHAR;

BEGIN  (* TAKEAPART *)
  S:= 'THIS IS A STRING';
  WRITELN ('LENGTH OF STRING = ',LENGTH(
  S),' CHARACTERS');
  WRITELN (S);
  FOR I:= 1 TO LENGTH(S) DO
    BEGIN  (* FOR..DO *)
      CH:= S[I];
      WRITELN (CH)
    END;  (* FOR..DO *)
END.  (* TAKEAPART *)
```

16.3 CONCAT

The CONCAT function can be used to append or join one string to another (or to join a series of strings together); the name of the function comes from the word **concatenate**, which means join together. The function parameters are the strings that are to be concatenated in the order in which they are to be joined. For example,

```
A := 'THIS ';
B := 'IS ';
C := 'A ';
D := 'STRING';
S := CONCAT (A,B,C,D);
```

combines strings A, B, C, and D into one string, S. Notice that strings A, B, and C all ended in blanks (spaces). If these spaces were not included, the words would all run together (THISIS-ASTRING).

In procedure ENTER (exhibit 14–9) we created a 13-character string and initialized it so that the first 8 characters were blank (spaces) and the last 5 characters were .TEXT. We then assigned the first 7 characters on a character-by-character basis (producing HIST234) and assigned the 8th character to be either N or G. The following program uses the CONCAT function to do the same thing without using a character-by-character exchange.

```
PROGRAM ADDON;

VAR
  PREFIX,SUFFIX,WHOLE: STRING;

BEGIN  (* ADDON *)
  WRITE ('ENTER 7 CHARACTER IDENTIFIER ');
  READLN (PREFIX);
  SUFFIX := '.TEXT';
  WHOLE := CONCAT (PREFIX,'N',SUFFIX);
  WRITELN (WHOLE)
END.  (* ADDON *)
```

Enter and run the program. You can use HIST234 as the 7 character identifier, just as we did in chapter 14. The result should be

```
HIST234N.TEXT
```

Note that the CONCAT function works with both N and the string variable SUFFIX. Thus, we could have used

```
WHOLE := CONCAT (PREFIX,'N','.TEXT');
```

or even

```
WHOLE := CONCAT (PREFIX,'N.TEXT');
```

In either case, we do not have to initialize the string first, nor do we have to do a character-by-character assignment. S(ave this program under the name ADDON and clear your workspace again.

16.4 POS

The POS function searches the specified string for a given substring and returns the character position (an Integer value) where the substring begins. The substring is the first function parameter and the string being searched is the second parameter. For example,

```
S := 'THIS IS A STRING';
N := POS ('A',S);
```

searches our familiar string S for the substring (letter) A. The Integer variable N is assigned a value of 9, since the letter A is the 9th character in the string. What would happen if we use N := POS ('S',S);? The letter S occurs three times in the string, but N would be assigned the value 4, because the first occurrence of the letter S is at the 4th character of the string. The POS function locates only the first occurrence of the substring. If we want to determine the position of the third S, we could use N := POS ('STRING',S);. The result (N = 11) would give us the position of the first character (S) of the substring (STRING) within the string S.

Can you predict the result of the following statement?

```
N := POS('THE',S);
```

In this case, N would be assigned a value of 0 since the word THE does not occur in the string.

In these examples, we have searched for the position of a letter or a whole word. What about the following statement?

```
N := POS('RING',S);
```

In this case, N would take a value of 13 because the substring RING is contained in the word STRING and begins at the 13th character of the string S.

G(et TAKEAPART and modify it so that it is the same as the following program:

```
PROGRAM SEGMENT;

VAR
  I,N: INTEGER;
  S: STRING;
  CH: CHAR;
```

```
BEGIN  (* SEGMENT *)
  S: = 'THIS IS A STRING';
  WRITELN (S);
  FOR I := POS('IS',S) TO POS('ST',S) DO
    BEGIN  (* FOR..DO *)
      CH := S[I];
      WRITE (CH)
    END;  (* FOR..DO *)
  WRITELN
END.  (* SEGMENT *)
```

Before you run this program, see if you can predict the results. It is obviously similar to the TAKEAPART program, but in this case, we use the POS function to extract only a segment of the string, the segment between the first character of IS and the first character of ST. The result would be:

```
THIS IS A STRING
IS IS A S
```

The first occurrence of IS is at the 3d character, and ST begins at the 11th character; therefore the loop indexes from 3 to 11, outputting the 9 characters shown above.

16.5 COPY

The COPY function copies a number of characters from a string, beginning at a specified character location. Thus, the COPY function can be used to extract a portion of a string without affecting the original string. For example,

```
S := 'THIS IS A STRING';
NEW := COPY (S,9,8);
```

will assign the substring A STRING to the string NEW by beginning at position 9 (the 9th character in the string S) and copying 8 characters.

In the preceding example, the starting position and number of characters were both specified as Integer values. We could achieve the same results without counting by using the following program line:

```
NEW := COPY (S,POS('A',S),(LENGTH(S)-POS
('A',S)+1));
```

The POS('A',S) function returns an Integer value of 9 for the beginning point. The expression (LENGTH(S)-POS('A',S) + 1)) is then evaluated as (16 − 9 + 1) to return a value of 8. While it is easier to count the characters in this simple example, the second expression would be preferable in longer strings.

In section 16.2 we wrote a program that broke our string down into its component characters and output each character on a separate line. The following program is similar, but it uses COPY to output strings that grow from one character to the total string, one character at a time.

```
PROGRAM GROWING;

VAR
   I: INTEGER;
   S: STRING;

BEGIN  (* GROWING *)
   S:= 'THIS IS A STRING';
   WRITELN ('LENGTH OF STRING = ',LENGTH(
   S),' CHARACTERS');
   WRITELN (S);
   FOR I:= 1 TO LENGTH(S) DO
      WRITELN (COPY (S,1,I));
END.   (* GROWING *)
```

Enter and run this program. The output should look like this:

```
LENGTH OF STRING= 16 CHARACTERS
THIS IS A STRING
T
TH
THI
THIS
THIS
THIS I
THIS IS
THIS IS
THIS IS A
THIS IS A
THIS IS A S
THIS IS A ST
THIS IS A STR
THIS IS A STRI
THIS IS A STRIN
THIS IS A STRING
```

16.6 DELETE

The DELETE procedure allows us to delete a number of characters from an existing string. The parameters for DELETE specify the string, the beginning position expressed as an Integer value, and the number of characters to be deleted. DELETE has the same form as COPY, but DELETE alters the original string. For example,

```
S := 'THIS IS A STRING';
DELETE (S,5,5);
```

would begin with the fifth character in the string (a blank) and delete five characters (IS A). This would leave S equal to THIS STRING.

Using the functions (LENGTH, CONCAT, POS, and COPY) and procedure (DELETE) we have covered thus far, write a program that will convert our strings (THIS IS A STRING) into a new string (NEW) which reads A STRING THIS IS. Write your program before proceeding.

While the program can have many different forms, the final test must be, does it accomplish the task? If your program differs from the one shown below but produces the same result, you have been successful.

```
PROGRAM SWITCH;

VAR
  S,NEW: STRING;

BEGIN  (* SWITCH *)
  S := 'THIS IS A STRING';
  WRITELN (S);
  NEW := COPY (S, POS('A',S), (LENGTH(S)
  -POS('A',S)+1));
  DELETE (S, POS(' A',S), (LENGTH(S)-POS
  (' A',S)+1);
  NEW := CONCAT (NEW, COPY(S,POS(' ',S),
  1), S);
  WRITELN (NEW)
END.  (* SWITCH *)
```

Note that in the last CONCAT function, we include a COPY of one character from the string, a space to separate STRING from THIS. Obviously, it would have been easier to count the positions and enter the Integer values than to use the POS and LENGTH functions, but this example illustrates the use of DELETE and all the functions we have covered thus far in the chapter.

16.7 INSERT

The INSERT procedure allows us to insert a string or substring into an existing string. The parameters for INSERT specify the string to be inserted, the target string, and the position of the insertion (an Integer value). For example,

```
S := 'THIS IS A STRING';
I := 'MUCH LONGER ';
INSERT (I, S, POS('STR',S));
```

will insert string I into string S at the position of the first character (S) of STR (the 11th character), resulting in the string

```
THIS IS A MUCH LONGER STRING
```

A more extensive insertion is shown in the following program:

```
PROGRAM INSERTION;

VAR
  S,I: STRING;

I := 'THIS IS A STRING';
I := 'MUCH LONGER ';
  INSERT (CONCAT(COPY(I,1,POS('H',I)),',
  ',I,' '), S,POS('ST',S));
  WRITELN (S)
END.  (* INSERTION *)
```

Can you predict the results of this program? While it is more efficient to incorporate all of the alterations on one line, the program would probably be easier to interpret if the changes were spread over several statements. Enter and run the program to see if your prediction was correct.

The string being inserted is the concatenation of four substrings:

```
COPY,(I,1,POS('H,I)
','
I (MUCH LONGER)
', '
```

The first substring copies the characters from position 1 to the position of the first H (i.e., the word MUCH) from string I. The second substring adds a comma and a space. The third adds the entire string I and the fourth adds another space. Thus, the result of the concatenation is MUCH, MUCH LONGER . This string is then inserted into our original string S beginning at the position of the substring STRING. The final result, as you have already seen, is the new string

```
THIS IS A MUCH, MUCH LONGER STRING
```

You should always remember that DELETE and INSERT are built-in procedures rather than functions and, like all other procedure calls, cannot be included in assignment statements.

FOCUS
On Problem
Solving

When a word processor performs an automatic **word wrap** (taking a word that extends beyond the right-hand margin and moving it down to the next line), it determines where the word begins by looking for the space preceding the word. Let's see if we can approximate this word wrap process on a simple string. For simplicity, we'll assume our line is only 20 characters long. We will enter a string longer than 20 characters and then let our program perform a word wrap on any words that extend beyond the right margin. There are two alternative approaches we could take to this problem. The first finds the position for the word wrap by starting at the 20th character and working backwards in the string until it finds a space. The second approach builds a new string up to a maximum of 20 characters by adding one word at a time from the existing string to the new string (again using the spaces to mark the ends of the words). Examples of both approaches will be presented to illustrate the different types of problems encountered by each approach.

We'll begin with the first approach, starting with the 20th character and working backwards. An algorithm for this problem might look like this:

1. Enter a string;
2. Determine the length of the string;
3. If the string is longer than 20 characters, then
   a. Find the last space preceding the 20th character;
   b. Split the string at the space;
   c. Repeat the process (steps 2 and 3) for the substring;

Further refinement of the second and third steps might take the following form:

2. Determine the length of the string;
3. If the string is longer than 20 characters then
   a. Beginning at position 21 and moving backwards:
      (1) If the character is a space:
         (a) Split the string at the space, making the first part a new string;
         (b) Remove the space from the end of the new string;
         (c) Output the new string;
         (d) Delete the first part of the string from the original string;
         (e) Repeat the process beginning at step 2;

Why do we start at the 21st space rather than the 20th space? This takes into consideration those occasions where the last character in the substring might be a space, i.e., if the 21st character is a space, the first 20 characters will fit within our margins. If the 21st character is not a space, the algorithm will simply proceed backwards until it finds a space. Coding the algorithm might produce a program similar to the one shown in exhibit 16–3.

Exhibit 16–3. Program WRAP

```
PROGRAM WRAP;

VAR
  S1: STRING;

PROCEDURE SPLIT(LONG:STRING);
  VAR
    SHORT: STRING;
    I,J: INTEGER;
  BEGIN  (* SPLIT *)
    I := 1;
    J := 21;
    WHILE LONG[J]<>' ' DO
      J := J - 1;
    SHORT := COPY (LONG,I,J);
    IF J = 21 THEN
      DELETE (SHORT,21,1);
    WRITELN (SHORT);
    DELETE (LONG,I,J);
    IF LENGTH(LONG) > 20 THEN
      SPLIT (LONG)
    ELSE
      WRITELN (LONG)
  END;  (* SPLIT *)

BEGIN  (* WRAP *)
  WRITELN ('ENTER A STRING OF AT LEAST 2
0 CHARACTERS');
  READLN (S1);
  WRITELN;
  WRITELN ('YOU HAVE ENTERED THE FOLLOWI
ING STRING:');
  WRITELN (S1);
  WRITELN ('MARGIN --              !');
  IF LENGTH(S1)>20 THEN
    SPLIT (S1)
  ELSE
    WRITELN (S1);
  WRITELN;
  WRITELN ('DONE')
END.  (* WRAP *)
```

Enter the program and run it. Use the following strings to test the program (you will have to run it three times):

```
THIS IS A STRING

THIS IS A LONGER STRING

THIS STRING IS APPROXIMATELY EIGHTY CHAR
     ACTERS IN LENGTH FROM BEGINNING TO END.
```

The first string is only 16 characters long and should be output on one line (without ever entering the procedure). The second string is 23 characters long and should be output on two lines. The third string is 79 characters long and should require five lines of output.

Notice that this program contains a recursive procedure call, i.e., the procedure SPLIT calls itself. This allows us to continue splitting the original string until it is less than 20 characters in length. Recursion will be discussed further in chapter 17. When you are sure the program runs properly, S(ave it under the name WRAP and clear your workspace.

The second approach is to extract words from the original string and use them to build a new string up to 20 characters in length. We can use spaces to mark the end of each word in the original string, but we will run into a problem when we reach the last word—it usually will not have a space following it. There are a number of different approaches we can take to solve this problem, but we will use a very simple one: we will have the program add a space at the end of the string. This will allow us to treat the last word in the same manner as every other word in the string. Our algorithm for this approach might be:

1. Enter a string;
2. Add a space at the end of the string;
3. While any subset of the original string remains:
   a. Extract the first word in the string;
   b. Delete the first word from the original string;
   c. If the length of a new string and the extracted word is less than 21 characters then:
      (1) Combine the word and the new string;
   d. If the length of the new string and the extracted word is not less than 21 characters then:
      (1) Delete the space at the end of the new string;
      (2) Output the new string;
      (3) Delete the new string;
      (4) Add the extracted word to the empty string;
4. If the original string has been completely deleted:
   a. Output the last new string

Step 4 is necessary to handle the last segment of the original string, which may not be 20 characters long and, therefore, not output by section 3d. Coding the algorithm would produce the program in exhibit 16–4. When you have entered and compiled this program, test it with the same strings you used to test program WRAP, i.e.

```
THIS IS A STRING

THIS IS A LONGER STRING

THIS STRING IS APPROXIMATELY EIGHTY CHAR
    ACTERS IN LENGTH FROM BEGINNING TO END.
```

Exhibit 16–4. Program WRAP2

```
PROGRAM WRAP2;

CONST
  MARK = ' ';
  EMPTY = '';

VAR
  S1: STRING;

PROCEDURE BUILD (LONG:STRING);
  VAR
    WORD,NEW: STRING;
    I,J: INTEGER;
  BEGIN  (* BUILD *)
    NEW := EMPTY;
    INSERT(MARK,LONG,LENGTH(LONG)+1);
    WHILE LENGTH(LONG) > 0 DO
      BEGIN  (* WHILE LOOP *)
        WORD := COPY(LONG,1,POS(MARK,LON
        G));
        DELETE (LONG,1,POS(MARK,LONG));
        IF LENGTH(CONCAT(NEW,WORD)) < 21
          THEN
            NEW := CONCAT(NEW,WORD)
          ELSE
            BEGIN  (* ELSE *)
              DELETE (NEW,LENGTH(NEW),1);
              WRITELN (NEW);
              NEW := WORD
            END;  (* ELSE *)
        IF LENGTH(LONG) = 0 THEN
          WRITELN (NEW)
      END  (* WHILE LOOP *)
  END;  (* BUILD *)

BEGIN  (* WRAP2 *)
  WRITELN ('ENTER A STRING OF AT LEAST 2
  0 CHARACTERS');
  READLN (S1);
  WRITELN;
  WRITELN ('YOU HAVE ENTERED THE FOLLOW
  ING STRING:');
  WRITELN (S1);
  WRITELN ('MARGIN --            !');
  IF LENGTH(S1)>20 THEN
    BUILD (S1)
  ELSE
    WRITELN (S1);
  WRITELN;
  WRITELN ('DONE')
END.  (* WRAP2 *)
```

This program should give the same results as program WRAP. S(ave this program under the name WRAP2. ■

16.8 LONG INTEGERS

There is one additional string procedure in UCSD Pascal, but before we look at it, we will examine the **long integer**, a special Integer data type that is available in UCSD Pascal. You may remember that normal Integer values can range from -32768 to 32767. These values are the smallest and largest Integer values that the Apple can represent in binary notation. Pascal actually has a built-in constant called **MAXINT** that defines the largest allowable Integer value. The value of MAXINT may vary with the brand of computer you are using, but on the Apple, MAXINT is always 32767. Pascal allows us to exceed these limitations by using special values called long integers. A long integer is declared in the variable declaration statement by appending a length to the data type Integer, for example

```
I,J: INTEGER[20];
```

This statement declares variables I and J to be of type Long Integer. What is the difference between a long integer and a normal Integer value? The normal Integer value is stored in the Apple in binary notation, while the long integer is stored as a decimal number, in this case up to 20 decimal digits. This means I and J could each have a maximum value of

99999999999999999999

The largest (or smallest) long integer we can declare is 36 digits long.

The major advantage of long integers is that they provide us with greater precision than ordinary Integers or Real numbers. For example, suppose we want to add the following numbers:

$$
\begin{array}{r}
3{,}845{,}600{,}700 \\
+ \qquad 4{,}290 \\
\hline
3{,}845{,}604{,}990
\end{array}
$$

The first number is too large to use a normal Integer value. But what would happen if we use Real numbers? Enter and run the program in exhibit 16–5 to find out.

When you run this program, you can see that the value of A is stored as 3.84560E9 and the value of B is stored as 4.29000E3. When added, these values produce a result of 3.84561E9 (3,845,610,000). The second result shows that the long integer method gives 3845604990 (3,845,604,990). The difference between these results is 5,010. While this difference is small in

Exhibit 16–5. Program
LONG

```
PROGRAM LONG;

VAR
   A,B: REAL;
   I,J: INTEGER[20];

BEGIN  (* LONG *)
   A := 3.8456007E9;
   B := 4.29E3;
   I := 3845600700;
   J := 4290;
   WRITELN ('A = ',A,'       B = ',B);
   WRITELN ('SUM = ',A+B);
   WRITELN;
   WRITELN (I+J)
END.  (* LONG *)
```

proportion to the total result, it is not a small number. Thus, long integers can be useful when we need accuracy to the nearest digit and we are working with extremely large numbers. If we were working with financial data, we would probably want accuracy to the nearest penny. By using long integers and treating all values as if they were in cents, we can obtain the accuracy we need, for example

```
PROGRAM ACCURATE;

VAR
   SALES,COSTS,PROFIT: INTEGER[36];

BEGIN  (* ACCURATE *)
   SALES := 3450890324;
   COSTS := 1872948713;
   PROFIT := SALES - COSTS;
   WRITELN (PROFIT)
END.  (* ACCURATE *)
```

In this case, you would simply have to remember that the result (1577941611) must be divided by 100 (mentally) to give a result in dollars and cents. If you want to get fancy, you could add a program segment to make the conversion for you. You would have to calculate two long integer values in that case, the dollar value and the cents value. The dollar value can be determined by dividing the result by 100.

```
DOLLAR := PROFIT DIV 100);
```

This would produce a value of 15779416. To determine the cents value, you can simply subtract the DOLLAR value (expressed in terms of pennies) from the original (PROFIT) value.

```
CENTS := PROFIT - DOLLAR*100;
```

To output the result in dollars and cents, we could use the following statement:

```
WRITELN (DOLLAR,'.',CENTS);
```

All of the normal Integer arithmetic functions except MOD can be used with long integers. You can also assign Integer values to a long integer variable or mix Integers and long integers in the same expression; the result will be a long integer, and the Integers will be converted to long integers before the expression is evaluated.

Long integer values can also be assigned to Integer variables as long as the value of the long integer does not exceed MAXINT. When assigning long integer values to an Integer variable, however, you must use the TRUNC function. If NORMALINT is an Integer and LONGINT is a long integer and we want to assign the value of LONGINT to NORMALINT, we might use the following program segment:

```
IF (LONGINT<MAXINT)AND(LONGINT>-MAXINT)THEN
   NORMALINT := TRUNC (LONGINT);
```

The IF..THEN statement protects us from those cases where the value of LONGINT is too large (greater than MAXINT) or too small (less than –MAXINT) to assign to an Integer variable. We might even want to add:

```
ELSE
   WRITELN ('VALUE OF LONGINT OUTSIDE
MAXINT RANGE');
```

so that we know what's happening when the program executes. Now that you have a better understanding of long integers, we'll move to the last string procedure available on the Apple, one not listed in exhibit 16–1.

16.9 STR

The STR procedure is a special built-in procedure that creates a string with the value of a specified integer. The parameters must specify the integer variable and the string name, for example

```
STR (LONGINT,INTSTRING);
```

assigns the value of the long integer LONGINT to the string INTSTRING. In section 16.9 we split a long integer value into dollar and cents parts and placed a decimal between the two separate values. If we use the STR procedure in combination with the other functions and procedures we have learned, we could add not only a decimal point, but a dollar sign and commas as well. We would first convert the value to a string, then add a decimal point to the left of the next-to-last character. We could then begin at the decimal point and insert commas every three characters to the left, as long as there was at least one character remaining to the left of the last comma. We could then complete our display by inserting a dollar sign at the beginning of the string.

If you would like to try your hand at writing a program segment to accomplish these tasks, do so before proceeding. The program shown in exhibit 16–6 uses the body of the AC-CURATE program shown in section 16.9 with some alterations and adds a procedure named DISPLAY to produce the desired effect.

The first statement in the procedure converts the long integer into a string. The second adds the decimal point. The third and fourth lines make up an IF..THEN statement that adds a comma

Exhibit 16–6. Program DOLLARS

```
PROGRAM DOLLARS;

TYPE
  LI = INTEGER[20];

VAR
  SALES,COSTS,PROFIT: LI;

PROCEDURE DISPLAY (AMOUNT:LI);
  VAR
    MONEY: STRING;
  BEGIN  (* DISPLAY *)
    STR (AMOUNT,MONEY);
    INSERT ('.',MONEY,LENGTH(MONEY)-1);
    IF LENGTH(MONEY)-3 > 3 THEN
       INSERT (',',MONEY,POS('.',MONEY)-3);
    WHILE POS(',',MONEY) > 4 DO
       INSERT (',',MONEY,POS(',',MONEY)-3);
    INSERT ('$',MONEY,1);
    WRITELN (MONEY)
  END;  (* DISPLAY *)

BEGIN  (* DOLLARS *)
  SALES := 3450890324;
  COSTS := 1872948713;
  PROFIT := SALES - COSTS;
  WRITELN (PROFIT);
  DISPLAY (PROFIT)
END.  (* DOLLARS *)
```

if there are more than three characters to the left of the decimal point. The fifth and sixth lines are a WHILE..DO loop that continues to add commas every three characters as long as there are four characters or more to the left of the previous comma. The seventh line completes the string by adding a dollar sign ($) preceding the value (string). As you can see from the program results,

```
        1577941611
    $15,779,416.11
```

the altered string is much easier to read than the original long integer value.

16.10 SUMMARY

In this chapter you learned about four built-in string handling functions and three built-in string procedures. The functions were: LENGTH, which returned the length of the string (number of characters including spaces) as an Integer value; CONCAT, which concatenates or joins two or more strings; POS, which determines the position of a specified character or the first character of a specified string in a designated target string; and COPY, which copies a character or set of characters from an existing string.

The three built-in procedures were: DELETE, which deleted a specified number of characters from a string; INSERT, which inserted another string or a substring within a designated string; and STR, which copied a long integer value into a string.

You also learned about a special UCSD Pascal data type, the long integer, which could be used to store Integer values up to 36 digits long. Because long integer values are stored in decimal rather than binary form, they can have up to six times as many significant digits as a normal Integer value or a Real data type. They are used primarily to gain additional accuracy when performing calculations with large numbers.

Review Questions

1. What are Pascal's built-in String functions?

2. What are Pascal's built-in String procedures?

3. What does LENGTH do? What are its parameters? Give an example of its use.

4. What does CONCAT do? What are its parameters? Give an example of its use.

5. What does POS do? What are its parameters? Give an example of its use.

SUMMARY of Pascal Syntax

Reserved Words	Built-in Procedures	Built-in Functions	Library Units
PROGRAM	WRITE	EOF	TURTLEGRAPHICS
USES	WRITELN	ABS	APPLESTUFF
CONST	READ	SQR	TRANSCEND
TYPE	READLN	SQRT	
SET..OF	NEW	ROUND	
PACKED	RESET	TRUNC	
ARRAY OF	REWRITE	EXP	
RECORD	PUT	LN	
FILE OF	GET	LOG	
VAR	SEEK	PWROFTEN	
FUNCTION	CLOSE	ATAN	
FORWARD	LOCK	SIN	
PROCEDURE	INITTURTLE	COS	*Boolean Constants*
BEGIN	PENCOLOR	ORD	
FOR..DO	MOVE	CHR	
TO	TURN	PRED	FALSE
DOWNTO	MOVETO	SUCC	TRUE
REPEAT	TURNTO	EOLN	
UNTIL	TEXTMODE	**LENGTH**	
WHILE..DO	GRAFMODE	**CONCAT**	
IF	PAGE(OUTPUT)	POS	
THEN	**DELETE**	**COPY**	
ELSE	INSERT	STR	
CASE..OF			
WITH..DO			
END			
DIV			
MOD			*Integer Constants*
NIL			
AND			
OR			**MAXINT**
NOT			
IN			

6. What does COPY do? What are its parameters? Give an example of its use.

7. What does DELETE do? What are its parameters? Give an example of its use.

8. What does INSERT do? What are its parameters? Give an example of its use.

9. What is a long integer? How does it differ from a normal Integer data type? How are long integers created?

10. What is MAXINT? What is the value of MAXINT?

11. What is the largest value that a long integer can have? Why are long integers more accurate than Real data types?

12. Describe a situation in which we might want to use long integers.

13. What does STR do? What are its parameters? Give an example of its use.

Programming Exercises	

1. Write a program segment that outputs each character of a String separately.

2. Write a program segment that extracts the first word in a string and outputs it to the screen.

3. Write a program segment that extracts the first word in a string and outputs it to the screen.

4. Write a program segment that inserts an asterisk after the first occurrence of the letter A within a string.

5. Write a program segment that inserts * MID * in the middle of a string.

6. Write a program segment that sums the values 34,567,293 and 88,914,006 and outputs the result to the nearest integer.

7. Write a program segment that sums the values 0.284,973,805 and 0.066,093,295, and then subtracts 0.198,774,316 and outputs the result correct to nine decimal places. (Hint: you may want to use the STR procedure.)

Diagnostic Exercises	

In the following exercises, explain what the result of each statement or set of statements will be if String variable ST is THE APPLE COMPUTER SPEAKS PASCAL and NS is VERY WELL.

8. a. POS('E',ST)
   b. POS('C',ST)
   c. POS('L',NS)
   d. POS('WELL',NS)

9. a. LENGTH(ST)
   b. LENGTH(NS)
   c. LENGTH(CONCAT(NS, ' INDEED'))
   d. LENGTH(CONCAT(NS,NS,NS))

10. WRITELN (LENGTH(ST)+LENGTH(NS))

11. WRITELN (CONCAT(ST,NS))

12. WRITELN (COPY (ST,POS('A',ST),7))

13. WRITELN (CONCAT(COPY(ST,POS('PA',ST),6),' ',
            COPY(ST,POS('PA',ST)+1,2),COPY(NS,5,5)))

14. DELETE (ST,1,4);
    INSERT (ST,COPY(ST,POS('S',ST),1),POS('R',ST)+1);
    WRITELN (ST)

15. INSERT (NS,CONCAT(COPY(NS,1,4),', '),1);
    WRITELN (NS)

16. REPEAT
       IF POS(' ',ST) > 0 THEN
          DELETE (ST,POS(' ',ST),1);
    UNTIL POS(' ',ST) = 0

Problems

17. Write a procedure that allows the user to input six words and then outputs those words in a single String, first in the order they were entered and then in reverse order. Be sure to leave a space between words.

18. Write a procedure that will allow the user to input a String and then remove all spaces from the String.

19. Write a procedure that will allow the user to input a String and then replace every occurrence of the letter A with an asterisk.

20. Using the built-in String functions and procedures, develop an algorithm for a program that (1) allows the user to input a String of up to 200 characters; (2) allows the user to input two words, which we'll call word1 and word2; and then (3) replaces all occurrences of word1 with word2.

21. Code and test the algorithm developed in problem 20.

17

Recursion, Searching, and Sorting

This chapter will expand on recursion, which we have used in some of the example problems in previous chapters. It will also introduce methods for searching and sorting lists of data. **Searching** means finding the location of a particular value in a list of values. **Sorting** means putting a list or table of values into some kind of order, typically ascending or descending, although sorting processes can also be used to alphabetize lists of characters or strings. There are numerous methods of searching and sorting lists; this chapter will review a sample of the more popular approaches. Most programmers do not develop new algorithms and procedures every time they need to sort a list. Once they have a procedure that works properly, they use it over and over again. This chapter will present the more common methods, so you can select one and use it whenever you need to sort or alphabetize a list.

17.1 RECURSION

As you have already seen, a **recursive** procedure or function is one that calls itself. A procedure or function can be recursive, but a program cannot be. Recursive procedures and functions are sometimes used in place of iterative loops, because they allow us to repeat an entire function or procedure rather than just a portion of it. They also allow us to define a function in terms of itself; this can be an extremely useful approach in some problem-solving applications. Keep in mind, however, that recursion is not an easy concept to master and it can produce erroneous results or program-terminating errors if used incorrectly. Recursion can also require more computer memory than some of Pascal's repetitive routines.

Let's look at an example. Pascal does not have a function that will raise a value to a power, e.g., X^5; we will write such a function, first using a normal iterative approach and then using a recursive function. Our iterative approach will use a FOR..DO loop (for simplicity, we will assume that the power P cannot be less than 1):

```
PROGRAM POWER;

VAR
  X,P,RESULT,I:INTEGER;

BEGIN  (* POWER *)
  WRITE ('INPUT X VALUE: ');
  READLN (X);
  WRITE ('INPUT POWER: ');
  READLN (P);
  RESULT := X;
  IF P > 1 THEN
    FOR I:= 1 TO P-1 DO
      RESULT := RESULT * X;
  WRITELN (X,' TO THE ',P,' POWER = ',RE
SULT)
END.  (* POWER *)
```

This program sets the value of RESULT equal to the value of X (the equivalent of P = 1) and then, if P is greater than 1, multiplies the value of RESULT by X P – 1 times, for example, if P = 5, RESULT is multiplied by X 4 times. Enter this program and then test it by entering 2 for the value of X and 5 for the value of P. In this example P = 5, so the loop produces

```
RESULT * X * X * X * X
```

which is equivalent to

```
X * X * X * X * X
```

or X to the 5th power, giving us an answer of 32.

Now we'll write the program using a recursive function instead of a loop (exhibit 17–1). In this program, the recursive function RESULT is used. Note that if P1, RESULT is assigned the value of the function RESULT(X,P – 1) * X for example, RESULT(2,5):= RESULT(2,4) * 2. Thus this assignment statement calls the function RESULT again, this time with the parameters X and P – 1 (2 and 4 in our example). In the new call, P has a value of 4, which is still greater than 1, so the assignment statement is executed again and the function is called with P equal to 3. This recursive calling continues until the value of is 1, then the ELSE branch of the loop is executed.

On the first pass through the IF..THEN statement, no value is assigned to RESULT, since RESULT(2,5) := RESULT(2,4) * 2 and RESULT(2,4) has no value at this point. But RESULT(2,4) is

Exhibit 17–1. Program POWER2

```
PROGRAM POWER2;

VAR
  X,P:INTEGER;

FUNCTION RESULT (VALUE,POWER:INTEGER):IN
TEGER;
  BEGIN  (* RESULT *)
    IF POWER > 1 THEN
      RESULT := RESULT(VALUE,POWER-1) *
      VALUE
    ELSE
      RESULT := VALUE
  END;  (* RESULT *)

BEGIN  (* POWER2 *)
  WRITE ('INPUT X VALUE: ');
  READLN (X);
  WRITE ('INPUT POWER: ');
  READLN (P);
  WRITELN (X,' RAISED TO THE ',P,' POWER
  = ',RESULT(X,P))
END.  (* POWER2 *)
```

a function call that will be evaluated as RESULT(2,3) *2; RE-SULT(2,3) will be evaluated as RESULT(2,2) * 2, and so on. Exhibit 17–2 shows the values of RESULT and POWER at each pass through the function. Since each assignment statement assigns RESULT the value of the next function call, the resulting value for each of the first four calls is undefined, i.e., it cannot be evaluated until the result of the next call is returned (and is defined). This means that the first IF..THEN..ELSE statement is not completed before the next one begins. In this situation, Pascal puts the first call result on hold until it gets the result of the second call, which is also put on hold until the result of the third call is obtained, and so on. Thus a number of values are left on hold. The uncompleted statements (and undefined results) are placed in a **stack**, in the Apple's memory.

When the function parameters are finally (2,1), the ELSE is executed and a value of 2 (RESULT: = 2) is returned. Once this value is obtained, the last undefined value on the stack (RESULT(2,1)*2) can be evaluated as 2*2 or 4. This result is then passed to the next call in the stack, producing 4*2 or 8, and so on, until every call in the stack has been evaluated. The last call in the stack thus produces our answer of 32.

The fifth recursive call, which causes execution of the ELSE portion of the statement, is known as a **limit call** because it is the last (or limit) of the recursive calls. Every recursive function or procedure must have a limit call. Without a limit call, the recursive process could in theory continue forever, producing **infinite recursion**. If the recursive calls create a stack, the process will not actually continue forever, because the computer will soon run out of memory space for the stack, resulting in a memory overflow error. Thus, it is important to remember that recursive procedures or functions *must* include an exit point, usually an IF..THEN branch, for the recursive calls; otherwise an error will result.

We should also note that although our examples seem to give us an easy solution to Pascal's omission of powers, they are of limited use. Because of the MAXINT limitation, we are limited to fairly small values in actual use. For example, if X is 7, the power to which we raise X cannot exceed 5 (7^5 = 16807).

Exhibit 17–2.
Evaluation of a
Recursive Function

Call Number	Power Value	Function Call	Resulting Value
1	5	RESULT(2,5)	RESULT (2,4) * 2
2	4	RESULT(2,4)	RESULT (2,3) * 2
3	3	RESULT(2,3)	RESULT (2,2) * 2
4	2	RESULT(2,2)	RESULT (2,1) * 2
5	1	RESULT(2,1)	2

17.2 SEARCHING TECHNIQUES

Searching means finding the location of a particular value in a list. There are two basic approaches to searching, the linear search and the binary search. The linear search can be used with any data set, but the binary search routine can only be used with an ordered list (all values in ascending or descending order).

Linear Searches

Suppose we have the following list (array) of fifteen values

37 14 86 11 92 43 77 82 29 38 95 64 51 60 16

and we want to find the position of the number 29 within the list. We could write a program that would compare the value we were searching for with each value in the list, beginning at one end of the list and moving toward the other end until a match is made. The program segment that does this might look like:

```
KEY := 29;
I := 0;
REPEAT
  I := I + 1
UNTIL KEY = LIST[I];
WRITELN (KEY,' IS AT LOCATION ',I,' IN T
HE LIST.');
```

The variable KEY is the value we are looking for. The counter I is initialized to zero, and then we use a REPEAT..UNTIL loop to index the counter until the Ith variable in our list is equal to the value of KEY. At that point, the program exits the loop and outputs the value of I, which corresponds to the location of KEY within the list. In this example, 29 was the 9th value in the list, so the program would execute the loop 9 times (making 9 comparisons). The values in the list were in no particular order, but we wanted to search in a logical manner, so we simply began at one end of the list and proceeded toward the other end. This process is called a **linear search**, since it moves through the list in a linear fashion.

In this example, we assumed our KEY value was in our list. If we were uncertain whether the KEY was in the list, we could modify our program segment to prevent an error and alert us to that fact:

```
KEY := 29;
LIMIT := 15;
I := 0;
WHILE I < LIMIT DO
  REPEAT
    I := I + 1
```

```
     UNTIL KEY = LIST[I];
  IF KEY = LIST[I] THEN
     WRITELN (KEY,' IS AT LOCATION ',I,' IN
     THE LIST.')
  ELSE
     WRITELN(KEY,' IS NOT IN THIS LIST');
```

The linear approach works equally well with ordered and random lists. If the list is long, however, and the value we are searching for is near the end of the list, the loop will have to be repeated many times before we find the value. For example, suppose we have an ordered list containing the numbers from 1 to 1000 (incremented by 1) and we are searching for the value 899. A program using a linear search must make 899 comparisons before it finds the value. In searching this list for values between 1 and 1000, we could say that on the average, the program will make 501 comparisons ((1 + 1000)/2) before terminating. Obviously, the longer the list, the more comparisons that will have to be made before the correct value is found.

Binary Searches

When the values in the list are ordered, a second search procedure known as the **binary search** can be used. The binary search divides the list of values in half by selecting a value in or near the middle of the list as a beginning point. If that middle value is lower than the value being searched for (KEY), the lower half of the list is discarded (ignored) and the process is repeated with the remainder of the list. If the middle value is greater than the KEY value, the upper half of the list is discarded. The process is repeated as many times as necessary until the correct value is found.

For example, if we were searching for the value 39 in the list of fifteen values below, we would first compare our KEY (39) with the middle value in the list (the 8th value), or 26.

2 6 11 14 19 23 24 26 29 30 31 35 39 41 49
                                ↑

Since our KEY value is greater than 26, we discard the first half of the list, including the 26. We would then compare our KEY with the middle value in the remaining list, 35.

29 30 31 35 39 41 49
            ↑

Since our KEY is still larger that 35, we again discard the lower end of the list, leaving

39 41 49
 ↑

This time the middle of the remaining list, 41, is higher than KEY, so we discard the upper end of the list, leaving

39

Although 39 was the 13th value in the list, the binary search process only took four comparisons (as opposed to 13 with a linear search) to locate it. This efficiency is even more apparent on longer lists. Remember our list of 1 to 1000 with a KEY value of 899? The first search would eliminate 1 to 500, the second 500 to 750, and the third 751 to 875. A linear search would require 875 comparisons (rather than 3) to eliminate those first 875 values.

Although the binary search is much faster in performance, there is a price: the program is more complex to write. In addition to subdividing lists and making comparisons, we must also keep track of where we are (location) in the original list. A program that performs a binary search is shown in exhibit 17–3.

Because we don't have an actual list, the program begins by using a loop to create a list of 1000 ordered values (1 to 1000 to make it easy for us to test the program). It then initializes the LO and HI values and evaluates the MID value. (The WRITELN ('MID = ',MID); statements and the COUNT variable are included in this example to make it easier for us to follow the process and to give us a count on the number of comparisons made before the search is completed.)

We then use the WHILE..DO loop to compare our KEY value to the value at the MID location of the list. If the values differ, we use an IF..THEN to see if KEY is greater than the LIST[MID] value. If it is, we assign a value of MID + 1 to LO (thus discarding the lower half of the list) and recalculate MID. If KEY is not greater than LIST[MID], it must be less than LIST [MID], (since the loop would not be entered if they were equal) and the ELSE statement is executed, setting HI equal to MID − 1 (thus discarding the upper half of the list) and recalculating MID. This process continues until KEY is equal to LIST [MID]. Enter and run the program. Test it with a number of different values. What is the largest number of comparisons required to locate a value? The value 899?

As you can see from your results, this is a much more efficient searching process for ordered lists. It takes 10 comparisons to locate 899 with a binary search, versus 899 with a linear search. In fact, 10 is the maximum number of comparisons a binary search will ever have to make to locate a value from a list of 1000 values; the average number of comparisons required will be 6! A binary search is definitely more efficient than a linear search, and as you saw in the example program, it is longer and more difficult to write.

Exhibit 17–3. Program
BINARYSEARCH

```
PROGRAM BINARYSEARCH;

VAR
   LIST: ARRAY[1..1000] OF INTEGER;
   KEY,LO,HI,MID,COUNT,I:INTEGER;

BEGIN  (* BINARYSEARCH *)
   FOR I:= 1 TO 1000 DO
     LIST[I] :=I; (* INITIALIZES LIST *)
   WRITE ('ENTER KEY VALUE --> ');
   READLN (KEY);
   LO := 1;
   HI := 1000;
   MID := (LO + HI) DIV 2;
   WRITELN ('MID = ',MID);
   COUNT := 1;
   WHILE KEY<>LIST[MID] DO
     BEGIN  (* WHILE..DO *)
        COUNT := COUNT + 1;
        IF KEY > LIST[MID] THEN
          BEGIN  (* IF..THEN *)
             LO := MID + 1;
             MID := (LO + HI) DIV 2
          END  (* IF..THEN *)
        ELSE
          BEGIN  (* ELSE *)
             HI := MID - 1;
             MID := (LO + HI) DIV 2
          END;  (* ELSE *)
        WRITELN ('MID = ',MID)
     END;  (* WHILE..DO *)
   WRITELN ('LOCATION = ',MID,'    NO SEA
     RCHES = ',COUNT)
END.  (* BINARYSEARCH *)
```

17.3 SWAPPING

The fact that the binary search routine works only with lists
that are in sequential order raises the question, can we use the
computer to take a list of randomly arranged values and rear-
range them into a sequential order? The answer to this question
is yes, this process is called **sorting**. Before discussing sorting,
however, we need to examine a more fundamental process
called **swapping**. To change the order of values within a list, we
will **swap** them, i.e., switch their positions. The swapping procedure is relatively simple. Suppose we have two variables, A
and B, and we want to swap their values. The algorithm

1. Assign B's value to A;
2. Assign A's value to B.

states what we want to accomplish, but it won't work in this form. If A = 5 and B = 10, step 1 would produce A = 10, and then step 2 would have no effect. We need to create a third variable, TEMP, store A's value temporarily:

1. Assign A's value to TEMP;
2. Assign B's value to A;
3. Assign TEMP's value to B.

With this algorithm, step 1 would result in A = 5, B = 10, and TEMP = 5. Step 2 would then produce A = 10, B = 10, and TEMP = 5. And step 3 would complete the swap, with A = 10, B = 5, and TEMP = 5. As you will soon see, this basic swapping procedure is an essential part of any sorting approach.

17.4 SORTING

There are many different methods that can be used to sort a list into a particular order. We will discuss only six of the more common approaches: bubble sort, modified bubble sort, selection sort, insertion sort, Shell's sort, and quicksort.

Bubble Sort

The most common type of sorting procedure is known as the **bubble sort**. The bubble begins at the beginning of the list and compares the first element in the list with the second. If the first element is greater than the second, they are swapped. Then the second element is compared with the third, and so on. This method is called a bubble sort because the higher values tend to rise in the list like bubbles.

We can illustrate the bubble sort with the following list:

86 53 67 29 14

On the first pass, 86 is compared with 53 and since 86 53, they are swapped:

53 86 67 29 14

The second value (now 86) is then compared with 67 and since 86 67, they are also swapped:

53 67 86 29 14

The process will continue until 86 is not greater than the next number in the list or until it is the last number in the list.

53 67 29 14 86

The process then repeats itself, starting with the first element in the list. Successive passes through the list are shown below:

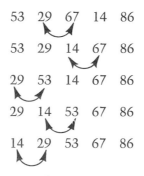

53   29   67   14   86

53   29   14   67   86

29   53   14   67   86

29   14   53   67   86

14   29   53   67   86

Because the process always returns to the first position after making successive comparisons and swaps, we must have some way to tell the computer when it has finished. An obvious method of determining whether or not the sort is completed would be to ask the question, were any swaps made in this last pass? If the answer to that question is no, we have finished the sort and can stop. Instead of this question, we will use the statement "there were no swaps made in the last pass" and use a Boolean variable to represent the responses True (the sort is completed) and False (continue the process).

Before proceeding, we will set up a list of values that we can use to test each of our sorting procedures. Clear your workfile, enter the Editor, and enter the following list.

```
86
53
67
29
14
92
 7
34
19
48
82
71
50
23
95
```

Once you have entered the list, Q(uit the Editor and W(rite the list to a file named MIXED. Then clear the workfile again and enter the program in exhibit 17–4. Procedure SORT performs the bubble sort. The main program inputs the values to be sorted and calls the SORT procedure. When you have the program entered, compile and run it. This procedure takes 154 comparisons to complete the sort. T(ransfer this program to your storage disk under the name BUBBLESORT.

Exhibit 17–4. Program BUBBLESORT

```
PROGRAM BUBBLESORT;

TYPE
  NOS = ARRAY[1..15] OF INTEGER;

VAR
  LIST: NOS;
  NUM,I: INTEGER;
  DF:TEXT;

PROCEDURE SORT (VAR VALUES:NOS; LIMIT:INT
EGER);
  VAR
    I,J,TEMP:INTEGER;
    FLAG:BOOLEAN;
  BEGIN (* SORT *)
    FLAG := FALSE;
    FOR I:= 1 TO LIMIT-1 DO
      BEGIN  (* FOR..DO *)
        IF VALUES[I] > VALUES[I+1] THEN
          BEGIN  (* IF..THEN *)
            FLAG := TRUE;
            TEMP := VALUES[I];
            VALUES[I] := VALUES[I 1];
            VALUES[I 1] := TEMP;
            FOR J:= 1 TO LIMIT DO
              WRITE (VALUES[J]:4);
            WRITELN
          END  (* IF..THEN *)
      END  (* FOR..DO *)
    IF FLAG THEN SORT(VALUES,LIMIT)
  END;  (* SORT *)

BEGIN  (* BUBBLESORT *)
  RESET (DF,'MIXED.TEXT');
  NUM := 0;
  WHILE NOT EOF(DF) DO
    BEGIN  (* WHILE..DO LOOP *)
      NUM := NUM + 1;
      READLN(DF,LIST[NUM]);
      WRITELN(LIST[NUM])
    END;  (* WHILE..DO LOOP *)
  CLOSE(DF);
  SORT(LIST,NUM)
END.  (* BUBBLESORT *)
```

Modified Bubble Sort

You may have noticed that in the BUBBLESORT program, the largest value "bubbled" to the end of the list by the time the

FOR..DO loop was completed once. The second largest value moved to the next-to-last spot on the list the second time the FOR..DO loop was executed, and so on. This means that each time the procedure exits from the FOR..DO loop, another value has moved to its correct location at the end of the list. Thus, further comparisons between these end values become unnecessary; any swaps are made closer and closer to the beginning of the list. We can eliminate these redundant comparisons and speed the excution of the program by reducing the number of comparisons by one each time we exit the FOR..DO loop. We can do this by changing the value of LIMIT after the end of the FOR..DO loop:

```
          ⋮
    END;   (* FOR..DO LOOP *)
  LIMIT := LIMIT-1;
  IF FLAG THEN SORT(NOS.LIMIT)
          ⋮
```

Make this change and run the program. This procedure only required 99 comparisons to complete the sort. This is a reduction of 55 comparisons (approximately 36%); it would be even more noticeable in a longer list. T(ransfer this program to your storage disk under the name MODBUBBLE.

Selection Sort

As you may have noticed in the bubble sort procedure, large values that start out near the beginning of the list must pass through each location between their original position and their final destination. The **selection sort** attempts to avoid this multiple swapping by selecting the lowest (or highest) value in the list and swapping it with the value in the first position. It then selects the second lowest value and swaps it with the value in the second position. This selection and swapping process continues until the next-to-last value has been selected and swapped. Using our earlier example

86   53   67   29   14

this procedure would search the list for the lowest value (14) and then swap it with the value in the first location (86), producing

14 53 67 29 86

It would then locate the second lowest value (29) and swap it with the value in the second location (53).

14   29   67   53   86

The next swap moves the 53 to the third location in the list, swapping it with the 67.

14   29   53   67   86

When the next value (67) is located, it is already in its correct location and the process is completed.

The SORT procedure in exhibit 17–5 illustrates the selection sort process. Change the name of your BUBBLESORT program to SELECTION and replace the SORT procedure with the one shown in exhibit 17–5. When you have made these changes, compile and run the program. While this procedure requires about the same number of comparisons as the previous one (in MODBUBBLE), it only requires 14 swaps (as opposed to 50 in MODBUBBLE). S(ave or T(ransfer this program with the name SELECTION.

Insertion Sort

The **insertion sort** takes a slightly different approach than the other sorting methods we have looked at. The insertion sorting procedure takes new values or additions to a list and inserts them at the proper location. It does this by comparing each value to be inserted with each value in the list, beginning at the first position in the list. If the value to be inserted is less than the existing value, the new value is inserted at either the last location in the existing list or at the location of the first value

Exhibit 17–5.
Procedure SORT

```
PROCEDURE SORT(VAR VALUES:NOS;LIMIT:INTEGER);

  VAR
    I,J,TEMP,SMALL:INTEGER;
  BEGIN  (* SORT *)
    FOR I:= 1 TO LIMIT-1 DO
      BEGIN
        SMALL := I;
        TEMP := VALUES[I];
        FOR J:= I+1 TO LIMIT DO
          IF TEMP > VALUES[J] THEN
            BEGIN  (* SELECT SMALLEST *)
              SMALL := J;
              TEMP := VALUES[J]
            END;  (* SELECT SMALLEST *)
        VALUES[SMALL] := VALUES[I];
        VALUES[I] := TEMP
      END
  END; (* SORT *)
```

that is greater than the one to be inserted. Before we make an insertion, however, all the values from the point of the insertion to the end of the list must be shifted to the right (or down) one location.

Let's use the numbers from our earlier example to see how the insertion sort works, but we will assume the values are entered one at a time, starting at the left.

86   53   67   29   14

The first value entered is 86, so it is placed in the first position in the currently empty list.

86
↑

The second entry is 53. It is compared with 86, and since 86 is greater than 53, 86 is shifted to the second location in the list and 53 is inserted at location 1.

53   86
↑   →

The third entry, 67, is compared with 53 and then 86. Since 86 is greater than 67, it is shifted again and 67 is inserted in its place

53   67   86
     ↑   →

The fourth value, 29, is compared with 53, and since 53 is greater, all three numbers in the list are shifted and 29 is inserted in the first location.

29   53   67   86
↑   →   →   →

The last value, 14, is compared with 29, so all the values in the list are shifted and 14 is inserted at the first location. This completes the entries, and we have a list that is in the proper ascending order:

14   29   53   67   86
↑   →   →   →   →

In an insertion sort, we have insertions rather than swaps, and the efficiency of the sort would depend on how many numbers are shifted each time. Because the insertion sort inserts each value once, the number of insertions will always equal the number of values in the list.

We will modify our INSERTION program once more, this time altering the order of the steps so that the insertion sort takes place after each value is read from the data file. The resulting program is shown in exhibit 17–6. (We assume that we

Exhibit 17-6. Program
INSERTION

```
PROGRAM INSERTION;

TYPE
  NOS = ARRAY[1..15] OF INTEGER;
VAR
  LIST: NOS;
  ENTRY,SHIFTS,NUM,I: INTEGER;
  DF:TEXT;

PROCEDURE INSERT (VAR VALUES:NOS;NEW,LIM
IT:INTEGER);
  VAR
    I,LOCATE:INTEGER;
    FLAG:BOOLEAN;
  BEGIN  (* INSERT *)
    IF LIMIT = 1 THEN
      VALUES[LIMIT] := NEW
    ELSE
      BEGIN
        FLAG := FALSE;
        LOCATE := 1;
        WHILE (NOT FLAG) AND (LIMIT > LO
        CATE) DO
          IF VALUES[LOCATE] > NEW THEN
            FLAG := TRUE
          ELSE
            LOCATE := LOCATE+1;
        FOR I:= LIMIT-1 DOWNTO LOCATE DO
          VALUES[I+1] := VALUES[I];
        VALUES[LOCATE] := NEW
      END;
    FOR I:= 1 TO LIMIT DO (* OUTPUTS *)
      WRITE (VALUES[I]:4); (* CURENT *)
    WRITELN (* LIST *)
  END;  (* INSERT *)

BEGIN  (* INSERTION *)
  RESET (DF,'MIXED.TEXT');
  NUM := 0;
  WHILE NOT EOF(DF) DO
    BEGIN  (* WHILE..DO LOOP *)
      NUM := NUM + 1;
      READLN(DF,ENTRY);
      WRITELN(ENTRY);
      INSERT(LIST,ENTRY,NUM)
    END;  (* WHILE..DO LOOP *)
  CLOSE(DF)
END.  (* INSERTION *)
```

know the total number of values to be added to the list; this is important because the list grows in length as each new value is added, and we must declare an array large enough to hold all the insertions.) When you have completed the modifications, run the program to test it. The correct order is achieved after the 15 insertions, and 50 shifts are required. As mentioned earlier, the insertion sort works well when values are entered into a list in random order, but the list is to be arranged in ascending (or descending) order. S(ave this program as INSERTION.

Shell Sort

The **Shell sort**, named for Donald Shell, its originator, uses an approach similar to the bubble sort. But instead of comparing adjacent items in the list, it creates a **gap** between items and then compares the list values across this gap. If the second value is smaller than the first, the items are swapped, and the comparisons continue. This process has the effect of moving larger values closer to the higher end of the list and smaller values closer to the lower end using fewer swaps than the bubble sort, which only moves a value one position at a time. Once all of the appropriate values have been swapped, the gap is reduced and the process is repeated again. This continues until the gap has been reduced to one and no more swaps can be made.

Using our original example

86   53   67   29   14

we first determine the gap by summing the first and last positions (1 and 5) and dividing (DIV) by 2. This gives us a gap of 3, so we compare 86 with 29 (the number 3 positions away); 29 is smaller, so we swap these values.

29   53   67   86   14

We then move to the second position and compare 53 with 14. Again, 14 is smaller, so the values are swapped.

29   14   67   86   53

The gap is then halved (GAP DIV 2), giving a new gap of 1. The comparisons across the new gap result in the swaps shown below:

14   29   67   86   53

14   29   67   53   86

14   29   53   67   86

Our list is now sorted. The Shell sort took a total of five swaps compared with bubble sort's nine swaps. The savings is even more substantial in longer lists.

The procedure for the Shell sort is shown in exhibit 17–7. Of course, the main body of the program would also have to be modified to include the procedure call

```
SHELL (LIST,NUM);
```

which would be placed outside of the loop used to read the data values from the MIXED.TEXT file. Modify one of your earlier programs to include this procedure and test it.

The Shell sort places our list of fifteen numbers in the proper order after 22 swaps. This is a savings of almost 60% over the 50 swaps required by the original bubble sort. S(ave this program as SHELLSORT.

Quicksort

The last sorting technique we will cover is **quicksort**, which is one of the fastest sorting methods used to sort lists of values. Quicksort begins by dividing the list of values to be ordered into

Exhibit 17–7.
Procedure SHELL

```
PROCEDURE SHELL (VAR VALUES:NOS;LIMIT:IN
TEGER);
   VAR
     I,J,GAP,TEMP:INTEGER;
   BEGIN  (* SHELL *)
     GAP:= LIMIT DIV 2;
     WHILE GAP)0 DO
        BEGIN  (* WHILE GAP LOOP *)
           FOR I:=1 TO LIMIT-GAP DO
             BEGIN  (*FOR..DO LOOP *)
                J:= I;
                WHILE J)0 DO
                   BEGIN  (* WHILE J LOOP *)
                     IF VALUES[J])VALUES[J+GA
                     P] THEN
                        BEGIN  * IF..THEN LOOP *)
                           TEMP:= VALUES[J];
                           VALUES[J]:= J+GAP];
                           VALUES[J+GAP]:= TEMP;
                           J:= J-GAP
                        END  (* IF..THEN LOOP *)
                     ELSE
                        J:= 0;
                   END  (* WHILE J LOOP *)
             END;  (* FOR..DO LOOP *)
           GAP:= GAP DIV 2
        END  (* WHILE GAP LOOP *)
   END;  (* SHELL *)
```

two sublists. One list will contain all of the lower values and the other all of the higher values. Ideally, the sublists will be split around the median value for the list. Unfortunately, the procedure necessary to locate and identify the median is almost as long and complex as the sorting procedure. We will therefore use an approach that arbitrarily selects a value from the middle of the list. If the numbers are in random order, any value could be selected, but a value from the middle of the list will produce faster results when the list is in some semblence of order to begin with.

Once we have two separate lists, one with the lower values and one with the higher ones, we will use the same procedure to split those lists into sublists of low and high values. We will repeat this process (recursively) until the lists have been subdivided repeatedly and each remaining sublist only contains one value.

In our familiar example

86   53   67   29   14

the middle value is 67. We now introduce two locational indexes, I and J. I marks the first value in the list, J the last vlaue.

```
86   53   67   29   14
↑                ↑
I                J
```

The value at I (86) is compared with the middle value (67). Because 86 is larger than 67, the index remains at 86. The value at J (14) is then compared with 67 and since 14 is less than 67, the J index remains at 14. The values at the index locations are then swapped and the I and J indexes are moved toward the middle of the list:

```
14   53   67   29   86
       ↑        ↑
  →   I        J   ←
```

The value at I (53) is again compared with 67; this time, because 53 is less than 67, the I index is moved one more position toward the middle.

```
14   53   67   29   86
            ↑    ↑
        →  I    J
```

The I value is now equal to 67, so the index remains there. The J value (29) is smaller than 67; therefore, is also fixed. The values at I and J are again swapped and the I and J indexes moved, resulting in

```
14   53   29   67   86
            ↑    ↑
          J    I
```

At this point J is less than I, so the list is split into two lists:

   14   53   29   67   86

As you can see, the first list contains the lowest values and the second list the highest. We will now repeat the process with the first list. The middle value will be 53. The I and J indexes are again placed at the ends of the list.

   14   53   29
   ↑   ↑
   I   J

Since 14 is less than 53, I moves to the next position (53), where it remains. J does not move because 29 is not greater than 53.

   14   53   29
       ↑   ↑
 →   I   J

The values at I and J are swapped and the indexes moved.

   14   29   53
       ↑   ↑
      J⇌ I

J is once again less than I, and the list is divided.

   14   29   53

Performing the operation on the two remaining pairs of figures (14 29 and 67 86) results in five separate one-digit lists:

   14   29   53   67   86

These lists cannot be subdivided further and they are in the correct order, so the process is finished.

The program code for this procedure is shown in exhibit 17–8. We also need to modify the procedure call to conform with QUICK and its parameters, and add the variable START and initialize it to 1. Enter this procedure within the basic program, make the other necessary modifications, and run it.

Quicksort sorts the list into the proper order with only 20 swaps; it is slightly faster than Shell sort and much faster than bubble sort. S(ave this program as QUICKSORT.

As we stated earlier in the chapter, most programmers do not create new sorting procedures each time they need to do a sort. Any of the sorting procedures you have learned could be saved in a file and inserted into a program needing a sorting procedure (see the Apple Pascal Reference Manual on C(opy F(ile). Or you could simply refer back to this chapter and copy these sorting routines as needed.

Exhibit 17–8.
Procedure QUICK

```
PROCEDURE QUICK(VAR VALUES:NOS,START,LIM
IT :INTEGER);
  VAR
    I,J,MID,TEMP:INTEGER;
  BEGIN  (* QUICK *)
    I:= START;
    J:= LIMIT;
    MID:=VALUES[(I+J) DIV 2];
    WHILE J>I DO
      BEGIN  (* WHILE J>I *)
        WHILE VALUES[I]<MID DO
          I:= I+1;
        WHILE VALUES[J]>MID DO
          J:= J-1;
        IF J >= I THEN
          BEGIN  (* SWAP *)
            TEMP := VALUES[I];
            VALUES[I] := VALUES[J];
            VALUES[J] := TEMP;
            I := I + 1;
            J := J - 1
          END;  (* SWAP *)
      END;  (* WHILE J>I *)
    IF START < J THEN
      QUICK (VALUES,START,J);
    IF LIMIT > I THEN
      QUICK (VALUES,I,LIMIT);
  END;  (* QUICK *)
```

FOCUS
On Problem
Solving

In all of our examples in this chapter, we have searched for or sorted numeric values. Since the Apple identifies the keyboard characters by their ASCII codes (which are integer values), we can also compare alphabetic characters, and thus we can search for or sort characters as well as numbers (digits).

We'll see how this is done by creating a program that will read a string from the keyboard, determine the frequency of occurrence of each letter of the alphabet in the string, and sort each character in the string alphabetically from A to Z. The algorithm will have three steps:

1. Input a string;
2. Count the occurrences of each letter in the string;
3. Sort the characters in the string alphabetically.

We will use procedures for steps 2 and 3. Developing the algorithms for these procedures would produce:

2. COUNTER:
   a. Establish a matrix for tabulating results;

      b. Initialize the matrix to zero;
      c. For each alphabetic character in the string;
         (1) Increment the results matrix by 1 for the appropriate letter;
      d. Output the results (matrix);
  3. SORTER:
      a. Bubble sort alphabetic characters in string;
      b. Output results.

Since we have already discussed sorting and bubble sorting, it would be redundant to develop an algorithm to bubble sort the string. However, we will add another refinement to our SORTER algorithm. Remember that we only want to sort the alphabetic characters (A to Z), but strings usually have spaces between words. Because we don't want to sort these spaces (which, incidentally, have lower ASCII values than the letter A), we'll create another procedure called EXTRACT to remove all spaces from the string. The algorithm for step 3 might then look like this:

  3. SORTER:
      a. Remove all spaces from the string;
         (1) As long as spaces remain in the string:
            (a) Remove the next space encountered;
      b. Bubble sort alphabetic characters in string;
      c. Output results.

Since we are working with characters (or their numeric representation), we can use **sets** of characters to simplify this problem. For example, algorithm 2.c.(1) says, "Increment the results matrix by 1 for the appropriate letter." By using a set of characters corresponding to the alphabetic characters, the statement

```
IF KEY IN ['A'..'Z'] THEN
    COUNT[KEY]:=COUNT[KEY]+1;
```

allows us to first test the character KEY to see if it is alphabetic and then to increment the COUNT element referenced by KEY.

A segment has been added to the EXTRACT procedure to replace all nonalphabetic characters with spaces just before the spaces are deleted. This will ensure that only the 26 alphabetic characters remain when the sorting routine begins.

The entire program is shown in exhibit 17–9. Notice that the routine that outputs the results from the COUNTER procedure uses WRITE to output each value and adds a WRITELN whenever J MOD 5 = 0. Since J is incremented with every WRITE, the WRITELN will be executed after every five WRITE statements. This has the effect of outputting five values per line.

Exhibit 17–9. Program
ALPHABETIZE

```
PROGRAM ALPHABETIZE;

TYPE
   CHARS = ARRAY['A'..'Z'] OF INTEGER;

VAR
   S:STRING;

PROCEDURE COUNTER (S:STRING);
   VAR
     KEY:CHAR;
     COUNT:CHARS;
     I,J:INTEGER;
   BEGIN  (* COUNTER *)
     FOR KEY:= 'A' TO 'Z' DO
       COUNT[KEY]:= 0;
     FOR I:= 1 TO LENGTH(S) DO
       BEGIN  (* COUNTING LOOP *)
         KEY := S[I];
         IF KEY IN ['A'..'Z'] THEN
           COUNT[KEY]:= COUNT[KEY]+1
       END;  (* COUNTING LOOP *)
     J:= 0;
     FOR KEY:= 'A' TO 'Z' DO
       BEGIN  (* COUNT OUTPUT *)
         WRITE (KEY:5,COUNT[KEY]:3);
         J:= J+1;
         IF J MOD 5 = 0 THEN
           WRITELN
       END;  (* COUNT OUTPUT *)
     WRITELN
   END;  (* COUNTER *)

PROCEDURE EXTRACT (VAR S:STRING);
   VAR
     I:INTEGER;
   BEGIN  (* EXTRACT *)
     WHILE POS(' ',S) > 0 DO
       DELETE (S,POS(' ',S),1)
   END;  (* EXTRACT *)

PROCEDURE SORTER (S:STRING);
   VAR
     I:INTEGER;
     TEMP:CHAR;
     FLAG:BOOLEAN;
```

```
BEGIN  (* SORTER *)
  EXTRACT(S);
  REPEAT
    FLAG:=FALSE;
    FOR I:= 1 TO LENGTH(S)-1 DO
      BEGIN  (* COMPARISON *)
        IF S[I] > S[I+1] THEN
          BEGIN  (* SWAP *)
            FLAG:= TRUE;
            TEMP:= S[I];
            S[I]:= S[I+1];
            S[I+1]:=TEMP
          END  (* SWAP *)
      END  (* COMPARISON *)
  UNTIL NOT FLAG;
  WRITELN(S)
END;  (* SORTER *)

BEGIN (* ALPHABETIZE *)
  WRITE ('ENTER A STRING ');
  READLN (S);
  COUNTER(S);
  WRITELN (S);
  SORTER(S)
END.  (* ALPHABETIZE *)
```

Enter and run this program. To test it, use the string below, which is used in many introductory typing classes because it requires the typist to use every key:

```
THE QUICK BROWN FOX JUMPS OVER THE LAZY DOG
```

Did your test results confirm this fact, i.e., was every letter found at least once?

The second portion of the program shows that we can sort alphabetically as easily as we sort numerically. Although we used the simple bubble sort in this case, the other methods can be modified to work equally well.

This concludes the sorting examples, so you can S(ave this program and T(ransfer any of the other example programs to your storage diskette if you haven't already done so. If you then want to R(emove these program files from your system disk, you can speed up the process by using **wildcards** in the file names. Answering the R(emove prompt with ?.TEXT or ?.CODE will cause the Filer to prompt you with each TEXT or CODE file name. Responding with a Y will delete the file and an N will keep it. After you have responded with a Y or an N to each file, you will be asked if you want to update the directory. ■

17.5 SUMMARY

In this chapter, you learned more about recursive functions and procedures and you also learned various searching and sorting routines. Recursion is a form of repetition that occurs when a function or procedure calls itself. When the recursive call occurs in the middle of a statement and the value of the function or procedure variable is still undefined, the computer creates a stack that stores the undefined function while the next recursive call is executed. The computer continues to place undefined functions or variables (uncompleted statements) on the stack until a limit condition is reached, causing the statement to be executed and ending the recursive process.

The searching routines we examined were the linear search and the binary search. The linear search simply begins at the beginning of a list and compares each value with the value we are searching for until it is located. The binary search, which can be used only with ordered lists, divides the list in half and compares the search value with the dividing value. Based on the results of that comparison, half the list is discarded and the remaining part of the list is divided again. This process is repeated until the search value is located. Binary searches are usually significantly faster than linear searches when searching long, ordered lists.

Sorting routines are procedures that sort the values in a list into some sort of order, usually ascending or descending. There are a wide variety of different sorting routines. This chapter reviewed six of the more common routines: the bubble sort, a variation of the bubble sort, the selection sort, the insertion sort, the Shell sort, and the quicksort. While these routines differ in their approaches, most of them employ the basic swapping procedure that was discussed in this chapter. In general, the faster the sorting routine is, the more complex the algorithm tends to be. Given the speed of the computer, sorting speed is a relative thing: A program that is twice as fast may save only one or two seconds when sorting a list of hundreds of values. Finally, you learned that you can sort lists alphabetically as well as numerically.

Review Questions

1. What is a recursive procedure or function?

2. With regard to recursion, what is a stack? A limit call?

3. What are the two basic searching techniques? How do they differ? Under what circumstances would you be likely to use each?

4. What is a swap? Why do we use a temporary variable when swapping?

SUMMARY of Pascal Syntax

Reserved Words	Built-in Procedures	Built-in Functions	Library Units
PROGRAM	WRITE	EOF	TURTLEGRAPHICS
USES	WRITELN	ABS	APPLESTUFF
CONST	READ	SQR	TRANSCEND
TYPE	READLN	SQRT	
SET OF	NEW	ROUND	
PACKED	RESET	TRUNC	
ARRAY OF	REWRITE	EXP	
RECORD	PUT	LN	
FILE OF	GET	LOG	
VAR	SEEK	PWROFTEN	
FUNCTION	CLOSE	ATAN	
FORWARD	LOCK	SIN	
PROCEDURE	INITTURTLE	COS	*Boolean*
BEGIN	PENCOLOR	ORD	*Constants*
FOR..DO	MOVE	CHR	
TO	TURN	PRED	FALSE
DOWNTO	MOVETO	SUCC	TRUE
REPEAT	TURNTO	EOLN	
UNTIL	TEXTMODE	LENGTH	
WHILE..DO	GRAFMODE	CONCAT	
IF	PAGE(OUTPUT)	POS	
THEN	DELETE	COPY	
ELSE	INSERT	STR	
CASE..OF	PAGE(OUTPUT)		
WITH..DO	DELETE		
END	INSERT		
DIV			
MOD			*Integer*
NIL			*Constants*
AND			
OR			MAXINT
NOT			
IN			

5. What are the popular sorting techniques?

6. The bubble sort is the most commonly used sorting routine. Explain how it works.

7. How does the modified bubble sort differ from the bubble sort?

8. Explain how the selection sort differs from the bubble sort.

9. The insertion sort is a specialized sorting routine. Why? Explain how it works.

10. The Shell sort is much faster than the bubble sort. Why? Explain how it works.

11. What is the fastest sorting routine discussed in the chapter? Explain how it works.

12. When the computer sorts alphabetically, it is actually sorting numerically. Explain.

13. When the computer sorts alphabetically, where are spaces placed?

14. In an alphabetic sort, would the number 1 or the letter A come first? Explain.

Because this chapter has simply illustrated a number of specific applications without introducing any new Pascal syntax or p-System commands, the usual EXERCISES and DIAGNOSTIC EXERCISES have been omitted.

Problems

1. Write a program segment that prompts the user for a value and then searches an array LIST for that value. If the value is not found, a message to that effect should be output.

2. Write a procedure that takes an array of values arranged in ascending order (12, 22,...m88) and inverts the array so that the values are in descending order (88,...,22,12). Do *not* use a second array.

3. We have two arrays, GRAD and NAME. GRADE contains the final average for 20 students and NAME contains the students' names. Although the lists are not in any particular order or sequence, the elements are matched, e.g., the 3d element in GRADE is associated with the 3d name in NAME. Write a procedure that will arrange the grades in sequential order from highest to lowest and then output the list of grades and the associated names.

4. We have a two-dimensional matrix with 10 rows and 2 columns. The first column contains values between 1 and 100. The second column contains the rank order of those values (from 1 to 10). Neither the values nor the rank order values are in any particular order. Write a procedure that will output the values in sequential rank order (beginning with 1 and ending with 10) without changing the actual order of the values in the array or creating a second array.

5. Write a procedure that will first create an array with the numbers from 1 to 1000 in it, then randomly swap values in the array 2000 times so that the digits are in no longer in any sequence. The array should then be written to a file.

6. Using the file created in problem 5, read the data back into an array and then sort the array using each of the six sorting routines covered in this chapter. Time each routine and compare the times.

7. Write an algorithm to create a graphics program that will: (1) generate the numbers from 1 to 100 in a random order; (2) display the numbers as points on the screen, where the X axis is the value of the digit and the Y axis is its current position in an array; and (3) show the movement of the values as the array is sorted. (When the array is completely sorted, the points on the screen should form a diagonal line at a 45° angle from the X axis.

8. Code and test the algorithm developed in problem 7.

18

Additional Apple Features— Graphics and Sound

This chapter covers some of the special Pascal features that are only available in UCSD and/or Apple Pascal. These features include additional graphics commands that were not covered in chapter 6 and the Apple's ability to produce sound. The additional graphics features allow us to adjust the size of the graphics screen, fill the graphics screen with a color, determine where the Turtle is located and what direction it is facing, determine whether a particular screen pixel is black or lighted, place text images on the graphics screen, choose different character fonts, and create our own graphics pictures (images) and draw them on the screen. The sound features use the Apple's speaker to produce sounds varying from a simple click to tones that approximate the notes of the musical scale.

18.1 VIEWPORT

The built-in procedure VIEWPORT allows us to adjust the current size of the graphics screen. It has the form

```
VIEWPORT (LEFT, RIGHT, BOTTOM, TOP);
```

The four parameters, LEFT, RIGHT, BOTTOM, and TOP, are Integer values that establish the X and Y boundaries for a desired viewport by specifying X (LEFT and RIGHT) and Y (BOTTOM and TOP) axis values. (Remember that the X-axis goes from 0 to 279 and the Y-axis from 0 to 191, with the 0,0 location at the bottom left-hand corner of the screen.) The statement

```
VIEWPORT (100, 179, 20, 171)
```

would establish a tall, narrow graphics screen in the middle of the screen, while the statement

```
VIEWPORT (30, 249, 80, 111)
```

would set a short, wide viewport (see figure 18–1). Once we have set the screen size using VIEWPORT, only those graphics

Figure 18–1.
VIEWPORT Examples

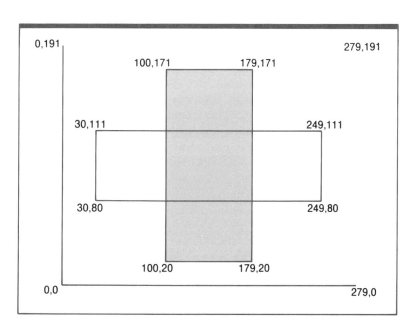

commands that take place within the viewport coordinates will be displayed.

Changing the viewport does not affect the graphics image that is currently on the screen, however. VIEWPORT, therefore, is a very convenient procedure to use when part of the screen has an image that we don't want altered. By simply changing the viewport so that the image we want to preserve is no longer within the viewport range, we in effect "lock" the image on the screen. Remember, however, that INITTURTLE resets the viewport to full screen.

18.2 FILLSCREEN

The FILLSCREEN procedure has the form:

```
FILLSCREEN (COLOR);
```

It has one parameter, COLOR, and does exactly what its name implies. It fills the screen with the specified color. The statement

```
FILLSCREEN (BLACK)
```

can be used to clear the screen. The advantage of using this statement over INITTURTLE is that the Turtle will not be returned to the center of the screen and the viewport will not be reset to full screen.

FILLSCREEN can be used with VIEWPORT to create a border around the screen. For example, the segment

```
INITTURTLE;
FILLSCREEN (ORANGE);
VIEWPORT (9,270,9,182);
FILLSCREEN (BLACK);
```

would first change the entire screen to orange (on a color monitor), then reset the viewport and change its color to black (clear it). This places an orange border around the screen. Although noncolor monitors will obviously not show an orange border, the procedure will still work; the border will simply be a shade of the normal text color (white, green, or amber).

FILLSCREEN uses the same colors that are available to the Turtle. This is because the TURTLEGRAPHICS library creates a new data type called SCREENCOLOR where

```
SCREENCOLOR = (NONE, WHITE, BLACK, REVERSE,
               RADAR, BLACK1, GREEN, VIOLET,
               WHITE1, BLACK2, ORANGE, BLUE,
               WHITE2);
```

When the REVERSE color is used with FILLSCREEN, it has a different effect than the other colors have. The statement

```
FILLSCREEN (REVERSE)
```

reverses the colors that appear on the screen. The REVERSE color pairs are BLACK and WHITE, GREEN and VIOLET, ORANGE and BLUE, BLACK1 and WHITE1, and BLACK2 and WHITE2.

18.3 TURTLEX, TURTLEY, AND TURTLEANG

TURTLEX, TURTLEY, and TURTLEANG are three built-in graphics functions. All three have no parameters. TURTLEX and TURTLEY return the current X and Y coordinates of the Turtle as Integer values. We can use these values to move the Turtle to a new location, for example,

```
MOVETO (TURTLEX + 20, TURTLEY + 20);
```

or to simply look ahead of a moving Turtle:

```
IF ((TURTLEX + 10) > 279) THEN ...
```

This statement could be used to look 10 units ahead of a Turtle moving horizontally toward the right. We could combine it with a segment that would give a warning if the Turtle was nearing the edge of the screen.

TURTLEANG, as you may have already guessed, returns the direction (angle) in which the Turtle is facing (0 means the Turtle is facing the right edge of the screen). The angle is given in degrees and is an Integer value between 0 and 359. We could modify the statement in the preceding example to consider the direction the Turtle is moving in, for example,

```
IF (((TURTLEX + 20) > 279) AND
   (TURTLEANG = 0)) OR
   (((TURTLEX - 20) < 0) AND
   (TURTLEANG = 180)) THEN...
```

This statement returns a TRUE if 20 units to the right of the Turtle's location is off the right edge of the screen AND the Turtle is facing right OR if 20 units to the left of the Turtle's location is off the screen AND it is facing left. We could also add a second statement to check for vertical movement.

18.4 SCREEBIT

SCREENBIT is a graphics function with two parameters. It has the form:

```
SCREENBIT (X, Y)
```

where X and Y represent graphics coordinates. The SCREENBIT function returns a Boolean value of TRUE if the location specified by the parameters is not BLACK and FALSE if it is BLACK. If we had drawn a border around the screen and were moving the Turtle, we could modify the last IF..THEN statement in section 18.3 to

```
IF (SCREENBIT(TURTLEX + 20, Y)
    AND (TURTLEANG = 0)) OR
    (SCREENBIT(TURTLEX - 20, Y)
    AND (TURTLEANG = 180)) THEN...
```

If the Turtle is facing right (ANG = 0), we look 20 units ahead of the Turtle; if we find a border (a nonblack pixel), the first two expressions evaluate as TRUE. When the Turtle is facing left and we look 20 units ahead and find a border, the second expressions evaluate as TRUE. Note, however, that this will only work if we are looking ahead fewer units that the width of the border. Otherwise, we may cause our look-ahead feature to "step over" the border without examining any of the pixels in the border area.

We can also use SCREENBIT to find the location of lines the Turtle has drawn on the screen, but this is not quite as easy because of the manner in which the monitor displays lines. To be certain of locating a line on the screen, we must check not only a particular pixel, but also the adjacent pixels in the direction of movement. Again, this is due to the peculiar manner in which monitors turn pixels on to create line images. (You may want to refer back to the discussion in chapter 6.)

18.5 WRITING TEXT ON THE GRAPHICS SCREEN

Apple Pascal allows us to write text onto the graphics screen using the built-in procedures WCHAR, WSTRING, and CHARTYPE. The text is actually drawn on the screen using the graphics procedures and an array of character images stored in the file SYSTEM.CHARSET. Each character drawn on the screen is 7 pixels wide and 8 pixels high.

The WCHAR procedure has one parameter and has the form

```
WCHAR (C);
```

The parameter C represents a keyboard character, which the procedure writes (draws) on the screen. The character will be drawn at the current location of the Turtle; the Turtle's X and Y coordinates will be the lower left-hand pixel of the letter. The color of the letter is not a function of the current PENCOLOR, however. The following segment would put the letter X near the upper right-hand corner of the screen.

```
PENCOLOR (NONE);
MOVETO (260,180);
WCHAR ('X')
```

The WSTRING procedure has one parameter and has the form

```
WSTRING (S);
```

where S is the string or String variable that is to be written onto the screen. Again, the Turtle's X and Y coordinates are the lower left-hand corner for the first pixel in the string. WSTRING actually uses WCHAR to draw each character in the string onto the screen, so each character in the string will again be 7 pixels wide. The following segment would place a string on the screen beginning near the lower left-hand corner.

```
PENCOLOR (NONE);
MOVETO(10,10);
WSTRING ('A STRING ON THE SCREEN')
```

Since WCHAR or WSTRING draws letters on the screen using the Turtle, the Turtle's location will change when these procedures are used. At the conclusion of either of these procedures, the Turtle will be at the lower right-hand corner of the last letter drawn. You can check this by adding the statement

```
WRITELN (TURTLEX, TURTLEY)
```

after the WSTRING segment shown above.

The CHARTYPE procedure has one parameter and has the form:

```
CHARTYPE (MODE);
```

This procedure is used to select the MODE to be used when writing characters to the screen. The parameter MODE is an Integer value between 0 and 15.*

MODE 10 is the default MODE. This MODE draws white characters on a black background. MODE 5, the complement of the array, draws black characters on a white background. MODE 6 (XOR) will draw a character on the screen, and then, if the character is redrawn at the same location, erase it, leaving the screen as it was before the character was drawn the first time. The following program would cause a message to be drawn and erased, thus briefly flashing the message on the screen.

---

*For a complete list of the sixteen MODE values and their effect, please refer to the Apple II Apple Pascal Language Reference Manual (Apple Computer, Inc. 1980) p. 97.

```
BEGIN  (* FLASH PROGRAM *)
  INITTURTLE;
  PENCOLOR (NONE);
  CHARTYPE (6);
  FOR I := 1 TO 10 DO
    BEGIN  (* MESSAGE LOOP *)
      MOVETO (100,100);
      WSTRING ('A FLASHY MESSAGE');
      FOR J := 1 TO 500 DO;  (* PAUSE *)
    END;  (* MESSAGE LOOP *)
  WSTRING ('DONE');
  READLN;
  TEXTMODE
END.  (* FLASH PROGRAM *)
```

The pause loop is included to slow things down. The MOVETO statement must be included in the message loop to ensure that the starting point for each string is the same. Without this statement, each string would begin where the last string ended, since the position of the Turtle changes each time a new character is drawn on the screen. Note that since the message loop is executed an even number of times, the message will not be on the screen at the termination of the loop.

Text that is drawn onto the screen is drawn over existing images on the screen. Likewise, moving the Turtle after text is placed on the screen may cause a line to be drawn through existing text (in any direction).

18.6 DRAWBLOCK

The DRAWBLOCK procedure is a special graphics feature that draws a graphics image using a packed array of Boolean values (which we must create). The DRAWBLOCK procedure has nine parameters and has the form:

```
DRAWBLOCK (SOURCE, ROWSIZE, XSKIP, YSKIP, WIDTH,
           HEIGHT, XSCREEN, YSCREEN, MODE);
```

SOURCE is the name of the two-dimensional packed array of Boolean that contains the image we want to draw on the screen. A Boolean array is used to either turn the pixels on (TRUE) or off (FALSE).

ROWSIZE is the number of bytes in each row of the array. It can be calculated using the formula

$$2 \; * \; ((X + 15) \; \text{DIV} \; 16 \;)$$

where X represents the number of pixels in the row. Thus, a row 12 pixels wide would have a ROWSIZE of 2 (2 * ((12 + 15) DIV 16) or 2 * (1)).

XSKIP tells the Apple how many horizontal pixels to skip

in the array. This allows you to copy a portion of the array rather than the whole array.

YSKIP tells the Apple how many vertical pixels (rows) to skip in the array. The image copied onto the screen is drawn from the bottom up, i.e., the first row in the array will be the bottom row of the image. Any rows skipped, therefore, will be from the top of the array but from the bottom of the image.

WIDTH tells the Apple how many pixels wide the image will be, i.e., how many columns of the array will be used. The columns counted for the WIDTH figure begin immediately after the columns counted for XSKIP.

HEIGHT tells the Apple how many pixels (rows) of the array will be used. Again, the HEIGHT is counted from the bottom of the image, after the rows skipped by YSKIP.

XSCREEN is the X-axis coordinate of the lower left-hand corner of the image.

YSCREEN is the Y-axis coordinate of the lower left-hand corner of the image.

MODE is the same MODE parameter discussed with the CHARTYPE procedure (see exhibit 18–1).

Let's look at a program that uses DRAWBLOCK. Suppose we want to draw an arrow on the screen. We will use a packed array of Boolean named PICTURE to hold our image and another array of Strings named IMAGE to create our picture. The example program in exhibit 18–2 shows how this is done.

In program ARROWPIC, procedure MAKEIMAGE creates the arrow image using nine strings of nine characters each. The procedure MAKEARROW then converts each character into a Boolean value. If the character is a space (' '), PIC[ROW,COL] is FALSE; an asterisk ('*') evaluates as TRUE. Each string, therefore, makes one row of Boolean values. Note that we use DOWNTO to create the Boolean array because the image will be drawn from the bottom up with the first row in the array as the bottom row of the image. By inverting the Boolean array, we thus produce an image that looks like our string array image (but condensed). You may have also noted that A[10–ROW] denotes one string in the array A of nine strings and that [COL] denotes a specific character in that string.

The first DRAWBLOCK call uses MODE 10, producing a light (white) arrow on a dark (black) background, while the second call uses a MODE of 5, producing a dark (black) arrow on a light (white) background.

Suppose we want to draw arrows pointing in other directions, e.g., left or right. Do we need to create new arrays of strings with the arrows pointing in the desired direction? The answer is no. Once we have the packed array of Boolean representing the arrow pointing upwards, we can easily use that array to produce others. Can you see how? Try to develop the algorithm that will use our original Boolean array to produce the image of an arrow pointing to the right. Then develop a similar

Exhibit 18–2. Program
ARROWPIC

```
PROGRAM ARROWPIC;

USES TURTLEGRAPHICS;

TYPE
  PICTURE = PACKED ARRAY[1..9,1..9] OF B
  OOLEAN;
  IMAGE = ARRAY[1..9] OF STRING;

VAR
  ARROW: PICTURE;

PROCEDURE MAKEARROW (VAR PIC:PICTURE; A:
IMAGE);
  VAR
    ROW,COL: INTEGER;
  BEGIN  (* MAKEARROW *)
    FOR ROW := 9 DOWNTO 1 DO
      FOR COL := 1 TO 9 DO
        PIC[ROW,COL] := A[10-ROW] [COL]
        <> ' ';
  END;  (* MAKEARROW *)

PROCEDURE MAKEIMAGE (VAR PICT: PICTURE);
  VAR
    LINE: IMAGE;
  BEGIN  (* MAKEIMAGE *)
    LINE[1] := '    *    ';
    LINE[2] := '   * *   ';
    LINE[3] := '  * * *  ';
    LINE[4] := ' * * * * ';
    LINE[5] := '*   *   *';
    LINE[6] := '    *    ';
    LINE[7] := '    *    ';
    LINE[8] := '    *    ';
    LINE[9] := '    *    ';
    MAKEARROW (PICT,LINE)
  END;  (* MAKEIMAGE *)

BEGIN  (* ARROWPIC *)
  MAKEIMAGE (ARROW);
  INITTURTLE;
  DRAWBLOCK (ARROW,2,0,0,9,9,TURTLEX,TUR
  TLEY,10);
  PENCOLOR (NONE);
  MOVETO (10,10);
  DRAWBLOCK (ARROW,2,0,0,9,9,TURTLEX,TUR
  TLEY,5);
  READLN;
  TEXTMODE
END.  (* ARROWPIC *)
```

algorithm for an arrow pointing to the left. Since not all images are as symetrical as our arrow, you should work with an arrow with only one flange

to ensure that your algorithms are correct. Your new arrays should produce the following images for right- and left-facing arrows:

You might want to diagram the matrices on graph paper to help you develop the algorithms (use the Boolean array rather than the original string array, since all of the Boolean arrays will be drawn on the screen in inverted form).

The two algorithms (for the arrows pointing to the right and left) should simply rotate the Boolean matrix 90°. To do this, they must switch row and column values and reverse the order of either the rows or columns (depending upon the direction desired). If the original Boolean matrix is represented by A, the right-facing arrow by R, and the left-facing arrow by L, the segment

```
FOR ROW := 1 TO 9 DO
  FOR COL := 1 TO 9 DO
    R[ROW, COL] := A[COL, (10-ROW)];
```

would produce the Boolean matrix for an arrow facing right and the segment

```
FOR := 1 TO 9 DO
  FOR COL := 1 TO 9 DO
    L[ROW, COL] := A[(10-COL), ROW];
```

would produce the Boolean matrix for an arrow facing left. Using these segments to write the new procedures MAKE-RIGHT and MAKELEFT, we could modify Program ARROW-PIC as shown in exhibit 18–3. In the last two DRAWBLOCK procedures, we specified the X and Y coordinates directly rather than as TURTLEX and TURTLEY. This program modification should add two arrows, one pointing right and one pointing left, a short distance from each other.

Exhibit 18–3. Program
ARROWPIC2

```
PROGRAM ARROWPIC2;

USES TURTLEGRAPHICS;

TYPE
  PICTURE = PACKED ARRAY[1..9,1..9] OF B
OOLEAN;
  IMAGE = ARRAY[1..9] OF STRING;

VAR
  ARROW,RIGHT,LEFT: PICTURE;

PROCEDURE MAKEARROW (VAR PIC:PICTURE; A:
IMAGE);
  VAR
    ROW,COL: INTEGER;
  BEGIN  (* MAKEARROW *)
    FOR ROW := 9 DOWNTO 1 DO
      FOR COL := 1 TO 9 DO
        PIC[ROW,COL] := A[10-ROW] [COL]
        <> ' '
  END;  (* MAKEARROW *)

PROCEDURE MAKEIMAGE (VAR PICT: PICTURE);
  VAR
    LINE: IMAGE;
  BEGIN  (*MAKEIMAGE *)
    LINE[1] := '    *    ';
    LINE[2] := '   * *   ';
    LINE[3] := '  * * *  ';
    LINE[4] := ' *  *  * ';
    LINE[5] := '*   *   *';
    LINE[6] := '    *    ';
    LINE[7] := '    *    ';
    LINE[8] := '    *    ';
    LINE[9] := '    *    ';
    MAKEARROW (PICT,LINE)
  END;  (* MAKEIMAGE *)

PROCEDURE MAKERIGHT (VAR R: PICTURE; A:
PICTURE);
  VAR
    ROW,COL: INTEGER;
  BEGIN (* MAKERIGHT *)
    FOR ROW := 1 TO 9 DO
      FOR COL := 1 TO 9 DO
        R[ROW, COL] := A[COL, (10-ROW)]
  END;  (* MAKERIGHT *)
```

Exhibit 18–3.
Continued

```
PROCEDURE MAKELEFT (VAR L: PICTURE; A: P
ICTURE);
   VAR
     ROW,COL: INTEGER;
   BEGIN  (* MAKELEFT *)
     FOR ROW := 1 TO 9 DO
       FOR COL := 1 TO 9 DO
         L[ROW, COL] := A[(10-COL), ROW]
   END;  (* MAKELEFT *)

BEGIN  (* ARROWPIC *)
  MAKEIMAGE (ARROW);
  INITTURTLE;
  DRAWBLOCK (ARROW,2,0,0,9,9,TURTLEX,TUR
  TLEY,10);
  PENCOLOR (NONE);
  MOVETO (10,10);
  DRAWBLOCK (ARROW,2,0,0,9,9,TURTLEX,TUR
  TLEY,5);
  MAKERIGHT (RIGHT, ARROW);
  DRAWBLOCK (RIGHT,2,0,0,9,9,120,50,10);
  MAKELEFT (LEFT, ARROW);
  DRAWBLOCK (LEFT,2,0,0,9,9,150,50,10);
  READLN;
  TEXTMODE
END.  (* ARROWPIC *)
```

The procedure in exhibit 18–4 uses MODE 6 to produce an image of a moving arrow. Three loops are used in this procedure. The first (I) loop repeats the routine 40 times. This increments the X coordinate in steps of 5, moving the position of the arrow from 25 (20 + 5) to 225. The second (J) loop repeats DRAW-BLOCK twice. The first call draws the image of the arrow on the screen. The second does the same thing, but because we are using MODE 6, it erases the first arrow. The third (K) loop serves as a pause to slow the computer down slightly before the arrow is erased. This series of images, quickly drawn and erased, creates the sense of movement. Adjusting the distance moved and the length of the pause between the two DRAWBLOCK calls will affect the smoothness of the movement.

These procedures and functions and those covered in chapter 6 can be combined to give a multitude of various graphics possibilities. Feel free to use your imagination and don't be afraid to experiment. These are the basic principles that are used in many of the popular computer games.

Exhibit 18–4.
Procedure FLIGHT

```
PROCEDURE FLIGHT (RIGHT: PICTURE);

   VAR
     X,I,J,K: INTEGER;

   BEGIN  (* FLIGHT *)
     X := 20;
     FOR I := 1 TO 40 DO
       BEGIN  (* I LOOP *)
         X:= X+5;
         FOR J := 1 TO 2 DO
           BEGIN  (* J LOOP *)
             DRAWBLOCK (RIGHT,2,0,0,9,9,X,
             20,6);
             FOR K := 1 TO 20 DO; (* PAUSE *)
           END  (* J LOOP *)
       END  (* I LOOP *)
   END;  (* FLIGHT *)
```

18.7 SOUND

The procedure NOTE, which is contained in APPLESTUFF, can be used to make the Apple speaker produce sound. NOTE has two parameters, PITCH and DURATION, and has the form

```
NOTE (PITCH, DURATION);
```

PITCH can be any Integer value between 0 and 50, while DURATION can be any Integer value between 0 and 255.

A PITCH of 0 is used for a rest (no sound); a PITCH and DURATION of 1, (NOTE (1,1) produces a click. PITCH values from 2 through 48 produce an approximate tempered chromatic scale. DURATION is used to determine the length of time a note is played. An eighth note will have a DURATION of about 50, a quarter note a DURATION of 100, and a half note a DURATION of 200. The following program illustrates the use of NOTE to produce different sounds.

```
PROGRAM SOUND;

USES APPLESTUFF;

VAR
  PITCH,DURATION, I, PAUSE: INTEGER;
```

```
BEGIN  (* SOUND *)
  WRITELN ('BUZZ');
  NOTE (1,100);
  WRITELN;
  FOR I := 1 TO 10 DO
    BEGIN  (* CLICKS *)
      WRITELN ('CLICK');
      NOTE (1,1);
      FOR PAUSE := 1 TO 500 DO; (* PAUSE *)
    END;  (* CLICKS *)
  WRITELN;
  WRITELN ('SCALE ');
  DURATION := 100;
  FOR PITCH := 2 TO 48 DO
    NOTE (PITCH,DURATION);
  DURATION := 50;
  FOR PITCH := 48 DOWNTO 2 DO
    NOTE (PITCH,DURATION)
END.  (* SOUND *)
```

Exhibit 18–5 shows the approximate musical notes created by the different PITCH values.

While the Apple approximates the musical notes, you will find that the small speaker in the Apple does have its limits. Try the program in exhibit 18–6. You may even recognize the tune.

Exhibit **18–5.** Musical Notes and PITCH values

Exhibit 18–6. Program
MUSIC

```
PROGRAM MUSIC;

USES APPLESTUFF;

VAR
  I,DUR: INTEGER;

PROCEDURE PLAY;
  BEGIN
    NOTE (32,DUR);
    NOTE (31,DUR)
    END;  (* PLAY *)

PROCEDURE PLAY2;
  BEGIN
    NOTE (29,DUR);
    NOTE (39,100);
    NOTE (34,DUR)
  END;  (* PLAY2 *)

BEGIN (*MUSIC *)
  DUR := 50;
  FOR I := 1 TO 3 DO
    NOTE (22,DUR);
  NOTE (27,100);
  NOTE (34,100);
  PLAY;
  PLAY2;
  FOR I := 1 TO 400 DO; (* PAUSE *)
  PLAY;
  PLAY2;
  FOR I := 1 TO 250 DO; (* PAUSE *)
  PLAY;
  NOTE (32,DUR);
  NOTE (29,DUR)
END.  (* MUSIC *)
```

18.8 ONE FINAL PROGRAM

To conclude this chapter and the book, we will look at one final program (see exhibit 18–7) that creates a simple game by expanding on the ZIGZAG program we developed earlier. In this game, the Turtle begins at the bottom of the screen and moves at a set speed, leaving a white trail behind it. The object of the game is to use the keys to keep the Turtle from running into the border at the edge of the screen or from running into its own trail for as long as possible. A built-in "clock" keeps track of the time. A turn ends when the Turtle crashes into the edge of the screen or its own trail. New turns will continue indefinitely until the Q (for Quit) key is pressed.

Exhibit 18–7. Program
GAME

```
PROGRAM GAME;

USES TURTLEGRAPHICS, APPLESTUFF;

CONST
  QUIT = 'Q';

VAR
  C: CHAR;
  FLAG, FLG: BOOLEAN;
  ANG,DIST,H,TX,TY,HISCORE,COUNT,DELAY:
  INTEGER;
  DISPLAY: STRING;

PROCEDURE STARTUP;
  BEGIN  (* INITIALIZE VALUES AND GIVE I
  NSTRUCTIONS *)
    FLAG := FALSE;
    FLG := FALSE;
    COUNT := 0;
    DIST := 5;
    ANG := 90;
    WRITELN;
    WRITELN ('R-UP       J-LEFT');
    WRITELN ('F-DOWN     K-RIGHT');
    WRITELN;
    WRITELN (' Q-QUIT (END GAME)');
    WRITELN;
    WRITELN ('SPEED:  1 = SLOW; 10 = FAST');
    WRITELN ('PICK A SPEED BETWEEN 1 AND 10');
    WRITELN;
    WRITE ('INPUT SPEED -->');
    READLN (H);
    DELAY := 101 - (10 * H);
    FOR H := 1 TO 1500 DO; (* PAUSE *)
  END;  (* STARTUP *)

PROCEDURE BORDER;
  BEGIN
    INITTURTLE;
    VIEWPORT (0,279,9,191);
    FILLSCREEN (WHITE);
    VIEWPORT (5,274,14,186);
    FILLSCREEN (BLACK);
    VIEWPORT (0,279,0,191);
    PENCOLOR (NONE);
    MOVETO (135,16);
    TURNTO (ANG);
    PENCOLOR (WHITE)
  END;  (* BORDER *)
```

Exhibit 18–7.
Continued

```
PROCEDURE EXPLODE;
  VAR
    A,B,C,D: INTEGER;
  BEGIN  (* EXPLODE *)
    C := TURTLEX;
    D := TURTLEY;
    B := 10;
    FOR A:= 1 TO 36 DO
      BEGIN  (* FOR..DO *)
        MOVE (50);
        MOVE (-50);
        TURN (B)
      END  (* FOR..DO *)
  END;  (* EXPLODE *)

PROCEDURE CHECK;
  BEGIN
    PENCOLOR (NONE);
    FOR H := 1 TO DIST DO
      BEGIN  (* FOR..DO *)
        IF H = 1 THEN
          MOVE (2)
        ELSE
          MOVE (1);
        TX := TURTLEX;
        TY := TURTLEY;
        IF SCREENBIT (TX,TY) THEN
          FLG := TRUE;
      END;  (* FOR..DO *)
    MOVE (-(DIST+1));
    PENCOLOR (WHITE)
  END;  (* CHECK *)

PROCEDURE MOV;
  BEGIN
    MOVE (DIST);
    IF FLG THEN
      BEGIN  (* IF..THEN *)
        EXPLODE;
        PENCOLOR (NONE);
        MOVETO (100,0);
        WSTRING ('BOOM');
        NOTE (20,100);
        FLAG := TRUE
      END  (* IF..THEN *)
    ELSE
      COUNT := COUNT + 1;
    FOR H := 1 TO DELAY DO; (* PAUSE *)
  END;  (* MOV *)
```

Exhibit 18–7.
Continued

```
PROCEDURE DIRECTION;
  BEGIN
    READ (KEYBOARD,C);
    IF (C <> QUIT) AND (NOT FLAG) THEN
      BEGIN  (* IF..THEN *)
        CASE C OF
          'R': ANG := 90;
          'F': ANG := 270;
          'J': ANG := 180;
          'K': ANG := 0
        END  (* CASE *)
      END;  (* IF..THEN *)
    TURNTO (ANG)
  END;  (* DIRECTION *)

PROCEDURE SCORE;
  BEGIN
    STR (COUNT,DISPLAY);
    TX := TURTLEX;
    TY := TURTLEY;
    PENCOLOR (NONE);
    MOVETO (175,0);
    WSTRING (DISPLAY);
    MOVETO (TX,TY);
    PENCOLOR (WHITE);
    IF (HISCORE < COUNT) THEN
      HISCORE := COUNT
  END;  (* SCORE *)

BEGIN  (* GAME *)
  HISCORE := 0;
  REPEAT
    STARTUP;
    BORDER;
    REPEAT
      REPEAT
        SCORE;
        CHECK;
        MOV
      UNTIL (KEYPRESS) OR (FLAG);
      DIRECTION
    UNTIL (C = QUIT) OR (FLAG);
    TEXTMODE;
    PAGE (OUTPUT);
    WRITELN;
    WRITELN ('SCORE = ',COUNT);
    WRITELN;
    WRITELN ('HIGH SCORE = ',HISCORE)
  UNTIL (C = QUIT)
END.  (* GAME *)
```

Although this game is not very sophisticated, it does offer some advantages over many other computer games. First, you can read the program to see how the game works, and second, if you don't like it, you can always change it yourself.

18.9 SUMMARY

In this final chapter, you have learned some of the additional graphics commands not included in chapter 6 and you have learned how to make the Apple generate sound. VIEWPORT can be used to set the size of the graphics screen, and FILLSCREEN fills the viewport with a specified color. The functions TURTLEX, TURTLEY, and TURTLEANG return the Integer values of the current X and Y coordinates of the Turtle and the angle it is facing. SCREENBIT checks the color of a particular pixel on the screen and returns TRUE if the pixel is any color but BLACK. WCHAR and WSTRING are procedures that allow us to write text onto the graphics screen, and we can even specify one of sixteen different MODEs using CHARTYPE. DRAWBLOCK allows us to draw images stored in a packed array of Boolean values onto the screen. Finally, you learned how to use the built-in procedure NOTE to create sounds ranging from a simple click to musical notes.

This concludes the Pascal syntax covered by this book. The rest is up to you. Programming proficiency comes with practice. This book has given you the tools you need. The more you use them, the more comfortable you will feel about them and the easier they will be to use in the future.

Review Questions

1. What is the purpose of the procedure VIEWPORT? What are its parameters?

2. What does the procedure FILLSCREEN do? How does it interact with VIEWPORT?

3. The TURTLEGRAPHICS library includes the declaration of a scalar data type named SCREENCOLOR. What is the purpose of this data type? How is it used?

4. Explain the purpose of the functions TURTLEX, TURTLEY, and TURTLEANG.

5. What does the function SCREENBIT do? How might it be used?

6. There are two Pascal procedures that allow us to write text on the graphics screen. What are they? How are they different from the normal text displays?

7. What is the purpose of CHARTYPE? How many MODEs are available with this procedure? How are they numbered?

SUMMARY of Pascal Syntax

Reserved Words	Built-in Procedures	Built-in Functions	Library Units
PROGRAM	WRITE	EOF	TURTLEGRAPHICS
USES	WRITELN	TURTLEX	APPLESTUFF
CONST	READ	TURTLY	TRANSCEND
TYPE	READLN	TURTLEANG	
SET OF	NEW	SCREENBIT	
PACKED	RESET	ABS	
ARRAY OF	REWRITE	SQR	
RECORD	PUT	SQRT	
FILE OF	GET	ROUND	
VAR	SEEK	TRUNC	
FUNCTION	CLOSE	EXP	
FORWARD	LOCK	LN	
PROCEDURE	INITTURTLE	LOG	*Boolean Constants*
BEGIN	PENCOLOR	PWROFTEN	
FOR..DO	MOVE	ATAN	
TO	TURN	SIN	FALSE
DOWNTO	MOVETO	COS	TRUE
REPEAT	TURNTO	ORD	
UNTIL	TEXTMODE	CHR	
WHILE..DO	GRAFMODE	PRED	
IF	VIEWPORT	SUCC	
THEN	FILLSCREEN	EOLN	
ELSE	WCHAR	LENGTH	
CASE..OF	WSTRING	CONCAT	
WITH..DO	CHARTYPE	POS	
END	DRAWBLOCK	COPY	
DIV	NOTE	STR	*Integer Constants*
MOD	PAGE(OUTPUT)		
NIL	DELETE		
AND	INSERT		MAXINT
OR			
NOT			
IN			

8. What does DRAWBLOCK do? Identify its parameters and explain what each one does.

9. DRAWBLOCK creates an on-screen image from a packed array of Boolean values. Explain how this is done.

10. The Boolean array used with DRAWBLOCK stores an inverted image of the actual picture that will be drawn on the screen. Explain.

11. Explain how an animated image can be created on the screen.

12. What does the built-in procedure NOTE do? What are its parameters?

Programming Exercises

1. Write a statement that will change the graphics screen to the left half of a 40-column screen.

2. Write a program segment that will turn the left half of a 40-column screen BLUE and the right half ORANGE.

3. Write a program loop that will create concentric rectangles of different colors on the screen.

4. Write a program segment that will determine the direction the Turtle is facing and how far it is from the left edge of the screen.

5. Write a statement that will determine the Turtle's current PEN-COLOR.

6. Write a program segment that writes the character X at the left edge of the graphics screen, halfway down.

7. Write a program segment that writes the character X at the right edge of the graphics screen, halfway down. The character should be black on a white background.

8. Write a procedure that creates arrays of Strings which can be used to create an image of an X and an image of an 0 to be used in a game of tic-tac-toe.

9. Write a procedure that will change the String arrays created in exercise 8 to a packed Boolean array.

10. Write a statement that will make the Apple sound any half note.

Diagnostic Exercises

Explain what each of the following statements or segments will do. If the statement is in error, explain why. (Assume the statement INITTURTLE preceeds these statements.)

11. a. `FILLSCREEN (1)`
    b. `VIEWPORT (50, 70, 150, 100)`
    c. `MOVETO (TURTLEY, TURTLEX)`
    d. `VIEWPORT (250, 270, 20, 170)`
    e. `TURN (TURTLEANG)`

12. a. MOVE (TURTLEANG)
   b. VIEWPORT (10,260, 10, 180);
      FILLSCREEN (RED)
   c. MOVETO (TURTLEX + 50, 80)
   d. SCREENBIT := FALSE
   e. IF SCREENBIT THEN
      MOVE (TURTLEX − 10);

13. a. WCHAR ('V')
   b. WCHAR (CHR(65))
   c. WSTRING ('G')
   d. WSTRING (B)
   e. WCHAR ('A');
      MOVETO (TURTLEX + 7, TURTLEY − 8);
      WSTING ('BOUT')
   f. CHARTYPE (16);
      WCHAR ('Y')

14. Assume we have a (10 × 10) packed array of Boolean named PICT.
   a. DRAWBLOCK (PICT,0,0,0,10,10,50,50,10)
   b. DRAWBLOCK (PICT,2,4,4,5,5,50,50,10)
   c. DRAWBLOCK (PICT,2,0,0,6,6,10,10,5)
   d. DRAWBLOCK (PICT,2,0,0,10,10,250,250,10)
   e. DRAWBLOCK (PICT,2,0,0,10,10,100,100,6)

15. a. NOTE (0,30)
   b. NOTE (30,0)
   c. NOTE (1,3)
   d. NOTE (24,50)
   e. NOTE (200,200)

Problems

16. Write a procedure that will create the image of a musical note using an array of Strings.

17. Write a program that will display the note created in problem 16 on the graphics screen and also play it on the Apple's speaker.

18. Write a procedure that creates a figure (car, rocket, etc.), and then write a program that animates the figure so that it appears to move across or around the screen.

19. Write a procedure for the GAME program in exhibit 18–7 that will place obstacles (small boxes) on the screen before the game starts.

20. Change the DELAY calculation in the GAME program (exhibit 18–7) so that the speed begins at level 1 and increases by 1 unit for every 50 units added to COUNT, i.e., the longer you play the game, the faster the Turtle moves.

21. Write a program that allows you to press a key (C, D, E, F, G, A, or B) and then plays the musical note corresponding to that key.

22. Develop a nonrandom pattern of movement for the GAME program in exhibit 18–7 and then modify the game so that the computer moves the Turtle following your pattern. You may want to enable the computer to look ahead for obstacles and turn to avoid them.

23. Write a procedure that creates a file and stores the 10 highest scores obtained while playing the game in exhibit 18–7. The file should also contain the name of the players obtaining each score. The procedure should be able to update the file as new top "top 10" scores occur.

Appendix A
Making Back-up Copies

Before proceeding with this book, you should make back-up copies of the Apple Pascal system disks (APPLE0:, APPLE1:, APPLE2:, and APPLE3:). You should then put the original disks away in a safe place and use the back-up copies. Disks do get damaged, accidentally erased, and worn out. Working with back-up copies protects you against such possibilities. You will need four blank disks, one for each copy. Once you have your system disks and your blank disks, you are ready to start. There are two different approaches to copying the system disks; we'll look at both.

A.1 MAKING COPIES USING THE APPLE DOS 3.3 SYSTEM MASTER DISK

Probably the easiest way to copy your Pascal system disks is to use the COPYA program on your Apple DOS 3.3 System Master disk. Place the System Master disk in Drive 1 and turn the Apple on. When you get the APPLE][prompt, enter RUN COPYA and hit the RETURN key. You will be prompted for the correct slot number with

```
ORIGINAL SLOT: DEFAULT = 6
```

Accept this default by pressing the RETURN key. You will then see

```
DRIVE: DEFAULT = 1
```

Press RETURN again to accept this default. Then press RETURN again when you see

```
DUPLICATE SLOT: DEFAULT = 6
```

You should then see

```
DRIVE: DEFAULT = 2
```

If your Apple has two disk drives, press RETURN to accept this value. If your Apple only has one disk drive, type a 1 (this tells the computer that you will be copying onto a diskette in Drive 1). You should then see the prompt

```
-- PRESS 'RETURN' KEY TO BEGIN COPY --
```

This is your signal to remove the System Master disk from the drive.

At this point, the procedure will differ slightly depending on whether you have one or two disk drives. You can proceed to the instructions that match your Apple's configuration.

One Disk Drive

If you are working with only one drive, you will have to switch your disks when the computer instructs you to do so. Press RE-TURN. You will be prompted to

```
INSERT ORIGINAL DISK AND PRESS RETURN
```

Put the system disk you want to copy into the drive (be sure to write-protect it first) and press RETURN. The program will read information from the system disk and then instruct you to

```
INSERT DUPLICATE DISK AND PRESS RETURN
```

Remove the system disk, place the blank disk in the drive, and press RETURN. The program will first initialize the disk and then begin to copy the system disk onto it. During the copying process you will be prompted to

```
INSERT ORIGINAL DISK AND PRESS RETURN
```

and to

```
INSERT DUPLICATE DISK AND PRESS RETURN
```

At these prompts, you should insert the appropriate disk and press RETURN.

When the copying process is completed, you will see the prompt

```
DO YOU WISH TO MAKE ANOTHER COPY?
```

Since you still have three more system disks to copy, type Y. Then insert the next system disk and begin the process all over again. You should label your copies as you make them, but do *not* write-protect them.

When you have copied all of the system disks, you can type N when asked if you wish to make another copy.

Two Disk Drives

If you have two disk drives, the copying process is relatively easy. Insert the system disk you want to copy in Drive 1 (be sure to write-protect it first) and a blank disk in Drive 2 and press RETURN. The program will then read the system disk and copy it onto the blank disk (initializing the blank disk first). You will then be prompted with

```
DO YOU WISH TO MAKE ANOTHER COPY?
```

Since you still have three more system disks to copy, type Y. Then insert the next system disk in Drive 1 and a new blank disk in Drive 2 and begin the process all over again. You should label your copies as you make them, but do not write-protect them.

When you have copied all of the system disks, you can type N when asked if you wish to make another copy.

A.2 MAKING BACKUP COPIES USING THE PASCAL DISKS

The second method, making copies using the Pascal disks is a slower process. In fact, making copies with the Pascal disks and one disk drive is an extremely slow process, so slow it would be faster to find a friend or associate with two drives to make the copies for you. The process will again be discussed in two sections, one for Apples with one drive and one for those with two drives. Before beginning, however, it would be a good idea to write-protect your original disks.

One Disk Drive

Place the APPLE3: disk in the drive and turn on the Apple. When the drive stops whirring, replace APPLE3: with APPLE0: and press RESET (or CTRL-RESET) or, if prompted by the screen, the RETURN key. When you see the COMMAND prompt at the top of the screen

```
COMMAND: E(DIT, R(UN, F(ILE, C(OMP, L(IN
```

or

```
COMMAND: E(DIT, R(UN, F(ILE, C(OMP, L(IN
K, X(ECUTE, A(SSEM, D(EBUG,?
```

remove APPLE0: from the disk drive and replace it with APPLE3:. Then type X. The prompt

```
EXECUTE WHAT FILE?
```

should appear. Respond with APPLE3: FORMATTER and press the RETURN key. The Apple will then prompt:

```
APPLE DISK FORMATTER PROGRAM
FORMAT WHICH DISK (4, 5, 9..12) ?
```

At this point, remove the APPLE3: disk from the drive and re-place it with a blank disk. Then type 4 and press RETURN. If you forgot to remove the APPLE3: disk from the drive, you will get a warning, for example

```
DESTROY DIRECTORY OF APPLE3 ?
```

Should this happen, you should type N (for No). If you have correctly inserted a blank disk, however, the computer will pro-ceed and tell you

```
NOW FORMATTING DISKETTE IN DRIVE 4
```

When the formatting process is done, the message

```
FORMAT WHICH DISK (4, 5, 9..12) ?
```

will appear again. Remove the blank disk and replace it with another (blank disk) and repeat the process until you have four blank disks that have been formatted. When you have four disks formatted, press the RETURN key without entering any number. You will then be prompted to

```
PUT SYSTEM DISK IN #4 AND PRESS RETURN
```

Remove the last formatted blank disk, replace it with the APPLE0: disk, and press RETURN. The Apple will respond with

```
THAT'S ALL FOLKS...
```

and the COMMAND prompt line will reappear at the top of the screen. You now have four blank formatted disks and are ready to begin making the actual copies.

Type F (which stands for Filer) and then type T (for Transfer). The Apple will then respond

```
TRANSFER?
```

You should then enter APPLE0: (don't forget the colon) and press RETURN. The Apple will then prompt

```
TO WHERE ?
```

You should respond with BLANK: (which is the name of the disk you want to copy APPLE0: to) and press RETURN. The Apple will then say

```
TRANSFER 280 BLOCKS  ? (Y/N)
```

This is really saying, do you want to copy the whole disk? Type Y. You will then be prompted with

```
PUT IN BLANK:
TYPE <SPACE> TO CONTINUE
```

Replace the APPLE0: disk with one of the blank disks and press the space bar. The drive will whir and the warning

```
DESTROY BLANK:   ?
```

will appear. Since we want to copy APPLE0: over BLANK: (in effect, destroying BLANK:), type Y. This will begin the copying process. You will then be prompted to alternately

```
PUT APPLE0: IN UNIT 4
TYPE <SPACE> TO CONTINUE
```

and

```
PUT BLANK: IN UNIT 4
TYPE <SPACE> TO CONTINUE
```

When the copying process has been completed, the message

```
APPLE 0:          --> BLANK:
```

will appear. This tells you that the contents of APPLE0: have been successfully transferred to BLANK:, which is now a copy of APPLE0:. You should now label the copy APPLE0: and put it aside. You can then repeat the process by typing T and then Transferring APPLE1:, APPLE2:, and APPLE3: to the remaining blank disks. Do *not* write-protect your new copies. When you have made copies of all four system disks, remove the last disk from the drive and turn the Apple off. You should now put your original system disks in a safe place and use your copies.

Two Disk Drives

Place the APPLE1: disk in Drive 1, the APPLE2: disk in Drive 2, and turn on the Apple. When the drives stop whirring, you should see the COMMAND prompt at the top of the screen

```
COMMAND: E(DIT, R(UN, F(ILE, C(OMP, L(IN
```

or

```
COMMAND: E(DIT, R(UN, F(ILE, C(OMP, L(IN
K, X(ECUTE, A(SSEM, D(EBUG,?
```

When you see this prompt line, remove APPLE2: from the Drive 2 and replace it with APPLE3: Then type X. The prompt

```
EXECUTE WHAT FILE?
```

should appear. Respond with APPLE3: FORMATTER and press the RETURN key. The Apple will then prompt:

```
APPLE DISK FORMATTER PROGRAM
FORMAT WHICH DISK (4, 5, 9..12) ?
```

At this point, remove the APPLE3: disk from Drive 2 and replace it with a blank disk. Then type 5 and press RETURN. If you forgot to remove the APPLE3: disk from the drive, you will get a warning, for example,

```
DESTROY DIRECTORY OF APPLE3 ?
```

If this happens, you should type N (for No). If you have correctly inserted a blank disk, however, the computer will proceed and tell you

```
NOW FORMATTING DISKETTE IN DRIVE 4
```

When formatting process is done, the message

```
FORMAT WHICH DISK (4, 5, 9..12) ?
```

will appear again. Remove the blank disk and replace it with another (blank disk) and repeat the process until you have four blank disks that have been formatted. When you have four disks formatted, press the RETURN key without entering any number.

You will then see the prompt

    THAT'S ALL FOLKS...

and the COMMAND prompt line will reappear at the top of the screen. You now have four blank formatted disks and are ready to begin making the actual copies.

Leave the last formatted blank disk in Drive 2 and type F (which stands for Filer) and then type T (for Transfer). The Apple will then respond

    TRANSFER?

You should then enter APPLE1: (don't forget the colon) and press RETURN. The Apple will then prompt

    TO WHERE ?

You should respond with BLANK: (which is the name of the disk you want to copy APPLE1: onto) and press RETURN. The Apple will then say

    TRANSFER 280 BLOCKS   ? (Y/N)

This is really saying, do you want to copy the whole disk? Type Y. You will then be prompted with

    DESTROY BLANK: ?

Since we want to copy APPLE1: over BLANK: (in effect, destroying BLANK:) type Y. This will begin the copying process.

When the copying process has been completed, the message

    APPLE0:   --> BLANK:

will appear. This tells you that the contents of APPLE1: have been successfully transferred to BLANK:, which is now a copy of APPLE1:. You should now label the copy APPLE1: and put it aside. You can then repeat the process by typing T and then Transferring APPLE0:, APPLE2:, and APPLE3: to the remaining blank disks. Do *not* write-protect your new copies. When you have made copies of all four system disks, remove the last disk from the drive and turn the Apple off. You should now put your original system disks in a safe place and use your copies.

Appendix B
ASCII Character Codes

Exhibit B–1. ASCII Codes

Code	Character	Code	Character
0	NUL	32	SP
1	SOH	33	!
2	STX	34	''
3	ETX	35	#
4	EOT	36	$
5	ENQ	37	%
6	ACK	38	&
7	BEL	39	'
8	BS	40	(
9	HT	41	)
10	LF	42	*
11	VT	43	+
12	FF	44	,
13	CR	45	–
14	SO	46	.
15	SI	47	/
16	DLE	48	0
17	DC1	49	1
18	DC2	50	2
19	DC3	51	3
20	DC4	52	4
21	NAK	53	5
22	SYN	54	6
23	ETB	55	7
24	CAN	56	8
25	EM	57	9
26	SUB	58	:
27	ESC	59	;
28	FS	60	<
29	GS	61	=
30	RS	62	>
31	US	63	?

Exhibit B–1.
Continued

Code	Character	Code	Character
64	@	96	
65	A	97	a
66	B	98	b
67	C	99	c
68	D	100	d
69	E	101	e
70	F	102	f
71	G	103	g
72	H	104	h
73	I	105	i
74	J	106	j
75	K	107	k
76	L	108	l
77	M	109	m
78	N	110	n
79	O	111	o
80	P	112	p
81	Q	113	q
82	R	114	r
83	S	115	s
84	T	116	t
85	U	117	u
86	V	118	v
87	W	119	w
88	X	120	x
89	Y	121	y
90	Z	122	z
91	[	123	{
92	\	124	|
93	]	125	}
94	^	126	~
95	__	127	DEL

Exhibit B–2. Meaning of Nonprinting ASCII Codes

Nonprinting Code	Acronym	Meaning
0	NUL	Null
1	SOH	Start of Heading
2	STX	Start of Text
3	ETX	End of Text
4	EOT	End of Transmission
5	ENQ	Enquiry
6	ACK	Acknowledge
7	BEL	Bell
8	BS	Back Space
9	HT	Horizontal Tab
10	LF	Line Feed
11	VT	Vertical Tab
12	FF	Form Feed
13	CR	Carriage Return
14	SO	Shift Out
15	SI	Shift In
16	DLE	Data Link Escape
17	DC1	Device Control 1
18	DC2	Device Control 2
19	DC3	Device Control 3
20	DC4	Device Control 4
21	NAK	Negative Acknowledge
22	SYN	Synchronous Idle
23	ETB	End of Transmission Block
24	CAN	Cancel
25	EM	End of Medium
26	SUB	Substitute
27	ESC	Escape
28	FS	File Separator
29	GS	Group Separator
30	RS	Record Separator
31	US	Unit Separator
32	SP	Space
127	DEL	Delete

Appendix C
Pascal Reserved Words

The following words or identifiers have special meanings in Pascal. If you try to use them as user-defined identifiers in your programs, they will cause compiler errors. Not all of these reserved words have been discussed in this book. For a further explanation of any of these words, see the *Apple Pascal Reference Manual*.[1]

Standard Pascal Reserved Words

AND	ARRAY	BEGIN	CASE	CONST
DIV	DO	DOWNTO	ELSE	END
FILE	FOR	FORWARD	FUNCTION	GOTO
IF	IN	LABEL	MOD	NIL
NOT	OF	OR	PACKED	PROCEDURE
PROGRAM	RECORD	REPEAT	SET	THEN
TO	TYPE	UNTIL	VAR	WHILE
WITH				

Apple Pascal Reserved Words

EXTERNAL	IMPLEMENTATION	INTERFACE
SEGMENT	UNIT	USES

[1]*Apple Pascal Reference Manual* (Cupertino, Calif.: Apple Computer Co., 1980)

The following words or identifiers name built-in data types, constants, functions, procedures, and file types. While they can be used as user-defined identifiers without causing compiler errors, doing so will preclude their use with their predefined meanings (e.g., if you declare a variable LENGTH, you will not be able to use the built-in String function LENGTH).

Predefined Identifiers

Types

BOOLEAN   CHAR   INTEGER   REAL   STRING   TEXT

Constants

FALSE   TRUE   MAXINT

Functions

ABS	BLOCKREAD	BLOCKWRITE	CHR	CONCAT
COPY	EOF	EOLN	IORESULT	LENGTH
MEMAVAIL	ODD	ORD	POS	PRED
PWROFTEN	ROUND	SCAN	SIZEOF	SQR
STR	SUCC	TREESEARCH	TRUNC	UNITBUSY

Procedures

CLOSE	DELETE	EXIT	FILLCHAR	GET
GOTOXY	HALT	INSERT	MARK	MOVELEFT
MOVERIGHT	NEW	PAGE	PUT	READ
READLN	RELEASE	RESET	REWRITE	SEEK
UNITCLEAR	UNITREAD	UNITWAIT	UNITWRITE	WRITE
WRITELN				

File

INPUT   INTERACTIVE   KEYBOARD   OUTPUT

The following words or identifiers are declared by the special Pascal library routines TURTLEGRAPHICS, APPLESTUFF, and TRANSCEND. If you call these routines with the USES statement, you cannot use these words as user-defined identifiers without causing compiler errors.

Turtlegraphics

Functions

SCREENBIT   TURTLEANG   TURTLEX   TURTLEY

Procedures

CHARTYPE	DRAWBLOCK	FILLSCREEN	GRAFMODE	INITTURTLE
MOVE	MOVETO	PENCOLOR	TEXTMODE	TURN
TURNTO	VIEWPORT	WCHAR	WSTRING	

Types

SCREENCOLOR
APPLESTUFF

Functions

BUTTON   KEYPRESS   PADDLE   RANDOM

Procedures

NOTE   RANDOMIZE   TTLOUT
TRANSCEND

Functions
ATAN   COS   EXP   LN   LOG   SIN   SQRT

Appendix D
Pascal Error Messages

Pascal errors can be divided into three categories: Execution Errors, I/O Errors, and Compiler Errors. Exhibits D-1, D-2, and D-3 summarize these errors.

If an error occurs while the program is compiling, pressing the E key will return you to the Editor for the error message and approximate location of the error. Run-time (execution) errors, however, are sometimes more difficult to diagnose. When a run-time error occurs, the program will stop and a message similar to

```
STACK OVERFLOW
S#1, P# 1, I# 18
TYPE <SPACE> TO CONTINUE
```

will appear on the screen. The message STACK OVERFLOW indicates that the computer ran out of memory. The S# gives the segment number of the program, the P# identifies the procedure or function within the segment, and the I# is the byte number within the procedure or function (or program) where the error occurred. (The main program will always have a P# of 1.)

By inserting

```
(* $L CONSOLE: *)
```

in your program just before the PROGRAM statement, the compiler option switch will be turned on and the Apple will generate a compiler listing and send it to the monitor as your program is compiled, for example

```
1    1    1:D    1    (* $L CONSOLE *)
2    1    1:D    1    PROGRAM EXAMPLE;
3    1    1:D    3    VAR
```

.
.
.

The first number is the line number, the second the segment number (S#), the third the procedure or function number (P#) and Lexical level (D indicates a declaration statement; all other statements will have a number indicating the nesting level of the statement), and the fourth the byte number (I#). The error message will appear when the statement causing the error is reached. This can be extremely helpful in locating run-time errors.

Exhibit D–1. Apple
Pascal Run-Time Errors

Error Code	Meaning
0	System error
1	Invalid index, value out of range, subscript or subrange value out of range
2	No segment, bad code file
3	Procedure not present at exit time
4	Stack overflow. Program ran out of memory. Put (*$S + *) at top of program to cause compiler to cause segment swapping
5	Integer overflow. Attempt to assign a value to an integer that is greater than MAXINT or smaller than—MAXINT
6	Divide by zero
7	Invalid memory reference
8	User break
9	System I/O error
10	User I/O error
11	Unimplemented instruction
12	Floating-point math error
13	String too long
14	Halt, breakpoint (without debugger in core)
15	Bad block

Exhibit D–2. Apple
Pascal I/O Errors

0	No error
1	Diskette has bad Block: parity error (CRC). (Not used on the Apple.)
2	Bad device (volume) Number
3	Bad Mode: illegal operation. (For example, an attempt to read from PRINTER:.)
4	Undefined hardware error. (Not used on the Apple.)
5	Lost device. device is no longer on-line, after successfully starting an operation using that device.
6	Lost file: file is no longer in the diskette directory, after successfully starting an operation using that file.
7	Bad title: illegal file name. (For example, filename is more than 15 characters long.)
8	No room: insufficient space on the specified diskette. (Files must be stored in contiguous diskette blocks.)
9	No device: the specified volume is not on line.
10	No file: The specified file is not in the directory of the specified volume.
11	Duplicate file: attempt to rewrite a file when a file of that name already exists.
12	Not closed: attempt to open an open file.
13	Not open, attempt to access a closed file.
14	Bad format, error in reading real or integer. (For example, your program expects an integer input but you typed a letter.)
15	Ring buffer overflow: characters are arriving at the Apple faster than the input buffer can accept them.
16	Write-protect error: the specified diskette is write-protected.
64	Device error: failed to complete a read or write correctly (bad address or data field on diskette).

Exhibit D-3. Apple
Pascal Compiler Errors

1: Error in simple type
2: Identifier expected
3: 'PROGRAM' expected
4: ')' expected
5: ':' expected
6: Illegal symbol (possibly missing ';' on line above)
7: Error in parameter list
8: 'OF' expected
9: '(' expected
10: Error in type
11: '[' expected
12: ']' expected
13: 'END' expected
14: ';' expected (possibly on line above)
15: Integer expected
16: ' = ' expected
17: 'BEGIN' expected
18: Error in declaration part
19: Error in < field-list >
20: '.' expected
21: '*' expected
22: 'Interface' expected
23: 'Implementation' expected
24: 'Unit' expected

50: Error in constant
51: ': =' expected
52: 'THEN' expected
53: 'UNTIL' expected
54: 'DO' expected
55: 'TO' or 'DOWNTO' expected in for statement
56: 'IF' expected
57: 'FILE' expected
58: Error in < factor > (bad expression)
59: Error in variable

101: Identifier declared twice
102: Low bound exceeds high bound
103: Identifier is not of the appropriate class
104: Undeclared identifier
105: Sign not allowed
106: Number expected
107: Incompatible subrange types
108: File not allowed here
109: Type must not be real
110: < tagfield > type must be scalar or subrange
111: Incompatible with < tagfield > part
112: Index type must not be real
113: Index type must be a scalar or a subrange
114: Base type must not be real
115: Base type must be a scalar or a subrange

116: Error in type of standard procedure parameter
117: Unsatisfied forward reference
118: Forward reference type identifier in variable declaration
119: Respecified parameters not OK for a forward declared
     procedure
120: Function result type must be scalar, subrange or pointer
121: File value parameter not allowed
122: A forward declared function's result type can't be
     respecified
123: Missing result type in function declaration
124: F-format for reals only
125: Error in type of standard procedure parameter
126: Number of parameters does not agree with declaration
127: Illegal parameter substitution
128: Result type does not agree with declaration
129: Type conflict of operands
130: Expression is not of set type
131: Tests on equality allowed only
132: Strict inclusion not allowed
133: File comparison not allowed
134: Illegal type of operand(s)
135: Type of operand must be Boolean
136: Set element type must be scalar or subrange
137: Set element types must be compatible
138: Type of variable is not array
139: Index type is not compatible with the declaration
140: Type of variable is not record
141: Type of variable must be file or pointer
142: Illegal parameter solution
143: Illegal type of loop control variable
144: Illegal type of expression
145: Type conflict
146: Assignment of files not allowed
147: Label type incompatible with selecting expression
148: Subrange bounds must be scalar
149: Index type must be integer
150: Assignment to standard function is not allowed
151: Assignment to formal function is not allowed
152: No such field in this record
153: Type error in read
154: Actual parameter must be a variable
155: Control variable cannot be formal or nonlocal
156: Multidefined case label
157: Too many cases in case statement
158: No such variant in this record
159: Real or string tagfields not allowed
160: Previous declaration was not forward
161: Again forward declared
162: Parameter size must be constant
163: Missing variant in declaration
164: Substitution of standard proc/func not allowed

Exhibit D–3.
Continued

165: Multidefined label
166: Multideclared label
167: Undeclared label
168: Undefined label
169: Error in base set
170: Value parameter expected
171: Standard file was redeclared
172: Undeclared external file
174: Pascal function or procedure expected

182: Nested units not allowed
183: External declaration not allowed at this nesting level
184: External declaration not allowed in inferface section
185: Segment declaration not allowed in unit
186: Labels not allowed in interface section
187: Attempt to open library unsuccessful
188: Unit not declared in previous 'Uses' declaration
189: 'Uses' not allowed at this nesting level
190: Unit not in library
191: No private files
192: 'Uses' must be in interface section
193: Not enough room for this operation
194: Comment must appear at top of program
195: Unit not importable

201: Error in real number—digit expected
202: String constant must not exceed source line
203: Integer constant exceeds range
204: 8 or 9 in octal number

250: Too many scopes of nested identifiers
251: Too many nested procedures or functions
252: Too many forward references of procedure entries
253: Procedure too long
254: Too many long constants in this procedure
256: Too many external references
257: Too many externals
258: Too many local files
259: Expression too complicated

300: Division by zero
301: No case provided for this value
302: Index expression out of bounds
303: Value to be assigned is out of bounds
304: Element expression out of range

350: No data segment allocated
351: Segment used twice
352: No code segment allocated
353: Nonintrinsic unit called from intrinsic unit
354: Too many segments for the segment dictionary

Exhibit D–3.
Continued

398: Implementation restriction
399: Implementation restriction
400: Illegal character in text
401: Unexpected end of input
402: Error in writing code file, not enough room
403: Error in reading include file
404: Error in writing list file, not enough room
405: Call not allowed in separate procedure
406: Include file not legal
407: Too many libraries
408: (*$S + *) needed to compile units

500: General assembler error

Appendix E
Apple Pascal Language System Files

The following files are normally stored on the Apple Pascal Language System Disks indicated.

APPLE0:

SYSTEM.PASCAL
SYSTEM.MISCINFO
SYSTEM.COMPILER
SYSTEM.EDITOR
SYSTEM.FILER
SYSTEM.LIBRARY
SYSTEM.CHARSET
SYSTEM.SYNTAX

APPLE1:

SYSTEM.APPLE
SYSTEM.PASCAL
SYSTEM.MISCINFO
SYSTEM.EDITOR
SYSTEM.FILER
SYSTEM.LIBRARY
SYSTEM.CHARSET
SYSTEM.SYNTAX

APPLE2:

SYSTEM.COMPILER
SYSTEM.LINKER
SYSTEM.ASSEMBLER
6500.OPCODES
6500.ERRORS

APPLE3:

SYSTEM.APPLE
FORMATTER.CODE
FORMATTER.DATA
LIBRARY.CODE
LIBMAP.CODE
SETUP.CODE
BINDER.CODE
CALC.CODE
LINEFEED.TEXT
LINEFEED.CODE
SOROCGOTO.TEXT
SOROCGOTO.CODE
SOROC.MISCINFO
HAZELGOTO.TEXT
HAZELGOTO.CODE
HAZEL.MISCINFO
CROSSREF.TEXT
CROSSREF.CODE
SPIRODEMO.TEXT
SPIRODEMO.CODE
HILBERT.TEXT
HILBERT.CODE
GRAFDEMO.TEXT
GRAFDEMO.CODE
GRAFCHARS.CODE
GRAFCHARS.TEXT
TREE.TEXT
TREE.CODE
BALANCED.TEXT
BALANCED.CODE
DISKIO.TEXT
DISKIO.CODE

Appendix F

Changing the Configuration for the Up and Down Arrow Keys

The following instructions will outline the procedure which may be used to reconfigure the Apple Pascal disks so that the up and down arrow keys may be used to move the cursor up and down rather than the CTRL-O and CTRL-L keys. Some newer versions of Apple Pascal sold for the IIe or IIc may already have these changes made. If they do not, the following instructions will help you to make these simple alterations.

If you have a two drive system, place the APPLE1: disk in drive 1 and the APPLE3: disk in drive 2 and boot the Apple (turn it on). If you have a one drive system, boot the Apple with APPLE3: and then APPLE0:; then place the APPLE3: disk back in the drive.

When the COMMAND prompt line appears at the top of the screen, press X for X(ecute and when asked what file to execute, answer APPLE3:SETUP. The screen will show

```
INITIALIZING..............................
..........................................
SETUP: C(HANGE  T(EACH  H(ELP  Q(UIT  [S.2]
```

press C for C(hange. The next prompt will be

```
CHANGE: S(INGLE)  P(ROMPTED)  R(ADIX)
    H(ELP)  Q(UIT)
```

press S for S(ingle. You will be prompted to enter "Name of Field:". Enter

```
KEY TO MOVE CURSOR UP
```

and hit ⟨RET⟩. The Apple will respond with the following information on the current key

```
OCTAL  DECIMAL  HEXADECIMAL  ASCII  CONTROL
  17      15          F         SI     ^0
```

The Apple will then ask if you WANT TO CHANGE THIS VALUE? (Y,N,!). Respond Y and when asked for "NEW VALUE:" press the up arrow key (this will show up on the screen as a ?). Press ⟨RET⟩ and the information on the new key will appear.

OCTAL	DECIMAL	HEXADECIMAL	ASCII	CONTROL
13	11	B	VT	^K

The prompt WANT TO CHANGE THIS VALUE? (Y,N,!) will reappear. Respond N for no if you have made no mistakes. This will take you back to the

```
C(HANGE: S(INGLE) P(ROMPTED) R(ADIX)
    H(ELP) Q(UIT)
```

prompt. Repeat the process, i.e. S for S(ingle and use KEY TO MOVE CURSOR DOWN as the field name. After the current values have been displayed

OCTAL	DECIMAL	HEXADECIMAL	ASCII	CONTROL
12	10	A	LF	^J

answer Y to change the values and press the down arrow key when asked for the NEW VALUE (remember, this will show as a ? on your screen). You should then see

OCTAL	DECIMAL	HEXADECIMAL	ASCII	CONTROL
14	12	C	FF	^L

Answer N to the prompt asking if you want to change the value and Q to the Change prompt. Then respond Q again to the Setup prompt. You will then see

```
QUIT: D(ISK) OR M(EMORY) UPDATE,
      R(ETURN) H(ELP) E(XIT)
```

(If you are working with a one drive system, place the APPLE0: disk back in the disk drive before proceeding.) Press D to update these changes to the system disk (APPLE0: or APPLE1:) and then E to exit the SETUP program.

Now press F to move to the Filer and L(ist the contents of your system disk. You will see two files with the same MISCINFO suffix, SYSTEM.MISCINFO and NEW.MISCINFO. The SYSTEM.MISCINFO file contains information which your Apple uses when it boots Pascal. Included in that information are the special key definitions. The file NEW.MISCINFO was created by the SETUP program and contains the new definitions which use the up and down arrow keys. You can now type R for R(emove and respond with SYSTEM.MISCINFO to remove (erase) this file. When asked if you wish to update the directory, respond Y (yes).

Then type C for C(hange and enter NEW.MISCINFO. When asked what you wish to change it to, enter SYSTEM.MISCINFO. This completes the change and should enable an Apple IIe or IIc to use the up and down arrow keys rather than CTRL-O and CTRL-L to move the cursor up and down. (If you would rather not remove the original SYSTEM.MISCINFO file, you can change it to some other filename, e.g. OLD.MISCINFO rather than removing it, but be sure to do so before changing NEW. MISCINFO.)

Answers to Selected Problems

Chapter Two

2. a) 7 b) 18
c) 17 d) 14
4. a) 93.2   b) 0.00154
c) 45760 d) 0.63
e) 8925000
6. a) 26 b) 6.5 c) 0.2 d) 10.8
e) 0.9
8. a) 2 b) 0 c) 2 d) 0 e) 3
10.
```
PROGRAM TEN;
BEGIN
   WRITELN ('NOW OR NEVER')
END.
```
12.
```
PROGRAM TWELVE:
VAR
   A:REAL;
BEGIN
   A := 49.65;
   WRITELN ('ANSWER = ',A)
END.
```
14. a) RESULT = 14 b) RESULT = 21 c) RESULT = 60
16. 2B—invalid identifier as program name, begins with digit; .8—constant value begins with decimal point; semicolon instead of colon between variables and data types; assignment statements both missing colcon in (:=); "RESULT"—single rather than double quotes needed; while not a fatal error, the semicolon is not needed between the WRITELN and END statements.

Chapter Four

2.
```
PROGRAM EXER2;
   BEGIN
      WRITELN (4.56 * 9.72)
   END.
```
4.
```
PROGRAM EXER4;
VAR
   VAL1,VAL2,RESULT:REAL;
BEGIN
   READ (VAL1);
   READ (VAL2);
   RESULT := VAL1 + VAL2;
   RESULT := RESULT * VAL1;
   WRITELN (RESULT)
END.
```

6.
```
PROGRAM EXER6;
VAR
   VAL1,VAL2,RESULT:REAL;
BEGIN
   WRITE ('ENTER FIRST VALUE -> ');
   READ (VAL1);
   WRITE ('ENTER SECOND VALUE -> ');
   READ (VAL2);
   RESULT := VAL1 + VAL2;
   WRITELN ('SUM OF VALUES = ',RESULT:12:2);
   RESULT := RESULT * VAL1;
   WRITELN ('SUM X FIRST VALUE = ',RESULT:12:2)
END.
```
8. a) A = 12.0, B = 72.3, C = 86.0
b) same as (a)
c) A = 12.0, B = 72.3, C = 608.0
d) A = 12.0, B = 608.0, C = 39.21
10. 92 1.73E1 (a space)
12. HERE IS A AND B TOO
14.
```
PROGRAM DISCOUNT;
CONST
   OFF = 0.27
VAR
   PRICE:REAL;
BEGIN
   WRITE ('ENTER PRICE ->');
   READLN (PRICE);
   PRICE := PRICE * (1 - OFF);
   WRITELN ('DISCOUNTED PRICE = ',PRICE:12:2)
END.
```
16.
```
PROGRAM TAXER;
CONST
   RATE = 0.07;
VAR
   PRICE,TAX,TOTAL:REAL;
BEGIN
   WRITE ('ENTER PRICE -> ');
   READLN (PRICE);
   TAX := PRICE * RATE;
   TOTAL := PRICE + TAX;
   WRITELN ('PRICE',PRICE:12:2);
   WRITELN ('TAX',TAX:14:2);
   WRITELN ('TOTAL',TOTAL:12:2)
END.
```

Chapter Five

2. (1) a) request the length of the room;
      b) get the length;
   (2) a) request the width of the room;
      b) get the width;
   (3) a) request the height of the room;
      b) get the height
   (4) a) add the length and the width;
      b) double the result of (a);
      c) multiply the result of (b) times the height;
   (5) output the result

4. The result should be 528 cubic feet.

6. (1) input amount of sale; (2) input cash tendered; (3) subtract value of (1) from value of (2); (4) output change due equal to (3)

8. (1) a) request the length of the room;
      b) get the length;
   (2) a) request the width of the room;
      b) get the width;
   (3) a) request the height of the room;
      b) get the height
   (4) a) add the length and the width;
      b) double the result of 4(a);
      c) multiply the result of 4(b) times the height;
   (5) a) multiply door width times height;
      b) multiply window width times height;
      c) double value of (b);
      d) sum values of 5(a) and 5(c)
      e) subtract value of 5(d) from value of 4(c)
   (6) output the result

Chapter Six

2. a) The turtle will move forward 60 units.
   b) The turtle will turn right 30 degrees.
   c) The turtle will turn left 120 degrees.
   d) The turtle will turn right 135 degrees.

4. a)
```
INITTURTLE;
PENCOLOR (WHITE);
MOVE (140);
```
   b)
```
INITTURTLE;
PENCOLOR (WHITE);
TURN (180);
MOVE (140);
```

6.
```
PROGRAM TRIANGLE;
USES TURTLEGRAPHICS;
BEGIN
  INITTURTLE;
  PENCOLOR(WHITE);
  MOVE(60);
  TURN(120);
  MOVE(60);
  TURN(120);
  MOVE(60);
  READLN;
  TEXTMODE
END.
```

8. ⌐

10. ✕

12.
```
PROGRAM EXER12;
USES TURTLEGRAPHICS;
VAR
  DISTANCE,ANGLE:INTEGER;
PROCEDURE DRAW;
  BEGIN
    MOVE(DISTANCE);
    TURN(ANGLE);
    MOVE(DISTANCE);
    TURN(ANGLE);
    MOVE(DISTANCE);
    TURN(ANGLE);
    MOVE(DISTANCE)
  END;  (* DRAW *)
BEGIN  (* EXER12 *)
  INITTURTLE;
  DISTANCE := 60;
  ANGLE := 90;
  MOVETO((139-DISTANCE DIV 2),(95-DISTANCE DIV 2));
  PENCOLOR(WHITE);
  DRAW;
  READLN;
  TEXTMODE
END.  (* EXER12 *)
```

14.
```
PROGRAM BORDER;
USES TURTLEGRAPHICS;
BEGIN
  INITTURTLE;
  MOVETO(0,0);
  PENCOLOR(WHITE);
  MOVETO(279,0);
  MOVETO(279,191);
  MOVETO(0,191);
  MOVETO(0,0);
  READLN;
  TEXTMODE
END.
```

16. Insert the following segment immediately after the DRAW statement in exercise 12: DRAW; DRAW; DRAW;

Chapter Seven

2.
```
FOR I := 1 TO 5 DO
    WRITE('* ');
    WRITELN;
```

4.
```
SUM := 0;
I := 0;
REPEAT
  I := I+1;
  SUM := SUM+I
UNTIL I = 20;
WRITELN ('SUM = ',SUM);
```

6. 1 2 3 4 5 6 7 8 9 10

8. 6
   7
   8
   9
   10
   11
   12
   13
   14

10. 1
    2
    ·
    ·
    ·
    10
    11

12.
```
*
* *
* * *
* * * *
* * * * *
* * * * * *
* * * * * * *
```

14. (no output since I is not less than 10)

16.
```
FACT := 1;
FOR I := 2 TO 7 DO
  FACT := FACT*I;
WRITELN('FACTORIAL OF 7 = ',FACT);
```

18. (1) for 5 rows of 9 columns (each column 2 characters wide):

print 4 blanks and 1 star in the first row;

print 3 blanks, 1 star, 1 blank, and 1 star in the second row;

print 2 blanks, 1 star, 3 blanks, and 1 star in the third row;

print 1 blank, 1 star, 5 blanks, and 1 star in the fourth row;

print 9 stars in the fifth row

Examining the rows for patterns, we can see that the first and last rows are unique. The first has one star, the last 9 stars. Rows 2–4 all have two stars. Thus, we can break (1) up into three subproblems:

(1) print 4 blanks and 1 star;

(2) a) print 3 blanks, a star, 1 blank, and a star;

b) print 2 blanks, a star, 3 blanks, and a star;

c) print 1 blank, a star, 5 blanks, and a star;

(3) print 9 stars

There are two patterns that appear in (2). The first set of blanks go from 3 to 1 in steps of 1 and the second set go from 1 to 5 in steps of 2. Refining (2) gives us:

(2) initialize b2 at −1;

for each row:

for b1 from 3 downto 1:

print b1 blanks;

foprint a star;

add 2 to b2 and print b2 blanks;

print a star;

20.
```
SECONDS := 0;
SPEED := 1;
REPEAT
   SECONDS := SECONDS +1;
   SPEED := SPEED * 2
UNTIL SPEED > 200;
WRITELN (SECONDS, SECONDS TO REACH ',SPEED, ' MPH');
```

Chapter Eight

2.
```
IF X > Y THEN
    WRITELN ('X IS GREATER')
ELSE
    IF X < Y THEN
       WRITELN ('Y IS GREATER');
```

4.
```
CASE (X-Y) OF
   -1:WRITELN('Y IS GREATER');
    0:WRITELN('X AND Y ARE EQUAL');
    1:WRITELN('X IS GREATER')
END;
```

6. a) TRUE b) FALSE c) FALSE d) TRUE

8. a) TRUE b) TRUE c) FALSE d) TRUE

10. a) TRUE b) FALSE c) TRUE d) TRUE

12.
```
PROGRAM PROB12;
CONST
   DISC = 0.10;
   LIMIT = 100;
VAR
   PRICE:REAL;
BEGIN
   WRITE('ENTER PRICE -> ');
   READLN(PRICE);
   IF PRICE > LIMIT THEN
     WRITELN('CASH PRICE = ',PRICE*(1-DISC):10:2)
   ELSE
     WRITELN('CASH PRICE = ',PRICE:10:2)
END.
```

14.
```
IF KEYPRESS THEN
   BEGIN
     READ(KEY);
     IF KEY = 'L' THEN
       TURNTO (0)
     ELSE
       IF KEY = 'T' THEN
         TURNTO (90)
       ELSE
         IF KEY = 'K' THEN
           TURNTO (180)
         ELSE
           TURNTO (270)   (* ASSUMING A G IS PRESSED *)
   END;
```

16.
```
PROGRAM PROB16;
VAR
  OLDTEMP,NEWTEMP:REAL;
BEGIN
  OLDTEMP := -999;
  REPEAT
    WRITE('ENTER TEMP -> ');
    READLN(NEWTEMP);
    IF NEWTEMP > OLDTEMP THEN
      BEGIN
        WRITELN('PROCESS CONTINUING');
        OLDTEMP := NEWTEMP
      END
  UNTIL OLDTEMP > NEWTEMP;
  WRITELN('PROCESS COMPLETED')
END.
```

Chapter Nine

2. EXER1(I,J)

4. EXER1(I,J,SUM)   and
   PROCEDURE EXER1(I,J:INTEGER; VAR SUM:INTEGER);

6. a) incorrect—parameters separated by ; instead of , b) correct, but (X,Y:REAL) would be better c) incorrect—, instead of ; between data types d) incorrect—no ; after VAR e) correct

8. a) yes b) yes c) yes d) no e) yes f) no g) no

10. 5 0 3

12. a) 2 b) 4 c) 18 d) 1 e) 18

14. PROCEDURE PROB14;
```
BEGIN
  IF VAL >= 0 THEN
    POS := POS + 1
  ELSE
    NEG := NEG + 1
END;
```

16. set largest value small and smallest value large; for each value:
   a) input value;
   b) if value greater than largest value then change largest value to input value;
   c) if value less than smallest value then change smallest value to input value; output results (largest and smallest values).

Chapter Ten

2. WRITELN(SQR(6)*6))   (216)

4. FUNCTION MULT(A,B,C:REAL):REAL;
```
BEGIN
  MULT := A + B + C
END;
```

6. a) 25 b) 1000 c) 3 d) 4

8. a) 1.29250   b) $-8.83455E-1$
   c) $-1.12152E-1$
   d) $-1.42547E-1$

10. a) no parameter list or data type b) no data type c) cannot have a variable parameter with a function; semicolon used between list and data type e) semicolon used between parameters A and B

12. A = 5   B = 6 C = 22

14. FUNCTION PAY(RATE,HOURS:REAL):REAL;
```
BEGIN
  IF HOURS <= 40 THEN
    PAY := RATE * HOURS
  ELSE
    PAY := RATE*40.0 + 1.5*RATE*(HOURS-40.0)
END;
```

16. FUNCTION BALANCE(OLD,PAY,NEW:REAL):REAL;
```
BEGIN
  IF OLD > PAY THEN
    BALANCE := (OLD - PAY + NEW)*1.015
  ELSE
    BALANCE := OLD - PAY + NEW
END;
```

18. generate a random number; divide the random number by 6; add 1 to the remainder.

20. if distance of current player is greater than 50 then winner is true.

Chapter Eleven

2. TYPE
   WEEK = (SUNDAY,MONDAY,TUESDAY,WEDNESDAY,THURSDAY,
          FRIDAY,SATURDAY);

4. VAR
   DAY:WEEK;

6. SOME will take a value of 120 which is outside the range and the program will terminate in an error.

8. LOW := [10..20,25,30];

10. 0 (zero)

12. No. Assignments cannot be made to a data type.

14. a) [1,3,5,6,7]   b) [2,4,8]
   c) [1..10,16]

16. a) [1,2,4,6,8,10..15,17..20]
    b) [3,5,7,9,16]
    c) [3,5,7,9] d) [ ]

18.
```
PROGRAM PROB18;
TYPE
   LETTERS = SET OF CHAR;
VAR
   ALL,CON,VWL:LETTERS;
   CH,ANS:CHAR;
   CHECK:BOOLEAN;
BEGIN
   ALL := ['A'..'Z']
   VWL := ['A','E','I','O','U'];
   CON := ALL - VWL;
   REPEAT
     WRITE('INPUT A LETTER OF THE ALPHABET -> ');
     READ(CH);
   UNTIL (CH IN ALL);
   WRITE('IS THE LETTER ',CH,' A CONSONANT (C) OR VOWEL (V)? ');
   READ(ANS);
   IF (CH IN VWL) AND (ANS = 'V') THEN
     WRITELN('RIGHT! IT''S A VOWEL');
   IF (CH IN CON) AND (ANS = 'C') THEN
     WRITELN('RIGHT!  IT''S A CONSONANT');
END.
```

Chapter Twelve

2. A: LIST;
    B: ARRAY [1..40] OF .... (data type)

4.
```
PROGRAM INITLIZE;
VAR
   MATRIX:ARRAY [1..5,1..5] OF INTEGER;
   I,J:INTEGER;
BEGIN
   FOR I := 1 TO 5 DO
     FOR J := 1 TO 5 DO
       MATRIX[I,J] := 0;
END.
```

6.
```
VAR
   PAR: PACKED ARRAY [1..20] OF CHAR;

FOR I:= 1 TO 20 DO
   IF ODD(I) THEN
     PAR[I] := '*';
WRITELN(PAR);
```

10. a) Yes b) Yes c) Yes d) Yes
    e) Yes

12.
```
PROCEDURE MATOUT;
VAR
   I,J:INTEGER;
BEGIN
   FOR I := 1 TO 5 DO
     BEGIN
       FOR J := 1 TO 5 DO
         WRITE(MATRIX[I,J]:4);
       WRITELN
     END
END;
```

14.
```
PROGRAM PROB14;
VAR
   I,J:INTEGER;
   MATRIX:ARRAY[1..5,1..5] OF INTEGER;

(* PROCEDURE MATOUT - PROB 16 - HERE *)

BEGIN
   FOR I := 1 TO 5 DO
     FOR J := 1 TO 5 DO
       IF (I=1) OR (I=5) OR (J=1) OR (J=5) THEN
         MATRIX[I,J] := 1
       ELSE
         MATRIX[I,J] := 0;
   MATOUT
END.
```

8a)

	10	9	8	7	6	5	4	3	2	1
A	[1]	[2]	[3]	[4]	[5]	[6]	[7]	[8]	[9]	[10]

b)

1	1	1	1	1	1	1	1	1	1
2	2	2	2	2	2	2	2	2	2
3	3	3	3	3	3	3	3	3	3
4	4	4	4	4	4	4	4	4	4
5	5	5	5	5	5	5	5	5	5

c)

0	1	2	3	4	5	6	7	8	9

d)

A:	1	2	3	4	5	6	7	8	9	10
B:	6	6	6	6	6	6	6	6	6	6

e) AAAAA

```
16. PROCEDURE SWITCH;
    VAR
      I,J:INTEGER;
      REVERSE:PKD;
    BEGIN  (* SWITCH *)
      FOR I := 1 TO 5 DO
        BEGIN  (* FOR..DO *)
          REVERSE := UP[I];
          FOR J := 1 TO 5 DO
            IF REVERSE[J] = '*' THEN
              REVERSE[J] := ' '
            ELSE
              REVERSE[J] := '*';
          UP[I] := REVERSE;
          WRITELN(UP[I])
        END;  (* FOR..DO *)
    END;  (* SWITCH *)
```

To test, add this procedure to Prob 19 with the procedure
call SWITCH immediately after ARROW (and add the ; after
ARROW).

d) Correct. Assigns the characters BIOGRAPHY to the packed array field SUBJ. e) Not correct. WITH REC[ ] DO TITLE := ... f) Not correct. WITH REC[I] DO AUTHOR := ... g) Correct. Assignes 'ANON' to REC[I] field AUTHOR h) Not correct. WITH REC[I] DO ADVENTURE := i) Not correct. CAT := NONFICT;

Chapter Thirteen

2.
```
TYPE
  TWO = RECORD
           FIRST:INTEGER;
           SECOND:ARRAY[1..10] OF REAL
        END;
```

4.
```
TYPE
  PLAYER = RECORD
              NAME:STRING;
              TEAM:STRING;
              AGE:INTEGER;
              BAVE:ARRAY[1..5] OF REAL
           END;
```

6.
```
VAR
  WORK:DEPT;

  WORK.NUMBER := 1234;
  WORK.STAFF[2].AGE := 35;
```

8.
```
TYPE
  ONE = RECORD
           CASE SIZE:INTEGER OF
             1 : ONE:INTEGER;
             2 : TWO:REAL
        END;
```

10. Yes, it is acceptable. It defines two records, one with two fields and one with three. Field names need not be unique between different records.

12. a) Not correct. Must specify subscript. b) Not correct. REC[12].ADVENTURE := ... c) Not correct. REC[50].ADVENTURE := ...

13.
```
TYPE
  TRUCK = RECORD
             LICENSE:STRING;
             WEIGHT:INTEGER;
             HOURS:REAL
          END;
VAR
  FLEET:ARRAY[1..28] OF TRUCK;
```

14.
```
PROCEDURE UPDATE;
  VAR
    I:INTEGER;
    HRS:REAL;
  BEGIN
    FOR I:= 1 TO 28 DO
      BEGIN
        WRITELN(FLEET[I].LICENSE);
        WRITE('HOURS ON ROAD THIS WEEK -> ');
        READ(HRS);
        FLEET[I].HOURS := FLEET[I].HOURS+HRS;
        IF FLEET[I].HOURS > 750 THEN
          WRITELN('*** SCHEDULE SERVICE ***');
        WRITELN
      END  (* FOR..NEXT *)
  END;  (* UPDATE *)
```

Chapter Fourteen

2.
```
REWRITE(INFO,'TEST.DATA');
```

4.
```
RESET(INFO,'TEST.DATA');
TEMP := INFO^;
```

6.
```
RESET(INFO,'TEST.DATA');
SEEK(INFO,5);
GET(INFO);
TEMP := INFO^;
WRITELN(TEMP);
```

8.
```
VAR
   NOS:TEXT;
BEGIN
   REWRITE(NOS,`MYFILE.TEXT');
   FOR I := 1 TO 3 DO
     WRITE(11*I:10);
     WRITELN;
   FOR I := 4 TO 6 DO
     WRITE(11*I:10);
     WRITELN;
   FOR I := 7 TO 9 DO
     WRITE(11*I:10);
     WRITELN;
   CLOSE(NOS)
END.
```
or we could use a fancy algorithm and the lines:

```
   FOR I := 1 TO 3 DO
     BEGIN
       FOR J := 1 TO 3 DO
         WRITE(11*(3*I+J-3):10);
       WRITELN
     END;
```

10. Not correct. The variable should be DFILE, not DF. This segment will open the file DFILE.DATA and write the value 64 to it.

12. Not correct. Cannot assign a Real value to an Integer variable. Will write value to file.

14. Not correct. Must close DFILE, not file name. Unless LOCK is used in the CLOSE statement, the file will not be saved when the program terminates.

16. Correct syntax, but intent in doubt. Opens file and gets value from it. Then gets second value, assigns it to NV and writes it to screen.

18. Not correct. LOCK not needed on files opened by RESET. Opens file, getting value, and assigns value to NV. Then gets next value in file, assigns value to NV and writes that value to the screen.

20.
```
PROCEDURE EXCHANGE;
VAR
   FV:FILE OF INTEGER;
BEGIN
   REWRITE(FV,filename);
   SEEK(FV,5);
   FV^ := 76;
   PUT(FV);
   CLOSE(FV,LOCK)
END;
```

22.
```
PROGRAM COMPARE;
VAR
   FIRST,SECOND:INTEGER;
   ONE,TWO:TEXT;
BEGIN
   RESET(ONE,`FILE1.TEXT');
   RESET(TWO,`FILE2.TEXT');
   REPEAT
     READ(ONE,FIRST);
     READ(TWO,SECOND);
     IF (FIRST = SECOND) AND NOT EOF(ONE) THEN
       WRITELN (FIRST);
   UNTIL EOF(ONE) OR EOF(TWO);
   CLOSE(ONE);
   CLOSE(TWO)
END.
```

Chapter Fifteen

2. PNTR$^\wedge$:= 43;

4. A$^\wedge$:= 12; B$^\wedge$:= 33; C := A; (where C is also a pointer variable) A := B; B := C;

6.
```
LINK = ^DATA;
DATA = RECORD
          NAME:STRING;
          GRADE:REAL;
          LETTER:CHAR;
          NEXT:LINK
       END;
```

8. a) 14 b) 10 and 10 (1.00000E1)
c) 36 and 36

10. a) A := B;
b) A$^\wedge$. NEXT := B;
c) A$^\wedge$.VALUE := 9;
d) C := A$^\wedge$.NEXT;
e) A$^\wedge$.VALUE: = C$^\wedge$. VALUE;
f) A$^\wedge$.NEXT$^\wedge$. VALUE: = 23;
g) A$^\wedge$. NEXT: = C$^\wedge$.NEXT;
h) A$^\wedge$.NEXT$^\wedge$. NEXT: = A;

```
12. PROCEDURE READFILE(VAR S,P:POINTER);
      VAR
        E:POINTER;
        DF:TEXT;
      BEGIN
        RESET(DF,'filename');
        WHILE NOT EOF(DF) DO
          BEGIN
            NEW(S);
            READLN(DF,S^.VALUE);
            P:=S;
            WHILE NOT EOF(DF) DO
              BEGIN
                NEW(E);
                READLN(DF,E^.VALUE);
                P^.NEXT := E;
                P := E
              END
          END;
        P^.NEXT := NIL;
        CLOSE(DF)
      END;
14. PROCEDURE MENU;
      VAR
        ANS:CHAR;
      BEGIN
        PAGE(OUTPUT);
        WRITELN('LINKED LIST PROGRAM');
        WRITELN;
        WRITELN('YOUR CHOICES ARE:');
        WRITELN('  (C)  CREATE');
        WRITELN('  (O)  OUTPUT LIST');
        WRITELN('  (A)  ADD ITEM');
        WRITELN('  (D)  DELETE ITEM');
        WRITELN('  (W)  WRITE TO FILE');
        WRITELN('  (Q)  QUIT');
        WRITELN;
        WRITE('ENTER YOUR CHOICE (LETTER) -> ');
        READ(ANS);
        CASE ANS OF
          'C': CREATE(S,P);
          'O': DISPLAY(S);
          'A': INSERTION(S);
          'D': DELETION(S);
          'W': SAVELIST(S)
        END;
        IF ANS<>'Q' THEN
          MENU
      END;
change program block to:
BEGIN
  MENU
END.
you might ask your students why, since the program block
only calls MENU, we made MENU a procedure rather than the
main program body. (Ans: we use a recursive call to MENU.)
```

Chapter Sixteen

2.
```
S1 := 'ONE ';
S2 := 'LONG ';
S3 := 'STRING';
S := CONCAT(S1,S2,S3);
```
4.
```
LOC := POS('A',S);
INSERT('*',S,LOC+1);
or   INSERT('*',S,POS('A',S)+1);
```
6.
```
VAR
  A,B,C:INTEGER[10];
BEGIN
  A:=34567293;
  B:=88914006;
  C:= A+B;
  WRITELN(C);
```
8. a) 3 b) 11 c) 8 d) 6

10. 41

12. APPLE C

14. APPLE COMPUTERS SPEAK PASCAL

16. THEAPPLECOMPUTERSPEAKSPASCAL

18.
```
PROCEDURE SPACEOUT;
  VAR
    S:STRING;
  BEGIN
    REPEAT
      IF POS(S,' ') > 0 THEN
        DELETE(S,POS(S,' '),1)
    UNTIL POS(S,' ') = 0;
    WRITELN(S)
  END;
```

20.
1. define 200 character string;
2. prompt for and get string;
3. prompt for and get primary word;
4. prompt for and get secondary word;
5. call REPLACE;
6. output string.
   REPLACE:
   for each occurance of the primary word: a) locate primary word in string; b) delete primary word; c) insert secondary word.

Chapter Seventeen

```
2. PROCEDURE INVERT(VAR LIST:ARRAY OF INTEGER;LIMIT:INTEGER);
   VAR
     I,MID,REM,LOC,TEMP:INTEGER;
   BEGIN
     MID:= LIMIT DIV 2;
     REM:= LIMIT MOD 2;
     LOC:= 2*MID+REM;
     FOR I:= 1 TO MID DO
       BEGIN
         TEMP:=LIST[I];
         LIST[I]:=LIST[LOC-I+1];
         LIST[LOC-I+1]:=TEMP
       END
   END:
4. PROCEDURE OUTORDER;
   VAR
     I,J:INTEGER;
   BEGIN
     FOR I:= 1 TO 10 DO
       FOR J:= 1 TO 10 DO
         IF MATRIX[ROW,2]:=J THEN
           WRITELN(MATRIX[ROW,1]
   END;
```

7. 1. call GENERATE;
   2. call DISPLAY; 3. call
   SORT;
   GENERATE;
   a) set up a 100 item list for
   values; b) set up a 100 item
   list for checking values;
   c) initialize checking list;
   d) repeat the following
   steps until 100 values have
   been added to the list:
   (1) generate a random
   number between 1 and 100;
   (2) if the number is not already in the list: (a) add the
   number as the next item in
   the list; (b) change the
   check list value to TRUE;
   (c) add one to a counter;
   DISPLAY;
   a) initialize the graphics
   screen; b) draw X and Y
   axis on screen; c) for each
   value in the list: (3) plot
   the point; (a) let X axis values equal the list values;
   (b) let Y axis values equal
   the list subscript value;
   SORT;

   a) use Bubble Sort procedure to sort list; b) as each
   value is exchanged: (1) call
   ERASE to remove old image before exchange;
   (2) call SPOT to place new
   image after exchange;
   ERASE;
   a) move to old point; b) re-
   draw old point with background color;
   SPOT;
   a) move to new point;
   b) draw new point in
   white;
   GENERATING 100 RAN-
   DOM NUMBERS');

Chapter Eighteen

2. VIEWPORT   (0,139,0,191);
   FILLSCREEN (BLUE); VIEW-
   PORT (140,279,0,191); FILL-
   SCREEN (ORANGE);
4. WRITELN('THE TURTLE IS
   FACING   ',TURTLEANG,'
   DEGREES');   WRITELN
   ('AND IS ',TURTLEX,' PIX-
   ELS FROM THE LEFT
   EDGE');
6. PENCOLOR(NONE);   MO-
   VETO(0,90); WCHAR('X');
8.
```
PROCEDURE XIMAGE(VAR XPICT:PICTURE);
VAR
  LINE:IMAGE;
BEGIN
  LINE[1]:='*        *';
  LINE[2]:=' *      * ';
  LINE[3]:='  *    *  ';
  LINE[4]:='   *     ';
  LINE[5]:='  *    *  ';
  LINE[6]:=' *      * ';
  LINE[7]:='*        *';
  MAKESYMB(XPICT,LINE)
END;
```

```
PROCEDURE OIMAGE(VAR OPICT:PICTURE);
VAR
   LINE:IMAGE;
BEGIN
   LINE[1]:=`  ***  ';
   LINE[2]:=` *   * ';
   LINE[3]:=`*     *';
   LINE[4]:=`*     *';
   LINE[5]:=`*     *';
   LINE[6]:=` *   * ';
   LINE[7]:=`  ***  ';
   MAKESYMB(OPICT,LINE)
END;
```

10. NOTE(25,200)

12. a) Moves the Turtle a number of pixels equal to its current angle. b) Sets the graphics screen slightly smaller than the full screen and produces and error because RED is not an acceptable color. c) Moves the Turtle to a point 50 pixels to the right of its current location and 80 pixels from the bottom of the screen. d) Incorrect. SCREENBIT is a function and cannot be assigned a value. e) Checks the color of the Turtle's coordinate and if the color is not BLACK, moves the Turtle a distance equal to its current X axis location minus 10, e.g. if the Turtle is at 100,50, it moves forward 90 pixels.

14. a) Incorrect. Specifies 0 bytes per row. b) Skips 4 rows and columns, then draws 5 rows and columns. The rows skipped will be rows 6–10. c) Draws 6 rows and columns in reverse color. d) Draws full image, but off the top of the screen. e) Draws full image in left center of screen in mode 6.

16.
```
PROCEDURE MUSIC(VAR MNOTE:PICTURE);
VAR
   LINE:IMAGE;
BEGIN
   LINE[1]:=`       ******';
   LINE[2]:=`       *     ';
   LINE[3]:=`       ******';
   LINE[4]:=`       *     ';
   LINE[5]:=`  **   *     ';
   LINE[6]:=` **** *      ';
   LINE[7]:=`*******      ';
   LINE[8]:=` ****        ';
   LINE[9]:=`  **         ';
   MAKESYMB(MUSPICT,LINE)
END;
```

18. This program will use a procedure similar to that in problem 16 to create a figure. Animation is achieved by using DRAW-BLOCK with mode 6 in a loop similar to that shown in the FLIGHT procedure in the chapter (section 18.6).

21.
```
PROGRAM PROB21;
USES APPLESTUFF;
TYPE
   OKNOTES = SET OF CHAR;
VAR
   KEY:CHAR;
   ACCEPT:OKNOTES;
   PITCH:INTEGER;
BEGIN
   ACCEPT:= [`A',`B',`C'..`G'];
   REPEAT
     WRITELN(`PRESS A KEY CORRESPONDING TO A MUSICAL NOTE');
     WRITELN(`OR PRESS ANY OTHER KEY TO EXIT');
     READ(KEY);
     WRITELN;
     IF KEY IN ACCEPT THEN
       BEGIN  (* IF .. THEN *)
         CASE KEY OF
           `C':PITCH:=20;
           `D':PITCH:=22;
           `E':PITCH:=24;
           `F':PITCH:=25;
           `G':PITCH:=27;
           `A':PITCH:=29;
           `B':PITCH:=31
         END;  (* CASE ..  OF *)
         NOTE(PITCH,100)
       END  (* IF .. THEN *)
   UNTIL NOT (KEY IN ACCEPT)
END.  (* MAIN PROGRAM *)
```

Index _____

Educational Linguistics/TESOL/ICC
Graduate School of Education
University of Pennsylvania
3700 Walnut Street/Cl
Philadelphia, PA 19104